The History of Civilization
Edited by C. K. OGDEN, M.A.

The Court of Burgundy

PLATE 1

After Rogier van der Weyden: Duke Philip the Good. Royal Palace, Madrid.

The Court of Burgundy

BY

OTTO CARTELLIERI

NEW YORK

BARNES & NOBLE, PUBLISHERS

First Published 1929
Reissued 1972

Published in the United States of America 1972
by Barnes & Noble, Publishers, New York, N.Y.

No part of this book may be reproduced in any form
without permission from the publisher, except for
the quotation of brief passages in criticism

ISBN 0–389–04456–3

Translated by

MALCOLM LETTS, F.S.A.

Printed in Great Britain

DEDICATED TO

FRAU EVA CARTELLIERI-SCHRÖTER

AUTHOR'S PREFACE

WHEN, more than twenty years ago, I began to work on the political history of the Dukes of Burgundy, I was fascinated by the extraordinarily rich and splendid culture of the brilliant court, at which dying Knighthood was celebrating its last triumphs. I therefore turned my attention to the spiritual and social questions, and now at last, having overcome all extraneous difficulties, I am pleased to submit the fruit of my studies. I remember with pleasure the stimulation afforded me by the works of Pirenne and Fredericq, of Coville and Huizinga, to mention only a few names. I have to thank especially the University Library of Heidelberg and the National Library in Karlsruhe for kind encouragement; the Head of the Département des Manuscrits of the Bibliothèque Nationale in Paris, M. Henri Omont, for valuable information; the publishing firm of Benno Schwabe and Co. in Basle for procuring works difficult of access; and finally Frau Eva Cartellieri-Schröter for untiring collaboration, and Professor Dr. W. Lenel and Dr. Klaus Graf v. Baudissin for help in reading the proofs.

OTTO CARTELLIERI.

CONTENTS

CHAP.   PAGE

      AUTHOR'S PREFACE vii

      LIST OF ILLUSTRATIONS xi

      TRANSLATOR'S PREFACE xiii

   I. INTRODUCTORY 1

  II. THE CARTHUSIAN MONASTERY OF CHAMPMOL 24

 III. THE GLORIFICATION OF TYRANNICIDE . . 36

 IV. THE RULER AND HIS COURT . . . 52

  V. THE KNIGHT 75

 VI. THE LADY 97

VII. JOUSTS AND TOURNEYS 119

VIII. FEASTS 135

 IX. THE LIBRARY 164

  X. LA VAUDERIE D'ARRAS 181

 XI. ART AND ARTISTS IN THE NETHERLANDS . 207

XII. CONCLUSION 241

      NOTES 245

      INDEX 274

      GENEALOGICAL TABLE   *At the end of the book.*

LIST OF ILLUSTRATIONS

PLATE   FACING PAGE

1. After Rogier van der Weyden : Duke Philip the Good. Royal Palace, Madrid . . *Frontispiece*

2. Choir of the former Carthusian Church, Champmol, after an engraving of the eighteenth century. Bibliothèque Nationale, Paris . . . 24

3. Claus Sluter : Duke Philip the Bold with John the Baptist. Former Carthusian Monastery, Champmol, near Dijon 30

4. Claus Sluter : The Fountain of the Prophets. Former Carthusian Monastery, Champmol, near Dijon 32

5. *Pleurants* at the tombs of the Dukes of Burgundy. Museum, Dijon 34

6. Unknown Master : Duke John the Fearless. Museum, Antwerp 38

7. Juan de la Huerta and Antoine Le Moiturier : Tomb of Duke John the Fearless and his wife Margaret. Museum, Dijon 50

8. Unknown Master : Charles the Bold holds a Chapter of the Golden Fleece. Miniature : Guillaume Fillastre, L'histoire de la Toison d'Or. Bibliothèque Royale MS. 9028,* Brussels . 58

9. Unknown Master : Jean Wauquelin presenting his work to Philip the Good. Miniature : Chroniques du Hainaut. Bibliothèque Royale MS. 9242 fol. 1,* Brussels 64

10. Giovanni Candida : Charles the Bold. Medal. Bibliothèque Nationale, Paris . . .
Privy Seal of Charles the Bold. State Archives, Lucerne . . . .
Seal of Claus Sluter. Archives de la Côte d'Or,* Dijon 76

11. Goblet of Philip the Good. Kunsthistorisches Museum, Vienna 84

12. Unknown Master : Christine de Pisan at work. Miniature : Christine de Pisan, La Cité des

PLATE   FACING PAGE

Dames. Bibliothèque Royale MS. 9236, fol. 3r,*
Brussels   100

13. Unknown Master : Garden of Love.   Miniature :
Guillaume de Lorris and Jean de Meung,
Roman de la Rose.   Harley MS. 4425, fol. 12,*
British Museum   106

14. Loyset Liédet : Duel.   Miniature : Histoire de
Charles Martel, Bibliothèque Royale MS. 6,
fol. 355v.* Brussels   120

15. Unknown Master : Anthony of Burgundy, the
Great Bastard.   Musée Condé, Chantilly .   . 126

16. Loyset Liédet : Banquet.   Miniature : Histoire
de Charles Martel.   Bibliothèque Royale MS. 8,
fol. 33v,* Brussels   136

17. Burgundian   Flower - carpet.   Historisches
Museum, Berne   150

18. Unknown Master : Charles the Bold.   Musée,*
Avignon   158

19. Loyset Liédet : Charles the Bold surprises David
Aubert at work.   Miniature : Histoire de
Charles Martel.   Bibliothèque Royale MS. 8,
fol. 7,* Brussels   172

20. Unknown   Master :   Disputation.   Miniature :
Martin Le Franc, Le Champion des Dames.
Bibliothèque Nationale, MS. franç. 841, fol. 31v,*
Paris   178

21. Unknown Master : Witches' Sabbath.   Miniature :
Traittié du crisme de vaulderie.   Bibliothèque
Nationale MS. franç. 961,* Paris   .   .   .   190

22. Unknown Master : Flag of the period of Charles
the Bold.   Historisches Museum,* St. Gall   .   208

23. Jan van Eyck : Giovanni Arnolfini and his wife.
National Gallery, London   222

24. Jan van Eyck : The Madonna of the Chancellor
Rolin.   Louvre, Paris   224

25. Rogier van der Weyden : Charles, Count of
Charolais.   Kaiser-Friedrich Museum, Berlin   . 234

Photographs marked * have been specially taken for this work.

TRANSLATOR'S PREFACE

PROFESSOR CARTELLIERI'S volume is the work of
a specialist dealing with a subject which has not received
much separate treatment. His *Philipp der Kühne* published
in 1910 is well known, and, as he tells us himself, his study
of the history of the House of Burgundy commenced more
than twenty years ago. In this volume, a translation of the
work entitled *Am Hofe der Herzöge von Burgund*, published
in 1926, he deals mainly with the by-ways of history, with
social life and manners, with art, literature, music, the
position of the knight and the lady, and with that strange
manifestation of the fifteenth century, the witch persecutions
in Arras, all of great importance for the proper understanding
of his subject. These matters, or some of them, are touched
on in Huizinga's *Waning of the Middle Ages*, but from a
different and less detailed point of view. The reader who
has these two works on his shelves will be well equipped
for the study of one of the most amazing episodes in history.

Through all the interplay of politics, extravagance and
tragedy which characterized the history of the Dukes of
Burgundy, Professor Cartellieri leads us with a practised
and scholarly pen. There can be few sources which he has
not tapped. He describes very vividly in Chapter III the
troubles and excitements following the murder of Louis
of Orleans in 1407, and that strange scene enacted at Paris
a year later when the royal Dukes, the Council, and a vast
number of notables assembled in the Hotel de St. Pol to
listen for hours to a rambling dissertation by Magister Jean
Petit on murder as a fine art. Then in 1419 came the death
of the murderer on the bridge of Montereau, and in an
incredibly short time we find ourselves, far removed from
violence, amidst splendour and magnificence at the court of
Philip the Good. The Duke's alliance with England enabled
him to extend his frontiers and renew the prosperity of
his Flemish towns. Under him the fortunes of Burgundy
attained their highest point. Philip's Court shone with a

magnificence unmatched in any other western kingdom. The towns were the scenes of endless festivities, of stately tournaments, banquets, and revels, and every form of extravagance, until it seems to the reader of to-day that no time can have remained for serious business and affairs of State. The court was the resort of half the chivalry of Europe, and there the Duke presided like another Arthur among his knights, not indeed a king but the envy of many crowned heads, the last great representative of feudalism. When he died in 1467 he was the wealthiest prince in Christendom, and his Duchy was in a state of incomparable prosperity.

The marriage of his son Charles the Bold to Margaret of York in 1468, brought Burgundy once again into intimate relations with England, and gives Professor Cartellieri's book a special interest for English readers. He has examined and digested the various accounts of the wedding festivities, which are scattered here and there among the chronicles of the period, and presents us with a striking picture of Bruges at its gayest and best. Many notables from England were present for the marriage, and one of the bride's attendants was Sir John Paston, who described the spectacles and entertainments in a charming letter to his mother. The marriage was a turning point in the history of both Burgundy and England. Its importance was seen two years later when Edward IV, driven from his kingdom, fled for protection to his brother-in-law and obtained his assistance to regain his crown. Very little is known of the Duchess's private life, but it was under her protection that Caxton learned the art of printing and produced his first book, and Englishmen, mostly Lancastrian refugees, were always present at Charles' court.

Unfortunately Charles the Bold was fated to destroy what his ancestors had built up. He was a man unlucky in his age, his temperament, his friends, and his enemies. For ten years he kept the world in perpetual commotion. He wanted to be King of Burgundy, King of the Romans, even King of England. Freeman in an illuminating essay says of him that his whole career was one simple embodiment of military force in its least amiable form. In the end he contrived the utter destruction of his fortunes, and died miserably before Nancy. Possibly he has had scant justice at the bar of history, for he was chaste, scrupulously just, of good faith, and a strict avenger of vice, but he could not mix with his fellows and even the gift of simple courtesy was denied him. Had he thought a little less of conquests and annexations and turned his mind to the selection of a husband for his only daughter the whole course of history might have been changed.

Professor Cartellieri has been good enough to revise his book for the purposes of translation. With his approval the detailed descriptions of some of the stage plays performed at court have been compressed, and a paragraph has been omitted here and there. The notes, which contain a mass of out-of-the-way information, have been for the most part translated as they stand, but if anything of importance has been omitted, a reference has been added to the page of the German edition where the abbreviated note can be read in full.

MALCOLM LETTS.

THE COURT OF BURGUNDY

CHAPTER I

INTRODUCTORY

. . . la très noble, resplendissante et opulente maison des Bourguignons, dont aujourd'hui sa renommée court par les sept climats ; sa clarté illumine les ténèbres du monde, et sa beauté décore le quartier d'occident . . .—JEAN MOLINET.

THE four dukes of Burgundy-Valois inspired Western Europe with their names. Seven incidents stand out in their history, all of them of decisive importance for these princes of the French royal house ; some of them advancing and strengthening ; others hindering and disturbing.

It is, however, no unprecedented occurrence which introduces these princes into history. In the second decisive battle of the Hundred Years' war at Maupertuis-Poitiers in the year 1356, Philip, a younger son of King John the Good, threw himself into the midst of the fighting to save his father's life. As a reward for his courage the Prince, already called the Bold by his contemporaries, received in the year 1363 the grant of the Duchy of Burgundy. This, too, was not unprecedented. Even if the policy of granting appanages to younger sons had by no means always held good in France, the kings still remained faithful to it. What gave the new dukes of Burgundy their peculiar character was their alliance with Flanders, " the richest, noblest, and greatest Duchy of Christendom."

Edward III, not satisfied with his conquests abroad, sought to extend his influence in the Netherlands by aspiring to obtain for one of his sons the hand of the widowed Countess Margaret, only daughter of Count Louis of Maele. The French Crown recognized the danger that threatened it, and was able, with the active help of the Papacy at Avignon,

1

to thwart the English plans.   It was this Duke Philip of
Burgundy who became the consort of the richest heiress
in Europe, and thereby future master of Flanders.   It was
indeed a momentous day when in the year 1369 the wedding
bells rang out at Ghent.

After the death of Louis of Maele in the year 1384, the
new lord, with French assistance, was able to assume the
government of his dominions, of which the eastern part,
the lordship of Flanders, belonged to the Empire.   The
French Crown once again seized the opportunity of making
its influence felt in the frontier territories.   What had the
Empire done to support the House of Wittelsbach when it
entered upon its heritage in Holland and Hainault, to assist
a Luxemburger when he married the heiress of Brabant ?
John d'Avesnes had already drawn Rudolf of Habsburg's
attention to the dangers arising to the Empire from the
neglect of the Netherlands.   But Germany still failed to
move when a French prince established himself in the
frontier lands and set to work to extend the influence of
France in Germanic countries.

Philip the Bold was well qualified to undertake the difficult
task with which he was faced.   When he died in 1404, the
foundations of the new Burgundian State had been laid.
He approached the Wittelsbachs and endeavoured to dislodge
the Luxemburgers from the duchies of Brabant and Limburg,
which were in time to pass as a Burgundian appanage to a
younger son.   On all sides connections of great importance
were secured, and by an advantageous treaty Burgundy
obtained ascendency in the Austrian possessions on the
Upper Rhine.

Philip the Bold, presaging the future greatness of his
house, sought to establish a strong and independent State.
He believed that as a French Prince, he could identify this
policy with the policy of France, for he regarded himself as
indispensable to the French throne, its chief support, indeed,
in place of the mentally afflicted King.   But it soon became
clear that the interests of the French Crown and of Flanders,
which became more and more the chief concern of Burgundy,
were by no means identical.   The Flemish people, whose cloth
manufactures were dependent on the free imports of English
wool, desired to remain neutral in the quarrels between

France and England. Could Duke Philip meet the wishes of his new subjects without endangering the interests of France as well as Burgundy ?

The possessions which Duke John inherited from his father and mother were the Duchy of Burgundy, Flanders with Malines, Artois, Rethel, Nevers, and Charolais.

William Brito is very eloquent in his praise of Burgundy, the fruitful land, abounding in sustenance of all kinds, in corn and wine. Its Duke is rich in treasure, but richest in weapons of defence and fighting men. Enraptured, he enumerates the beautiful towns : Châtillon, the ornament, of the Allobroges, the bulwark of the Empire, watered by the Seine's clear stream ; Autun, the ancient town, which once hid Legions within her walls, and was faithful to the followers of Romulus.

The Merovingians had chosen Chalon-sur-Saône as their chief town. Under the Capetians Dijon became the capital of Burgundy. The strength of its walls had already been praised by Gregory of Tours ; later, they provided a welcome protection to the monks against the fury of the Normans. Not far distant from the town soared the venerable Abbey of St. Bénigne. Cluny's earlier fame was brought into remembrance by this mighty house of God, so splendid, "that it might have served the angels as a habitation." At Cîteaux, the fame whereof had been carried by a son of Burgundy, Bernard de Clairvaux, into all countries, the Dukes found their final resting places.

Of the numerous markets, those of Chalon and Autun were the most popular ; iron, salt, and ropes, stuff and cloth from Châtillon were sold there. The wine trade played an important part ; in particular request by connoisseurs was the red wine of Beaune, " which only too easily fires heated minds to warlike deeds." Without the wines of Beaune, writes Petrarch, indignantly, the Cardinals of Avignon can no longer live ; for them there is reason enough not to return to Italy.

The principal traders were the Jews, and, after their banishment, the Lombards ; the road once built by Agrippa sent north and south the goods which were not entrusted to

the Saône and other water-ways. St. Jean-de-Losne negotiated
by way of *Franche Comté* the trade with Germany.

Burgundy had been regarded in its business of traffic and
exchange as better suited than any other province to unite the
north and south of France. As if fate had selected this
task for the young Duke Philip, it procured for him the
possession of the most northerly province in the Kingdom.

" The Count and the people of Flanders," says Froissart,
" feared no power on earth, nor were they astonished at
anything ; so abundantly were they furnished and provided
with gold, silver, riches, and all kinds of goods." By sedulous
industry, the inhabitants had overcome the barren nature
of their country ; they reclaimed the lands from the sea
and protected them with dykes which had already excited
the admiration of Dante ; they changed the water-courses,
deepened and widened the river beds, and prevented the
silting up of the harbours ; they transformed barren wastes
into fruitful fields and rich meadows.

" The country, washed by the waters of the Scheldt, is
rich in pastures, full of large and small cattle ; it is distinguished by the most noble cities and harbours, all
excellent," so in the thirteenth century were its praises
sung by an Englishman (Bartholomew Anglicus).

Among its towns, Ghent, Bruges, and Ypres, the " drie
lede von Vlaenderen " stand out predominant ; they are
conscious of their strength, for between them they carry the
whole structure of Flanders.

" Ghent is the town most to be reckoned with in Flanders,"
writes Froissart, who by his journeys and his indefatigable
questionings was well qualified to instruct his readers on
foreign conditions, " decisive by its power, council, gentry,
dwellings and position, by all things, indeed, which one can
think of to make a good and noble town. Three water-
courses serve her ; the Scheldt brings her corn from Hainault,
and wines from France, the Ley corn from Artois and the
Lieve, over dams and sluices, brings her goods from the sea."

Bruges had developed into a great world-market. In the
ports of the Zwin, in Sluys, in Muiden, lay at anchor the
galleons of the Genoese and the galleys of the Venetians and
Florentines, the cogs from Hamburg, Lübeck, and Danzig,
the fishing-smacks of the herring-fishers. Lighters and

barges hurried to and fro to take the goods to the ware-houses and to the market-stalls in Bruges, which proudly throughout maintained its staple-rights. Before long the burgesses gave up navigation on their own account and took little part in wholesale trade, in order to become middle-men and brokers, and to devote themselves to their guests as money-changers and hosts, as inspectors and porters. The strangers, who came from all parts of the world, soon acquired their own houses which in time filled whole streets. In the Carmelite monastery the counting house of the Hanseatic League held its meetings and energetically upheld the interests of the German merchant. All kinds of commodities were offered for sale at Bruges : groceries and luxury-wares from the Orient, the forest-produce of the northern districts, English wool and coal, precious metals from Bohemia and Hungary, Russian pelts, sailcloth from Navarre, gold brocade from Tartary, and costly silks, sugar from Morocco, and fruits from Granada and Andalusia. The fiery wines of Cyprus and Burgundy were stored beside the mild growths of the Rhinegau and of Poitou.

A record of the beginning of the thirteenth century notes forty-four nations who sent their produce to Bruges. And no vessel returned home empty : all were loaded with the famous cloth, the *vestes dominis gestandae*, which on account of its unequalled quality was everywhere in great demand. At one time, in spite of unfavourable conditions, no fewer than two thousand active looms were to be counted in Ghent. More than 92,000 leaden seals were used annually in Ypres for the official marking of stuffs. The people of Ypres, with that extravagant splendour which only Gothic architecture can display, set up their Cloth Hall on the *groote markt*, the soaring pinnacles, the over-elaborated decoration speaking visibly to them of their greatness. Local patriots compared their town with Paris, and even with Rome and Constantinople.

Under such broad and opulent conditions, the development of town life, rich in colour and many-sided, was extraordinary. The good qualities of the citizens were highly praised by contemporaries, although their overwhelming pride and their short tempers brought them into disrepute. The Belfry, the sign of municipal freedom, stood forth boldly in their

streets, but too often its bells called the citizens to arms
against their rulers and the nobility.   The towns lost no
opportunity to break down the power of the Counts.   And
even if they did not succeed in becoming, as their German
sisters, free Imperial towns, States within the State, they
enjoyed, nevertheless, an independence never attained by
the towns in France.   It was unfortunate for them that their
craving for freedom was overshadowed by their pride.   In
Flanders there was never complete peace, for the Flemings
disturbed themselves even when their rulers left them to
their own devices.   At one time they fought against the
Counts, at another against their neighbours in the country
districts whose ascendancy was a never-failing cause of jealousy
to the towns.   Sometimes they fought amongst themselves,
one great man against another, the rich against the poor.
Within the town, the patricians opposed the gilds.   The gilds
on their part were dissatisfied with the part they played in
the government of the community.   The cloth-workers
opposed the gilds whose interests were not their own.   In
spite of their glorious exploits at Courtrai and Mons-en-
Pévèle, the workers had not attained to any economical
independence, and they endeavoured incessantly, a sacrifice
to wholesale industry, to shake off the yoke of the cloth
and wool dealers who oppressed them.   Then again, among
the clothworkers, the weavers and fullers were continually
at variance.   Hard and rough fellows always in revolt against
authority, their hands were ever ready to grasp and use a
knife.   Only too often were their masters to experience this.

Under Duke John the Fearless the inevitable disintegra-
tion began.   The Duchy of Burgundy which gave its name
to the race and to the State, receded more and more into the
background.   Flanders became the heart of the Burgundian
State and commenced its fight with France for independence.
A curious dispensation forced the Count-Dukes to sympathize
for once with their subjects.   This was due mainly to the
party-disputes which at that time were becoming more and
more violent in France.   When King Charles VI lost his
reason, no formal regency was appointed.   A council of
regency was considered sufficient, and the princes of the

blood composing it commenced to quarrel among themselves for the controlling influence. A dangerous rival to Duke Philip the Bold arose in the person of the King's talented brother ; for Louis of Orleans not only arrogated to himself the first place at Court ; he was occupied at the same time in founding on the eastern frontier a State, which should serve to support his ambitious schemes. What one prince built up the other destroyed. If Burgundy made terms with the Emperor Rupert and Henry IV of England, then Orleans allied himself with King Wenzel and King Richard. If Burgundy supported the withdrawal from the Avignon obedience, then Orleans sided with Pope Benedict XIII. Rumour had it that Louis intended taking his Pope to Rome and crowning himself Emperor.

The proud ship with the fleur-de-lis shaped an irregular course. " Chance reigns in France and not human knowledge " cries Jean de Montreuil in despair, not forgetting politics in his humanistic studies.

In order to assert himself against Louis of Orleans, Duke John called the Flemings to his aid, but they named their own terms. In spite of intrigues and opposition, the Duke was forced to negotiate a treaty of commerce with England, which was to remain effective in case of war between the French and English, thereby securing the neutrality which his subjects demanded. Not long afterwards, in the autumn of 1407, he went further and in the manner of a *rinascimento principe* caused Louis of Orleans to be assassinated.

Civil war now broke out, and for decades the Burgundians and the Orleans faction, which called itself after its leader Count Bernard d'Armagnac, were arrayed one against the other. France suffered the most terrible calamities. Party-strife raged more furiously there than formerly in Italy when Ghibelines and Guelfs destroyed each other.

The war, carried on with senseless fury, killed all nobler feelings. Both opponents entered into dealings with the enemy of the kingdom and made secret terms. The peace treaties were *paix de malice fourrées* ; they were as quickly broken as they were with difficulty secured. When the weapons were at rest, word and paper war continued : manifestos were distributed broadcast to whip the people on to madness. The antagonists were accused of every evil thing. Both parties struggled for the person of the sick and helpless ruler in whose name every kind of cruelty was perpetrated. Once when the Burgundians had Charles VI in their hands, they gave out that the Armagnacs were striving to exterminate the royal house and to impose a new king upon the people. During the Burgundian reign of terror in Paris, the Armagnacs were regularly excommunicated every Sunday with pealing of bells. Holy images were adorned with the cross of St. Andrew, the party-sign of the *Bourguignons*. It was rumoured that at mass and baptism, priests crossed themselves obliquely.

On their side, the Armagnacs branded Duke John as Lucifer's deputy on earth and accused him of devilish arts. The opponents vied with each other in infamous deeds. No crime was too vile; no misdeed too light to attract the most horrible punishment. There was one principle which triumphed, the principle of revenge ;—an eye for an eye, a tooth for a tooth.

The result was that men coarsened and became like beasts. After the Burgundians had again made themselves masters of the capital, a horrible carnage took place in the streets and houses of Paris : " *Et il y eut une femme grosse qui feut tuée, et veoit-on bien bouger ou remuer son enfant en son ventre, dont disaient aucuns inhumains : regardez ce petit chien qui se remue.*"

With what tragic words have such writers as Christine de Pisan, Alain Chartier, Charles of Orleans, and Georges Chastellain portrayed the desperate condition into which France had fallen. " Not mine is the victory," cried King Henry of England, after Agincourt, " God metes out divine judgment to the French."

Very sadly writes Chastellain :—

> Dieu ne fit oncques deux Troyes, ne deux Romes,
> Ne fera-il deux Frances, quant faillie
> Sera la nostre, assez ja affoiblie.

It was Duke John's wish to defend the *bien public* of France. He fought with the courage of despair for predominance. Did he understand that at the same time he was freeing Flanders from French influence ? In their blind hatred the Armagnacs could not see that they were paving the way for far worse things in France than the

Duke of Burgundy and his despotism. In striving to turn him out of France they forced him to unite with England and helped him to found the very power, which again and again was to bring the French monarchy to the verge of ruin. Moreover, in the midst of party-strife, a Burgundian national feeling came to birth ; side by side with French aims and ideals rose those of Burgundy. Men, like the author of the *Pastoralet* and the *Geste des ducs de Bourgogne* wrote in French, but in their thoughts and aspirations they were no longer Frenchmen.

The fourth decisive event, like the third, in the history of Burgundy, was a murder. It brought the severance of Burgundy from France to fulfilment. With the consent of the Dauphin, afterwards King Charles VII, John the Fearless was slain on the bridge of Montereau-faut-Yonne in the year 1419. Once when King Francis I was being shown the skull of John in the crypt of Champmol, a Carthusian monk pointed to the hole left by the murderer's sword and said : " *Sire, c'est le trou par lequel les Anglais passèrent en France.*"

The necessities of the hour again threw Burgundy into the arms of England whether the new Duke Philip (the Good) wished it or not. If he delayed, then the Armagnacs, who had seized the person of the Dauphin, would join hands with the English King, and Burgundy could never hope to withstand such a combination. Murderous revenge was then a holy duty, and the people expected and demanded it. Paris, for a long time already the decisive voice in the land, together with a great part of the realm, supported Duke Philip, and after long and painful hesitation, in the year 1420, he concluded the Treaty of Troyes and fought with England, the arch-enemy of France, against the " King of Bourges ". A second moral defeat for chivalry had been achieved : on the Burgundian shield the murder of the Duke of Orleans was already indelibly engraved. Now the principle of unqualified honour and allegiance received a blow from those who had set themselves up as its most passionate devotees. But in drawing his sword against his feudal lord, Duke Philip the Good placed himself as an independent prince

the equal of the French and the English Kings, as sovereign
beside sovereigns.   He had no thought of sacrificing himself
for England.   The alliance for him was nothing more than
a necessary evil.   After the early death of King Henry V
in 1422, he refused to undertake the Regency of France in
place of Henry VI, then a minor.   He did not care even to
accept the English Order of the Garter.   When an English
Prince, Duke Humphrey of Gloucester, endeavoured, as
husband of the Countess Jacqueline, to secure Holland,
Zeeland, and Hainault, and thereby to make a bid for the
heritage of the Wittelsbachs in the Netherlands, Burgundy
turned still further aside from England.   As soon as the
political situation permitted, as soon as Joan of Arc had led
the troops of the Dauphin from victory to victory, Duke
Philip the Good made his peace with Charles VII, who by
his anointing and coronation in Rheims in 1429, revealed
himself to the French people as their true King.   If, after
the murder of Montereau, public opinion cried out for revenge,
it now approved wholeheartedly the breaking of the treaty
with the hated *caudati*, the tailed Englishmen, for whom no
term of abuse was too violent.

   The Treaty of Arras was a great triumph for Burgundian
policy.   At a European peace-congress, such as the world
had not seen until then, in the presence of two Cardinals,
of the Legate of the Pope, of the Council of Basle and of the
ambassadors of all the most important kings and princes,
Philip the *Grand Duc d'Occident*, deigned to return to his
obedience to his overlord.   The murder of the Duke of
Orleans sank into oblivion, the murder of Duke John of
Burgundy, on the other hand, was to be inscribed in the
imperishable annals of history.   In Montereau a chapel and
a Carthusian monastery were to be founded : a cross was to
be set up on the ill-omened bridge.   A requiem in Montereau
and a mass in the Carthusian monastery were to perpetuate
the memory of the crime.   And not only in Montereau and
in Dijon, but also in Paris, in Flanders, in the most distant
foreign parts, in Rome, in Santiago di Compostela, in
Jerusalem, more churches and more memorials were to
commemorate the   dreadful   deed.   Then   followed   an

unprecedented humiliation for the French Crown. At St. Vaast, in the presence of all the people, a councillor in the name of the King of France knelt before Duke Philip and solemnly craved his pardon.

But never again was there any true agreement between the Royal House and the Count-Dukes. Never could France forget the defeat she had suffered at Arras. Duke Philip could not bring himself to appear at Court and attend King Charles as premier peer and vassal. Paris was always ready to remind the Duke of his position, and the summons to Court never failed to move Philip to great wrath. On one occasion, when a councillor appeared at Ghent to cite him to Paris, the Duke cried out in his rage : "*Je me plaings à Dieu et au monde des torfais, injures et rudesses que vous m'avez fait et faites tous les jours . . . mon intention n'est point de le souffrir plus, mais m'en vengeray une fois si je puis ; et prie à Dieu qu'il me doint tant vivre que j'en puisse prendre vengeance à l'appetit de mon cœur.*"

Philip the Good regarded himself as a man born to be King. His intentions were perfectly clear when he caused himself to be freed for life from all feudal dependence on the French King : when he announced himself " by God's grace " ; when he founded the Order of the Golden Fleece, which emperors and kings were proud to wear.

The Treaty of Arras put an end to the unnatural alliance with England ; solemnly the Cardinals released the Duke from the oath he had sworn to King Henry V. The political advantage to be derived from the Treaty were self-evident, for it gave the Duke the possession of the Somme towns. But the Treaty brought with it also qualities of peculiar significance ; for peace returned to the Burgundian land, peace, which throughout France was desired with every fibre of their beings by the sorely-afflicted people. Here was indeed a prince beloved of God, who freed his subjects from the fury of war.

Peace, then, entered the Burgundian land. But it must not be assumed that complete quiet reigned. There were risings here and there, and the troops of mercenaries which were now released from service brought the usual horrors to the Duke's dominions. But these sufferings and plagues seemed small and insignificant compared with the terror

of war in the neighbouring states.   France, strong again
with the victories which the Maid had given her, strove
valiantly to loosen the fetters which two decades of restless
warfare had imposed on her.   The party feuds which had
been rife also in Holland, now reached England, which was
ravaged by civil war.   The Empire, too, was in a deplorable
condition.   As a result of the increasing development of
the territorial states, the Emperor was powerless to impose
peace at home or to concentrate his army upon any one point
abroad.   It seemed like magic, like God's will, when Duke
Philip contrived for thirty years to keep his kingdom free
from foreign wars.   In his chronicle, Georges Chastellain
lets the princes pass in review ;   one understands why it
was, in spite of all his weaknesses, that Philip received
the palm.

The Duke's most passionate desire was to recover the Holy
Land from the infidel.   When Henry V of England was
stricken down in the midst of his brilliant career, the thought
that troubled his last hours was that he had failed to free the
Lord's sepulchre.   Philip strove to succeed where others
had failed.   He saw himself as the pillar of western ideals.
He longed to avenge the insults which had been showered
on the Cross.   The crusading fever left no rest to princes and
people, to thinkers and poets, and if Philip succeeded, sultan-
ships and kingdoms would pale before the name of Burgundy.
Enthusiastically the papacy extolled the champion, of whom
it thought so highly.

Philip foresaw no difficulties from the Empire, even if
Burgundy was to cause considerable anxiety to the Emperor.
" *Nimis alte volat* " ;   thus high does Duke Philip soar in his
flight, cried Sigismund in his rage.   Philip's grandfather
had asked no leave of Germany when he induced the Duchess
Joan to transform Brabant and Limburg into a Burgundian
appanage for a second son, and Philip himself was even less
concerned when in 1421 he obtained the Margravate of
Namur, or when, after the early failure of the Burgundian
collateral line in 1430, he seized Brabant and Limburg,
or again when in 1433 he compelled the Countess Jacqueline
to resign her inheritance to him.

So once more were German fiefs to come under the
Burgundian banner ;   Brabant and Limburg, long stepchildren

of the Empire, with their thriving industry and agriculture, with their rich mines and quarries, their great cattle farms, Soignes with its splendid woods ; Holland and Zealand with their luxuriant meadows, pastures, and marshlands, reclaimed with infinite labour from the sea, with their intrepid mariners, their world-famous shipbuilders and their busy fishermen, all passed into Philip's hands. It was said of the Dutch that they fished more silver and gold out of the sea, than other men could dig with the sweat of their brows from the unwilling earth. Holland, supported by the arms of Burgundy, could now increase her sea-power without restraint from the Empire and in the face of the Hanseatic League. Now, too, there flowed into the ducal treasury the revenues of Hainault and Namur, the whole wealth of the Ardennes, iron, lead, and coal from the mines, marble and chalk from the quarries, saltpetre and vitriol, sulphur and gold.

Nothing that the Emperor Sigismund could say, no threats, no warnings, could change what was ordained. Of what use were the Imperial letters to the Countess Jacqueline in the war against her cousin if they were unsupported by the Imperial armies ? Sigismund might declare war on the " Rebels and Traitors ", but he could undertake no campaign commensurate with the dignity of the Empire. The German princes, sufficiently occupied with the Hussite troubles, had no intention of embarking upon adventures on the western borders from which no profit was ever likely to accrue.

Burgundy was not unprepared to make concessions, and promises of all kinds were forthcoming. But Sigismund, always pressed for money, placed his demands too high, and confused his rights as German King with dynastic matters. This was a great mistake. Burgundian diplomacy was prepared to consider the Emperor as such, but not the helpless dynast. Soon after Sigismund's death his own heritage, the Duchy of Luxemburg, together with the Countship of Chiny, was incorporated into the Burgundian dominions.

Thus Philip the Good remained in undisputed possession of the Netherlands. He paid homage neither to Sigismund, nor to Albert II, nor to Frederick III. Yet it would still have been to his interests to come to terms with them.

It was a mighty estate, therefore, which belonged to the
House of Burgundy. Though it could cheerfully compete
with any kingdom of the West, it was never a compact whole,
but merely a loose structure of disorganized states. The
lands which had gradually passed under the dominion of
the Count-Dukes were of great variety, differing among
themselves in nationality, in political, economic, and social
conditions. The Flemings had little in common with the
Walloons in the Netherlands. The Walloons again were
utterly different from the French inhabitants of Burgundy.
Everywhere were differing laws and varied methods of
administration. As soon as the Count of Flanders stepped
over the borders of Brabant or Holland, his official authority
changed. The inhabitants of the various provinces regarded
each other without interest. When their aims did not
coincide, all pretence of friendship vanished. How could
the wine-growers of Burgundy understand the aims of the
fishermen and sea-folk of Holland and Zealand ? How many
Flemings knew the mother-land of their counts ? Dijon,
and with Dijon the whole of Burgundy, could not but feel
slighted when it remembered the rise of Bruges and Brussels,
now the chosen dwelling-places of the ruler ; and Bruges
itself was to watch with helpless anger while Antwerp,
little by little, usurped her coveted position as the market
of the world.

If the work of Philip the Bold, so well begun, was to endure,
the multitude of different states had to be welded into some
semblance of unity. Philip allowed himself to be called the
Grand Duc d'Occident, yet " King " Philip would have had
a very different meaning. In the beautiful illuminated
manuscripts of the ducal library much could be learnt
concerning the ancient Lotharingians, the *regnum Lotharii*,
which had once devolved upon the great grandson of Charlemagne. The remembrance of this had never quite
disappeared. Brabant still proudly called himself *Duc de
Lothier*, a survival of the days, it was said, when his territory
embraced the whole of the land between the Meuse and the
Scheldt.

The ancient middle kingdom was to blossom again under
a new name ; and but for the difficulties which negotiations
with the Emperor always entailed the ideal might well

have been realized.   There had already been delays and
difficulties as to the obligations of homage, from which
Philip desired to be relieved, and now lengthy negotiations
were entered into with the Emperor Frederick III concerning the creation of a Burgundian kingdom.   But these
also came to no effective conclusion.   All the arts of the
Duke's diplomats were powerless against Habsburg passivity.
The Emperor Frederick took no steps against the unlawful
appropriator of Imperial fiefs : he was not likely to encourage
a vassal's ambitious designs for kingship.

Philip had, therefore, to seek his compensations elsewhere.
He began by preparing for the great work of unification
within his dominions.   In spite of the separatist policy of
the towns, which were always on the watch against the
tendencies of their princes towards absolutism, he developed
the constitution built up by his grandfather, and laboured
above all for centralization.   Not only did the several
dominions receive an admirable system of justice and
accounts, but centres of government were established whose
enactments were effective throughout all the Duke's
possessions.   A permanent Council supported the Prince,
first as a Council of State and supreme Court of Justice,
later, under Philip's son, as Council of State alone, beside
which the Court of Justice at Malines, the supreme court
for the whole of the Netherlands, functioned independently.

Under Duke Philip the States General met for the first
time in 1463; and to this assembly the delegates from every
part of the dominions had been summoned.   Although
organized primarily in order to simplify the financial administration, and although the simultaneous assembly of the
provincial delegates was far from forming a national parliament, nevertheless, the States General contributed not a
little to that policy of centralization which was the Duke's
most cherished ambition.   The Netherlanders, who regarded
all innovations with the greatest suspicion, saw this clearly.
The convocation of the General Assembly was regarded
with considerable disfavour, and it was only with great
reluctance that they sacrificed their ideals of independence
to the centralizing demands of their ruler.

It was necessary, therefore, to proceed with great caution,
for the State of Burgundy required money—endless money.

Stately as were the demesnes, imposing as were the revenues
from tolls of all sorts, from court-fees, taxes on seals, and such
like, there was always need for more. The ruler was dependent
on the *bedes* or aids extracted from the nobility, the clerics,
and the towns. Taxation became in time permanent, but
as the taxes increased, the incidence was more evenly
distributed.   Contemporaries estimated the revenues of
Duke Philip in 1455 at nine hundred thousand ducats. At
that time Venice controlled a like sum, Florence a fourth,
Naples a third, and the Pope and Milan one-half.

In the Treasury countless specimens of artistic industry,
beautiful manuscripts, paintings and carpets, gold and silver
vessels, and ornaments, were gathered together. They
formed, at a time when an ordered currency was not
established, an excellent investment. In times of necessity
the equivalent for considerable sums was always at hand.
Philip the Good established a special treasury in the castle
at Lille to meet the needs of war. He had splendid coins
minted ; the golden *Philippus* or *Ryder* and the silver
Vierlander all testify to the sound economic condition of
his dominions.

To his subjects Philip the Good was the sun of their
existence. He was one of those fortunate men who charm
by the force of personality alone. It was his ambition to
revive the old ideals of chivalry, for in the ranks of knighthood *sans peur et sans reproche* he looked to find the champions
he needed for his ambitious schemes. Before long lords and
gentlemen from all quarters came flocking to the Court of
Burgundy. No monarch could show the like. Philip outshone
even René of Anjou and Charles of Orleans. As once in the
time of the daughters of Queen Eleanor of England, knights
and warriors flocked to Blois and Troyes to sing their love
songs at the feet of the Countesses Alix and Marie, now the
flower of chivalry from Germany and England, from Italy
and Spain, hurried to the Court of the first peer of France.
The Count of Horn declared at the feast of the Pheasant, that
he would rather serve the Duke of Burgundy than the
Emperor himself, although he held his possessions as vassal
of the Empire. A Count of Salm, a Lord of Ferrara served

as lords in waiting at the Burgundian Court. Under the eyes of the very pattern of knighthood the sons of the noble and illustrious men came to learn discipline and manners, and to win their spurs.

Western Europe beheld the splendours of the Burgundian court with wonder, for a counterpart of the Italian Renaissance seemed to be blossoming in the North. Feast gave way to feast in brilliant succession. Every pastime known to the century was exploited. The pleasures of the table were followed by hunting expeditions, feats of arms, by pageants, dances, and mummeries. But amidst all this riot of gaiety and mirth the impression remains of something planned and considered as if every extravagance was subjected to some higher purpose.

The princes vied with each other in the magnificence of their gifts, nor were they sparing in their rewards to trusted servants and counsellors at home and abroad. A royal state demanded royal splendour, and this unparalleled display of luxury served greatly to enhance the already remarkable prestige of the House of Burgundy. All Europe was witness when Philip the Good sent out his ships and men to the East, and when at the Feast of the Pheasant at Lille, with royal pomp, he took the Cross himself with his paladins. This example of boundless extravagance shows society at its best and at its worst. It seems as if the art of ceremonial was greater than the art of good manners, for it was only with difficulty that quarrels, wild drinking, and sexual licence could be restrained.

The most gifted artists left the Court of France and came to Burgundy to spread the fame of the Count-Dukes. At a time when Ghiberti and Donatello were working in Italy, Claus Sluter was busy with his masterpieces in the Carthusian Monastery at Dijon. The Fleming, Jan Van Eyck, attached himself to the Court, holding a position under Philip the Good not unlike that occupied by Rubens in the time of Albert and Isabella of Austria. Rogier van der Weyden, who like Robert Campin came from Tournai, established himself in Brussels. Hans Memling was working at Bruges, and Hugo van der Goes at Bruges and Ghent. It will always redound to the credit of the Dukes of Burgundy, that at a time when France and Germany were careless of such things, they drew to their

Court the most distinguished intellects on this side of the Alps ;
a greater loss to Germany than to France, for the French
princes were represented at the Court of Burgundy and were
able to share in the intellectual development which they
found there.

The Netherlanders distinguished themselves also as
musicians ; they introduced important novelties and soon
became famous and influential.   Poets and men of letters
found in the Count-Dukes intelligent and generous patrons.
Eustache Deschamps and Christine de Pisan began to carry
the praise of the House of Burgundy from country to country
and set an example which the numerous court-poets were
glad to follow.   Monstrelet, working on the lines of Froissart,
portrayed in show and stately diction the pageantry of peace
and war.   Olivier de La Mache strove to paint a picture of
the glittering world of chivalry to whose charms he too had
succumbed.   Georges Chastellain, *la perle et l'estoille de tous
les historiographes,* had his own apartments in Philip's palace
at Valenciennes " *pour mettre par escript choses nouvelles et
moralles, aussi mettre en fourme par manière de cronique fais
notables dignes de mémoire advenus par chi-devant et qui
adviennent et puevent souvantes fois advenir* ".   This author
turned to the nobility, the patricians.   The craftsmen sought
rather a Flemish chronicler, or took pleasure again in the
simple words of Jan Ruysbroek, who knew better than
any other how to rouse the religious perceptions of the
working classes.

Neo-Latin and Germanic literature existed side by side,
without permeating each other ; but it was otherwise with
the languages themselves.   Since the middle of the fourteenth
century Flemish had borrowed from the French numerous
technical expressions in the province of law and administration which have survived to the present day.   On the other
hand in many places, as in the Liège district, Flemish
expressions found their way into the speech of the Walloons.

French was the language of the Court, the nobility and the
patricians, and the higher administration.   But the rulers
were not anxious for any great movement towards France.
They recognized Flemish as the official language, learnt it
themselves and required a knowledge of it in their officials.
At the same time it was necessary for every ambitious

man to know French. The Flemish merchant, too, was well
advised to learn it. He was thus on terms of familiarity
not only with the Parisian, but also with the North-German,
the Nuremberger, and the Augsburger, who, for the most
part could speak French, but not Flemish. In this way
the language of French literature, which had conquered the
whole of the French dominions made its way into foreign
parts. Christine de Pisan claimed for it that it was *la plus
commune par l'universel monde.*

As we have seen, Philip the Good made it his business to
free himself from Germany and France, and to found a
sovereign border state. It was his aim to assert the authority
of the Crown over the antagonistic power of the states, to
free himself from every feudal and communal tie. Even if
the task was not fully accomplished when Duke Philip
died on 15th June, 1467, he still had reason to be satisfied
with what he had achieved. He was conscious of his mistakes.
But his subjects were grateful for his care of them, and they
acknowledged and reverenced him as the father of his
people. Once when the news of his illness reached Abbeville,
the magistrates ordered the bells to be rung, the citizens
streamed to the churches to pray to God for the recovery
of their ruler. They remained all night in the churches,
weeping, and burning hundreds of candles. The news of
his death threw his dominions into something like despair.
The mournful tidings spread like wild-fire throughout
Franche-Comté. Little children ceased their play and cried
bitterly in the streets.

Thus it was that a Burgundian State began to be formed,
and a Burgundian public spirit came slowly into being.
Philip the Good, the equal of his grandfather in many
things, in many ways his superior, was well fitted to carry
on his great work. Not unjustly did Justus Lipsius in the
sixteenth century appraise him as the *conditor Belgii.*

In a poem of Jean Molinet Philip the Good thus extols
himself :—

> J'ay creu ma seigneurie de Brabant, de Limbourg,
> Namur, Haynau, Hollande, Zélande et Luxembourg.
> Contrariez si m'y ont Allemans et Anglois.
> Deboutez je les ay, par armes et par droictz . . .
> Du même temps François, Anglois me defièrent,
> Et l'Empereur aussy ; du mien riens ne gaignèrent . . .

Par trois fois fut requis pour gouverner l'empire . . .
Mais par Charles septiesme j'euz guerre à grant desroy.
Il me requist de paix, dont il demoura roy . . .
Loys, filz dudict Charles, fugitif et marry,
Fut par moy couronné, quant cinq aus l'euz nourry.
Edouard, duc d'Jorch, chassé vint en ma terre ;
Par mon port et faveur il fut roy d'Angleterre.

Charles the Bold would have liked to follow in his father's footsteps, but he was one of those unhappy persons, the victims of their own impulsive natures, who offend everyone and awake suspicion everywhere. Philip understood how to wait ; his contemporaries called him also *l'assuré*. What he endeavoured to attain with much thought and care, even with considerable hesitation, his son, inflamed with the wildest passions, strove to obtain instantly. A man without consideration for others, he could brook no opposition. He treated people mistakenly, drove his subjects into opposition, and alienated his friends.

The Netherlands question was now bound to reach a climax. Even in the lifetime of his father, as his deputy, Charles instigated the *Ligue du Bien Public*, and sword in hand at Montlhéry in 1465, advanced against his King and feudal lord—an event of lasting consequence. There was no longer any question of a secret, hidden struggle with France ; it was open and declared war.

At the reception of the Burgundian deputies at Dijon in 1473, after the Chancellor had spoken, Duke Charles delivered himself thus : " *et n'oublia pas de parler du Royaume de Bourgoigne que ceux de France ont long temps usurpé et d'icelluy fait duchié que tous les subjects doivent bien avoir à regret ; et dit qu'il avoit en soy des choses qu'il n'appartenoit de sçavoir à nul qu'à luy.*"

Charles never desired to rank as a Frenchman, as a prince of the blood. The great grandson of Philip the Bold, who had regarded himself as indispensable to the support of the French throne, Charles declared that he would rather have six French Kings than one. Again and again he led his armies against his feudal lord. He forced him to be present in his train when he wreaked his vengeance on the towns-people of Liège who had been shamelessly betrayed by France. With the cross of St. Andrew round his neck, amidst the cries of *Vive Bourgogne*, King Louis rode into Liège; even the humiliating act at St. Vaast in Arras paled before this. It was only by concentrating all his strength and employing every art and means that, thanks largely to the mistakes of his impetuous opponent, Louis was able to save the throne of Valois amidst the storm of war which broke over France.

Charles, victorious over the French King, in possession of the Somme towns, the key to France, now turned his eyes towards Germany, for him the land of unbounded possibilities. He measured his deeds by those of a Caesar or a Hannibal.

"*Il désiroit grand gloire qui estoit ce qui plus le mettoit en ses guerres que nulle autre chose ; il eust bien voulu ressembler à ces anciens princes dont il a esté tant parlé après leur mort*," says Commines. The pecuniary embarrassments of Sigismund procured him the Rhenish provinces of Austria. The langravate of Sundgau and Pfirt came in the year 1469 under Burgundy's administration and with them Charles acquired the "*ingang und slüssel Teutscher nacion*" (the entry and key to the German nation). The plans to obtain a footing on the Upper Rhine, visualized first by Philip the Bold, then by John the Fearless, seemed now in hope of realization.

Disputes in the ducal House of Gelders offered another welcome opportunity, and in 1473 Charles became master of the Dukedom, whose projecting extremity between the Meuse and the Moselle had been a constant threat to Brabant as well as to Holland. By this means the State of Burgundy advanced also on the Lower Rhine.

But neither the burning to ashes of the episcopal city of Liège nor the conquest of Gelderland deprived the Emperor Frederick of his peace of mind. There were no warlike operations, only negotiations. For the hand of the Duchess Marie, Charles's only child, was too charming a prize to be missed. Charles increased his demands. For him it was no longer sufficient to rule as King over his numerous provinces, he desired to become King of the Romans, vice-regent of the Emperor. In order to be crowned with the royal crown, he came in the autumn of 1473 to a meeting with the Habsburgs in Trèves. But he left the town an

uncrowned King.   The war, too, which he waged against
the Empire, ended in defeat : for eleven months Neuss, with
heroic defence, withstood all attacks.

In 1475 Charles turned against Lorraine, for this important
entrance gate into France was necessary to his schemes.
Then down into Provence.   How long before the Count-
Duke could ride on his own roads from Holland to the
Mediterranean ?

In a wild frenzy, Charles swept on with his fantastic plans.
Everywhere opponents sprang up, everywhere were signs
of treachery and deceit.   Charles did not perceive them, or
did not wish to perceive them.   In his own lands he was
threatened with sedition and revolt.   The policy of centralization, continued with too great severity, had aroused intense
exasperation.   Both the Netherlands and the Duchy of
Burgundy condemned these wars of conquest and refused
subsidies.   The military forces were totally inadequate.
The standing army raised by Charles was too small for his
purpose, and his mercenaries proved wholly unreliable.

Catastrophe followed with sinister rapidity.

The last decisive event in the history of the four Burgundian
Dukes was, to the astonishment even of contemporaries, the
war with the Swiss in 1476.   Charles' Upper Rhine policy
having brought him into conflict with them, he now set out
to enforce his will.   With most eager attention the whole
of the West awaited the issue of this unequal struggle between
the arms of chivalry and the free sons of the mountains.
There were some mighty battles—and then the disturber
of the world vanished from the sight of men.   Already
defeated at Grandson and Morat, on 5th January, 1477, at
Nancy, he lost both the battle and his life.   King Louis,
l'araignée universelle, who had waited long for his revenge,
marched his armies into Burgundy, and seized the Duchy
for the French Crown.

Charles left as his heir no experienced warrior or statesman, but a young and unexperienced girl, Marie of Burgundy.
No faithful subjects, holding fast with all their might to
the memory of their ruler, mourned his death ; one and all
exulted in the sudden end of despotism.   The separatist

spirit of the Communes was aflame once more. In Flanders, Ghent, Bruges, and Ypres the people again took command, and Charles's devoted counsellors expiated on the scaffold the grasping folly of their master.

The State of Burgundy was created amidst the fury of universal conflict. Was it to perish in another conflict equally furious and universal ?

CHAPTER II

The Carthusian Monastery of Champmol

Les armes des conquérans sont ternies, leurs heaumes sont cassés et leurs lances brisées, mais leurs noms, ensemble leurs glorieux faicts, sont escripts en lettres d'or et demeurent à perpétuité.—JEAN MOLINET.

AT the period when the Carthusian Monastery came into being, there was as yet no artist in the modern sense of the word. According to the divinely inspired division into appropriate estates or orders, the artist belonged to the artisans. A long time was to elapse before the artist attained the position that was his due, or until his profession was recognized. Painters and sculptors worked for their daily bread in the same way as the artisans made useful articles. They had in the same way to submit to the restraints imposed by the gild. The number of journeymen was fixed. Nightwork was frequently forbidden and indeed often impossible because painters and sculptors were obliged to serve with the watch. The overseers examined each finished work, and considered the methods by which it was produced; in the case of a picture, for instance, whether the prescribed colours had been employed, whether gold-leaf had really been laid on silver and not, dishonestly, on tin.

Though strict regulations served to protect the interests of the purchaser and guard him against fraud, they opened the door also to oppression on the part of the gild overseers. Only too easily, under the semblance of justice, could they satisfy their desire for personal revenge, advance their favourites and exclude their rivals. Moreover, through the gilds, the magistracy possessed additional powers which might easily be abused. In Paris where the *jurés* as a rule found effective support in the *prévôt des marchands*, even Colart de Laon was compelled to adapt a Dutch picture, destined for the Louvre, to suit the Parisian style. An artist who did not conform to the statutes ran the risk of having his work burnt before his eyes. If a holy person was represented, any part of the picture which aroused objection

PLATE 2

Choir of the former Carthusian Church, Champmol, after an engraving of the eighteenth century.   Bibliothèque Nationale, Paris.

[face p. 24

had to be erased. Yet in spite of this, it was imperative for strangers to become members of the gild. To remain outside the organization was often to forfeit every kind of protection. These reasons help to explain why men like Jehan Pepin of Huy and Hennequin of Liége, who lived in Paris, found it necessary to acquire their rights as citizens.

In Paris in the fourteenth century, a distinction was made between the *peintres-imagiers* or figure-carvers and moulders, the *enlumineurs* or miniaturists, and the *selliers,* or sadlers. It was the *selliers* who were really the originators of all formal pictures for they made chairs, chests and tabernacles, and then painted them. It was only after the rebellion of the Maillotins, when new statutes were enacted, that the *peintre-sellier* ceased to exist, and the painter himself was no longer obliged to make the objects he was to adorn.

Masters with established reputations were very jealous of their secrets, and kept the results of their experiments and experiences strictly to themselves. Some had a room which no one else could enter ; others made their pupils swear not to divulge what they saw. A collaborator of Jacquemart de Hesdin, Jan van Holland, guarded the secrets of his colours so closely that once, when he suspected an assistant of having broken open his box, a fight with daggers ensued, and an artisan was left dead on the spot. Nor were these outbursts unusual. Among the artists, as among other craftsmen, there were hot-headed youths, never satisfied with their wages, and ready on the slightest provocation to draw their weapons. Christine de Pisan extolled the Paris artists (upon whom, indeed, she had to rely for the ornamentation of her works) as *les souverains du monde en la science de peintrerie,* but at the same time censured them for their unbridled, and dissolute lives.

There was one means only of escaping the restrictions of the gilds, and that was by the grace of princes. An artist who could claim the favour of some king or prince, or become his court-painter or sculptor, his varlet-de-chambre, was a man freed from all restraint. Under the protection of his master he could work as he pleased. If a varlet-de-chambre he enjoyed additional privileges, the right of approach to his prince at any time, and permission to use a seal, like the nobility, by virtue of which he could buy in his master's name the colours and other materials which he needed for his work, and issue valid receipts for his purchases. There were financial advantages as well ; a fixed yearly salary kept the artist free from the cares of daily life which so sorely troubled his professional colleagues. The petitions to the magistracy of Dijon, praying for relief from taxation, reveal the misery of the artists who had no claim to princely protection. The wife of one must work as a midwife; a harp-player has broken his leg during his service with the watch ; a painter complains bitterly of the demands of the city that he shall practise cross-bow shooting, a proceeding which will involve him in heavy expense, especially as this year he has been elected master of the shooting contests.

The freedom from taxation enjoyed by the ducal varlets, a privilege which Claus van Werve maintained vigorously and acrimoniously against the Dijon magistracy, was a matter of vast importance to the court-artists. Claus, in his opinion, was assessed too highly, but was nevertheless required to pay : an official, in fact, had dared to seize goods in his house by way of pledge. His petition leaves nothing to be desired in the way of clarity and force. " I complain to God and the whole world of the wrong that I have suffered." He has been four or five times too highly taxed. " This time " he continues " I will refrain from producing the open letter of the lord Duke in which he grants me, with other permanent officials, freedom from taxation . . . In accordance with his will, he keeps me in Dijon to execute his commissions." If they do not listen to his complaints, it is his intention to appeal to the Duke by word of mouth and in writing. " I shall know well " he says " how to fix the day and hour for an audience."

Those artists who could not boast the Duke's patronage had to adopt a milder tone. A musician, who played the flute and tambourine for dances in Dijon, presented his petition to the tax-authorities in rhymed verse ; he promised :—

> Et pour vous une chanchonette
> Dira qui sera joliette,
> Et du tabourin vous fera
> Certes danser quand vous plaira.

Their worships entered into the jest and replied :—

L'on remet au suppliant tous les impostz
Dont ceste requeste fait mencion à six gros.

But an artist who entered the service of a prince was
by no means always free from troubles and difficulties.
The painter Broederlam, being exceptionally skilful in
handling stuffs, had to make thousands of pennons and
small flags for the campaigns. Beaumez once supplied
two thousand of them, and painted a carriage for the ladies
of the court. Maelweel painted the tourney harness for
Duke John, Bellechose made armorial escutcheons for
candles and torches, and painted the castle door, as well as
Jacquemart, the celebrated clock, formerly brought as war-
booty to Dijon from Courtrai. In addition, there was the decoration of walls, ceilings, fireplaces, beams, and coping stones
of the castles. Broederlam worked for three years in the
celebrated gallery of Hesdin palace and ornamented Ypres
castle with frescoes. This mechanical work was paid for
on a mechanic's scale. The master, who decorated the Hall
of the Lamb in the castle of Germolles with lambs and
thistles, and drew no fixed salary, received five francs for
every hundred lambs, and two and a half francs for every
fifty thistles. The court artist had, moreover, to render
a strict account of his work, but with this difference.
He had to do not with the gild overseers, but with a commission of court officials, among whom brother artists
were frequently to be found. Even the artisans who distinguished themselves in the more pedestrian tasks received
commissions which gave their imagination freer play. Thus
when a call came from a prince to an artisan, even from the
greatest distance, there was no hesitation, no delay, off he
started on his travels.

Sight-seeing was at all times the best education for an
artist. A strong, inherent craving for the road came to all
who desired to make a name for themselves, to escape from
the narrow restrictions of the home.

On ne voit rien qui ne vas hors

says an old French proverb ; and another :

Travelling has taught me what I did not learn at home.

Life on the road presented an attractive and varied picture.
People of all sorts were always coming and going. There
were gentlemen on horseback, ladies of quality in silk-hung
litters with their armed escorts ; magistrates and prosperous
merchants ; heralds and pursuivants in their gaily-coloured
coats ; pedlars ever ready to unpack their wares ; students
seeking knowledge with adventure, always on the look-out
for a pretty face ; pilgrims whose bearing matched the
proverb :—

> Pèlerin qui chante
> Larron espouvante

Clerics offering relics for sale ; condemned malefactors,
candle in hand, praying aloud and singing, on their way to
some pilgrimage church. Play-actors sang on the roads the
verses which in the castles were to bring them money and
renown ; gipsies watched for a favourable opportunity to
steal a horse ; beggars with feigned infirmities appealed to
the charity of passers-by. Rogues and vagabonds turned
order into riot, while everywhere were the *caymands,* who
kidnapped little children, and blinded them to make a profit
for themselves out of their misfortune. Quacks and charlatans
cried their wares, seeking profit from fools and simpletons.
At night an inn welcomed the rich man, and if the single
chambers were engaged, there was always a bed to be had
in the common room. As for the poor they slept in the
woods or in the fields, consoling themselves with the
rhyme :—

> Qui n'a couché au vent et à la pluye,
> Il n'est digne d'aller en compagnie.

Frequently this bed was very hard :—

> Duquel estoient les courtines
> Toutes de chardons et d'espines,
> Et la couche de terre dure,
> Le chevet de grosses racines,
> Et de ronces la couverture.

The discomfort was willingly endured, if only one was
spared robbers and thieves. In this situation, the poor man
had the advantage of the rich :—

> Qui porte argent, porte sa mort,

says a poet.

And then when night with its terrors was past, another
day dawned, shining brightly, as the sunset had foretold :—

Rouge vespre et blanc matin
Rend joye au cœur des pèlerins.

" For the soul's salvation nothing suffices like the prayers
of pious monks, who, for love of God, of their free will
choose poverty and shun all the vanities of the world."
Thus runs the charter of 15th March, 1385, by which Duke
Philip the Bold founded the monastery of Champmol.
Seeing that the Carthusians pray incessantly, day and night,
for the salvation of souls, and the prosperous increase of the
public welfare, and the advancement of princes, the Duke is
pleased, under God's mercy, which has preserved him from
childhood until now, to endow from his own private purse,
a Carthusian monastery for twenty-four monks, five lay
brothers and their prior, in honour of the Holy Trinity.

These were the pious reasons which moved him. Unwritten
and unrecorded were the temporal ones : to secure for
himself and his descendants a lasting memorial, worthy of
their fame. The documents of the period, in other respects
dry and uninspiring, provide evidence of the Duke's unceasing
personal interest in the erection of this monument. A picture
of the Apostles by Jan Maelweel pleased him so much that
he had it placed every day in his Oratory. The carved altars
of Flanders had attracted his notice, and similar altars had
to be constructed for his Carthusian monastery.

The work was begun in the year 1377, on the site of
Champmol, " about the range of two arrow shots from
Dijon " ; in the following year the ground was acquired.
In the absence of her husband, Duchess Margaret and her
eldest son with solemn ceremony laid the foundation stone,
and five years later, on Trinity Sunday, 24th May, 1388, the
church was dedicated to the service of God. A few weeks
afterwards the monks were able to take possession of the
monastery.

Drouet de Dammartin was the architect. He had been
previously in the service of King Charles V and the Duke de
Berry, and the castle at Sluis had been his work. An excellent
opportunity was offered now for him to show his skill. For
the Carthusian monastery, which was to shelter twice the
usual number of monks, comprised a vast number of buildings,

while the church was to be a shrine of uncommon splendour. The finest and most expensive material was procured, and four hundred workmen were constantly employed.

Before the church was dedicated, Drouet de Dammartin had returned to the Court of the Duke de Berry, and soon afterwards an artist, who was subsequently to become world-famous, took over the control. This was Claus Sluter, a native of Holland, who had worked under the Fleming, Jean de Marville. He had soon, however, become independent, and held the office of *ymagier et varlet de chambre* to the Duke. On his seal two birds, with outspread wings, hold a key.

He had already received many signs of the Duke's favour. He enjoyed a grant from the ducal purse and had his own quarters which he was able to enlarge and alter, near the castle at Dijon, close to the offices of the administration and the dwellings of the Lord Treasurer and other officials. The Duke had sent him to the Court of the Duke de Berry at Mehun-sur-Yèvre, so that he might study the works of the celebrated André Beauneveu of Valenciennes, who had erected monuments for the royal crypt. "*Il n'avait pour lors meilleur ne le pareil en nulles terres ne de qui tant de bons ouvraiges fuissent demourés en France ou en Haynnau dont il estoit de nacion et ou royaulme d'Angleterre.*" Thus Froissart praises meistre Adryen. There were other opportunities for travel as well. Official commissions took Sluter to Paris to buy alabaster from the Genoese, then to Dinant and to Malines, where supplies of glass and marble could be obtained.

For a time Sluter seems to have put his hand to everything, to have been active both in and out of Dijon, but his attention was now concentrated above all on the completion of the Carthusian Monastery. In time a stately and beautiful building arose, but to-day only the portal, a winding stair, and the Prophet's fountain, survive to remind us of its vanished splendour.

The exterior of the church was remarkable for its gargoyles, on which the stonemason's fantasy could spend itself in wanton pleasantries, without incurring the censure of the Church. On the belfry shone a copper cross and a cock, for which Bouvignes had supplied the ore. Above the choir stood an angel holding the ducal banner. On the portal the

PLATE 3

Claus Sluter : Duke Philip the Bold with John the Baptist.   Former Carthusian Monastery,
Champmol, near Dijon.

[face p. 30

founder and his consort were perpetuated. These figures are Sluter's work.

Duke Philip kneels on the left, a slight smile upon his face, suggestive rather of a well-to-do merchant recalling some successful enterprise, although the costly mantle trimmed with ermine discloses the princely rank of the worshipper. Behind the Duke stands his patron saint, John the Baptist, a life-like and compelling figure.

The image of the Duchess, on the other side, is unfortunately so damaged that her features can no longer be discerned. It would have been interesting to know how Sluter had portrayed this energetic, haughty, and imperious lady, whose anger even her husband was glad to avoid. Margaret has invoked the protection of St. Catherine, who stands behind, guarding her anxiously.

Near them, in the centre of the portal, absorbed completely in her happiness, stands the Virgin, gazing at the Divine Child. A lovely figure, but so different in conception and execution that it must indeed be the creation of another artist. If this is Sluter's work, then the influence of the South had drawn him into its magic circle and vouchsafed to him a glimpse of the flowing grace of Italian art in all its beauty.

The interior of the church must have presented a splendid sight. From the rose-window on the west side, the great window in the choir beneath the statue of the Trinity, and from thirty other windows light streamed in through the richly-coloured panes, illuminating the church with its screen, the three chapels, the high altar with its copper candelabra, the richly carved pulpit, and the lectern : an eagle holding two serpents in its claws. Sluter carved the sculptures, well-known painters like Jean de Beaumez, Jan Maelweel, and Henri Bellechose decorated the altars with pictures, and ornamented the cloisters. From the roof of the church huge lanterns were suspended. The Angel Chapel near the choir was used as the oratory of the Duke and Duchess. It had two floors ; on the walls of the lower was a gallery of angels holding coats of arms ; a winding stair led to the upper oratory. In the sacristy the vessels, robes and stuffs were stored.

Most of these works of art, such as Sluter's figures and the

portraits of the founder and his successors, have disappeared.
Only a few pictures still remain : Christ in the arms of God
the Father, the martyrdom of St. Dionysius, which was
perhaps painted by Maelweel and Bellechose, the Life of
St. George, as well as the two carved altars by Jacques de
Bars, the outer wings of which were decorated by Broederlam,
with scenes from the life of Christ and the Virgin. To prevent
the altars from being affected by damp, thick canvas screens
had been erected at the back.

While the work on the portal was still proceeding, Duke
Philip gave his favourite *imagier* a second commission : the
erection in the large transept of a monumental fountain,
with the representation of the crucifixion. Here, the monks
as they paced up and down in prayer, were to be reminded of
the vanity of all earthly desires. The gloomy verse of Job,
" *Putredini dixi ; pater meus est, mater mea et soror mea
vermibus*," was inscribed out of sight over the transept. Here
in accordance with the directions of St. Bruno were the graves
of the Carthusians. Here, too, in the crucifixion of Christ, was
a memorial in stone for the monks and visitors, the ducal
family, and the host of pilgrims who streamed there. Later
a hundred days' indulgence was granted to those who at the
Cross implored the grace of God.

Sluter, with his nephew, Claus van Werve, executed his
task in a very characteristic fashion. In the centre of the
fountain, which is more than twenty-three feet wide, a
powerful column supports a hexagonal pedestal, whereon
in six recesses stand Moses, King David, and the prophets,
Jeremiah, Zachariah, Daniel, and Isaiah. On the capitals
of the pillars which separate the recesses from one another,
six angels rest their feet ; they are taking refuge, like
frightened birds under the protecting cornice over which the
Calvary rises. At the foot of the mighty crucifix are
seen Mary, Mary Magdalen, and John, mourning. Of the
Calvary only the head of Christ remains. Moses and the
Prophets, however, are still intact and enable us to realize
something of the genius of the master who created them.

With overpowering directness these figures personify the
predictions and lamentations inscribed on their stoles. They

PLATE 4

Claus Sluter : The Fountain of the Prophets.   Former Carthusian Monastery, Champmol, near Dijon.

stand there, mourners rather than judges. Many a time Sluter must have wandered through the narrow streets of Dijon's ghetto to find the models he required.

Moses, as he appeared to Israel when he descended from Mount Sinai with the Tables of the Law—the ruler, the sage, with flowing beard and horned forehead. With commanding presence he passes the inexorable sentence, while his eye seems to search out the future which is unveiled to him :—

Immolabit agnum multitudo filiorum Israhel ad vesperam.

David adorned with the royal crown leans sadly upon his harp and makes complaint :—

Foderunt manus meus et pedes meos, numerarunt ossa.

Jeremiah holds the Holy Writ, submissive to unalterable fate. A supernatural inner sorrow speaks from his face and words :—

O vos omnes qui transitis per viam, attendite et videte si est dolor sicut dolor meus.

Zachariah, bent under his burden of woe, sinks his head and bemoans the heartlessness of men :—

Appenderunt mercedem meam triginta aureos.

Daniel, erect, utters his prophecy, the only one who presumes to sit in judgment.

Post hebdomadas sexaginta duas occidetur Christus.

Lastly, Isaiah, shaken to his inmost soul, an old man, bald-headed, with long beard and deeply furrowed brow. There he stands like one who has experienced all the miseries of earth :—

Sicut ovis ad occisionem ducetur, et quasi agnus coram tondente se obtumescet et non aperiet os suum.

With sweet childlike grace, the angels take up the prophet's song of lamentation and bear it heavenwards. The sorrowful figures, who raise their hands, clasp them together across their breasts, or press their clenched fists to their cheeks, are very moving in their delicacy and naturalness.

When Sluter and Werve had completed their work, Jan Maelweel and his assistants were called in to heighten their effects with colour.

Moses was given a red tunic and a golden mantle lined with blue ; while gold stars, leaves and lace ornamented the draperies of many folds, an effect which the artist had doubtless observed at the Mystery Plays. As the account books reveal, a copper halo which ornamented the head of the Magdalen had been made by a goldsmith.   Jeremiah's nose was adorned by spectacles of gilded copper.

Sluter, with his delight in colour, also shared the contemporary taste ; nor did he hesitate to proclaim the fame of his master and of the ruling house, even on the Cross itself.   The extremities of the arms of the Cross, almost 10 feet long, bore the coats of arms of Burgundy and Flanders. They appeared, too, on the pillars of the fountain.   The hexagonal pedestal displayed on the gilt cornice the sun's rays bearing the initials P. M. P.   The church, likewise, showed crests in the glass of the windows, on the walls, on the banners and the lanterns ; on the altar beside the angels with the implements of the Passion, were other angels bearing the Duke's coat of arms and crest.

Not content with his mighty accomplishment, Sluter started once again in the Carthusian monastery upon his third great work, the sepulchral monument of Philip the Bold.   The plan of this originated with Jean de Marville.   At his death, however, only the stonemason's work had been finished.   Sluter undertook the execution of the figures, but the work did not proceed.   He was stricken with sickness and, an ageing man, he retired to the monastery of St. Etienne at Dijon.   Not long afterwards, on 27th April, 1404, Duke Philip died far from his native duchy, in the small town of Halle, near Brussels, whose miracle-working Madonna he had invoked for his recovery.

In spite of the oppressive load of debt, left by the Duke, the interment took place in the most magnificent manner. Gold and silver table ware was pawned.   Dino Rapondi, the versatile merchant, banker, and moneylender, was once again ready with his help, and himself advanced a large part of the money which was needed.

The embalmed corpse rested under a covering of gold brocade, which bore in the middle a red velvet cross.   Stately banners of blue material fluttered at the four corners of the hearse drawn by six horses.   On the garments of the sixty torch-bearers, 150 coats of arms were sewn.

Behind the coffin walked John, the new Duke, with his

PLATE 5

Pleurants at the tombs of the Dukes of Burgundy.   Museum, Dijon.

[*face p.* 34

two brothers, Anthony and Philip, and his brother-in-law, Count William of Osterbant. After them came an almost countless following of office-holders of the Court, distinguished nobles, knights, esquires, pages, administrative officials, clergy, bishops and monks, physicians and apothecaries, quartermasters and couriers, employés of the kitchens, chambers, and stables. All the mourners had received their mourning garments from Duke John.

From town to town, from place to place, the imposing procession passed on, and finally, on 16th June, 1404, the burial took place in the Carthusian monastery. Here, in fulfilment of the wishes of the dead man, whose body was clothed in a Carthusian's habit, all pomp was avoided. The Order showed its gratitude to its exalted patron by the bestowal on him of the title of *monachatus*, a special mark of ecclesiastical favour.

A slab of black marble was placed temporarily on Philip's grave. Sluter felt himself still strong enough to execute the memorial. He pledged himself to the new Duke to complete it within four years. But it was not to be. At his death the huge blocks of alabaster for the figures lay still unhewn. Claus van Werve, who had completely absorbed his uncle's methods, carved the figures and finished the memorial in about seven years. In ceremonious Court raiment which covers his armour, Duke Philip lies on the marble sarcophagus, at his feet a lion, at his head two angels holding his helmet ornamented with lilies. By his skilful colouring, Maelweel contrived to increase the impression of splendour. Around the tomb an alabaster gallery was constructed; and in the recesses stand the *Pleurants*, clergy in cowls, laymen in hoods, personages of the most diverse rank and condition, portrayed as the artist may have observed them in the funeral procession, some overwhelmed with grief, some sedate and solemn, others thoughtless and inattentive. To let the mourners appear on the tomb was no new idea, but here the artist has shown us figures drawn from the world in which he lived.

The foundation stone of the Burgundian State was laid. Duke Philip, who had once been called " the Landless ", left behind possessions " to the value of a kingdom ". His glory was proclaimed far and wide by the Carthusian Monastery of Champmol.

CHAPTER III

The Glorification of Tyrannicide

Dame convoitise est de tous maulx la racine.—JEAN PETIT.

ON the morning of 24th November, 1407, the news spread through Paris that the King's brother, Louis, Duke of Orleans, had been attacked in the night and most cruelly murdered. In a few days all Paris knew that John of Burgundy, a cousin of the Duke, had instigated the foul deed in order to rid himself of a rival who everywhere opposed him. The crime recalled the methods of the Italians. But no Italian ruler, who had commissioned such a murder, would have confessed in a moment of weakness, as did John, that the devil had instigated him to commit the outrage.

What were the real facts ?

The antagonism between Burgundy and Orleans was of long standing. It had shown itself during the lifetime of Philip the Bold, and since his death the feeling had been greatly intensified. Was a matter of importance to be debated the cousins invariably fell out with one another. John watched with growing resentment while Louis increased his position at Court. He saw himself disregarded, and was conscious that in many ways he was his cousin's inferior. Nor did Louis' dissolute life interrupt his political ambitions. He had in him something of the nature of a Sardanapalus : with every excess he seemed to renew his strength, and he pursued his ends with great tenacity of purpose. Realizing that he could never hope to be a match for such a man, John, without consulting his counsellors, resolved upon his assassination.

Great as was the indignation among the other princes of the blood, they lacked the courage to take up arms against the murderer. They feared the temper of the people of Paris, for great discontent prevailed in the city on account of the extravagant and unguarded conduct of Duke Louis and

Queen Isabeau. Orleans was suspected of having laid hands on State moneys to support his extravagant mode of life and to further his political enterprises. Duke John, on the other hand, was regarded as a friend of the lower classes. They looked to him for reforms in the administration and especially for some alleviation from the heavy load of taxation. In university circles, too, there was no regret for the murdered man, since his support of the Avignon Pope had given bitter offence there. His enemies made no secret of their feelings : " A blessing on him who struck this blow," they cried, " for had Orleans lived the whole kingdom would have been ruined." The princes, whatever their feelings, were forced from the path of violence into that of negotiation.

In the meantime Duke John had not remained idle. Having sought refuge in Flanders, he decided to acknowledge the deed anew : this time publicly. He was not to express regret, but to justify the act as necessary for the welfare of the King and the State. With this purpose he appeared before his subjects at Ghent. A ducal councillor read the justification aloud. Copies of this memorial, which has not been preserved, were spread broadcast ; anybody who desired could obtain one. The " members " promised aid, and made a grant of money ; and Duke John could now confidently await events.

With a large escort and numerous troops, he appeared at Amiens in January, 1408. In the picturesque fashion of the age he spoke his mind to the world at large. Over the doors of his quarters, to the right and left of his coat of arms, he caused two lances to be painted ; the one with a blunted point for jousting, the other sharpened as if for battle. In between was to be seen the carpenter's plane, the device which he had assumed when Louis of Orleans had threatened him with a knobbed stick. To him who desired peace he would offer peace. Failing that he was prepared for war.

Nearly two weeks were spent in conferences, interrupted only by the usual festivities. The Duke de Berry, the King of Sicily, and the royal councillors required that John should petition the King for pardon and mercy. This he declined to do. Indeed, he demanded that the crime should be ascribed to him as a merit. He was represented by skilled advocates. Master Jean Petit, later to become notorious, and four other

masters of the University of Paris, declared publicly in a
second justification, which has likewise disappeared, that
Duke John would have been guilty of sin if he had suffered
Louis of Orleans to live. They were ready, they said, to
defend this thesis against all comers. Duke John, for his
part, announced that he was willing and anxious to appear
before the King of France to vindicate himself.   Any
semblance of agreement was out of the question, and the
parties went their several ways, having accomplished nothing.

It was during these days that a strange pamphlet found
its way into the Burgundian Chancery, a bombastic manifesto
in the Latin language, proclaiming to kings and dukes, to
all lords, spiritual and temporal, the glorious deed of the
Duke of Burgundy, and setting forth the true facts concerning
the death of Louis of Orleans. After a lengthy introduction,
in the mazes of which the author appears to have lost his way,
Plato, that most ardent supporter of the common-weal,
appears with other witnesses to prove that disturbers of the
peace and enemies of civil order must be exterminated. Holy
Writ itself directs that an offending eye or foot shall be
plucked out or cut off.

A sign from God, the pamphlet continued, had moved
John to champion the honour of the royal house and to take
up arms against a villain, in comparison with whose crimes
the atrocities of the ancient world grew pale. Compared
with Louis and his devilish accomplices, Phalaris and his bulls,
Diomedes and his steeds, and Procrustes with his torture-
bed, sank into insignificance. Crime after crime is recited in
endless succession.

" We ask you mortals," the writer continues, " what was
to be done to this criminal who threatened King and State
with ruin ? He despised all rights, divine and human. He
showed no reverence to the King's judges, feeling himself
already a King. None dared to oppose him. We call God
and mankind to witness that out of regard for the welfare of
the King, the princes and the whole nation, which was ever
dearer to us than life itself, we refrained from strife and war,
from which neither victor nor vanquished would have
emerged unscathed. Conscious of our obligations to the
Crown, we were compelled, in order to avoid shedding innocent
blood, to consent to the eclipse of the Duke of Orleans.

PLATE 6

Unknown Master: Duke John the Fearless.   Museum, Antwerp.

[face p. 38

We were mindful of the fact that the Greeks decreed divine honours to tyrannicides, that tyrannicides, as we read in the chronicles, have filled the whole world with their glory. But we in truth sought not glory ; only the deliverance of the King and State. The deed had been too long delayed. Nothing, neither kinship or covenant could restrain us, nothing could prevent what was ordained. Let truth shine forth by virtue of her light."

This manifesto, it seems, was not published. In any case, this third justification gives some indication of what the Court was to expect when John appeared before the King. By the sophistry of schoolmen a deed of jealous hatred was to be transformed into a pious act of State.

Weary of the negotiations, Duke John now entered St. Denis at the head of a small army. The princes at once gave way, and declared their agreement with the proposal that John should be allowed to present his case publicly before the King. He entered Paris with a strong escort, and was received with great enthusiasm by the people, who cried " Noël " after him in the streets, as if he had been a conqueror. But prudence was still necessary. In the Hôtel d'Artois a room was hastily constructed in a tower which safeguarded the Duke by day and night.

At length the momentous day arrived, Thursday, 8th March, 1408, on which the ceremony was to take place. In solemn procession John proceeded to the Hôtel St. Pol. Among his companions, the Duke of Lorraine attracted notice. No princes of the blood were present, however, but the people once more acclaimed the Duke with shouts of welcome.

Hours elapsed before the procession reached its destination. When the last of the train had left the Hôtel d'Artois the leaders had already reached the royal palace. The hall was entered from the courtyard through a window. Each comer had to establish his identity. Duke John had been obliged to furnish beforehand a list of his escort.

In spite of the strict control, however, a few well-dressed people, a few clerks from the University, and a few citizens, of whom actually only four were admitted, succeeded in forcing their way in.

Already between six and seven in the morning Duke Louis of Guyenne, the eldest son, as representative and heir presumptive of the sick King, had appeared at the palace. Around him were grouped the Duke de Berry, Louis of Anjou, the King of Sicily, and other princes. The Rector of the University, members of the Great Council, of the *Parlement* and the Exchequer, were also in attendance. Duke John was the last to appear, and when he had entered, the window was bricked up and the hall was isolated. John wore a red velvet garment covered with gold-leaf, and lined with grey fur; when he moved his arms, his armour flashed out from under his wide sleeves. After formal greetings, John took his place between the Duke de Berry and the Duke de Bretagne, to the extreme annoyance of the latter, who had already refused to attend him.

On the left side of the hall was the advocate's tribune. Six steps led up to it, and here the Chancellor of the Duke, the bishop of Tournai, and the officials took their places with the barons and gentlemen beside them. The opposing tribune was reserved for the provost of the city with his sergeants, the royal chancellor and members of the Royal Council and the *Parlement*.

At last, at about ten o'clock, everything was ready and the speaker could begin. All eyes were directed to the man, to whom a very thankless and delicate task had been entrusted.

Jean Petit, a Norman, a graduate of the Collège du Trésorier, had, as a writer and orator, interposed with passionate zeal in the schismatic conflicts. In disputations he even seems to have defeated Jean Gerson, who is said never to have forgiven him. Petit was under special obligation to the House of Burgundy. He had received the means to pursue his studies from the ducal treasury and was bound by special oath to Duke John. He had recently been appointed a member of his council with a yearly salary. He accepted the duty now entrusted to him with considerable reluctance, for he knew that the undertaking might cost him his head, if his master were to withdraw his protection. Nevertheless, the Duke's commands must be obeyed. Petit was a blunt, vigorous and impetuous man, and he conducted his case in characteristic fashion. He was, he said, conscious of his defects: " . . . *quant . . . je me regarde impourveu de sens, povre de mémoire, feble d'engin et très mal appoinctié en parole, une très grande paour me fiert au cuer, voire si grande que mon engin s'esbahist et ma mémoire s'enfuit, et ce peu de sens que je cuidoie avoir m'a jà du tout laissé.*" And then having removed his hood, Jean Petit knelt and prayed the princes not to be offended at any words that might fall from him on behalf of his master, and immediately began his speech.

Duke John, he said, in obedience to his King and Sovereign, appeared most humbly before his Majesty in order to testify his reverence. Twelve obligations induced him to do this. As next of kin, as blood relation, as vassal, as subject; furthermore, as knight, baron, count and duke, as peer and Dean of Peers, and consequently, next the Crown, as chief dignitary of the kingdom, and finally as father-in-law of the Dauphin and of the Princess Michelle. These twelve obligations, as well as his father's deathbed exhortations, compelled him not only to serve, obey, love and honour the King, but also to defend and avenge him. Nothing would cause Duke John more heartfelt sorrow than that the King should condemn any one of his actions. And since, at the instigation of malicious persons, the King might be offended at the death of the Duke of Orleans, although the deed was committed for the great welfare of the King, his children and the State, John prayed the King most humbly to let his disapproval vanish, and to extend to him, as loyal vassal, subject and cousin-german, once more his grace and goodwill.

After the petition came the justification. Petit took as his theme the words of Paul the Apostle, *Radix omnium malorum est cupiditas*, bringing thus most skilfully into prominence the primary sin of covetousness. This vice, he said, had already engaged the special attention of many theologians, *cupiditas* appeared to desire to compete with *superbia* for precedence. Petit divided his speech into two parts, the *majeur* and the *mineur*; the former into four, the latter into three divisions.

In the first division of the *majeur*, Petit sought to prove the accuracy of the Bible words. In the second, he discussed the theory of crime against majesty, differentiating between crimes against divine majesty : in the first place those committed by heretics and idolators, in the second those by schismatics. Next came crimes against temporal majesty : firstly against the King, secondly against the Queen, thirdly against the King's children, and fourthly against the community. Both kinds of crime, being very horrible and unnatural, were justly visited with extraordinary punishment. Even after his death an evildoer could be pursued for crime against majesty. If found guilty by the judge, his corpse was to be exhumed and burned ; his property confiscated, and his children were deprived of their inheritance.

His hearers could by now guess the goal at which Petit was aiming. Any remaining doubts were removed by the examples which followed. As instances of apostasy he cited Julian the Apostate; who, indeed, could have become a Pope, but declined on the ground that the profit was too small ; the monk Sergius, who from lust of money became a Mahommedan ; and Prince Zambri who denied our Saviour.

In loud tones the praise of Phineas resounded through the Hall, Phineas, the priest's son, who, uncalled for, of his own motion, slew Zambri the Israelite and his Midianite mistress, most lovely of all women, on their couch of sin. Though no name had as yet been mentioned, the significance of the illustration can have been lost upon no one, and all eyes, we may be sure, were turned upon the Duke of Burgundy.

The examples of the third division were equally clear. " Covetousness turns men into traitors." Lucifer, the most perfect being God ever created, was thrust from Heaven because he aspired to equality with his Maker. Absalom was killed because he rebelled against his father ; Queen Athalie because she attempted the murder of her grandson in order to acquire the sovereignty for herself. Was it necessary to search further for precedents or to name others, such as St. Michael, or Joab, or that valiant bishop who saved the rightful heir to the throne against the wicked conspiracy of Athalie ?

In order to make his case still clearer, Petit in his fourth division, examined eight universal propositions which he

labelled truths. The third is very significant : In accordance
with morality, with natural and divine law, it is permitted
to every subject, without command or injunction, to kill an
infamous traitor or tyrant, or to suffer him to be killed. It
is not only permitted, but even commanded when the traitor
or tyrant has assumed such power that the ruler cannot
summon him before his judges.

Jean Petit was at no loss for lack of proof. In honour of
the twelve Apostles, he quoted a dozen judgments from the
Fathers and philosophers, from the Civil and " Imperial "
law, as well as from the Bible. St. Michael and the Apostle
Peter, Thomas Aquinas, John of Salisbury, Aristotle
and Cicero, Moses and Phineas, even Boccaccio, all appear as
witnesses for the defence.

The fifth " Truth " also deserves attention. Amidst the
strange farrago of superstition and delusion, of scholastic
erudition and Burgundian party interests, one assertion is
surprising. Petit declares that although contracts, promises
and oaths must be observed even if prejudicial to the con-
tracting parties, yet, if found to be against the interests of a
prince or his family, they can be ignored. Surely Petit, in
enunciating this new doctrine of political necessity, must
have been influenced by Burgundian statesmanship which
considered it essential that property amassed by feudal
methods, should be welded together by non-feudal expedients
and cemented by political means.

Nine corollaries, which once again summed up the crimes
against divine and human majesty of the first, second and third
degree, concluded the main portion.

The second part, the *mineur*, specified the man who had
committed the crimes cited in the corollaries.

Louis of Orleans, he said, was so possessed by his greed
for vain honours and temporal wealth that he aspired even
to procure the crown of France for himself and his progeny.
Yielding to the temptation of the devil, his lust of tyranny
was such that he attempted to destroy the King and his
kindred by sorcery.

While the first part of the harrangue was intended rather
for the learned, the second appealed directly to the multitude.

Petit did not enlarge upon the nature of the crimes against
God, but dwelt on those against the King. First of all he gave

an account of the attempts by Orleans " the criminal " to
murder the King with the aid of the devil.   Superstition,
which threw its spell over all classes of people, was responsible
in this case for the wildest excesses.   In picturesque language
Petit related how early one Sunday morning an accomplice
of Orleans, an apostate monk, had procured a sword, a dagger,
and a ring to be consecrated, or, to speak accurately,
desecrated by two demons.   When these sons of Hell, Heremas
and Estramain, who were dressed in conspicuous green, had
finished their work, the bodies of certain men, who had been
hanged a short time before, were fetched under cover of
darkness from the gallows at Montfaucon.   The ring, which
shone as red as scarlet, was thereupon placed in the mouth
of a corpse, while the sword and dagger were thrust through
the heart in order to acquire magic properties.

A few days later the sword, dagger, and ring were returned
to Louis together with a small bag of bone meal from the
corpse.   Orleans wore this for some time next his heart
until one of his intimates heard of his secret and betrayed
it to the King.   But his doom was sealed.   Orleans pursued
the meddler with his hatred, and although closely related to
the Royal House, he had him banished from the kingdom.
Since that time none at Court had dared to offer any opposition to the Duke.

One crime followed another.   Did not the same apostate
monk give Duke Louis a wand of cherry wood which had been
dipped in the blood of a red cockerel and a white chicken, and
which possessed such magic powers that no woman could
resist the advances of its owner ?   Orleans procured the staff
in Easter week, as if with special intent to wound his Saviour
and to honour Satan.   In return, the Prince of Hell showed
his gratitude by heaping afflictions on the unfortunate King.
Charles fell so seriously ill at Beauvais that he lost his nails
and almost all his hair.   Then at Le Mans his mind became
deranged.   " Tear the sword out of my heart !   My brother
Orleans has done this.   I must kill him ! " cried the unhappy
man, who had wrought continuously for his brother's good.
" Orleans the criminal " was supported also by the Duke of
Milan, Gian Galeazzo, who had married his daughter
Valentine to Louis with the sole object of securing the crown
of France for his grandson.   If proof of this be demanded,

said Petit, consider the words which the Duke of Milan had
called out after Valentine at her departure : " Only as Queen
of France will I see you again."

On the advice of Philip de Mézières, the French prince
had sought to emulate his father-in-law.   Just as Gian
Galeazzo had deceived his uncle Bernabo by his hypocrisy
so Orleans had duped King Charles.   His life had been
nothing but dissimulation.   The pious intercourse with the
Celestines, his devotions, his five or six masses daily, were
all deceptions.   And what took place in secret ?   By day
the most diabolical plots were hatched with Mézières.
At night there were drinking bouts, dice playing, and
familiarities with loose women.   And what at first occurred
in secret soon took place openly and shamelessly.

Thus was Orleans guilty of crimes of the first degree
against divine and temporal majesty.   Petit adduced evidence
also of crimes of other degrees.   Louis had attempted the
life of the King with poison.   At the notorious fancy-dress
ball, *bal des sauvages*, he himself performed the lackey's
duties solely in order to be able to set fire to the King's dress
with his torch.   It was a miracle that the King escaped a
terrible death by fire, for several noblemen perished.   Orleans
had further concluded an iniquitous alliance with Henry of
Lancaster, as a result of which the French King was to suffer
the same fate as Richard II of England.   The Queen and the
royal children had also been attacked.   Had not Orleans
sent a poisoned apple to the Dauphin, now recently deceased ?
By chance it fell into the hands of his own little son, who
had perished lamentably.

Why did Orleans show such loyalty to Benedict, " le
Pappe de la Lune " ?   Was it not in order to induce the
Pope to declare the sick King and his issue incapable of
ruling, to release his subjects from their oath of allegiance,
and to proclaim Louis as the legitimate successor ?   The
criminal had plotted against the common weal no less than
against the Crown.   For years he kept in his pay bands of
mercenaries under arms who had ravaged and pillaged
without mercy, extorting money from loyal subjects for the
support of the country's enemies.

At length Petit had come to the end.   In his submission
he had proved clearly that Orleans had committed crimes

against majesty of the first, second, third and fourth degrees, in order to procure for himself the crown of France. He claimed, therefore, that the Duke of Burgundy was in nowise to be censured. The King must not only submit to what had taken place, but must expressly approve it. John, like the Archangel Michael and Phineas was to be lauded and recompensed. The King should load him with honours and riches, and proclaim his loyalty by letter patent, and by writings throughout the realm, for such without doubt was the will of God. The audience must have sighed with relief when Petit sat down. He had spoken for about four hours, very monotonously, without raising or lowering his voice.

At Petit's request, Duke John now formally and expressly acknowledged him as his representative, and once again the advocate declared that his master reserved to himself the right of revealing further crimes and misdemeanours at a more convenient time and hour. Thereupon the whole assembly broke up.

In their opinions of the justification, copies of which were soon circulated, the Burgundians and Orleanists were more strongly than ever at variance. Moderate and reserved men found also much in it for stricture. The prudent monk of St. Denis considered the defence by no means established. Unfortunately he does not criticize the justification in detail. He says simply that he will leave the masters of theology to dispute the alleged proofs among themselves, whether they were reasonable or merely ridiculous. And so it was with many others. The judicious were forced to acknowledge how cunningly Petit had played upon the feelings of the masses; how skilfully events, which had aroused popular indignation, had been exaggerated and exploited, and with what subtlety the empty gossip of the Court had been turned to his advantage. The stories of magic can have surprised nobody, for the Court itself had called in magicians to cure the King. But Petit had perverted well-known facts, and omitted much that might have been urged in favour of Orleans.

Whether the justification was substantiated or not, the hearers and readers were in agreement on one main point. Petit's harrangue was not so much a defence of the Duke

of Burgundy as a detailed indictment of Louis of Orleans.
It was a skilful move, originating probably in the commands
of John, that only the dead man should be attacked. Everyone else was ignored, including the unpopular Duchess
Valentine of Milan. Petit even broke a lance in defence
of Queen Isabeau, and praised the rule, as guardian, of the
Duke de Berry. The tactics adopted by the Duke and his
advocate were completely successful. The King having
temporarily recovered his reason, received the Duke in
audience, and was graciously pleased to accord him a full
and complete pardon. The royal act of clemency was received
with feelings of astonishment and some discontent, but there
was no open hostility. It was considered wise not to exas-
perate the Duke still further. Had not John threatened
new revelations ? Even the Queen had her reasons for
desiring that certain things should not be uttered. It was
necessary to rest and gain time until the murderer had
departed from Paris.

At length in July the Duke's enemies could breathe again.
Disorders had broken out in the bishopric of Liège which
compelled John to leave Paris. His opponents now straightway commenced their attack. Queen Isabeau threw in her
lot with the Orleanists and placed herself at their head.
She induced the King to cancel the letters of pardon. In
great state she returned to Paris, with the Dauphin on horseback at her side. The widowed Duchess Valentine returned
also with her eldest son Charles and renewed her demands
for justice. This time her request was granted.

On 11th September, 1408, there gathered in the Louvre
the same personages as had listened but a short time before
to Petit's glorification of tyrannicide. Only the Duke of
Burgundy and his supporters were absent. The assembly
was now to listen to the advocate of the widow and orphans
of the murdered man.

Thomas, the Abbot of Cerisi, mounted the tribune and
began a long and notably effective speech. He dwelt in the
first part on the obligation of the King, if peace was to be
preserved in the State, to administer justice to his subjects
with an even hand. Against the dark background of treason

and murder, hypocrisy and insensate desire of power, the figure of justice was brought out into brilliant relief. The blood of Abel cried to heaven for vengeance.

Cerisi allowed the dead man to rise from the grave and cry his grievous wrongs to the King. " My Lord and brother, see how I have suffered death for your sake. Behold my body which was trampled on and thrown in the mire of the street. Consider my severed arm, my scattered brains. Look and see if there be any sorrow like unto my sorrow. Alas ! It did not suffice my enemy to cut short my life. He surprised me treacherously and so suddenly that I was in danger of eternal damnation ; and still not satisfied, he strives to defame me and my house by shameful calumny."

In the second part, which he likewise divided into six articles, Cerisi denounced the crime of the Duke, basing his arguments on the text : *Radix omnium malorum est cupiditas.*

John, he said, had no right or authority to set himself up to judge Louis whom he should have honoured as brother of the King. John was himself a tyrant and ruled tyrannically. How could John, if he were not a hypocrite, continue to wear the Order of Louis ? He had moreover confessed his guilt. He had fallen on his knees before King Louis of Sicily and the Duke de Berry, imploring counsel and aid, confessing that he committed the deed at the instigation of the devil. How could this confession be reconciled with the allegation that his action was good and right ? Why the concealment of the deed ? Why the hurried flight to Flanders ?

Jean Petit's pamphlet with which Cerisi reached his third and last part, was, he said, a tissue of untruths. The Duke of Orleans never attempted to make away with the King, nor his wife nor children ; nor had he ever conspired against the commonwealth. And so the zealous Abbot, instead of challenging his opponent to prove his accusations, sought merely to refute them by denial. Several points were rather clumsily conceded, and his attempt to excuse Louis' dealings with the necromancers on the ground of the Duke's youth and inexperience must have sounded somewhat strange. Still, his endeavour to bring the University into the arena by appealing to the theological and medical faculties was very skilful, and his defence of the Orleanist party was striking and fairly successful. He was followed by a jurist, Guillaume

Cousinot, the councillor and advocate of the Duchess of Orleans who proposed the punishment to be meted out to the murderer : disgrace, a fine of a million gold shillings, imprisonment, and banishment. Should France, which had been a shining example to foreign countries, no longer be the stronghold of justice ? English, Germans and other foreigners had come formerly to the Court of France in order to enforce their rights. France would exist, St. Remigius had said at the baptism of Clovis, so long only as there was justice within her borders.

Sentence as demanded was passed, but never executed. Contrary to the expectations and hopes of Queen Isabeau and the Duchess Valentine, John emerged victorious from his conflict with the people of Liège. He won a brilliant victory near Othée, and his courage there earned for him the proud title of " the Fearless ". The Court considered it advisable to leave Paris, and the civil war which then broke out was to engage the activities and distract the thoughts of France for many years.

But the Duke of Burgundy had been pilloried as a traitor and a common murderer, and he could not possibly submit to the disgrace. The Burgundian council considered the plan of countering the reply of the Abbot of Cerisi by a reasoned rejoinder. In a third public assembly the deed was again to be justified in the King's presence. Petit and other learned men received instructions to issue a challenge to the Abbot of Cerisi. The Compact of Chartres had indeed patched up a reconciliation between the parties, but as the Burgundian Court jester sarcastically remarked, this *paix fourrée* was not lasting. At the New Year, Duke John distributed some remarkable emblems which took the shape of a mason's level. " *La quelle chose estoit en signification . . . que ce qui estoit fait par aspre et indirecte voie, seroit aplanyé et mis a son reigle, et le feroit mestre et mectroit a droicte ligne.*" Petit now saw his opportunity, by disposing of his opponent, to acquire wealth and property. With passionate zeal he set to work to answer the " greenhorn " who had attempted to refute his arguments and had fallen into error after error. The Abbot, he alleged, was not a man of learning, he had taken no degree ; at the most he had delivered a theological lecture. He had presumed to cast doubts on Petit's orthodoxy. He was ready at any time to justify himself before the Church or the University of Paris.

To anyone who can enjoy scholastic quibbles, these prolonged and tedious disputes between the learned rivals may have their interest. But the historian will lay them aside with considerable disappointment. Petit affords little positive material, he merely advances new accusations. The Burgundian agents, even if they had succeeded in discovering further crimes, could carry the matter no further. It seemed useless to come forward with fresh charges against the Duchess Valentine, who was then dead and could not refute them. But Petit pursued her as he pursued Louis of Orleans into the grave. He demanded that the bodies of Louis and Valentine, for their crime against the King, should be exhumed and handed over to the judge.

One point, however, is remarkable. Duke John's confession that he committed the murder at the instigation of the devil, was recalled. The admission, made in a moment of weakness, fear and excitement, contained an avowal of guilt. As their was no guilt there could be no confession.

But Petit's hopes of appearing once more at the bar of public opinion in order to substantiate anew his justification of tyrannicide and destroy his opponent, were not fulfilled. Duke John declined a *disceptation de replique*, and Petit died unnoticed.

" Would that I had never studied," he is said to have exclaimed at the approach of death. Was he allowed a presentiment that his work would disturb the minds of men for many years, or even that it would engage the attention of the General Council at Constance ?

When fortune turned in favour of the Armagnacs and they made their victorious entry into Paris, Jean Gerson, the illustrious theologian and chancellor of the University, at a Synod held in 1414, procured the condemnation of the doctrines laid down by Petit as heretical. Duke John appealed and the matter was referred to the Council. The Burgundian

Plate 7

[face p. 50

Juan de la Huerta and Antoine Le Moiturier : Tomb of Duke John the Fearless and his wife Margaret.   Museum, Dijon.

diplomats left no stone unturned to influence the judges. Splendid jewels and the finest produce of the Burgundian vineyards were dispatched to Constance. But after endless and embittered negotiations an anonymous and confused collection of points regarding the justification of tyrannicide was condemned by the Council fathers, while the Commission of Faith quashed the judgment of the Paris Synod. Silence was enjoined on the disputants lest at any time the conflict might break out afresh.

Thus ecclesiastical differences were made to serve the ends of politics. Consumed by their hatred the opposing parties rushed on from violence to violence. Not even the appearance in France of King Henry V could put an end to civil war. At the third decisive battle, near Agincourt, on 25th October, 1415, the banner of Duke John, the premier peer of France, was absent. The Emperor Sigismund, whose mind was always stimulated by difficulties, vainly attempted to play the part of mediator in Paris, but Burgundy continued his negotiations with the country's enemy. Duke John, having met the English King at Calais, again made himself master of Paris, while Henry V planted his standard on the battlements of Rouen. It seemed as if the work of Philip Augustus was to come to naught. King Charles and his Queen fell into the hands of John and had to serve his will. The Armagnacs seized the Dauphin Charles, who was essential to them if their methods were to be legalized. For Burgundian diplomacy the question grew ever more pressing : either reconciliation with the Armagnacs or open alliance with England. On 10th September, 1419, a further meeting was to take place at Montereau-faut-Yonne between the Dauphin and Duke John to discuss terms of settlement ; but here the treachery of Duke John was requited, and murder was repaid by murder. With the connivance of the Dauphin, the assassin of Louis of Orleans fell beneath the blows of the Armagnacs.

CHAPTER IV

THE RULER AND HIS COURT

Le prince en la chose publique
Est comme sang dedens le corps.
Le sang mauvais fait vie oblique
Et jette enfin l'esprit dehors ;
Le bon rend les esperis fors
Et donne aux membres nourreture.

MARTIN LE FRANC.

THE death of his father presented the young Duke Philip with an extremely delicate task. Not only had his father's assassination left him in alliance with England, a condition of things from which even Duke John had recoiled, but owing to his father's imprudent policy the inheritance which was now thrust upon him was bound to be a troubled one. The murder of Louis of Orleans had aroused a great deal of criticism, even in the Burgundian camp itself. The quibbling justification of Master Petit was by no means universally popular. Duke John had, moreover, done much to offend the aristocratic representatives of absolute government. In order to hold his own in Paris he had allied himself with the Cabochians whose leader was a butcher named Caboche, and he had so far forgotten his dignity as to give public expression of his sympathy on the death of Legois, another butcher. These fraternal advances were difficult to reconcile with the ducal policy in Flanders, where under the eyes of John himself the delegates from Ghent and Paris exchanged hoods and swore mutual help and support. Even the Abbot of Cerisi had reproached Burgundy with courting popular favour.

A new orientation of Burgundian policy was now necessary. Not another word was heard concerning the murder of the Duke of Orleans ; not another word of the justification of tyrannicide which might possibly bring Philip, a ruler proud of his orthodoxy and a champion of the Church, into conflict with the Holy See.

The Burgundian State was to be supported by the nobility rather than by the people. Philip the Good had recourse to

his grandfather's principles of government. A glorification
of the ideal of knighthood commenced. Free from all fetters,
inwardly restored, chivalry was to renew its strength.

Philip the Bold was a native of France. In agreement
with the French King and owning his support, his Flemish
policy was naturally influenced by French views. In no
other country at that time had the idea of monarchy
so strongly developed as in the dominions of Louis VI,
Philip Augustus, Saint-Louis, and Philip the Fair. Although
the occupant of the French throne was insane, the ship of
State was being skilfully piloted towards that harbour upon
which, since the time of Suger of Saint-Denis, the eyes of
French statesmen had been fixed. At a period of the greatest
domestic confusion France had done what an *Imperator* would
never have presumed to do. Relying on her ability to rule
the Church alone, she had refused obedience to her Pope
at Avignon.

In France a halo encircled kingship; we can speak almost
of the existence of a religion of kingship. As soon as the ruler
had been anointed at Rheims with the holy oil from the
ampulla, which was reputed to have been brought by the
dove to the baptism of Clovis, he was endowed with immediate
divine powers. By the laying on of hands, the wearer of the
French crown could heal the sick. The Capet legend celebrated him as a Priest-King, as God's viceroy.

Brought up in the belief of the sovereign's divine mission,
Philip the Bold came to the Netherlands and sought to
introduce this conception into his Franco-German feudal
territories. The ruler is absolute; in him the State is personi-
fied; all power submits to his will. A deeper meaning lies
in the formula, *Car ainsi nous plaist-il estre fait*, which
is to be found in the Burgundian State documents.

Philip's grandson claimed a reverence that amounted to
adoration. The Church raised no objection, but in fact
approved the claim. Gerson, unable to withstand the pressure
of the court theologians, allowed the prince a company of
guardian angels of special rank. With that strange sanctifi-
cation of daily life which was one of the features of the age,
the Bible was invoked for the glorification of the Sovereign,

and texts which spoke of God the Father and of Christ were freely applied to the Duke.

This conception of divine kingship was brought into prominence at the entry of Philip the Good into Ghent in the year 1458. Biblical experts had been consulted, and they had sought high and low for texts appropriate to the occasion. A venerable figure in imposing raiment, intended perhaps to represent the prophet Haggai, clasped a book bearing the words :

Ecce venit desideratus cunctis gentibus et replebit gloria eius domum Domini.

Isaiah was represented with the text : *Ecce nomen Domini venit de longinquo* ; and with another from the psalter : *Respice Domine in servos tuos.* By the side of a young girl, wringing her hands and imploring the Prince's grace, stood a shield with the verse :—

Inveni quem diligit anima mea.

On one occasion, after similar festivites in Arras, Jacques du Clercq had been moved to write : *"Bref, si Dieu fust descendu du ciel, je ne sçays si on en euist austant fait ne peu plus faire d'honneur que on feit audit duc."*

These ideas which took root and flourished under Philip the Good continued to exist, in spite of all the storms that broke over the Burgundian State long after the premature death of Charles the Bold. When Philip's great grandson, Philip the Fair, visited Franche Comté, he was received with unexampled enthusiasm. *"Long live Burgundy,"* was shouted so loudly in Dôle, writes an eye-witness of the entry, " that it was difficult to hear the trumpeters. So many people crowded into the streets at Gray that the sovereign could scarcely be seen. It seemed as if they had God himself by the feet."

The ruler was surrounded with the greatest pomp ; nothing was too good for him. What the Duke and the members of his family required for their daily needs, was furnished from the finest material, whether in the matter of garments or domestic utensils. From prayer-book and sword down to children's toys and toothpicks, everything was overlaid with gold and silver or sparkled in a blaze of jewels. The sovereign's hand might touch nothing common, and even the homeliest articles were made and beautified by famous craftsmen and artists.

The *Grand Duc d'Occident*, with his exaggerated self-esteem, and his almost divine attributes, claimed his own code of morality. He bestowed his favours upon numerous ladies although his motto, " *aultre n'aray* " might well have imposed on him at least a show of fidelity to his consort. Lambert of Ardres could have reproached him, as once he did the Count of Guines, with a mode of life not unlike that of Jupiter or Solomon. Chastellain was much troubled when in his character study of his master, he has to make mention of *le vice de la chair*. Philip the Good assured himself of the forgiveness of Heaven, and with this and with the Duke's eminent qualities, which occasioned their enthusiastic praise, the court clergy had to be content.

Philip's mistresses, however, never appeared publicly, nor can they be shown to have exercised any influence on his government. They were not seen at Court and their names are hardly mentioned by the chroniclers. But for the scrupulous bookkeeping of the Exchequer they would have fallen into total oblivion. Nevertheless if Isabella, Philip's third wife, the clever and haughty Portuguese princess, was not forced to meet her rivals officially at Court, the Duke's numerous bastards served to remind her constantly of the unhappiness of their married life. These children of illicit intercourse were brought up and maintained in the same way as the legitimate offspring. They bore the ducal coat of arms, the bar sinister alone proclaiming their illegitimacy. The daughters appeared at Court festivities, the sons played an illustrious rôle as generals, diplomats or princes of the Church. La Marche, whose attention was struck by the fact that " *sur toutes les nations du monde, les Germaniens et Allemans font petite extime des bastards et bastardes* ", made a collection in his memoirs of the great deeds done by bastards from remotest times ; and no one saw any reason for comment when Bishop John of Cambrai, an illegitimate son of Duke John the Fearless, was entrusted with the duty of christening Marie, the daughter of Charles the Bold.

The Duchess Isabella, who had known how to aid her husband even in the most delicate political negotiations, could not forget the slight to which she was exposed. She withdrew entirely from Court. Without taking vows she

lived like a nun, reappearing only at Philip's bedside when he
was taken ill.

Society at Court saw no reason to reproach Philip with his
private life : indeed, the courtiers, both lay and cleric, and
the citizens followed his example, thinking doubtless that
what was right in their sovereign was permissible for themselves. The countless patents of legitimacy tell their own
story. The scrupulous chastity of Charles the Bold was neither
respected nor understood, and when, on his marriage, he
put aside the habits of his youth the most disgraceful slanders
were circulated concerning his private life.

The children, like the wife, had to submit to the Duke's
will. When Philip the Good, at the close of his life, fell under
the influence of the ambitious family of Croy, who were
playing a dangerous game with France, he broke utterly with
his son, who dared to contradict him, and cut off his appanage.
Chastellain observed with the greatest concern the conflict
between father and son, which could benefit no one but the
King of France, and gave a sigh of relief when the quick-
tempered and obstinate prince was pardoned by his father.

It was obvious that a prince such as Philip the Good
could not continue as a vassal. Burgundy was to be
independent of France, the most formidable opponent,
independent of England, independent of the Empire, at that
time the least dangerous ; independent of them all. Philip's
plans became clear during the course of his conflict with
France. The successes of the Maid of Orleans paved the way
for a transformation of the political situation, for a victory
for France and a consequent weakening, even if there was
no defeat, of England. Philip longed ardently for the dissolution of the hated alliance.

On the occasion of his marriage with the Infanta of Portugal
in 1430, in the presence of a brilliant company assembled
at Bruges, Philip the Good made his great gesture in the cause
of chivalry. The Flanders King-at-Arms proclaimed that the
Duke had founded the Order of the Golden Fleece. This was
to be no mere mark of distinction, or device like the plane
that Duke John had borne, but an established Order with
a fixed number of members with regular chapters, as in the

case of Orders instituted by sovereigns. Duke Philip, who had rejected the Order of the Garter, could now wear his own Order, which Emperors and Kings were later proud to assume, the chief decoration and honour of the House of Burgundy.

The *Toison d'Or* was established, according to the articles of its foundation " from the great love which we bear to the noble order of chivalry, whose honour and prosperity are our only concern, to the end that the true Catholic Faith, the Faith of Holy Church, our Mother, as well as the peace and welfare of the realm may be defended, preserved and maintained to the glory and praise of Almighty God our Creator and Saviour, in honour of his glorious Mother, the Virgin Mary, and of our Lord, St. Andrew, Apostle and Martyr, and for the furtherance of virtue and good manners."

On St. Andrew's Day, 1431, the first solemn Chapter was held. There were processions to church, and solemn masses in honour of St. Andrew : the gown of the Order, bright scarlet lined with ermine, the mantle adorned with gold embroidery, the hood with a long band. Solemn requiem masses were said also for the dead ; the dress of the Order on this occasion being a mantle and hood of black. State processions on foot and on horseback were succeeded by State banquets, at which the Duchess was present with her ladies, and to which envoys and guests of high rank and representatives of the magistracy had been invited.

The ruling Duke was always to be Master and Sovereign of the Order. Four officers, a chancellor, a secretary and a treasurer served under him. As the first Master, Philip the Good assumed the collar with its famous device. The links of the chain were intended to represent steel and flint with flashing sparks ; a representation of the Golden Fleece served as pendant. The knights were bound always to wear the chain openly, but when in armour the pendant sufficed alone.

The number of the knights was to be strictly limited. In addition to the Master only twenty-four, later thirty, noble knights, without fear and without reproach were to be admitted. The Order was of unique merit and acknowledged no rival. With the exception of emperors, kings and dukes, no one was allowed to wear another Order beside it. The founder desired to chain and bind the knights indissolubly

together in this *fraternité amiable*. The noblest deeds of
knighthood were demanded. On the other hand, the noblest
privileges were accorded to its holders. On account of his
great love and as proof of his confidence, the founder bound
himself, unless secrecy were necessary, to undertake no
war nor any other important engagement without first consulting the majority of the knights. He went so far as to
admit no exception to his rule, and the knights were always
free to criticize his actions. Charles the Bold had on two
occasions to submit to strictures in matters of government.
At the eleventh Chapter, held in May, 1468, at Bruges,
the following *remontrances* were advanced against him:
" the Duke speaks with undue severity to his servants ; he
does not curb his impatience in his dealings with princes ;
he is over-zealous." Then followed the requests. Charles
is asked not to oppress his subjects so grievously as hitherto
when preparing for war, to be gracious, moderate and candid,
to provide equal justice throughout his dominions, to keep
his promises, to shield his people from war so long as possible,
and if notwithstanding he decides to go to war, to be advised
judiciously beforehand. In the year 1473 at the next Chapter
these representations were repeated ; and on both occasions
Charles was obliged to listen—how difficult this must have been
to a man of his temperament we can readily understand.
And we learn that he answered to the satisfaction of the
whole assembly.

The conduct of each individual member was subjected
to minute examination, and culprits were proceeded against
without mercy. In the Church of Our Lady at Bruges,
above the pew of the Count de Nevers, himself a Burgundian
prince, a black shield, in place of his coat of arms, still
proclaims the shame of his expulsion from the Order, while
at the outer door of the church, the reversed shield of the
Sire de Crèvecour provides additional evidence of the strict-
ness with which the actions of the knights were scrutinized.

Pope Eugenius IV greeted the foundation of the Order
with enthusiasm and hailed the knights as resurrected
Maccabeans. Constant reminders of the old spiritual ideals of
chivalry survive in the statutes of the Order. Even here the
Church asserted her rights, and in deference to them the Duke
conceded that the Chancellor and Secretary should always

PLATE 8

Unknown Master: Charles the Bold holds a Chapter of the Golden Fleece. Miniature: Guillaume Fillastre, L'histoire de la Toison d'Or Bibliothèque, Royale MS. 9028, Brussels.

[face p. 58

be selected from the ranks of the clergy. This *nouvelle religion* was expressly dedicated to the protection of the Church. The knights had to bind themselves to attend the Master personally if he took up arms in defence of the Christian faith, or the dignity and freedom of Holy Church or of the holy Apostolic See in Rome. Heresy, indeed, was one of the three offences punishable with expulsion. It attracted the same penalties as treachery and cowardice in battle.

Later the influence of the Church became still more pronounced. At the foundation of the Order the story of Jason, who at Colchis with Medea's help had wrested the Golden Fleece from dragon, serpent and bull, was taken as its model. But Bishop Jean Germain would not suffer this pagan legend to survive, and replaced it by the Bible story, according to which, Gideon, decked with the Golden Fleece, with God's help had overcome the Philistines. There was no objection on the part of the knights, who were disposed to feel that Jason's treatment of Medea was scarcely consistent with the ideals of the Order. Moreover, the claims of the Church were persistent and could not be denied.

Jason, however, did not disappear entirely from the scene. He still survived to rival Gideon in frescoes in the castle at Hesdin and elsewhere in tapestries. At the Feast of the Pheasant it was Jason who figured most prominently in the masques. In literature, too, the rivalry was apparent. Raoul Lefèvre takes Jason's side. He is made to appear in a *Vision à face tristre et désolée* and to exclaim to the writer: " *Journellement (je) laboure en douleur enrachinée en tristesse pour le déshonneur dont aucuns frappent ma gloire, moy imposans non avoir tenu ma promesse envers Médée . . . si te prie que tu faces ung livre ou ceulx qui ma gloire quièrent flastrir, puissent congnoistre leur indiscret jugement.*"

An anonymous writer, on the other hand, takes the view that nothing could excuse Jason's violation of faith, and Duke Philip himself is warned against the wiles of Jason the deceiver. Guillaume Fillastre, a very versatile prelate, wrote a work on the six known fleeces. He was at pains to discover a religious significance in the pagan legend and found it symbolical of almost every Christian ideal and institution. In his view Jason was the embodiment of generosity.

It is manifest that Philip the Good was concerned how to live in harmony with the clergy. As champion of the Church and protector of the Holy See, says Chastellain, Philip was ever to be found on the side of the Pope. The Duke does not appear to have been at all troubled concerning the Pragmatic Sanction of Bourges. He was ever ready to aid in the extirpation of heresy. On the other hand, he looked to the Church he supported to further his political ambitions. He claimed the wealthiest benefices for his bastards and favourites. He obtained by force of arms the bishopric of Utrecht for his son David, and maintained Guillaume Fillastre, in the face of great opposition, in the episcopal see of Verdun, later in that of Toul, brought him to Tournai and procured for him in addition the dignity and revenues of the Abbey of Saint-Bertin at Saint-Omer.

Philip the Bold had already made over the sepulchral church of his House to monks of the strictest rule. He had thought even of ending his days in the habit of a Carthusian monk. Philip the Good spent hours at his devotions. Even the call of battle had to pass unheeded while he prayed. He was secretly a most generous benefactor. He took particular delight in *choses trajans à dévotion.* Stores of the most costly articles used in divine service were kept in his treasury, and his library contained an extraordinary number of ecclesiastical and theological works.

It is true that the House of Burgundy produced no saint, no Peter of Luxembourg—a lonely figure amidst a crowd of warlike contemporaries. But there were still members of the ducal House who could set an example to the world by the piety of their lives.

Anne, Philip's sister, was much beloved by the Parisians on account of her kindness and beauty.

> Ce fut la perle de beaulté
> Et l'esméraude de léesse,
> Le fin saffir de léaulté ;

writes Martin le Franc, who could not grasp why she could have been allowed for political reasons to marry the Duke of Bedford, an Englishman. The Duchess Anne was conspicuous for her charity. She became infected with the germ of a fatal malady on the occasion of a visit to the poor at the *Hotel-Dieu* during an epidemic of plague. At her request the clergy of Notre Dame displayed in solemn procession the reliquary of St. Geneviève and invoked God's help for her, but in vain ; it was her fate to die young.

Isabella, Philip's third wife, was also a great benefactress and mediator. In homage to her, Martin le Franc dedicated the verse :—

> Chascun la dame bénissoit
> Pour sa doulceur, pour sa sagesse.
> Vive la dame, et bénit soit
> Qui nous donne tele princesse !

Beatrice of Portugal, wife of Adolph of Cleves, who was so dear to Duke Philip that her death was concealed from him during his illness, wore a hair shirt next her skin beneath her brocaded robes. She fasted much and slept, we are told, in her husband's absence, upon straw. Yet to the unsuspecting she appeared to be more worldly than the rest. It was a common practice also for the ladies and gentlemen of the Court to withdraw from time to time, and retire into the strictest seclusion.

St. Andrew was the most honoured among the saints. According to the legend, King Stephen the Burgundian, a *moult bon catholique*, procured the cross on which the saint had suffered martyrdom to be brought to Marseilles and adopted it as his device. The Dukes retained it and even in the turmoil of battle invoked the protection of the saint. *Nostre-Dame de Bourgogne et Montjoie Saint Andrieu* was their rallying cry. Philip the Bold had a splinter of the cross sent to Brussels and his grandson decreed that the Chapter of the Golden Fleece should be held on St. Andrew's Day. It was only for practical reasons that another date was afterwards selected.

Particular devotion was paid also to St. Jodocus, the Breton King's son. Philip the Good chose him as patron saint for one of his sons, and after his early death dispatched to St. Josse, a favourite place of pilgrimage near Étaples, a number of rich gifts, amongst others an image of the child wrought in gold.

When Duke Philip was once seriously ill, he dedicated to St. Hadrian, the patron saint of Geraardsbergen, a wax figure of a kneeling man, which weighed some sixty pounds.

The living, too, who were noted for their piety were

always honoured at the House of Burgundy. St. Colette
Boellet was a recipient of many ducal favours. On the
occasion of the German journey of Cardinal Nicholas of
Cues, Duke Philip the Good made the acquaintance of the
Carthusian Dionysius or Denis of Ryckel, whose reputation
for piety was unequalled. He was looked up to as monk and
prior, as an ascetic and visionary, and as a man of learning
and a writer. He was the theological encyclopaedist of
his age, an omnivorous reader, able and willing to give advice
to all. In one of his ecstasies he foresaw the dreadful miseries
which the Turks were to inflict upon the West, and never ceased
to direct his attack against the false doctrine of Mohammed
and to invite Duke Philip to go up and vanquish the enemies
of the Faith. It was to the Duke, that *inclytus devotus ac
optimus princeps et dux*, that Dionysius dedicated his work,
' *de vita et regimine principum* '.

When in the evening of his days, Dionysius, as Prior,
received the commission to found a new Carthusian monastery
in the Campine, Charles the Bold displayed the greatest
interest in the undertaking. After a hard and thankless
conflict, which exhausted his remaining strength, Dionysius
returned once more to his beloved solitude : " A happy and
holy life, godly and free, a pure and angelic life, light of the
soul, friend of knowledge, ornament of the Church, lover of
peace and quiet."

In an age when men—especially those of exalted rank—
still considered it their right to allow their passions free and
unfettered play, the greatest importance attached to the
observance of forms was bound to lead at times to
grave breaches of decorum. A most unseemly incident
occurred at the coronation banquet of King Charles VI at
Rheims in the year 1380. Louis of Anjou, as the King's
eldest uncle, claimed the seat of honour beside him ; Philip
the Bold made a similar claim as premier peer of the realm.
The escorts of both parties were preparing to come to blows
when Philip thrust his brother abruptly aside and took the
coveted place.

Even in the life of the citizens the most scrupulous forms of
politeness were observed. In the street long parleys and

wrangles would take place as to who was to walk on the right hand, who was to lead the way, or who should first enter the house. In church disturbances were caused by disputes concerning precedence at the Sacrifice or at the kissing of the Pax, the small tablet which was handed round at Mass after he Agnus Dei.

The aristocrats, the princes, and the ruler himself laid still greater stress on etiquette. The slightest deviation from prescribed rules, if not due to ignorance, was regarded as a deliberate intention to offend. Duke Charles strongly objected to the Constable of Saint Pol having a naked sword borne before him, a right which he claimed appertained to the sovereign alone. When Louis the Dauphin, on his flight in the year 1456, arrived in Brussels and was received in the absence of her consort by the Duchess Isabella, she would not suffer the King's son to give her precedence. For more than a quarter of an hour she resisted, " Monseigneur," she said finally, " you appear to desire to make me a laughing stock since you ask me to do what is not seemly." In the Dauphin's presence the Duchess would never have exercised the privileges of the highest princes. At the reception, after the christening of her granddaughter Marie, she herself made the *essai,* kneeling and still kneeling offered the dish of sweets to the Dauphin. Even after the coronation of Louis XI, when it was clear that he was preparing for war against Philip the Good, despite the fact that in his direst need the French King had found refuge and hospitality at the Court of Burgundy, the Duke never charged him with ingratitude nor forgot the respect which was due to him as Sovereign. Charles the Bold, obstinate and head-strong as he was, always paid the strictest attention to matters of ceremony and precedence. At his meeting with the Emperor Frederick III at Trèves in 1473, he was received at some distance from the town by the Emperor himself and lengthy discussions at once arose as to how the entry was to take place. Charles wished to ride respectfully behind the Emperor ; Frederick invited the Duke to ride by his side. A whole hour was spent in discussions ; in the meanwhile a heavy rainstorm came on and soaked them to the skin. It is significant that notwithstanding the bad weather, Charles, unlike the Emperor, did not assume his mantle, pride not permitting him to cover

up his jewels and decorations.   He also forbade his followers
to don their cloaks.

On his ceremonial visit to the Imperial lodgings, Charles
knelt before Frederick ; very unwillingly he allowed himself
to be persuaded to enter the chamber at the Emperor's side.
At his farewell there was a fresh interchange of compliments.
Frederick accompanied his guest, in spite of the latter's opposition, to the courtyard ; whereupon, taking the Emperor by
the hand, Charles led him up the staircase back into the hall.

Even on the scaffold the strictest rules of etiquette were
observed.   When the Bastard de la Hamayde was executed
he was first arrayed, in consonance with his rank, in a fine
silk doublet.   At the execution of the Constable of Saint-Pol,
none of the privileges of birth and high rank were forgotten.
The victim wore mourning, having recently lost his wife,
a sister of the Queen of France.   Silver-embroidered lilies
gleamed on the scaffold ; the praying cushions, and the
bandage for the eyes, were of crimson velvet.   No ordinary
executioner would suffice.   A man was selected who had never
filled the office previously.   One thing which the Burgundian
Court could never forgive was that the Armagnacs had
buried Duke John, after his assassination, in doublet, hose and
shoes only, in complete disregard of all prescribed forms.

Duke Philip and his son submitted themselves unconditionally to the laws of etiquette and demanded a like
submission from their servants, from the highest to the lowest,
from the chancellor to kitchen-boy.

A great master has protrayed in a miniature a solemn
audience at which Jean Wauquelin, kneeling, presents his work
with the deepest homage to the Duke.   An icy atmosphere
pervades the room.   Beneath a canopy of damask, stands
the Duke in majestic isolation, a ruler from head to foot,
transcending all other mortals.   He is superbly clad in robes
and hood.   At his feet lies an Italian greyhound.   His son,
the Chancellor, and the other officials and courtiers are
grouped together at a fitting distance awaiting a sign from
their master.

Every detail of life at Court was very strictly regulated.
The guiding principle was that nothing was dishonourable

Plate 9

Unknown Master: Jean Wauquelin presenting his work to Philip the Good. Miniature: Chroniques du Hainaut. Bibliothèque Royale MS. 9242 fol. 1, Brussels.

[face p. 64

if it was done in the service of the sovereign. It was the greatest honour to serve the prince in his most intimate and private affairs. Two matters were of supreme importance, firstly to protect the prince from injury, and secondly to show him due respect. Here again the spiritual exercised an influence over the temporal. Just as no one shrank from an apotheosis of the sovereign, so in matters of ceremony no one hesitated to borrow examples from the holy observances of the Church. In the description of the *quatre estaz que servent le corps et la bouche du prince*, the *panetiers* and cup-bearers are mentioned first. The justification for their office is that what they do is done in honour of the Holy Sacrament and in memory of the dear Body and Blood of Jesus Christ. Many details seem to have been copied from the Mass itself. At the same time precaution was absolutely necessary. The possibility of poison could never be ignored.

The napkin with which the prince dried his hands was kissed when the *sommelier* delivered it to the *panetier*; in the same way the *valet-servant* touched with his lips the handles of the two large knives, which were laid at the Duke's place at table, the *fruitier* in like manner kissed the torch which was intended for the ruler. Bareheaded, the valets and pages carried the dishes from the kitchen to the dining hall, the squires knelt frequently before the prince. The manner in which the various articles were to be held was carefully prescribed, the salt-cellar between the foot and girdle, the drinking vessel at the foot. When the prince had finished drinking, the cup-bearer received the cup with great reverence.

The chronicler Olivier de La Marche, who served the House of Burgundy also as diplomatist and soldier, actor and stage-manager, has left us a valuable description of life at the Court of Charles the Bold and of the rules of conduct and the order of precedence which had to be observed.

He commences first with the service of God and the ordering of the ducal chapel. A bishop supervised the chapel, supported by forty clergy, priests, confessors and musicians. Before the prince left a town upon his journeys the almoner had first to present him with a list of those who were to receive gifts.

Next came the Council. Here the chancellor was supreme. A bishop served as his deputy, and numerous officials, four knights, eight *maîtres de requêtes*, fifteen secretaries, *huissiers* and quartermasters were in attendance to execute his orders.

Public audiences were held two or three times a week. These were open to all, and here the poor and lowly could present their complaints against their betters. Duke Charles sat on his throne on a raised daïs beneath a canopy of tapestry. Two *maîtres de requêtes* and an *audiencier* knelt before him and presented the petitions, while a secretary also on his knees, took note of the proceedings. The whole Court, the household, the princes of the blood, and envoys, had all to be present, often much to their annoyance. But not one of them we are told, would have dared to absent himself.

A special council dealt with all matters relating to war which de La Marche regards as a separate branch of justice. He calls it Justice of the Strong Hand. The chancellor, the first chamberlain, and the comptrollers of the Court were among the members. Many of the court officials possessed at the same time military rank. Thus in case of war the first *panetier* and the first cup-bearer were squadron leaders and their esquires were attached to them.

The *maître de la chambre aux deniers* controlled the treasury. The ordinary expenditure for the household and the salaries exceeded 400,000 *livres* a year. The ordinary budget of the war treasurer amounted to 800,000 *livres*, the extraordinary budget as a rule to 160,000 *livres*. The *argentier*, who had to defray the cost of the legations and journeys, as well as the necessary gifts and the wardrobe, spent at least 200,000 *livres* a year. The Duke frequently took part in the meetings of the Treasury. He signed all authorizations for gifts, as well as the accounts and documents. He sat at one end of the board and calculated like the others, with this difference that whereas the officials used silver counters for reckoning, the Duke had counters of gold.

The *garde des joyaux* and his assistant had the custody of the jewels, the gold and silver services, the prince's private savings, and the sacred vessels of the chapel ; they controlled between them probably a million in gold.

In the household the Grand Pensioners came first. These included six dukes and twelve princes, marquesses, counts, and numerous other representatives of the nobility and knighthood, most of whom appeared on the list of the daily expenditure. The expenses of the household of the Duchess and her ladies, which were kept separately, amounted to 40,000 *livres* yearly.

The first chamberlain kept the key of the sovereign's chamber as well as the privy seal, and he carried his banner into battle. He was reverenced and obeyed as the Duke's deputy.

The *grand maître d'Hôtel* enjoyed privileges in Burgundy which differed from those in the other ducal territories. He was especially prominent at the four great feasts of the year. At the service of the table, he walked in front of the bearers of the dishes, with raised sword. Five comptrollers maintained order in the palace.

Sixteen esquires of the best families were constantly in attendance on the prince and slept in close proximity to him. When the prince retired at the conclusion of the day's work the esquires provided for his entertainment. Some sang, others read romances or tales aloud, others spoke of love and military glory.

Six physicians were in attendance at table and advised the Duke as to what meat was especially suitable for him. They frequently took part in the meetings of the Council. The four surgeons in chief were always extraordinarily busy, *car le prince est chevalereux*. Wounded men were constantly to be found at the castle, and fifty other surgeons attended to their needs. They likewise were busy men. Charles allotted also one surgeon to every company of 100 lances. Two *épiciers* had charge of the drugs and medicines, the sweets and medicated wines.

Most of the forty *valets de chambre* were permanently employed as barbers, tailors, and shoe-makers. Painters made tabards, banners and standards, others shared with the *sommeliers* the responsibility for the rooms and beds.

The order of service at table was very detailed and complicated. The duties were shared by the first *panetier*, the first *échanson* and the first *écuyer*, each of whom was attended by fifty esquires, while nobles, pages and servants were always in waiting for special duties. A good memory and a most complicated system of training were necessary if all the rules of order and precedence were to be observed. Food and drink were brought in in solemn procession. All eyes were upon the prince ; a nod sufficed and the cup-bearer presented the wine. When he bore the cup to the table, he held it on high above his head so that it should be untouched by his breath.

The court household, disposed according to rank, ate separately in different rooms. All were required to finish before the Duke in order to be ready to wait on him at table and pay him homage.

The most elaborate regulations preserved the prince against the danger of poisoning. Food and drink were examined and tasted beforehand. A silver ship was placed before the prince, which contained alms. Beside it stood the silver *tranchoirs*, the salt-cellar, a small silver wand, and a piece of a unicorn's horn for testing dishes.

Duke Charles drank only much-diluted wine. Indeed, there can have seldom been a prince who took so little wine himself, and yet disposed of so much. At least a thousand casks a year were needed for the Court.

The esquires had certain privileges appertaining to their office. If the prince ate in public, all the meat which remained belonged to the *écuyer tranchant*. On feast days, however, it was distributed otherwise : to the holy man who preached, to the court-blacksmith who had shod the Duke's horse, or to the *armoyeur*, who had cleaned his armour. Nor were the poor forgotten. Boiled and roast meats were constantly distributed among them by special servants.

The management of the kitchen was entrusted to two esquires. The cook was in command " *C'est mestier subtil et sumptueux et qui toute seureté sent.*" This important personage was chosen with great care and deliberation by the comptrollers of the Court. He had at times the right to appear personally before the ruler, and was permitted to serve him with the earliest truffles or herrings.

During the service, the cook sat enthroned on a high stool in the kitchen between the buffet and the fireplace so that he might see and control his servants. In one hand he held a large spoon, primarily for tasting the soup, but he used it also for purposes of correction or to eject intruders. The vast kitchen with the huge fireplaces which Philip the Good installed in the castle at Dijon serve still to remind us of the scene of the master-cook's activities and the extent of his dominion. Twenty-five persons were constantly employed as special cooks for the joints and soups, keepers of the store-rooms, stokers and fuel attendants, polishers and apprentices.

A *sausserie* and the *fruiterie*, which in addition to home-grown and southern fruits, had to supply wax and tallow for the innumerable candles and torches, were maintained close to the main kitchen, but separate from it. The demand for lights at high festivals and processions must have been extraordinary. At the Feast of the Purification of the Virgin Mary the whole ducal household, from the highest to the lowest, walked candle in hand behind the prince and his relatives, who themselves bore special lights on which their arms and devices were displayed.

In like manner, fifty esquires, as well as pages, the *pale-frenier*, blacksmiths, couriers and musicians, quartermasters and servants were under the orders of the *écuyer de l'écurie*. In battle this official took up his position beside the prince and bore the standards. At solemn entries he carried the sword of state ; at jousts and tourneys he had charge of the decorations to be worn by the Duke with the sole exception of those of pure gold and precious stones.

In the herald's office, six kings-at-arms, eight heralds and four pursuivants were employed. If a pursuivant had given satisfaction for seven years the Duke christened him personally with wine and promoted him herald. If the herald rose to the dignity of a king-at-arms, it was the Duke who crowned him with the herald's crown. This was composed of silver-gilt and set with sapphires, signifying, with that passion for religious symbolism which was a characteristic of the age, that the king-at-arms should turn his mind from earthly to heavenly wealth, of which the sapphires were the visible emblems. Of the kings-at-arms, he of the Golden Fleece held the first and most honoured place. His pursuivant was called Fusil. The other kings-at-arms were named after the various territories owing allegiance to the prince. The gifts which were bestowed at feasts when the heralds cried " largesse, largesse ", were allotted half to the heralds' office and half to the twelve trumpeters and ten musicians.

It was the privilege of the noblest in his territories to protect the prince from danger. His bodyguard consisted of 126 esquires of rank assisted by the same number of archers.

They were commanded by a captain. Under him were the chiefs of the four squadrons, and these squadrons in their turn were divided into four *chambres* or messes. Then came the officers, archers, *coutilliers*, trumpeters and a chaplain. All were paid monthly. A special body-guard of archers, which comprised sixty-two men, was placed under two further captains.

In view of the unfortunate experiences of his predecessors with their mercenaries and communal militia, Charles established in 1471 a standing army on the French pattern, without, however, entirely discarding his mercenaries. The " lance " served as the military unit and consisted of the mounted man-at-arms, three mounted archers, a crossbowman, the *coulevrinier* and the *picquenaire*. The knight maintained at his own expense a page and a mounted *coutillier*. One hundred " lances ", that is 900 men, 600 mounted and 300 on foot, composed a " band ", which was divided into four squadrons and each squadron was again subdivided into four *chambres* or messes. In 1473 the standing army consisted of 2,000 " lances ", that is of 18,000 men, not reckoning infantry and artillery. Duke Charles himself commanded the " lances ", and the conductors or commanders of companies received their commissions direct from him.

La Marche did not profess to treat of military matters in his work : " *pour ce que le duc Charles qui a ses ordonnances mis sus, a labouré en sa personne si notablement et fait mettre par escript les ordonnances de sa guerre si bien, si notablement et a tous mystères esclarci en telle forme que mon escripture ne sembleroit après que temps perdu.*"

In *Les honneurs de la Cour* written by Aliénor de Poitiers we have an excellent supplement to the work of Olivier de La Marche. From her seventh year upwards she lived at the Burgundian Court and was initiated by her mother, a Portuguese countess, who had left her native land with the Infanta, into all the niceties of Court ceremonial.

The laws of precedence were always in the foreground, occupying and exciting people's minds at every hour of the day. Jeanne de Harcourt, Countess of Namur, who instructed the Duchess Isabella in the customs of the Court, had on one occasion been led from her place by King Charles VII in the midst of a state wedding banquet and conducted to the Queen's table. Her seat might suffice for the wife of the Count of Namur, but not for a kinswoman of the King. The deciding factor was always the degree of relationship to the throne of France and if there was any contest or dispute the Duke decided the matter himself.

The ceremonial observed at births, christenings and deaths was so rigorous as to be almost overpowering. Every expression of joy and sorrow gave way to the strictest conventions : the prince triumphed over the human being.

Aliénor describes in detail the apartments assigned to Isabelle de Bourbon, the second wife of the Count de Charolais, at the birth of her daughter, Marie, in 1457. A state apartment hung with tapestries presented by the city of Utrecht, in which a bed of state had been set up, led into birth chamber and the adjacent nursery, in each of which stood two similar beds. Three curtains called *travarsaine* had been hung up, whereas the Queen of France could claim four. The sideboard had four shelves with gold and silver service, but the one placed in the apartment of Duchess Marie at the birth of her son Philip in 1478 had five ; in the case of a countess three only were allowed. The room of Charles' consort was hung with green silk, that of the Duchess Marie with green samite ; a coverlet of ermine was reserved exclusively for queens and princesses of high rank. Only ladies were allowed to offer spices and wine in the birth-chamber.

When in mourning princely personages put on black, the King alone wore red.

The Countess of Charolais after the death of her father remained six weeks in her apartments lying on her bed in morning attire. The bed was covered with white cloth, while the walls were draped with black. And thus she received her visitors.

Aliénor de Poitiers and Olivier de La Marche treat of these matters as if they were officers of State debating the most delicate political problems. In their opinion the preservation of ceremonial was as essential as obedience to God and to the sovereign. No changes could be tolerated. " As may be seen daily all kinds of things are now done differently in

many places," writes Aliénor with indignation, " but this
should not be allowed to change those honourable institutions
which are the outcome of due and proper reflection." In
another passage she becomes pessimistic. " At the present
hour," she writes, " each one does as he likes ; but such
irregular observances will certainly lead to disaster."

All matters of fashion were determined by the ruler. Duke
Philip submitted to its yoke and enforced his will upon
others. When in 1462 he was compelled, owing to illness,
to lose his hair, he is said to have ordered the nobles to
follow his example. Possibly this was an expression of a
wish rather than a direct order ; in any case more than five
hundred nobles promptly shaved their heads, and the unscrupulous and ambitious Peter of Hagenbach, who was later to
become notorious, was charged with the duty of seeing that
the Duke's wishes were obeyed.

A few years later a reaction took place and fashion decreed
that men should wear long flowing locks falling into their
eyes : this in spite of the biblical injunction : " Doth not
even nature itself teach you that if a man have long hair
it is a shame unto him ? " And with the fashion for longer
hair, a change in dress took place. Men wore indecently
short and padded pourpoints of velvet or silk. The shirt
could be seen through the slits of the leg-of-mutton sleeves.
The cap was absurdly small, the pointed shoes ridiculously
long. The gowns, which were very full and long, reached
down to the ankles. Men hung gold chains about their neck :
women wore gold neck bands. They had commenced to
abandon their long trains and trimmed their dresses instead
with a silk girdle and a wide edge of fur. The *hennin* rested
on the round cap-shaped head-dress, from which depended the
long butterfly veils. It is said at a later date that Frederick I,
Count Palatine, out of patience with the extravagant
Burgundian dress, ordered it to be worn by his court fools
in order to make it unpopular with his courtiers.

It is curious to see the violent contrasts of the age reflected
in the fashions. Garments were either too long or too short.
There was no harmony, no breadth, and little comfort :
only extravagance and exaggeration. Flowing lines were

sharply broken by cords and girdles at the waist. There was in everything an absence of repose, coupled with an ill-bred display of wealth and ostentation.

By the marriages of Philip the Good and Charles the Bold with foreigners, Portuguese and English fashions came into prominence and took their place beside the Burgundian, French and Italian modes. The gentlemen who were sent to Portugal to negotiate her match found the costume of the Infanta Isabella very strange ; she wore in addition to a mantle slashed on both sides, a blue velvet *chaperon* and on the top of that a Brabant *chapel*, " Some, it was said, took her for a knight."

Martin Le Franc, with his restless critical mind, dedicates numerous verses to the absurdities of fashion. While the Adversary in his *Champion des Dames* reproaches the ladies for the innumerable appliances, the salves, powder and paint which they employ to beautify themselves, the Champion on the other hand makes merry about the fops.

> Vous soliez robes porter
> Jusques à la jambe demye
> Ores les faictes excourter
> Sur les genouls, ne faictes mye ?
> En tant que se le vent fremye
> On peut veoir vos petits draps,
> Vierge du Puy ! Vierge Marie !
> Vous me faictes croisier les bras.

The household of the Court of Burgundy with its princes, high dignitaries, knights, esquires, officers, soldiers, music-players, craftsmen, servants, and male and female dwarfs and fools, was a State within a State. This subsidiary State was not based like the Flanders communes, proud of their freedom, on the idea of opposition to the prince. It was founded on the principle of unconditional and unqualified submission. Again and again the life at Court was subjected to mordant criticism. Bitter words had been uttered by Pierre de Blois, while Jean de Montreuil and the learned men associated with him treated the old theme in the same manner as Alain Chartier, the famous poet, in his work *Le Curial*. Jean Meschinot devised the following verses :—

> La cour est une mer dont sourt
> Vagues d'orgeuil, d'envie orage . . .
> Malebouche y fait maint dommage,
> Ire esmeut débas et oultrage . . .
> Qui les nefs gittent souvent bas,
> Traïson y fait son personnage :
> Nage aultre part pour tes esbas . . .

Yet in spite of all warnings against the slavish service demanded by the prince, in spite of exhortations against the sacrifice of freedom and of will, there does not seem to have been any shortage of young men anxious to adventure their lives and fortunes at the Court of Burgundy.

CHAPTER V

The Knight

Qui fist Lancelot et Artus
En armes si aventureux,
Tristan, Percheval et Pontus,
Sinon qu'ilz furent amoureux ?
Bibl. Nat. franc. 12476 fol. 85 v.

THE Burgundian knighthood claimed an origin peculiar to itself. It asserted that knighthood was a privilege of birth, an order exclusively noble and not a professional order. The knight was noble, the great majority belonged to the old families, though there were cases of course of individual ennoblement.

Olivier de La Marche differentiates between *gentils hommes, nobles hommes et non nobles*. The *gentilhomme* is the descendant of noble men and noble ladies : he continues the race by suitable marriages. The *noblesse qui est commencement de gentilesse* is acquired in a variety of ways. The prince can ennoble the holder of high office or the proved warrior ; he can ennoble by bestowal of the accolade and the grant of letters patent for loyal services, considering always the claims of honour and of wealth. La Marche ranks nobility by letters patent as the lowest, even if he concedes that the old nobility had its foundation in the possession of great riches.

The newly ennobled, he points out, must keep themselves at first modestly in the background ; one example will suffice. At jousts which were only open to champions of proved achievements, evidence of ancestry was always demanded. Jousts such as these were frequently confined to knights with four ancestors. Once, at an assault at arms, thirty-two pennants displaying the coats of arms of his ancestors were flown on the pavilion of Jacques de Lalaing.

The division of human society into ranks was determined by God from the beginning. The *estats* or *ordres*, by which the various pursuits and callings were indicated, the separation into classes, the single and married, the poor and rich, the sinner and saint ; these divisions were all based

75

upon a divinely-ordered plan, outside which nothing could exist and to which all must submit, even if the traditional separation showed signs of becoming obsolete. The old verse still held good :—

> Triplex ergo Dei domus quae creditur una
> Nunc orant, alii pugnant aliique laborant.

The attitude of Chastellain, who was descended from the Castellanes of Aalst, is very characteristic.

In the same way as men have received from God different faces, so, the chronicler asserts, have they received from Him different professions, dispositions and characteristics. He allowed some to be born for agriculture and socage, others for municipal government, others for commerce, some for the service of the Church, and finally others, such as esquires and knights, barons and princes, dukes and kings, for the maintenance of the order of nobility. When Chastellain in another passage happens to mention the citizens of France, whom he elsewhere praises, we read : " *Pour venir au tiers membre qui fait le royaume entier, c'est l'estat des bonnes villes, des marchans et des gens de labeur ; desquels ils ne convient faire ni longue exposition que des autres pour cause que celuy estat mesme ne le requiert, et que de soy il n'est gaires capable de hautes attributions, parcequ'il est au degré servile.*"

Thus wrote a native of Flanders, who knew well what the communes had achieved at Courtrai and what significance attached to a man such as James van Artevelde. Chastellain, a calm and ordered thinker, born among the ranks of the inferior nobility, was nevertheless incapable of doing justice to the *vilain*. The cleft between aristocrat and citizen was indeed nowhere more remarkable than in the land of the four *Lede*.

Molinet, too, who continued the work of Chastellain, held the same views. In his " Earthly Paradise " he attempts to show that the sun, moon and planets are symbolical of the different orders of mankind. The moon, as being the lowest satellite and nearest to the earth, corresponds to the peasants of lowest origin. Mercury represents those engaged in commerce, Venus denotes the bourgeoisie, who give themselves freely *à la dame oiseuse, aux jeus, aux devises, aux esbas et tous les fols délits mondains*. The sun is the Church and it is indeed a matter for surprise when Molinet allows

PLATE 10

Giovanni Candida : Charles the Bold.
Medal. Bibliothèque Nationale, Paris.

Privy Seal of Charles the Bold.   State Archives, Lucerne.

Seal of Claus Sluter.   Archives de la Côte d'Or, Dijon.

the rays of the Catholic faith to illumine not only the nobility but also the citizens, merchants and peasants. The aristocracy corresponds to Mars, princedom (in the person of Maximilian) to Jupiter, and the old nobility (in the person of the Emperor Frederick III) to Saturn, *fort tardive, située au septième estaige.*

The lofty conception of knighthood is reflected in the adoption into the Order of popular saints such as St. Michael, St. George, St. Ursus ; knights' belts were bestowed on biblical personages when they were thought worthy of the honour. The captain of Capernaum was so favoured, as was also Joseph of Arimathea, who had released the Saviour from the Cross. According to the opinion of the learned they were well worthy of a place in the *compaignie des chevaliers.*

When the election of a ruler is in question, declares an aristocratic writer, no better choice can be made than from among the ranks of the knights.

It is notable that when *vilains* are mentioned, no attempt is made to distinguish between the various kinds of citizens ; the aristocrat displays contempt towards the plebeian, whether he is dealing with a wealthy banker, able to finance a campaign, with some influential patrician whose authority could effect the most important changes in the policy of his native city, or with some lowly workman without a penny in his pocket. Rich citizens considered it a signal honour if their daughters were thought worthy of alliance with a ducal archer or servant. In order to escape being married against her will, a thirty-four year old widow of a furrier at Arras became the wife of a man of twenty on the day of her husband's funeral. Philip the Good demanded unconditional obedience in such matters, and once, when a rebel brewer at Lille who had dared to question the ducal orders was trying to dispose of his daughter's hand on his own account, the Duke immediately broke off his stay in Holland and embarked on a stormy crossing from Rotterdam to Sluis in order to set things right.

The more the Church insisted that with death, the leveller, all matters of earthly superiority were at an end, the greater became the desire of the worldly-minded to enjoy to the full the blessing of their superior rank while they lived. But they must have viewed with considerable disfavour the popular representations of the Last Judgment or a Dance of Death

on a churchyard wall, in which their claims to special treatment were openly and even deliberately ignored.

> Où sont les princes de la terre ?
>
> Où est le bon roy d'Engleterre
> Artur et son courage fier,
> Et Lancelot, bon chevalier,
> Qui fut garde de son honneur ?
> Ils sont mors comme vng laboureur.

The nobility claimed even the exclusive privilege of profane
cursing and swearing. " What," says the nobleman to the
peasant, " do you, a mere commoner, presume to give your
soul to the devil and deny God ? "
Molinet is consumed with indignation against the rich
bourgeoisie, living comfortably within their solid walls and
their perpetual grumbling against the nobility :—

> " Vous menez le bon temps en paisible asseurance,
>   Et ils sont aux hutins en mortelle souffrance ;
>   Vous dormez ès cités, bien couvers et repos,
>   Et ils couchent aux champs, toujours le fer au dos.
>   Vous rêvez en espoir d'augmenter vostre estage,
>   Et ils meurent pour vous et pour votre héritage."

The *Sirventes* of Bertran de Born serves to remind us that
the old hatred of the *vilain* remained unchanged, even if
the tone grew milder.

The noble's dislike of the citizen is shown in the emphatic
warnings uttered by aristocratic writers against confiding
any secrets to people of lower rank. It was a matter of great
irritation to the nobility when a prince like Philip the Good
allowed himself to be on confidential terms with the artists
and scholars at his Court and even entrusted them with
important commissions. We would give a good deal to-day
to know the details of the secret missions undertaken by
Jan Van Eyck on behalf of his master. The miniatures of
the period show that Philip the Good and his son were in
the habit of visiting their servants to watch them at their
work. Nothing definite is known about these visits, but it
is pleasant to think that the conversation on these occasions
was frank and free and that the prince allowed himself to be

instructed in matters which had no reference to state-craft. The prince, however, never took the decisive step of inviting the artists to take part in Court festivals. Nor could he have done so. Court society would not have tolerated such a step, even though the title and rank of a *varlet de chambre* had been conferred upon a citizen like Jan Van Eyck. This was done doubtless to facilitate the artists' intercourse with courtiers, as well as in consideration of his distinguished merits, but there was no question of equality.

The prince was to look exclusively to the knight for his real support. If proof is desired, we need only consider the *Rosier des Guerres*. This quaint little book was written for the glorification of knighthood, at a time when its steady decline had set in. It enjoyed such popularity and attained such celebrity that its authorship was ascribed to no less a personage than Louis XI, who was certainly under no delusions as to the value of knighthood. Sir Walter Scott, who always lays great stress on contemporary detail, quite rightly finds a place for the *Rosier* in his "Quentin Durward".

When we recall the misfortunes which befell French knighthood during the Hundred Years War, it is not a little surprising to find that the author of the *Rosier*, though he breaks here and there with tradition, still champions the presumption that the knight was an indispensable military factor in war. The old complaint about the citizens :—

> " Il vous ont par leur foy, grand loiauté jurée
> Mais amour de commune est mout tost trespassée."

was still current. In moments of the greatest danger the Duke of Burgundy had frequently been deserted by communal troops ; his knights were therefore of special value to him, since he could rely implicitly on their loyalty. Treachery in a vassal was to be condemned with the utmost severity. John the Fearless was greatly blamed when he forbade his vassals to assist Charles VI at Agincourt even though he was at the time at variance with his King and suzerain. John's own brother, Anthony, who had hitherto upheld him, could not bring himself when the test came to withhold his support from France, and met a hero's death at Agincourt. His own son, Philip, regretted in his old age that he had not been present. Courtiers had concealed from him the day of battle, lest he might be brought into conflict with his father.

The love of adventure and fighting might well be of out-standing importance, but the decisive factor was the loyalty and obligations of the vassal. "*Prince qui est bien aimé de ses nobles, ne peut succomber. Il est riche de précieuse chair et a de sang à commandement, comme d'eau en mer,*" says Chastellain. The saying still held good, "*Li cuers d'un homme vaut tout l'or d'un pays.*" Of the Lalaing family alone seven members lost their lives in thirty years in defence of the House of Burgundy. Here, too, the relationship was based on reciprocity ; *pro summa fidelitate summus amor* and *pro summo amore summa fidelitas.* Philip the Good recognized the importance of his nobility. Charles the Bold, on the other hand, did not. The poor nobleman was absolutely dependent on princely favour if he was to meet the cost of life at Court. If the Duke refused his patronage, there was no alternative for him but to seek another master and this happened frequently under Charles the Bold. In order to save them-selves from their creditors, many nobles were forced to listen to the enticements of Louis XI, who was sparing neither in gold nor lands. The hatred which Charles aroused by his thoughtless conduct is shown by the letter of a certain nobleman who had deserted the cause of Burgundy. When reproached with complicity in an attempt on the Duke's life, he publicly protested his innocence and gives vent to his rage in the most horrible accusations against his former master : "*La cause qui m'a meu . . . est pour les très-viles, très-énormes et déshonnètes choses que le dit Charles de Bourgogne lorsque j'étois devers lui, fréquentoit et commettoit contre Dieu nostre créateur, contre nature et contre nostre loi, en quoi il m'a voulu attraire et faire condescendre d'en user avec lui.*" Charles leads a dreadful life "*dont l'énormité est si grande que par la seule parole l'air en est corrompu et infect*".

Immediately on Charles' accession the nobles recognized that changes were imminent : that "*le temps du présent estre tout autre, tout dur et estrange envers l'autre passé et que nouvelles gens estoient en cours et le maistre de nouvelle dure mode tenant ses gens serfs et sous verge et crémeur*".

Many of the complaints concerning the innovations which accompanied the proposed reforms appear to be exaggerated. There is not much of importance in the protests at the frequent audiences, when the nobles were locked up for hours

as if they were listening to a sermon. But Charles' brusque
and imperious bearing seemed fated to drive his subjects
into opposition. Even in his dealings with the nobles, from
whom he required the highest standards of conduct, he appears
to have gone out of his way to offend the people by his violent
and capricious judgments ; and this in an age which knew
little of justice and nothing of equal rights for all, and was
prepared to applaud either a cruel sentence or a complete
pardon.

The sensation caused by the judgment on the Bastard
de la Hamayde was extraordinary. This handsome youth
had so far lost control of himself as to commit a heartless
murder, and he had foolishly neglected to offer satisfaction
to the kindred of his victim. The right of private revenge
had never been disputed in Hainault, and no very serious
notice of the crime was taken by the nobility. But Charles
threw the culprit into prison and swore by St. George that
he should die. Tremendous excitement prevailed. The
Hainault nobles made his cause their own, and great pressure
was put upon the Duke to exercise his prerogative of mercy.
But he was adamant, and the Bastard was condemned to be
executed like a common criminal. On the way to the scaffold
attempts were made by the women present to save the victim's
life by invoking an ancient privilege and offering to marry
him. But the Duke's orders were imperative. De la Hamayde
died bravely, and his head and body were then exposed on
the wheel between the remains of two common murderers.

Such an event might well dismay the nobles. Charles
had made it clear that he was ready to lay hands on men of
birth and to punish them like other criminals. This was an
offence against their honour, and if their honour was taken
from them what remained ?

The motto composed for Francis I, " *Tout est perdu fors
l'honneur* " sums up the attitude of knighthood in general
towards misfortune. " Honour above everything " stood in
invisible letters on the shield and banner of every true
knight. The French King John the Good was terribly
mortified when Louis of Anjou, his own flesh and blood,
whom he had left behind in England as hostage, broke his

parole and secretly made his way home.   The disgrace
had to be wiped out ; the King sacrificed his liberty and
straightway returned to imprisonment.

The aristocratic author of the *Enseignements paternels*
impressed on his son with great emphasis : " *on ne doit pour
mort, pour vie, pour chevance, ne autrement faire chose contre
honneur.*"   It was better to die honourably than to live in
shame.   " I would rather see you die gloriously in battle
than that you should return in dishonour."   May *Beau Sire
Dieu* grant that his son shall always live nobly.

The laws of chivalry required that an opponent should always
be honoured if he had shown himself worthy of his vows.   A
Hainault nobleman who had joined the English and wore the
Order of the Garter, received unstinted praise, because he
fought to his last breath and scorned to seek safety in a
neighbouring castle.

The same fiction required the same devotion from high
and low alike.   It was demanded of the prince that he should
be ready to lay down his life for his people if occasion
demanded such a sacrifice, since affairs of state and conflicts
between nations were still regarded as the ruler's individual
concerns.   Just as Richard II proposed to Charles VI that
the quarrels between England and France should be settled
by a duel, so Louis, Duke of Orleans, regarding himself as
the avenger of the House of York after Richard's mysterious
death, challenged Henry of Lancaster as a usurper.   What
had become of Richard ?   " *Où est sa vie ? où est son corps ?
ne le scet Dieu, ne le congnoist le monde ! . . . Vous mentez et
toutefoiz que ce direz, vostre bouche fera sa coustume qui est
remplie de mensongez et de très haulte faulseté—vous mentez
par vostre faulse et très desloyal gorge.*"

Philip the Good wished to engage in single combat with
Duke Humphrey of Gloucester, who as consort of Countess
Jacqueline of Holland, dared to dispute his claim to the
Netherlands.   In his challenge he alleges as the cause,
" *pour éviter effusion de sang chrestien et la destruction du
peuple dont en mon cuer ay compacion* " ; later he adds :
" *que par nos corps sans plus ceste querelle soit menée à fin,
que y aler avant par voies de guerres, dont il convendroit mains
gentilshommes et aultres, tant de vostre ost comme der mien
finer leurs jours piteusement.*"

The preparations for the combat were made with great solemnity : no detail was omitted. But it did not take place. Later Philip proposed to fight a duel with Duke William of Saxony, with whom he wished to settle some question in connection with Luxemburg. But this also did not take place. These princely duels may appear only as a *beau geste* to posterity, but they were certainly taken seriously by contemporaries. Duke Philip the Good went into training and practised fencing daily with the most skilful fencing masters.

But there could be no honour without virtue. In ancient Rome whoever wished to enter the temple of *Honos* had first to visit that of *Virtus*. According to the author of the *Instruction d'un jeune prince*, this principle holds good for the Order of Knighthood. The knight was required to wear his gold and gems not only outwardly but to shine inwardly like a burning lamp. Much had been written concerning knighthood since the enthusiastic eulogy of the *nova militia* resounded in praise of the Templars. It is, however, important to note that the influence of the Church was no longer so marked, and that knighthood was shedding its clerical trappings. Some de-christianization of the knightly ideal in fact occurred, and no objection was made to the knighthood of Saladin the Moslem.

It was during the zenith of knighthood that John of Salisbury wrote his *Policraticus*. He indicates the obligations of knighthood : protection of the Church, the up-rooting of dishonesty, respect for the priesthood, guardianship of the poor against injustice, the preservation of peace in the land, willingness on the part of the knight to shed his blood for his neighbour and if necessary to lay down his life for him. These lines might have been written in the fifteenth century. One thing is wanting : the devotion to womanhood, which played so prominent a part in the knight's life. The author of the *Instruction d'un jeune prince* deals with this aspect of chivalry very strikingly. He takes as his pattern a thirteenth century tract, which describes the French knight Hue de Tabarie, Prince of Galilee, instructing the Sultan of Babylon on the subject of knighthood. The knight makes

clear to Saladin the four chief duties of the perfect knight.
(1) He must avoid that place where false justice is
administered or treachery plotted ; (2) he must not lend his
presence to any company in which a lady is slandered or
improperly advised ; (3) he is to fast on Fridays in memory
of the day of the Lord's affliction ; (4) he is to hear mass
regularly and to take holy communion.   In another passage
the same writer sets out the qualities which are as essential
to the knight's condition as his girdle and golden spurs,
his men and trusty arms.   These are to follow truth
and courage, generosity and moderation, to leave plundering
and covetousness, to be constant in military exercises,
and strict in the observance of church duties.   Chastellain
is equally clear.   Truth and courage, a sense of shame and
generosity are the essential qualities of every true knight.

So extraordinary were the demands upon the knight that
the motives which induced him to undertake the obligations
of his calling must now be considered.   In the foreground
stood the glowing impulse for renown.   The passion for
personal prowess is illustrated as early as the twelfth century
in the case of a knight, apparently of French origin.   He
is consumed with the desire to equal the giants of old and
to be named in the same breath with the heroes of whom
Greeks, Romans, Israelites, and those Christian races who
had lived in the twilight of history and saga, were wont to
sing and tell.   Hero-worship was passionately fostered.
In the course of time a definite circle of heroes was formed,
which took its place beside the Round Table : Hector, Caesar,
Alexander, Joshua, David, Judas Maccabaeus, Arthur,
Charlemagne, Godefroy de Bouillon.   To the nine heroes
an age which delighted in symmetry added nine heroines.

Nor were the exploits of recent history forgotten.   Gilles
de Chin, Gilles de Trazegnies, whose deeds were richly
embellished by legend, enjoyed great renown.   Memorial
crosses and stones like the *Croix Pèlerine* proclaimed to
later generations the history of innumerable tourneys and
jousts.   The royal honours shown to the Constable Du
Guesclin made a very deep impression in the ranks of knighthood.   Like a scion of the Lily, the brave commander was

PLATE 11

Goblet of Philip the Good. Kunsthistorisches
Museum, Vienna.

interred in Saint-Denis and a few years after his death a splendid memorial service was held. The Bishop took as the text of his sermon, the passage from the Bible : *nominatus est usque ad extrema terrae.* Two of the Constable's swords were preserved in the Burgundian treasury and were found worthy of a place next the sword of St. George and the tusk of a wild boar *qui l'on dit la dent du sanglier Lorrain Garin.* This was in its way a recollection of the relic worship which so often occurs in the history of religious and knightly observances.

When Louis of Orleans had the banqueting hall at Coucy decorated with the statues of the heroes, he added as a tenth hero that of Du Guesclin. But the special object of hero-worship at the Court of Burgundy was Hercules. He was considered the progenitor of the race. This hero was to be met with everywhere ; his deeds were celebrated in tapestries which were carried on lengthy journeys to decorate hall and tent. Innumerable books, illustrated with life-like miniatures, told the story of his wondrous adventures and experiences. Articles of use in daily life, chests, shrines, and swordhilts, kept alive the memory of knightly deeds. When the body of Henry V was brought to London, the head harness of one horse bore three golden crowns on a blue shield, the coat of arms of King Arthur. In the *Pas de la Belle Pélerine*, the heroine's knight appeared as Lancelot du Lac with the latter's shield *à la bande de Benouhic* ; another presented Palamedes. On the stone Perron hung the shield of Tristan de Leonnois. At the funeral of Charles the Bold the victorious Duke René of Lorraine assumed, in addition to his robe of mourning, a long golden beard (another example of the purely superficial and ornamental influence of the antique) as the victorious heroes of old were wont to do.

Love went hand in hand with the desire for glory. In his love for his adored lady the seeker after adventure realized the attainment of his ambition. In her name he dared the deed which was to admit him into the company of the elect. No difficulty was too insuperable, no burden too heavy, no sacrifice too humbling. In the *Mémoires de Boucicaut* we read of Lancelot and Tristan. " *Amour . . . faict oublier toute peine et prendre en gré tout le travail que on porte pour la chose aimée.*" The knight did not shrink from the life of an ascetic or a monk whose chastity he ridiculed and despised. The energetic became apathetic, the strong became weaklings who spent their days in weeping and complaining. The knight gladly saw himself suffer, and was content that the world should see it too. When Jean de Chassa appeared at the *Pas de l'Arbre d'Or* as *chevalier esclave*, he related in a letter which was read aloud the sorrows which he endured by reason of his lady's coldness.

The lady for whom the knight was content to languish saw no reason for pity in his sorrows. She demanded his undivided service, and if she was to be his she was to be won by force of arms. The general injunction to protect and defend the weak was whittled down to a single object : to free pursued and oppressed womanhood from distress and danger and, as rescuer, to earn his lady's gratitude. The knights' example was St. George the Cappadocian champion, who killed the monster and freed the princess ; the old dragon-killer of heroic saga had been arrayed in Christian attire. It was the knight and his lady who now played at being Perseus and Andromeda.

An esquire or knight without his lady-love was unthinkable. Few could have faced the laughter which greeted the foolish young Jehain de Saintré when he blushingly and tearfully confessed to the Dame des Belles Cousines that his mother and sister were his loves.

In the domain of gallantry the Burgundian nobility looked to their prince as their pattern and example. Philip the Good was especially glorified as a worshipper of ladies. The Portuguese, Vasco Mada de Villalobos, declared in his prologue to the "*Triomphe des Dames*" which another Portuguese, Vasco Fernandez, Count de Lucena, had translated into French, that the dedication was rightly offered to Duke Philip as the pillar, the protector and invincible defender of the honour and nobility of the female sex, and eulogized him as "*le plus loyal serviteur d'amours et des dames qui au siècle vive.*" The following may be read in the *Livre du Cuer d'amours espris* :—

Je Phelippes de Bourgongne, tel est mon nom tenu,
Qui en amer me suis tout mon temps maintenu,
Où le dieu d'Amours m'a doulcement soustenu.

.   .   .   .

Et pour ce que je sçay, par estre combatu
Des batailles d'Amours, que j'ay esté vaincu.
En plusieurs nations, où me suis embatu,
Je me suis en présent aù dieu d'Amours rendu.

Society was quite willing to allow Philip his numerous
mistresses, and the people acclaimed him when he openly
displayed his gallantry. When his pretty niece, the Duchess
of Orleans, came on one occasion to fetch him in Paris, he
quickly mounted her horse, in order not to keep her waiting,
and placed her in front of him, " *et commencèrent à trotter
parmy les rues, en grand joye de tous les voyants qui alloient
disant : Et velà un humain prince ! velà un seigneur dont un
monde seroit estoré de l'avoir tel ! Qui bénoit soit-il, et tous ceux
qui l'aiment. Et que n'est tel nostre roi et ainsi humain !* "
Chastellain tells us that at the entry into Utrecht, after the
town's resistance was broken, Duke Philip rode in state
armour " *regardant fièrement comme un lion, espécialement
sur les hommes, mais en passant devant les dames qui estoient
assisses aux fenestres et qui lui firent les honneurs, il leur
tourna bénignement l'œil et le chief un peu.* "

In battle the bliss inspired by the proximity of the lady
to her knight was lacking. From the camp at Neuss where
snow and ice lay thick on the tents, where there were no
soft Dutch beds on which to repose, where the mud of the
roads was knee-deep, Philip de Croy, Count of Chimay,
recalling the luxurious days of the past, was moved to write :
" *Où est le diner loumé au son de la cloche ? Hélas ! où sont
dames pour entretenir, pour nous amonester de bien faire,
ne pour nous enchargier emprinses, devises, volets ne
guimpes ?* "

But joust and tourney afforded a welcome substitute for
war. The sight of so many and beauteous ladies exalted
the courage and the desire of innumerable young knights
and esquires. The cavalier Boucicaut, proud of his dress
and appearance, well mounted and equipped, caught a look
from his lady's eyes and attacked his opponent with such
fury that many of the onlookers were unhorsed by the force
of the encounter.

Fashion and convention demanded that ladies should always be present at the tourneys and permitted them to take part in the banquets which followed. Even the Duchess was present on occasion. During the *Pas de l'Arbre d'Or* at Bruges, Margaret of York appeared several times among the spectators. What happiness to unhorse your opponent under the very eyes of your lady and to receive at her hands the reward of your skill and valour! Her veil, a ribbon or glove fluttered on helmet or armour, and recalled to her enraptured champion, to use the language of the troubadour, her honey-sweet breath, and the milky fragrance of her skin. If a wise discretion required it, the language of adoration gave way to colours, flowers, and gems, all with their special symbols and secret meanings. While the happy lover wore green and violet as a sign of his *amoureuse lyesse*, the knight *fasché et ennuyé du monde* could give expression to his melancholy by appearing in the lists in red and black, and by displaying flowers as tokens on his tabard, or on the trappings of his horse.

That the Church soon began to oppose the tourneys was due undoubtedly to their erotic character, but the prevailing passion was too strong to suffer interference ; it had existed longer than knighthood itself. Did Philip de Mézières, that untiring herald of the Crusades, also recognize the dangers of a lady's service ? It is certainly remarkable that he desired to allow the knights of his Order *de la Passion* to marry and imposed on them not the obligation of chastity but a vow of marital fidelity. Christine de Pisan energetically rejected the *folle amour* and warned married ladies against the protestations of adoring knights.

It would be extremely interesting if some writer could have given us an insight into the mind of the lady of the period. What were her thoughts, what did she feel, and how did she judge her knight's demeanour ? Much as we hear of the man, we are told very little about the woman. She hardly ever emerges from the mysterious shadows of her bower into the light of day. This is all the more to be regretted, since just at that time the conflict kindled by the *Romance of the Rose* was being waged anew and raged passionately round the character, influence, and significance of woman. Christine de Pisan, the first Frenchwoman to champion her sex's rights, by her warmhearted defence of despised womanhood, provoked a number of attacks, but she succeeded also in obtaining a juster conception of the position of women in general. This can be seen even in the *Cent Nouvelles Nouvelles,* which was written in the first place for the world of pleasure.

Life at the Court of Burgundy was extremely costly. How could the knight afford to live there ? On what did he subsist ? There was no work which could be paid for in money. The right to earn was exclusively the vilain's. A knight must be able to command an assured income or boast a lord to fill his pockets for him. Untroubled by earthly cares the hero was to spend his life without any thought of gain : his motto still, as in the days of the Troubadours, *Joie aimer.* There were nobles even in France who were not ashamed to make money by trading, but there, as elsewhere, they were not prominent and met with no recognition.

In war-time pay and ransom played a great part in the life of the knight and helped him to pay his way. Eustache Deschamps has well described with what impatience the paymaster is awaited in the camp : *Et quant venra le tresorier* is the constant refrain of the poem. Ransom, however, was considerably more important than pay. The sober thinking author of the *Enseignements paternels* explains to his son that beside a good marriage and the prince's service there is a further means of attaining wealth ; he may during war-time with good luck capture a prisoner of such wealth and importance that the ransom alone will suffice to free him from care for the rest of his days. Perhaps the anonymous writer was thinking of the enormous sums which John the Good had to pay to Edward III in order to secure his release from imprisonment. To raise three million gold shillings the French King was forced to resort to desperate means ; " he sold his own flesh and blood," by marrying one of his daughters to Gian Galeazzo Visconti against payment of 600,000 gold shillings. No objection was made to the exploitation of captives : Charles of Orleans was to experience that there was, indeed, a distinctly practical side of knighthood, which to the modern critic does not harmonize well with the ideal.

In peace time, when this source of revenue failed, the knight errant, " *un povre aventurier en qui n'a que perdre* ", was forced to seek a substitute in the prizes of joust and tourney. The *grands seigneurs* might smile and mock at the professional *tournoyeurs*, who were quite ready to pawn helmet and armour in time of need ; but they tolerated in them conduct and lapses, which in the case of a non-noble, they would have publicly denounced. The mutual interests of their order kept them silent.

The contrast between the knightly ideal and reality was to become more marked as time went on. Honour required that the knight should never refuse battle when it was offered by his opponent. Tactical and strategic necessity, however, frequently demanded that the challenge should be refused. Philip the Good allowed the army commander to get the better of the knight when he avoided a battle three times in one day. He even allowed his magnificent and conspicuous armour to be worn in battle by one of his knights. He arrived at such decisions with great difficulty ; they deprived him of his sleep ; for it was Philip's boast that he preferred death to dishonour. But even in Philip's case sober political reasons were at times thrown into the background by the joy of battle. In order to encourage his followers, he galloped alone far ahead of his troops to the attack, and at the siege of Melun he took up his position in the trenches like King Henry V, and engaged an opponent.

The catastrophe at the battle of Nicopolis was largely occasioned by the demand of the French knights, that they should fight in the front line. The practical needs of the moment, as King Sigismund of Hungary pointed out, required that experienced esquires should take their place, but he was overruled. Again and again attempts were made to make practical use on the battlefield of the fighting methods of the tourney. It was with the greatest reluctance that the French knights were persuaded to follow the example of the English, and dismount from their chargers in order to fight on foot. Eustache Deschamps, it is curious to note, fails to see the significance of this change of tactics, although he is not often at fault. He taunts the knight with dismounting in order to run away more easily. The remark of Jean de Beaumont at Agincourt shows how incapable the knights were of accommodating themselves to changed circumstances. King Charles, he said, ought not to accept the aid of the Paris craftsmen, for then the French army would be three times as strong as the English ; and that would contravene the principles of knightly honour.

The knight's vows in which the influence of the Church is shown just as clearly as the influence of love, were by no means always harmless or trifling. In 1454, at the Feast of the Pheasant, knights and lords, after the wine had flowed freely, came forward and took, in the presence of the ladies, the most extravagant oaths in the name of God, the Virgin Mary and the Pheasant. Philippe Pot vowed to keep his right arm uncovered and not to sit at table on Tuesdays until he had fought successfully against the Unbelievers. Duke Philip found it necessary expressly to forbid that part of the vow relating to the arm-covering, but this did not prevent Louis de Chevalart declaring that as soon as the army reached a distance of only four days' march from the enemy, he would wear no covering on his head and would bare his right arm to the glove until he had faced an Unbeliever. " My horse's head," vowed another, " will never turn back until the banner of the Turk is thrown down or conquered."

Other obligations were more harmless. Some imposed physical penance on themselves. Thus the esquire, Guillaume de Martigny, who had formerly undertaken to wear a piece of his armour day and night until he had met a Turk, now vowed in addition that he would wear a hair shirt from the day of departure onward, that he would not sit at table on Saturdays, nor drink wine nor sleep in a bed. Jean de Rebremettes, another esquire, pledged himself that if before the Crusade his mistress had not granted him her favours, then on his return he would marry at random the first lady he met who had 20,000 shillings, provided she was agreeable to the match. For the most part these oaths were taken very seriously. The English knights may be

recalled to memory, who, on the expedition to France kept
one eye covered until they had proved their courage in battle.

Duke Philip considered it necessary to intervene and forbid
unnecessary recklessness.   Often, too, a little reflection served
to restrain the knight's exuberance without any interference
from the Duke.   But the Feast of the Pheasant with its
fort oultrageuse et desraisonable depense, was intended to
have a definite political object ; to gain knights and lords and
especially those who were reluctant and over-critical, for
the campaign against the enemies of the Cross.   The fusion
of the crusading ideal with the romance of chivalry was
deliberate and intentional.

The Crusade of Philip the Good did not take place, but it
is interesting to reflect what might have happened had he
set out for the Holy Land as he ardently desired to do.
Of this at least we may be sure.   Philip with his shrewdness
and moderation would never even have started for the East
unless there had been a reasonable probability of success.

The Burgundian knighthood created its own ideal type :—
Jacques de Lalaing, *le bon chevalier*, the brightest ornament
of Philip's Court, who lost his life when only thirty-two years
of age in battle with the men of Ghent.   When we recall
the glorious names which are linked up with the fortunes of
the House of Burgundy, we may well ask how it came about
that this young man whose achievements were in no sense
remarkable should have been singled out for special honours.
Possibly the very fact that Lalaing had performed no
particularly daring feats may have caused him to be regarded
as the pattern of the ordinary everyday knight.   For society
lived under perpetual restraint : it obeyed and was forced to
obey the dictates of its own artificial creations in the matter
of courtesy and fashion.   Lapses from precedent were scarcely
to be tolerated.   Without the strictest rules and ceremonies
it would have been difficult to curb the exuberance of the
hot-heads who affected to consider that the giants were still
at war with the knights.   Individual achievement was only
encouraged within perfectly definite limits.

This is probably the reason why Lalaing's life seemed
sufficiently memorable to be described in detail,   Jean Le

Févre, Seigneur de Saint-Remy, Toison d'Or King-at-Arms, glorified the young knight's heroic deeds in a letter addressed to his father. This letter, indeed, formed the foundation of the *Livre des faits*, which was at first ascribed to no other than Chastellain.

The *Livre des faits* is written for the world of chivalry, and contains a scrupulously exact description of Lalaing's assaults-at-arms, a detailed account of his armour, his lances, axes, and daggers. At the same time an attempt is made to sketch in the outlines of his character. The tone is comparatively unpretentious: the author has determined apparently that his hero is not to be a god; therein lies the value of the *Livre des faits* in comparison with such a work, for instance, as the biography of Marshal Boucicaut. The contrast between Boucicaut and Lalaing on the one hand, and the warrior presented to us in the *Jouvencel*, on the other, is very remarkable, for there we meet a specimen of knighthood which is new to us:—the French officer-nobleman who belongs definitely to the future.

Lalaing, we are told, was fair as Paris, pious as Æneas, wise as Ulysses, and passionate as Hector; but when once he had established his superiority over his opponent, he was singularly gentle and humble. Thus the chronicler eulogizes him. *Courtois, débonnaire* and *humble* are outstanding epithets.

Lalaing was very carefully brought up by his parents, and never omitted to hear mass every morning. As *mignon* of Duke John I he was initiated at the Court of Cleves into the mysteries of chivalry, and such was his progress that he was soon seen everywhere in the lists. He was also a knight-errant. We see him next preparing for the pilgrimage to the Holy Land, having first magnanimously abandoned his right to his father's castle in favour of his younger brother. No ordinary steed sufficed for such a paladin. He appeared on a splendid charger in stately array which Duke Philip and his father had provided for him, notwithstanding the fact that he was unable to pay his debts.

A knight-errant indeed, but not an empty-headed adventurer like Ulrich of Lichtenstein, nor a bizarre hidalgo like the immortal Don Quixote. Lalaing felt himself undoubtedly at home in the world, long vanished, of the

romances of chivalry.   It is true that he strove after
a splendid revival of knightly ideals, but this energetic and
clear-headed youth never took a false step nor sought to
achieve the impossible.   With a seriousness beyond his
years he avoided every extravagance which might render
him objectionable or ridiculous in society.   At the joust
of the *Fontaine aux Pleurs,* which seems very strange to us
to-day, he hit the taste of his contemporaries.   It made
him famous all over the West.   Jousting was his passion ;
his most ardent wish was to fight in the lists thirty times
before his thirtieth year.

> J'ai vu, estrange chose,
> Chevalier sous trente ans
> Combattre en lice close
> Vingt et deux nobles gens,
> Par tant de foys diverses
> Comme il y a de noms,
> Sans foulle et sans traverses :
> Ce qu'oncques ne fit homs.

Lalaing did not pursue sport for sport's sake ; the joust
for him was not an end in itself.   When his lord and duke
summoned him he hastened joyfully to the battlefield and
took his place among the bravest of his fellows.   He was
employed also in diplomatic services and was ready when
called upon with wise and varied counsel.   His biographer
presents him to us as a youth, prudent and reserved, amiable
but dignified, a member, it might be said, of the Spanish
grandezza.   We cannot imagine Lalaing laughing heartily
or enjoying life without restraint.

The young knight travelled far and wide.   By order
of the Duke he visited the Courts of Navarre, Castile, Portugal,
Aragon, Rome, and Naples ; his passion for jousting frequently
embarrassed his hosts.   He crossed the sea and in Scotland
measured his strength against a Douglas.   Germany he
reserved for later years.   At his death the rough draft
of a challenge was found in a chest, from which it is clear that
Lalaing desired to carry off a goblet from the Imperial table.
If no nobleman disputed his right to it, he purposed to
challenge the German knights and esquires to a contest in
the lists with the coveted goblet as a prize.

As envoy of the *Grand Duc d'Occident* and a member of
Burgundian Court society, Lalaing was received with honour

and distinction everywhere. He was perfectly at home
and at his ease whether at a bull-fight or at a royal banquet.
He took his place with address and dignity on the left
of the King of Portugal at table, led the Queen to the
dance and received, in accordance with custom, a kiss
at parting.

Lalaing, " who called Roland's arm and sword his own,"
treated his opponents, especially when vanquished, with
magnanimity. Once in a joust with an Englishman he fought
with axe alone, without vizier or sword, " *de quoy il fit folie*,"
for his left arm was badly injured. He dropped the axe
and threw his opponent skilfully to the ground. " (*Il avoit*)
le derrière tout découvert," and Lalaing could have given him
his death blow with a thrust of his knife, but he declined
to do so. When the Englishmen alleged later, without
foundation, that he had not fallen with his whole body and
consequently refused to send his glove to Lalaing's lady,
the victor declined to pursue the matter and even sent the
vanquished Englishman a diamond.

> Cy gist celui qui clair plus que l'ivoire
> Prit chasteté pour pilier de sa gloire,

Thus Chastellain wrote his epitaph.

Lalaing was once presented to two princesses, the Duchess
of Calabria, and Mary of Cleves, Duchess of Orleans, who
while still very young, was wedded to the aged prince. Both
ladies succumbed to the charms of the youthful knight, who
did not shrink from appearing as challenger at the joust in
place of two experienced knights. At the assault-at-arms he
rode into the lists wearing on his helmet the gift of one of
his ladies, a veil shimmering with pearls falling to the ground,
and on his left arm the favours of the other, a sleeve gleaming
with jewels, a proceeding which aroused much comment.
But both duchesses still desired to have him as their *passe
temps*. At the banquet, which followed, he appeared
among the lords and ladies, *le viaire frais et coloré comme
une rose*, in spite of all his exertions, and took his seat
between the two whose favours he had worn. Secretly the
one slipped a diamond-ring, the other a ruby ring, into his
hand. It speaks much for his skill and address that Lalaing
managed to retain the favour of both ladies, nor did he
demand from either what he could easily have obtained.

At his early death in 1453, Lalaing was universally mourned. He seemed to have been one of those rare natures who go through life without envy in themselves and without inspiring envy in others.   Olivier de La Marche complains bitterly against the malice of fortune which too frequently cuts off the finest flowers in their prime.   So it was in this case, but one consolation remained :—" the renown of the virtues, disposition, and chivalry of Lalaing will be perpetuated not only by his contemporaries and in their memories, but also as long as writings exist in this world."

Jacques de Lalaing did not fall, as he had dreamed, in glorious battle with an antagonist of equal rank.   He was killed most unromantically by a cannon-ball.   Can the conflict between the knightly ideals of the fifteenth century and the claims of practical reality be better illustrated ?

CHAPTER VI

THE LADY

Se bien veulx et chastement vivre
De la Rose ne lis le livre.

CHRISTINE DE PISAN.

NO other than Petrarch described the *Romance of the Rose* as the most striking poem ever conceived by French genius. Yet seldom has a book exercised such a baleful influence. It was read again and again, and copied repeatedly by industrious hands and illustrated by the most gifted miniaturists. Thus the mordant and poisoned words in which Jean de Meung, who continued the work of Guillaume de Lorris, scourged the female sex, secured the widest circulation, and held public opinion under their spell.

Qu'il est veritez senz doutance :
Fame si n'a point de science ;
Vers quanqu'el het e quanqu'ele aime :

might have been chosen by the highly gifted and youthful writer as his motto. He cannot do enough to surpass the Roman satirists. The character of an unfinished work has rarely been so changed by its continuator. *Toutes fames serf et eneure*, may be read in Guillaume de Lorris. Many found in Guillaume de Lorris' poem a rosebud, the personification of the virgin, which the lover has to gain by prowess ; it fades and dies at his audacious touch and sensual look.

Cynically, with seductive rhetoric, Meung preaches the emancipation of the flesh and pleads for sexual communism :—

. . . Toutes pour touz et touz pour toutes,
Chascune pour chascun comune,
E chascun comun à chascune.

An ardent cry resounds, the sharpest protest against ecclesiastical doctrines which saw the ideal of life in the mortification of the flesh. Unbridled enjoyment of love is demanded ; all the punishments of hell await those unwilling to observe the commands of nature and love. Brazenly and shamelessly the hypocritical and panderous old woman offers her wicked counsel as to how the rose may most easily be plucked.

Meung furnished his work with a mass of historical, mythological, cosmic, alchemic, astrological, and theological knowledge, and many read it enthusiastically who would have quickly laid aside a work of simple eroticism. It is strange indeed, but whoever sought advice in the *Romance of the Rose* on the *ars amandi,* was brought at once into contact with every conceivable problem which had plagued human knowledge. And again, the seeker athirst for knowledge, who sought it at the same source, was thereby initiated into the mysteries of the *ars amandi.* What Gothic architecture attained in the *style flamboyant,* was to be observed in literature at the turn of the thirteenth century. The guiding principle was imbedded in a profusion of forms, often of the most bizarre kind.

Jean de Meung was utterly opposed to the Troubadours who glorified the unstilled unsatisfied desire of love in an ecstacy of suffering. While courtly love might lead to the apotheosis of the adored lady, whose spiritual conquest was sufficient, the baser demand for the destruction of virginity led to the degradation of woman, who, being conquered, lost her value. A lady who, in spite of all temptations, can defend her honour does not seem to exist for Jean de Meung.

There was some opposition here and there, but it could not drown the applause which greeted de Meung's conception of love. Mahieu, a cleric of Boulogne-sur-Mer, openly approved it in his *Lamentationes,* which attained a wide circulation in the French translation by Jean Le Fèvre of Ressons. Le Fèvre—like Jean de Meung before him—was to regret later his contribution to the subject, and in the *Livre de Léesce,* the " Book of Merriment " contritely and solemnly recalled it.

> De femmes sommes tous venus,
> Autant les gros que les menus.
> Pourquoy celluy qui en dit blasme
> Doit estre réputé infâme.

But the seed had in the meantime taken root and flourished. Personal misfortune had turned Mahieu into an ardent misogynist. By his marriage to a widow, he had committed bigamy and lost his stipends . . . in addition he lived unhappily with his wife. His desperation found comfort in abuse. He roundly declared that God the Lord had himself condemned all womankind :—

> Leur nature à mal les excite,
> S'aucune en y a qui bien face,
> Ce li vient d'especial grâce.
> Si tost que femme fu fourmée.
> Elle fu contre moy armée ;
> Tollir me voult ma région
> Des cieulx par sa sédition.

Small wonder that there would be no women in Paradise. Adam, on the day of Judgment, would receive back the rib from which God created Eve.

Mahieu called to mind all the evils which his wife had brought him, and exclaimed :—

> Elle ressemble au basilique
> C'est un serpent dont Dieu te gart
> Les gens occist de son regart.

And again :

> Il n'est nul bien que femme face,
> Ainçois le destruit et efface
>
> .   .   .   .   .   .
>
> C'est la mère de tout orage
> Tout mal en vient et toute rage.

Many followed willingly the example set by Jean de Meung and Mahieu. The satirical literature cultivated by the citizen class delighted to tilt at woman and her honour, and employed in the main very heavy and ugly missiles. The married woman was the chief victim of attack: the spinster and the child escaped with comparative immunity. Only the nun, like the monk, attracted notice and met with approbation or abuse. Péronelle d'Armentières is one of the most interesting exceptions. She was immortalized by her beloved and adored Guillaume de Machaut in *Le Livre du Voir-Dit*. Her love romance shows that *Demies Vierges* existed even in those days.

As no successful literary champions appeared to defend the honour of women, it was left to Christine de Pisan to enter the lists in defence of her sex.

Dire necessity forced her to become an authoress and poetess. Born in Venice, she was the daughter of a physician and astrologer of Bologna, whom Charles V had invited to

the French Court. A cruel fate deprived her in early life of
a kind father and a loving husband :—

> Com turtre suis sanz per toute seulette

she complains, and calls to her husband in memory of their
happy marriage :—

> Hélas, quel infortune amère
> Tombe sus à femme et quelle misère,
> Quant pert mary bon et paisible,
> Qui d'amour l'amoit . . .

Compelled to earn her daily bread and to provide for her
mother and three children, the slumbering forces in Christine
burst forth into the choicest flowers. Though she had been
reared in comfort, and had been widowed at the age of 25,
she bravely faced the task of steering " through stormy seas
the ship which had lost its pilot ".

> Hèlas ! où donc trouveront reconfort
> Pouvres vesves de leurs biens despouilliées.

With great industry she applied herself to those learned
studies into which she had been initiated by her father.
She was the first to call the attention of literary circles in
France to the work of Dante, and before long she was able
to offer her own writings to an admiring public. In
accordance with the custom of the age, she presented or
dedicated her works in magnificent manuscripts to the
King and Queen, the Dauphin and Dauphiness, the dukes of
Berry, Burgundy, and Orleans, the King of Navarre. The
Court evinced great interest in the gifted writer, Duke Philip
the Bold took her under his care, and at his earnest entreaty
Christine wrote the life of Charles V of France, for whom she
entertained the greatest admiration.

" *De toutes les nacions du monde, je l'ose dire sans flaterie,
car il est vray, n'a tant bénignes princes, ne tant humains qu'il
y en a en France,*" wrote Christine. She knew that her position
was established in France, and she declined proposals and
requests to go to Milan or England : " *je tiens que de tous les
pays de chrestienté, c'est cellui où il fait communément meilleur
habiter et tant pour la bénignité des princes sans cruaulté,
comme pour la courtoisie et amiableté des gens d'icelle nacion,
et toutes-foys ce ne dy-je mie par faveur, comme je n'en soie
pas née.*"

When later the conflict between Burgundy and Orleans

PLATE 12

Unknown Master : Christine de Pisan at work. Miniature : Christine de Pisan, La Cité des Dames. Bibliothèque Royale MS. 9236, fol. 3r, Brussels.

broke out, she repeatedly raised her voice against the continuance of the strife, warning the opposing parties and praying for the deliverance from distress and danger of the land which had become her second home.

The frankness and noble passion shown by Christine in her political writings are apparent also in her efforts to overthrow her detested opponents, Jean de Meung, Mahieu, and their followers, and to secure justice and respect for women.

> Elle fut Tulle et Catton,
> Tulle car en toute éloquence
> Elle eust la rose et le bouton
> Catton aussi en sapience,

so runs the eulogy of Martin Le Franc at a later date.

Hers was a thorny task. The age revelled in a strong, healthy sensuality, and exhibited it openly and unblushingly. The chroniclers sympathized freely with the love adventures of their heroes. When, after waiting impatiently, King Charles VI and Isabeau celebrated their nuptials, Froissart remarks jestingly: "*Si furent en déduit celle nuit, che poés vous bien croire.*" The age was content to tolerate sexual excess. Chastellain writes placidly of the Constable of Saint-Pol that he was an *assez heureux et merveilleux solliciteur de Madame Vénus*. Matters of this kind were treated quite frankly and naturally. Even holy things were humanized. In the Burgundian Treasury there was a golden Madonna richly ornamented with gems : on a small door being opened, the Holy Trinity was seen in the womb of the Virgin. It may seem strange to us when we read in Chastellain that a countess "*représentait le ventre de sa feu mère*". It was left to later generations to withdraw the bridal night from curious eyes behind an impenetrable curtain : in those days it was their friends' privilege to accompany the young couple with song and jubilation to their chamber, and to wait outside until a cry proclaimed the consummation of the marriage. Christine herself had no scruples in recalling in one of her poems the circumstances of her own bridal night.

There was a danger, of course, under these conditions that woman might come to be regarded merely as a sexual necessity for man, and the nurse and attendant of his children, instead of taking her place as his legal, moral, and spiritual equal and companion. Nor was the Church concerned that its priests by glorifying at the cost of marriage the virtues of chastity and virginity, and regarding woman merely as a temptress, were contributing to her degradation.

Tertullian had condemned woman root and branch. Lothair de Segni, later known as Pope Innocent III, in his work *De contemptu mundi*, recognizes no joys but only the sufferings of motherhood : *Concipit mulier cum immunditia et fetore, parit cum tristitia et dolore, nutrit cum angustia et labore, custodit cum instantia et timore.* Jean de Varennes, the *saint-homme de Lié*, whom even Gerson had to oppose, discovered twenty-two or twenty-three separate and individual sins connected with matrimony.

But the enormity of her task did not alarm Christine. She attacked Jean de Meung and the " *aliez du Romans de la Rose* " and accused them of judging woman-kind as a whole by the depraved creatures of their acquaintance. She could not, she said, otherwise explain the shameless insults levelled at the female sex by Meung, who went so far as to maintain with Juvenal, that an honourable woman was scarcely to be found, and that when found she was as easily recognizable as a black swan.

How could Mahieu allege that God had judged woman unfavourably. Our Saviour deemed a woman worthy to give him birth, but there was no man equally worthy to be his father.

In her study of Mahieu's work, Christine noted very sorrowfully the unreasoning attacks on woman which were made on all sides, and felt at times great unhappiness that she had not been born a man. It was at such a moment as this that, as she tells us, *Raison, Droicture,* and *Justice* appeared to her, and urged her to build a *Cité des dames,* which would be strong and unassailable. In this work she recalls the deeds of brave and noble women, and points out that the reproaches levelled against them were no less applicable to men. She attacks with great energy and skill the general allegation of the moral and mental inferiority of woman and sets herself the task, like Boccaccio, in his work *De claris mulieribus,* of compiling a survey of representative and celebrated women of history. In the *Livre des Trois Vertus,* which Christine intended for use by her female contemporaries as a breviary in their hours of distress and danger, she expands the same ideas and draws the same conclusions.

If Christine ever allowed herself to be amused she might well have smiled to read the *Purgatoire des mauvais marys*, in which an anonymous author condemns Mahieu, the most infamous of mankind, to suffer all the tortures of the damned :

> Voyci Matheolet le vil,
> Dampné en pardurable exil
> Pour avoir des dames mesdit.
> Oncques plus villain ne nasquit,
> Oncques coquin ne fut plus ort,
> Et selon le commun recort,
> En tous ses fais il est infâme
> Et puant en corps et en âme.

Christine adopted the tactics of her opponents and paraded her learning freely. She drew on all the customary *livres d'auctorité*, the Bible, the Church Fathers, the classics, Roman and ecclesiastical law, legends and romances, in order to demolish argument by counter-argument, and confound her enemies from their own books. She demanded in the first place a sufficient education for the female sex, which was as necessary to a woman as to a man. Thus she opposed Philippe de Novare and his followers who claimed that only nuns should be allowed even the rudiments of learning, " for much evil has arisen through women being taught to read and write."

Olivier de La Marche addresses himself at a later period to young girls :—

> Vous, josnes filles, qui désirés honneur,
> Laissiés la lettre, tout ouvraige et escolle ;
> Se beau maintien qui tant est de valleur,
> Aprenez le et le faites de ceur
> Pour avoir loz qui légier court et volle.
> Car je juge d'escript et de parolle.
> Qu'i n'est au monde tel trésor ne chevance
> Milleur pour femme que bonne contenanche.

Christine, however, is of opinion that those who cannot defend themselves are most easily and lightly attacked. The men knew only too well why they were anxious to keep women in ignorance. She demanded also a more humane treatment for married women, whose husbands frequently threw them into complete seclusion, as if they were slaves in a Moslem harem.

Christine considered it disgraceful that men should strike their wives, particularly in public. She exclaims with emphasis :

Fay toy craindre à ta femme à point
Mais gard bien ne la batre point.

And in another passage :

Selon ton pourvoir vestz ta femme
Honnestement et si soit dame
De l'ostel après toy, non serve.

The times were passed, indeed, when even poets could speak of such things without a blush.

It is not surprising that Christine, by her courageous conduct should have aroused the most bitter opposition. New followers and new defenders of the *Romance of the Rose* appeared as if by magic. From the circle of French scholars who were inspired by the first rays of Humanism a very skilful advocate arose in the person of the learned secretary of the King and provost of Lille, Jean de Montreuil. Supported by his friends, the brothers Gontier and Pierre Col, he proclaimed his message to the world in dignified Ciceronian epistles. Overflowing with enthusiasm for the work of Jean de Meung, Montreuil strove to gain the approval of Christine de Pisan by an impassioned eulogy. As a complete humanist he was fully conscious of the learning and ability of the *fille de l'étude*. But all approbation disappeared when Christine dared in all modesty to turn the tables and declared that the *Romance of the Rose* deserved nothing better than destruction. This was too much. The vain and overbearing scholar could tolerate anything except contradiction. Beside himself with rage, he compared Christine to a Greek *meretrix* who had calumniated a philosopher.

It was of great moment to Christine when in 1402, Jean Gerson, the famous professor and Chancellor of the University of Paris, condescended to take part in the controversy. He condemned the *Romance* as a work of utter depravity from beginning to end. His methods were somewhat different. He attacked Jean de Meung in the name of morality and religion ; Christine, that *insignis virago* had belaboured the writer in the name of woman, but their goal was the same. If he possessed the only surviving copy of this *Romance*, were it worth a thousand pounds or more, wrote this passionate man, he would burn it at once. Even if his own brother had written it, he would pray for him indeed, but as for one already damned. The brilliant literary and artistic qualities of the *Romance of the Rose* appealed to him not at all.

How could Jean de Meung, this *Fol amoureux*, presume to scoff at what was lofty and sublime, at married and cloistered life, and glorify without restraint the unbridled pleasures of the flesh ? That those who shared his opinions had the impudence to quote scripture in support of their false doctrines, thereby tempting the ignorant to follow in their footsteps, only magnified the vileness of their crimes.

Christine found help also outside the world of learning, which was of great assistance to her, since it came from the leaders of society. Chivalry, too, which was pledged heart and soul to the honourable service of love, sent able disputants to her aid.

The famous Marshal Boucicaut with twelve other knights, founded the Order *de l'écu verd à la dame blanche* for the protection of ladies and more especially of widows. Very charming is the anecdote which comes from Genoa, and might just as well have been related of the age of Louis XIV. In the streets Boucicaut politely bowed to two ladies who had greeted him as the French King's viceroy. "*Monseigneur*," asked his companion, "*qui sont ces deux femmes à qui vous avez si grans révérences faictes ?*" "*Huguenin dist-il, je ne sçai.*" Lors lui dist : "*Monseigneur, elles sont filles communes.*" "*Filles communes,*" dist-il, "*Huguenin, j'ayme trop mieux faire révérence à dix filles communes que avoir failly à une femme de bien.*"

Christine de Pisan was deeply grateful to the Marshal for his support, and more powerful assistance was at hand. At Epiphany, 1401, when the contest was running high, Duke Philip the Bold in conjunction with the Duke de Bourbon, begged the King's permission to found a court of love, " in order during the vexatious and distressing plague epidemic to pass the time more agreeably and to create new pleasures," a sentiment which seems to suggest that its author was not unfamiliar with the *Decameron*.

The statutes of this literary society were drawn up with great exactitude and considerable pedantry ; recalling in some respects the *Puys d'amour*, which enjoyed remarkable popularity in Amiens and Arras, in Valenciennes and Tournai. The court was to be assembled in the name of the virtues of humility and modesty, and in honour, praise, and service of all ladies and virgins. It was presided over by a prince of love, who directed the proceedings of the court and occupied much the same position as the *Baronnye des Dieu d'Amour* in the *Romance of the Rose*.

> Si deus d'Amours, senz terme mettre
> De leu ne de tens en sa letre
> Toute sa baronie mande,
> Les uns prie, aus autres comande,
> Qu'il viègnent à son palement.

Surprisingly enough the sovereign of love was not a lord of high degree, nor a prince of the blood, but an esquire and cupbearer to the King, Pierre d'Hauteville, Lord of Ars, a man of no particular position at Court. Was it intended by this to emphasize the fact that love knows no differences in rank ? The document lays down specifically that in the court of love no post was to be regarded as inferior, and that the order of enumeration in the register of dignitaries was to be governed by the rule of precedence at the court of love itself, regardless of pedigree, profession, power, or wealth.

The Grand Conservators were no other than Charles of France, Duke Philip, and the Duke of Bourbon. Next in order came the ordinary conservators, men of rank, such as Duke Louis of Bavaria and Ingolstadt, brother of Queen Isabeau, Count William of Holland and Hainault, Louis of Orleans, and Jean de Nevers. These princes of the court of love again were succeeded by twenty-four knights and esquires as ministers, and the secretaries and servants of the King who had experience and knowledge of the science of rhetoric. Then came the lesser dignitaries, the presidents, grand-masters of the hunt, councillors, auditors, legates, knights and esquires of honour, keepers of the rolls and registers of love, secretaries, masters of requests, and wardens of the parks. All names and coats of arms were to be entered in a register, and the deeds of the Order were to be deposited for safe keeping in an abbey.

PLATE 13

Unknown Master: Garden of Love. Miniature: Guillaume de Lorris and Jean de Meung, Roman de la Rose. Harley MS. 4425, fol. 12, British Museum.

[face p. 106

The meetings were to be held in Paris. The assembly hall was to be decorated with the members' coats of arms. At the Sunday festivals, summer and winter alike, the shields of the sovereign and ministers were to be wreathed with evergreen, an emblem of perpetual joy. The ministers swore to hold a festival, a *puy d'amours*, at two o'clock every Sunday, wherever they might happen to be. Two golden diadems were selected as prizes, and these were to be bestowed impartially, without regard to rank or reputation. The presiding minister was to choose the refrain and had himself to produce a ballad. All ballads were registered by the court officials. The gentlemen concerned can have found little difficulty in complying with these requirements, since every true lover was expected to prove himself a poet. As Charles of Orleans expressed it very prettily at a later date :—

> Le sixiesme point et le derrenier
> Est qu'il sera diligent escollier,
> En aprenant tous les gracieux tours,
> A son povoir, qui servent en amours,
> C'est assavoir à chanter et dansser,
> Faire chançons et balades rimer,
> Et tous autres joyeux esbatements.

On the following St. Valentine's day, 14th February, 1401, when the little birds began to sing their songs at the approach of spring, the sovereign of love held his festival in Paris. A stately banquet was to unite all subjects in merry-making, and amorous discourse. After the solemn reading of the statutes by virtue of which the court had come into existence each member was to produce a love ballad. These were read aloud and then submitted to the judgment of the ladies. Ballads with false rhymes or faults of composition were rejected. To the Church, too, was given that which was the Church's due. In honour of St. Valentine mass was celebrated with organ and choir.

Every year in the month of May, and on one of the five festivals of the Holy Virgin, " mother of the angels and intercessor for all loving hearts," further celebrations were to take place at which love songs and *sirvantes* were to be produced. The sovereign of love was also expected to hold jousts in the merry month of May, and, indeed, was compelled to do so when requested by his loving subjects.

Other regulations exhibit the passion for detail and thoroughness which characterized the age. From these it was clearly demonstrated that the assembly was quite prepared to sit and function as a court of justice, having jurisdiction in affairs of love. Thus rules were framed to meet the requirements of members who desired to settle their little differences of opinion and conduct. Each party might present a formal pleading not exceeding twelve paragraphs of twelve lines each. But all pleadings had to be written on paper with a sufficient margin, and even the colour of the ink was prescribed. The presidents, or one of them, might give judgment only on St. Valentine's day.

The questions which were likely to come before the court are illustrated in the book of the *Cent Ballades*. In this work Jean le Seneschal converses with Marshal Boucicaut and two companions as to whether preference should be given to lasting and true love, or to love which was inconstant and light-minded. Finally they summon all true lovers as judges. The Duke de Berry, the brother of the King, as yet still Duc de Tourain, and others who appeared later as members of the court of love make answer, each in his own fashion. The majority gives judgment in favour of constant love. The Duke de Berry delivers himself as follows :—

> On peut l'un dire, et l'autre doit on faire.

But Jean de Mailly dissents and reserves his right to pay tribute to either, and thus found later a partisan in Alfred de Musset.

> Nous aimons, c'est assez ; chacun a sa façon . . .
> Et la femme qu'on aime aura toujours raison.

Two very important regulations remain to be mentioned. " As all nobles and others who are worthy of the passion of love must decorate their hearts with virtues and pleasing qualities to the end that they may be of good repute, and as the court and sovereignty of love are based on the two virtues of humility and modesty, and have been founded in honour and praise of all women and virgins," therefore the sovereign of love forbade the composition of any poems, rhymed or unrhymed, which depreciated or calumniated women and virgins, or the utterance of anything offensive in regard to them. Moreover, attacks on other members of the court of love were on no account to be permitted.

An offender was punished by being condemned as dishonourable. In the eyes of this world he was to be regarded as dead. As a lasting memorial of his shame his name was to remain on the register of the court, but the colours were removed from his coat of arms, and ashes took their place. For the glory of his fame was extinguished and he was to be accursed for all time.

The court of love attracted the greatest interest. A register of a later period shows that more than 700 members were enrolled; another register numbers more than 600. The persons enumerated did not, it is true, all belong to the court at the same time : their membership extends over a period of twenty-five years. All classes of society are represented, princes of the blood, nobles, prelates, scholars, and citizens. Burgundians were in the majority, the friends of the Dukes de Berry and Orleans in the minority.

We should like to have much fuller details of these sittings of the court. They would help us to realize what went on in the quiet of those lovely gardens depicted for us in the miniatures of the period. When Guillebert de Mets in his interesting description of Paris enlarges on all the wonders to be found there, he lays special stress upon the sovereigns of love, whose *galans et musiciens* knew well how to compose all kinds of verses, and to sing and play tunefully on instruments of music. At the bidding of his adored lady, a Savoyard poet sent his work to Paris for the opinion of the sovereign of love.

It is with a certain amount of astonishment that we find Jean de Montreuil as well as Pierre and Gontier Col among the members of the *Cour amoureuse*. Did fashion and convention compel them to join or was it due to vanity lest they should be absent from so illustrious a circle ? It may well have been policy on the part of Duke Philip and his lords to attempt to moderate the angry feelings aroused by the disputes concerning the *Romance of the Rose,* and to clothe the controversy in the court attire of a *débat amoureux.* If such an intention existed, it was certainly not completely successful.

Soon after the death of Duke Philip there was a great commotion among the members of the Court. Regnault d'Agincourt attempted to abduct the beautiful young widow of a shopkeeper.   A priest aided the well-conceived plan, and twenty horses were employed.   Louis de Chalon, Count de Tonnerre, eloped with a court lady of the Duchess of Burgundy, and married her after disowning his wife.

Here again we meet the ever-recurring contrast between the ideal and the practical, for great men still indulged their desires without scruple and without shame.   The code of honour prescribed by the court was openly ignored, and the noble service of ladies gave way to the demands of depravity and vice.

It was unfortunate for Christine and those who shared her opinions that the greatest lady in the land, the cynosure of all eyes, should have scandalized her contemporaries by her example, both as Queen, and as wife and mother.   A brilliant future seemed in store for Elizabeth of Bavaria, when in 1385 the young King Charles VI gave her his hand and placed her on the throne of France.   Her husband soon fell ill.   His mind became deranged, and although he was to enjoy considerable periods of sanity, he was never able to overcome his infirmity, and was always childishly weak and helpless.   Queen Isabeau, as she was called, might have played a prominent part in politics, but she lacked the necessary gifts of statesmanship, and she had no ambition.   These failings would have been readily excused, but unfortunately she was not strong-minded enough to take the only other course which was open to her :   to lead a life of dignified retirement befitting a Queen who could not rule, and to earn the love and gratitude of her children.

A very affecting picture of the King and his surroundings is presented to his readers by the *Religieux of Saint-Denis*, who contrived mysteriously to conceal his name.   The courtiers found the King in a condition of shocking neglect ; he ate and slept irregularly and refused to wash or change his linen.   His body was covered with sores and swarming with vermin.   A wound which he had received in an outburst of rage had developed into an evil-smelling ulcer.   The princes and princesses were in urgent need of maternal care and control.   The heir to the throne once complained to his father that his mother had not kissed him for three months.

The affectionate intimacy once so noticeable in the royal couple vanished entirely when the King became ill, and gave way to feelings of the strongest aversion. Isabeau feared and loathed the sick man. During his attacks, Charles refused to see his consort, who excited him. He hated her and everyone connected with her. He tried to strike the Bavarian attendants and even raised his hand against the Queen herself. Isabeau consented willingly to her husband taking Odette de Champdivers as his mistress. But she now lost all control over herself. At a time when thousands were starving in the streets, she spent frivolously and extravagantly, and wasted vast sums upon follies of all kinds. Isabeau seemed to be possessed by a demon of pleasure, and she succumbed readily to the charms of the most elegant cavalier at Court, a fascinating and experienced deceiver of women. Louis, her husband's brother, whose wife she banished, became her admirer and friend, and was her untiring partner at festivals and amusements. A wild passion for excitement carried her from extravagance to extravagance. She strove by every means to deaden her sorrow and home-sickness. Even if Isabeau was innocent of adultery, she most seriously compromised her dignity as wife and Queen. Louis and she, conscious of their power, cared little for Court ceremonial or popular opinion. The complaints grew louder and more insistent. The Duke attempted to silence slanderous tongues. An unpremeditated word might supply the hangman with a victim, but rarely has such vile abuse been hurled at a crowned head in any country. In the case of a Queen and in a land which revered its kingship so highly, it is almost unthinkable. This Marie Antoinette, too, remained always a stranger to her husband's people. The Parisians, it seems, could not forgive her love of her native land, and her figure, perhaps, may not have accorded with the type of beauty which Eustache Deschamps described in his blunt and coarse verse :—

" Gresle corps, gros cul et poitrine,"

but the people certainly thought her ugly. It was thus, perhaps, that popular aversion was strengthened ; the too susceptible Parisians might have forgiven much in a lady who appealed to them as beautiful and sympathetic.

" Go about for once disguised and you will soon hear
what is spoken of you," said Jacques Legrand, the Augustine
monk, in a public sermon. " Lady Venus wields the sceptre
at your Court ; drunkenness and dissipation are her companions," and France's Queen had no alternative but to
submit to what she heard. What a different picture from
that drawn by Christine de Pisan, the picture of an ideal lady
in a stately castle ! In obvious contrast to the old woman of
the *Romance of the Rose*, Christine lets Prudence Mondaine
describe the loyal and loving wife, who understands how to
suffer patiently even an uncouth and inconstant spouse and
to resist every temptation of a *folle amour*. She shows us the
anxious mother and self-controlled preceptress of her children,
the strict but just ruler of her servants, the exact and painful
mistress and housekeeper, well able to protect her husband's
rights and even to defend his castle, if need be, in his
absence.

Another lady of the House of Wittelsbach was to cause
considerable sensation at that period. This was Jacqueline,
the last scion of the collateral line of the Netherlands, whose
destiny it was to intervene in the mighty struggle between
France and England. Widowed at 16 years of age by the
death of the Dauphin, this gifted and sympathetic child of
princely descent was married in 1418, for political reasons,
in spite of Pope and Emperor, to Duke John of Brabant,
holder of the Burgundian appanage of a second son.
Jacqueline, however, contrived to burst the fetters that
chained her to an uncouth weakling, and sought protection
in England. There she offered her hand to the witty and
brilliant Duke Humphrey of Gloucester, and endeavoured
with an almost masculine strength and determination to
preserve her inheritance. But Philip the Good could not
suffer Gloucester to obtain a footing in the Netherlands and
establish a *contrescarpe* for England. Four times he took
the field with his forces against his kinswoman, whose up-
bringing and education were identical with his. Shamefully
betrayed by Gloucester (whose passions, quickly inflamed,
were quickly extinguished) with one of her Court ladies,
Jacqueline laid down her arms, and finally, in 1433, renounced

her hereditary territories in order to save the life of her fourth husband, to whom she had been secretly married. Franz of Borselen was to bring her the happiness hitherto denied her ; the woman triumphed over the princess.

Did not her romantic fate present to adventurous knights and lords the beau-ideal of a woman, ever newly threatened and ever again to be rescued ? A writer might have found here the most splendid material for a romance : but he would have had no readers at the Court of Burgundy. For relentless reasons of State compelled the Duke, who aspired to be the champion of knighthood and chivalry, to take up arms against a woman.

The same necessities and the same principle were present in Philip's treatment of Joan of Arc. Policy compelled the Duke to hand over the Maid to the English, and thus to the Inquisition. All her glorious achievements, from the success at Orleans to the coronation and annointing at Rheims, by which solemn act Charles VII at length became the true King, lord of his country ; all this was to vanish in the blazing flames of the stake, and to be remembered only as a devilish delusion.

After her capture, Duke Philip had the Maid brought before him ; what, we may well ask, was in his mind on that occasion. Monstrelet was present, but alleged later that he did not remember hearing what was said. This brevity in one who in other matters was so diffuse, is a bitter disappointment. Did Philip or any of his counsellors at that moment realize how much they owed to the peasant girl of Lorraine ? Did they recognize that the enfeeblement of England, brought about by the Maid's victories, enabled them to rid themselves of an inconvenient ally and renounce the hated Treaty of Troyes ?

The statesman may well have remembered these things, but not the knight. It was an intolerable thought for every knight, whether Burgundian, French, or English, that the triumphs of the one side and the defeats of the other were not connected with the name of any illustrious champion, but were due solely to the efforts of a peasant girl. The jubilant verses with which Christine de Pisan greeted *La Pucelle* found no echo in the ranks of chivalry :—

> Hée ! quel honneur au féminin
> Sexe ! Que (Dieu) l'ayme, il appert,
> Quant tout ce grant peuple chenin
> Par qui tout le règne est désert,
> Par femme est sours et recouvert,
> Ce que pas hommes fait n'eussent . . .

Threateningly the poetess calls to the English :—

> Si rabaissez, Anglois, vos cornes,
> Car jamais n'aurez beau gibier
> En France . . .

And when she presses the rebels to return to their allegiance, the Burgundians might well have taken her message to their hearts.

Christine de Pisan did not live to see the shameful end of the Maid. But if the behaviour of the Queen aroused her violent disapproval, her peace of mind would have been still further disturbed by the appearance at Court soon after Isabeau's death in 1435, of another lady, this time *la belle Agnès*, France's uncrowned queen. The Court was now to witness a phenomenon hitherto unknown in France : *la maîtresse attitrée*, overwhelmed with estates and revenues, stretching out her hand for the sceptre. . . . "*Entre les belles elle estoit tenue pour la plus belle du monde ; et fut appelée damoiselle de Beauté tant pour celle cause, comme pour ce que le roy lui avait donné la maison de Beauté delez Paris,*" thus writes a chronicler. Boldly and shamelessly Agnès Sorel sought to forget the loss of her honour in passionate sensuality and wild pursuit of pleasure. It would seem as if this frail beauty was able to foretell the gruesome death which was soon to end her reign of glory. By her arts, her amiability, and her ability constantly to contrive fresh distractions, she was able to rescue Charles VII from his melancholy. Courtiers, clinging to the customs and manners of the past, watched with horror the unaccustomed commotions and disturbances at Court, which mocked at good breeding and made short work of ceremonial.

What martyrdom must Queen Marie of Anjou have suffered !

en vertueuse souffrance
Où temps du commun desarroy
Elle a monstré plus de vaillance
Que sage prince ne fier roy.

exclaimed Martin Le Franc, in respectful admiration.

Charles VII's Queen had to endure that Agnès Sorel, a girl of inferior family, appeared at Court daily, attired as a princess ; she occupied better apartments than the Queen herself, used more beautiful beds and carpets, and received better table-service, wore finer jewels and had a larger household. France's Queen had to suffer that the beautiful Agnès received the visits of the nobility and even of the princes of the blood. And as if that were not enough, she had to allow her husband's mistress to take a seat at her own table and to entertain her. Agnès wore trains a third longer than any princess in the land, her hair ornaments were taller by a half than any others, and her robes far more costly than those of the Court ladies. She invented all kinds of extravagant costumes which might serve to seduce and allure the senses. She bared her shoulders and her bosom. Day and night she meditated on trifles which might tempt others from the path of virtue and demonstrate to chaste ladies that honour, shame, and purity were better lost.

Chastellain scourges Charles' mistress with words which bite home like the lash of a whip. He might be an executioner, driving with blows a naked and branded criminal from the town. A master, perhaps Jehan Fouquet, painted for Notre Dame in Melun a peculiarly subtle and lascivious Madonna ; the old tradition may be true that the features of Agnès were copied for the Mother of God. A royal treasurer presented the work and was unable to conceal his passion for the fairest of the fair : *Tant elle vaut celle pour qui je meurs d'amours.*

Chastellain had to be careful in his criticisms, since Lady Sensuality ruled also at the Court of Burgundy. It is characteristic that Antoine de la Sale, or whoever was the author, places the scene of his *Cent Nouvelles Nouvelles,* which was especially written after the model of Boccaccio's *Decameron,* at the court of Philip the Good. The Duke himself and a succession of courtiers descend to obscenities whose one aim was to ridicule the mysteries of sex. It is permissible, however, not to take these pictures of daily life too seriously.   This literary *genre*, too, was fiction, an exaggeration of much that was good and bad.   Had there been an over-emphasis in the ideals of love, a coarse joke soon brought back the sobriety of every-day.

Nor must it be overlooked that Duke Philip never forgot his dignity, and that his love adventures never gave rise to gossip, as in the case of Louis XI.   It was related publicly of that King that he went out nightly in the streets of Paris seeking adventure.   Noblemen did not recoil from acting as panders and introducing him to the company of complaisant women.

Paris was the city of pleasure, for the natives as well as for the crowds of strangers always within its walls. Foreign princes and lords possessed their own stately palaces in the city, and could take part in its amusements according to their wishes and inclinations.

Lady Venus' public and private handmaidens played a great part in the life of Paris. At that time the prostitutes numbered 3,000 ; they had to live in certain quarters, and might not reside elsewhere. This prohibition, however, was constantly ignored, and these women managed to settle in other streets, where as proprietors of taverns and shops, they plied their trade without restraint. They were required to avoid anything conspicuous or luxurious in their attire, but this prohibition was also disregarded.   Like honest women, they flaunted their furs and scarlet, and on their way to church, the most beautiful Books of Hours (which they could not read) were carried before them.   In order to be in the fashion and be able to wear the coveted dress with train and silver girdle, they often contracted marriage with some associate and were thus untouched by the royal decress.   If, however, the authorities enforced the regulations, the constables brought the offenders before the judge ;   collar, fur sleeves, and train were torn off, the valuable silver girdle was seized and devoted to charitable purposes, and the victim was lucky if she escaped without further punishment, for the justice administered to these women was pitiless and unmercifully severe.

Christine de Pisan must have suffered deeply when she beheld the life and activities of her women-contemporaries, whom destiny had allowed to fall so low. " The whole world despises you so greatly, that every decent person avoids you like one excommunicated, and looks the other way in the street so as not to see you " : thus Christine addresses the courtesans in her *Livre des Trois Vertus*. " Raise yourselves up out of the dirt. Go back to decent work."

Christine placed her talents at the service of noble and chaste womanhood. The poetess in her would have mourned indeed had she lived to see a poet, François Villon, with a brow kissed by genius, dedicate his verses to those dishonourable women who had given him pleasure and pain ; the *Hetaira* has even won a place in poetry.

François Villon, full of hatred against a society in which his frivolity would not let him gain a foothold, could not exist without his love adventures. Again and again he succumbed to the allurements of Parisian women, whom an Italian celebrated by declaring that they were capable even of seducing a Priam or a Nestor. Impudent and penitent, lascivious and pious, full of life and gloomy meditation, he passed abruptly from one mood to another :—

> Tout aux tavernes et aux filles

is his life's motto.

Cynically he speaks of his mistresses :—

> S'ilz n'ayment fors que pour l'argent,
> On ne les aime que pour l'eure.

He shows us the wench in her immodest dress,

> . . . fillettes monstrant testins.
> Pour avoir plus largement d'ostes.

He immortalizes the memory of Marion l'Idole, of Jehanne de Bretagne, pupils of that strange Paris school,

> où l'escollier le maistre enseigne,

of tall Margot, who had a house near Notre-Dame, where stabbing affrays and fights were only too frequent.

He lamented bitterly that old age and death should claim even women. What a picture of sorrow is drawn in the aged and abandoned courtesan, the *Belle Heaulmière*, who once had at her feet Nicholas d'Orgemont, the epicurean canon of Notre-Dame. Formerly a picture of beauty and brilliance, now a figure of ugliness and misery. Very sadly Villon asks :—

> Corps fémenin, qui tant est tendre,
> Poly, souef, si précieux,
> Te fauldra il ces maux attendre ?
> Oy, ou tout vif aller ès cieulx.

His love adventures were at times unfortunate. The *amant remys et regnye* was not always treated with respect.

> De moy, povre, je vueil parler :
> J'en fus batu comme à ru toiles,
> Tout nu, ja ne le quier celer.

Infidelity, too, he experienced :—

> . . . celle, qui n'en amoit qu'un
> D'iceluy s'eslongne et despart,
> Et aime mieux amer chascun !

On one occasion he exclaims in a rage :—

> Je regnie Amours et despite ;
> Je deffie à feu et à sang.

He thus maliciously presents a *faulse beauté* :—

> Ung temps viendra qui fera desséchier,
> Jaunir, flestrir vostre espanye fleur . . .
> Las, viel seray, vous laide, sans couleur.

But he cannot be angry for long ; when he makes his will, it is his desire to leave the most beautiful thing that his poverty has left him to his mistress,

> Je laisse mon cuer enchassée
> Palle piteux, mort et transy :
> Elle m'a ce mal pourchassié,
> Mais Dieu luy en face mercy.

His happy memories speak in tones that have never resounded since and will never resound again. They might even have reconciled Christine, who once wrote :—

> . . . car nos esperiz
> quant mors seront et periz
> Les corps, croy qu'ils s'aimeront
> Et ensemble demourront.

A gleam of genius and transfiguration lies in these verses of Villon. Time and place vanish in the darkness. The features of the woman are no longer recognizable, the untamed activity of the vagabond is at rest, but the rapturous love of his adored mistress lives on for ever.

> Deux estions et n'avions qu'ung cuer.

CHAPTER VII

Jousts and Tourneys

Main tendre tient mal espée, et chief bien peignée porte mal le bacinet.—
ENSEIGNEMENTS PATERNELS.

> " And on the morwe, whan that day gan springe,
> Of hors and harneys, noyse and clateringe.
> Ther was in hostelryes al aboute ;
> And to the paleys rood ther many a route
> Of lordes, up-on stedes and palfreys.
> Ther maystow seen devysing of herneys
> So uncouth, and so riche, and wrought so well
> Of goldsmithrie, of browding, and of steel ;
> The sheeldes brighte, testers, and trappures ;
> Gold-hewen helmes, hauberks, cote-armures ;
> Lordes in paraments on hir courseres,
> Knightes of retenue, and eek squyeres
> Nailinge the speres, and helmes bokelinge,
> Gigginge of sheeldes, with laynere lacinge ;
> Ther as need is, they weren no-thing ydel ;
> The fomy stedes on the golden brydel
> Gnawinge, and faste the armurers also,
> With fyle and hamer prikinge to and fro ;
> Yemen on fote, and communes many oon
> With short staves, thikke as they may goon ;
> Pypes, trompes, nakers, clariounes,
> That in the bataille blowen blody sounes . . ."

WHOEVER reads these verses from Chaucer's *Canterbury Tales*, might well imagine himself transported to the Burgundian Court in the midst of the elaborate preparations for an assault at arms, so astir are they with life. The poet has contrived to reproduce the excitement which ran riot in the streets and seized in its grip knights and esquires, indeed every member of the community as the time of the contest drew near. These verses form an excellent supplement to the reports and criticisms of the chroniclers. Under Philip the Good and Charles the Bold, the assaults-at-arms and jousts enjoyed remarkable popularity, whereas the massed tourney fell more and more into disuse. The contests on foot with sword or axe excited the greatest interest : " *les joustes . . . ne requièrent point telle glorification comme font les armes, là ou sont les honneurs avecques les périls.*" The *Pas de l'Arbre Charlemagne,* the *Pas de la Belle Pèlerine,*

119

the *Pas de la Fontaine aux Pleurs*, the *Pas du Perron Fée*, the *Pas de l'Arbre d'Or*, the *Pas de la Dame Sauvage*, to name only the most celebrated, caused a stir in the whole of the West, and expert jousters from far and near flocked to the Court of Burgundy. Expiring chivalry was celebrating its last triumphs. Italians, Spaniards, Englishmen, and Germans came to oppose the Burgundian champions. Jacques de Lalaing, that favourite of the Court of Burgundy, wandered far abroad in search of adventure. The tournaments bore an international character and increased the cosmopolitan tendencies of the nobility which were frequently noticeable during the course of the Hundred Years' War in France.

Jousts played a part in the life of a knight hardly inferior to the combats in actual and open warfare. For many perhaps they played a greater part, since in the case of jousts, the contests were held according to well-established rules and regulations. It was entirely a question of personal strength and presence of mind, of courage and skill. Fatal accidents, such as those which were already becoming general from the use of cannon, were not common at tourneys. But the danger was not less, since skilled fighters employed only the keenest weapons. Each detail connected with the " proud and dangerous profession of arms ", was treated with the utmost seriousness. Everything remarkable had to be recorded, and Olivier de La Marche regarded it as his natural duty to act as reporter at jousts. " It would be a sad pity and loss if such assaults-at-arms were passed over in silence or forgotten. It were cowardly of me if I restrained my pen from describing to the best of my ability all the noble feats that I have seen."

The joy of battle and pleasure in physical exercises caused even the nobility at times to disregard the barriers they had erected between themselves and the citizens. At a shooting festival at Oudenaarde in 1408, which lasted twenty-one days, John the Fearless appeared and " *moeste selve zÿnen boghe draghen op zÿnen hals* " (and had to hang his own bow round his neck). A number of noblemen belonged to the Guild of St. Joris there. The Great Bastard led the cross-bowmen of Lille to the shooting-match at Tournai. The knights, it is true, were wont to make fun of the citizen's jousts. Jehan Germain, describing the assaults-at-arms in

PLATE 14

Loyset Liédet: Duel. Miniature: Histoire de Charles Martel, Bibliothèque Royale MS. 6, fol. 355 v., Brussels.

[face p. 120

the Friday market at Ghent, tells us that " it is rather the bursts of laughter than the blows which cause the opponents to fall ". On the other hand, the nobility at times must have been pleased to find an appreciation of the profession of arms among the citizens, since their own stately jousts and tourneys were frequently ridiculed and even condemned. Eustache Deschamps did not spare his criticism :—

> On se destruit pour un pou de plaisance
> Où nul bien n'a fors sotie et folour,
> Orgueil de cuer, vaine gloire et despence
> Que les chétis veulent nommer honnour,
> Où chascun pert ; du bien commun l'amour
> Cesse et perist, dont maint sont malostrus.
> Jouste et tournois en guerre n'est qu'erreur.
> Que ne laissons vanité pour vertus ?

It was therefore of the greatest importance that the clergy should put no difficulties in the way of the Burgundian knights and lords. While elsewhere they were utterly opposed to duelling and refused holy burial to the slain, they were always ready, out of regard for the Dukes of Burgundy, to tolerate assaults-at-arms. Individual clerics were present as spectators ; and one Burgundian lord could boast a prelate among his train, the bishop of Langres. On their side, the champions were never forgetful of the rights of the Church. Before the beginning of his *Pas*, Lalaing heard three masses, and before the commencement of each assault, it was his custom to make the sign of the Cross with his " banderole ", as did likewise the others. He worshipped the Holy Virgin so profoundly, " *que pour l'amour d'elle il avait pris le mot et devise de la nonpareille.*"

Skill in arms was of course the decisive factor, but the leaders were always ready to invest the joust with an atmosphere of romance. The writers could not exist without their heroes ; illustrious historical personages, allegorical figures like those presented by the *Romance of the Rose*, mythological forms, savages, male and female, giants and dwarfs, unicorns and other fabulous animals, were invoked in order to introduce an element of the miraculous and the mystical.

With the consent and support of Philip the Good, Jacques de Lalaing instituted the *Pas de la Fontaine aux Pleurs*, remaining a whole year in Chalon-sur-Sâone for this purpose. He deliberately selected this town because in the jubilee year of 1450, many pilgrims from France, England, Spain, and Scotland were passing through it on their way to Rome. Lalaing had a richly-furnished pavilion built in the Faubourg Saint-Laurent on an island of the Sâone. The picture of a mysterious weeping woman hung beneath a Madonna. The tears fell into a basin borne by a unicorn, which held also three shields sprinkled with blue tears ; whoever desired to succour the *Dame de la Fontaine aux Pleurs* had to touch one of the shields, the white one if he desired to fight with the axe, the violet shield if he desired to fight with the sword, and the black shield if he was to fight mounted with the lance. The Herald Charolais was installed in the pavilion as guardian. Toison d'Or, King-at-Arms, acted as the judge. Numerous contests were fought, and in order to introduce variety into the proceedings, Lalaing, on divers occasions, arranged to dispense with particular parts of his armour.

Amongst those taking part was a Sicilian, Jean de Boniface, whose countersign ran thus : *Qui a belle dame, si la garde bien.* As he had the misfortune to fall, a golden bracelet was sent to him in conformity with the rules of the contest. He had to wear it a whole year unless he chanced to meet with a lady or maiden, who could open the lock and thus lay claim to his services.

Here again the knights rivalled each other in display. La Marche as eye-witness has left us the most enthusiastic accounts of his impressions. When the tent of a champion was opened, he was seen in full armour, seated on a costly chair, his " Banderole " on his arm, about to complete his prayer, with his followers around him. " In truth, he resembled a Caesar or a *Preux* in his triumph." The prizes distributed by Lalaing, axe, sword, and lance, were of gold. Two luxurious banquets, the second being arranged in honour of the ladies of Chalon, formed a worthy conclusion to the *Pas d'armes*. Huge *entremets* presented the town with its churches and belfry, its walls and bridge, as well as the pavilion, with its " mysteries " and finally the founder and his opponents.

The knight Claude de Vaudrey, a councillor and chamberlain of Charles the Bold, held the *Pas de la Dame Sauvage* at Ghent in 1470, in the presence of the Court. The letter of invitation itself sounded very romantic; the *Compaignon de la Joyeuse Queste* presents his respects to all emperors, kings, dukes, and princes, together with all those who deserve to hear of noble deeds, and acquaints them of his adventures, so that his action may be better understood and welcomed. Going forth on his first adventure, he left the wealthy kingdom of *Enfance* and came to a wild poor, and sterile land called *Jeunesse*. Long time he wandered there, living only on his thoughts and feelings, and on hope, which was his favourite food. In the wide plain of *Plaisance*, which lies between the castle *Beauté* and the noble mountain *Grâce*, called *Bonne Renommée*, he was attacked and almost mortally wounded by the guardian of this place, the knight *Regard*. He owed his recovery entirely to the care of a hermit in the *Eremitage Bel-Accueil*. There he was visited by the lady of the fierce guardian, who, conversing, gave him healing medicine. She was a Savage Lady; her lovely fair hair covered her whole body and formed her sole attire; blossoming branches adorned her head. Won by her beauty, compassion, and courtly behaviour, the convalescent begged to be allowed to serve her. She refused, however, with mild severity, but promised him a more favourable answer after he had taken food at a spot suitable for the acquisition of virtue and fame, and had gained a world-wide reputation for his knightly and noble skill. Thereupon, leaving the Savage Lady, he hastened through the painful solitudes of the *Pensées* and the morasses of the *Imagination*, until he had drawn up the conditions of a *Pas* with blunted weapons. As servant of the *Dame Sauvage* and with the consent of his master, the Duke of Burgundy, he apprizes the nobility of his intention and invites them to the contest; each emprise to include a single tilt and seventeen sword-cuts.

Claude de Vaudrey, who, as security for the service of the *Dame Sauvage*, affixed his seal to the letter and statutes, caused a great stir by the manner of his entry into the arena. In front strode two savage men with trumpets and large blue banners, one of which bore V V in letters of gold, the other the same device in letters of silver, probably an allusion to the motto of the family : " *J'ai Valu Vaulx et Vauldray.*" They were followed by two more savage men, carrying similar banners and leading white palfreys, whereon on gold-brocaded saddles, savage ladies were mounted. Around their necks they wore the prizes for which the combatants were to strive. The savage men and women were entirely covered with golden hair ; the women, alone, wore a curiously cut upper garment. At the conclusion of the *Pas*, which passed off in triumph, Claude de Vaudrey promised to communicate the names of those who had taken part to the *Dame Sauvage.*

At the marriage of Charles the Bold to Margaret of York, jousts and a tourney were held, at which excessive splendour was displayed, and Anthony, the Great Bastard of Burgundy, half-brother of the Duke, held the famous *Arbre d'Or* against all comers.

The fable on this occasion was as follows :—the Lady of the *Ile cellée* entreated the Bastard, her rescuer and deliverer from dire distress, to undertake three things for love of her ; firstly, himself to break 101 lances or to suffer them to be broken against him ; secondly, to make or suffer 101 sword-cuts ; thirdly, to decorate a Golden Tree from her treasury with the coats of arms of illustrious champions. In addition to the Golden Tree, which appears continually in the decorations, the noble king's daughter promised to place at the prince's disposal her pursuivant *Arbre d'Or*, a dwarf, and the giant of the *Forêt douteuse*, whom she held captive. In a letter written on the 8th January, 1468, at her Castle of *Bonne Espérance*, she craved permission of the illustrious, victorious and mighty Duke Charles to allow the emprise to be undertaken at his Court, well known to be the most distinguished and chivalrous in the world.

The Duke having given his consent, the market-place of Bruges was prepared for the tourney. High barriers were erected on all sides, and behind them were the tribunes for the spectators. Two gates, decorated with a golden tree, were set up ; one near the chapel of St. Christopher bore a golden hammer, the other, on the further side towards the Town Hall, was ornamented with two small towers. On these trumpeters were seated, wearing the livery of the Bastard, which was red with a golden tree on the sleeves ; white pennants bearing the same sign fluttered from the towers and from the trumpets.

Opposite the ladies' seats on the side of the great *Halles*, the Golden Tree was to be seen, a magnificent fir with gilded trunk. A kind of pulpit stood next to it intended for the dwarf, Master Peter, who together with the giant and *Arbre d'Or*, the pursuivant, was responsible for the regulation of the contests. An inscription was to be seen on the platform, which was built on three pillars, one green, one yellow, and one violet.

In addition, there were two tribunes for the judges, the heralds, including the Garter King-at-Arms and numerous others. Every lance had to be measured in the presence of the judges.

On 3rd July, 1468, the wedding day itself, the jousting was to begin. Owing to the celebrations at the entry, and the dinner having been unduly prolonged, the *Pas d'Armes* did not commence until a late hour. After the ladies had rested and changed their dresses, they proceeded on horseback, in carriages or litters to the lists, where a dense mass of people had assembled for the spectacle.

Duke Charles appeared attired in a long gold embroidered robe lined with marten fur, with wide, open sleeves ; large golden bells tinkled on his horse. The Duchess was at the window of one of the houses which had been splendidly decorated. She was dressed in a crimson and gold brocaded gown lined with ermine, and wore a golden crown on her head.

It was late in the afternoon when Adolph of Cleves, Lord of Ravenstein, a cousin of the Duke, arrived. He desired on the first day to match himself with the Bastard alone. His pursuivant knocked three times with the golden hammer on the gate which was opened by *Arbre d'Or*, whose white coat of arms also displayed the golden tree. In order to preserve the fiction of the *Pas*, the captain who had to defend the entrance accompanied him with six of his bowmen. In answer to the question as to the stranger's business, the pursuivant announced the name of Ravenstein, his master, and presented his coat of arms, which *Arbre d'Or* received kneeling, with great respect. After it had been approved by the judge, it was hung on the Golden Tree. Arbre d'Or wrote the name of the new arrival on a board and returned to the gate. This time he was followed by the dwarf, who led in the giant fettered with a chain. The bearded dwarf was dressed in a *beret* of flowers, and a long gown, half of white damask, half of scarlet figured satin ; the giant was clad in a small Provençal hat, a strangely-cut brocaded robe, and high-heeled shoes to make him appear taller. He carried a wooden sword in his hand.

Thereupon the ceremony of the entry began. First of all came the trumpeters and tambourine-players, and the officers-at-arms, and with them was a knight dressed as a counsellor in blue velvet, and mounted on a mule which was likewise decked out with blue velvet ; then followed the Lord of Ravenstein in a litter. This was blue and white, the Ravenstein colours, lined with gold brocade, and decorated with his arms and motto and a number of silver ornaments. Two noble steeds, their harness ornamented with blue velvet and thick silver nails, bore the litter ; mounted on them were small pages also dressed in blue velvet and yellow boots without spurs, with their whips in their hands. The litter was furnished with great cushions of crimson velvet. A Turkish carpet formed the back-cloth.

Adolph of Cleves, who was attended by four stately knights in blue surtouts, wore over his armour a long robe lined with ermine, with a wide turned-down collar and slit sides and sleeves ; on his head was a black velvet *beret*. He had the appearance of a worn-out veteran knight.

Behind the litter a liveried servant led the tourney-steed, upon whose blue and gold brocade trappings silver bells and the golden letters of the device were set in splendid contrast. This steed was followed by a sumpter with portions of the armour in two baskets covered with black velvet, between which a little fool peeped out.

Having reached the ladies' presence, the knights opened the litter and Adolph of Cleves stepped out. Olivier de La Marche—for he was the counsellor on the mule—made the welcoming speech, and begged, on his master's behalf, that the ladies would permit him to joust once again in spite of his great age and his resolution to bear arms no more. After

PLATE 15

Unknown Master : Anthony of Burgundy, the Great Bastard.   Musee Condé, Chantilly.

[*face p.* 126

the ladies had welcomed him, Ravenstein went the round of the barriers, in the course of which he made a deep obeisance before his coat of arms on the Golden Tree. Fully equipped with all his armour, he returned at last in solemn procession to the lists.

Thereupon the trumpets resounded for the challenger. A tent of white and gold damask with numerous embroidered golden trees, with a green velvet border and a fringe of violet and gold damask was pushed into the lists. The flag was fixed in a big golden apple, which crowned the roof. Six knights and two esquires rode beside the tent. The half horse-trappings of violet velvet were bound with white serge ornamented with golden studs, from which hung silver bells. There was no lack of heralds and trumpeters, for beside those who were employed in Ravenstein's service there were others who attended in the hope of attracting notice and rewards.

When the tent had reached the end of the barriers, the Bastard Anthony rode out in full armour. He carried a green shield, which never left him during all the days of the *Pas*, however frequently he might change the trappings of his steed. The choice of green was intended as homage to the newly-wedded couple.

> Il te fauldra de vert vestir
> C'est la livrée aux amoureulx,

so runs an old folk-song.

In the meantime the dwarf on his platform had turned the sand-glass which ran for half-an-hour, the time fixed for each contest. He then gave the signal with his horn, the two knights couched their lances and the tilt began. When the horn sounded once again the contest was over. As the Bastard could show more broken lances than the Lord of Ravenstein, whose horse had failed him at the end, he received a golden circlet as his prize. Before the champions parted, they attacked each other again, in honour of the ladies, with stout cudgels, which also showed the golden tree on a white ground, but this time without touching each other.

On this day no further assault-at-arms took place; it was too late and too dark. The banquet was approaching, choice delicacies of the table and wonderful performances

were in prospect.   The next day after dinner the jousting
recommenced and continued for nine days.

The scenes of magnificence and splendour which unfolded
themselves during the celebrations must have dumbfounded
even those who were familiar with the luxury of the Court
of Burgundy.   Duke Charles, who attended regularly as a
spectator, set a gorgeous example in the matter of dress.
The short crimson velvet coat, which he wore on the second
Sunday, was richly covered, like the trappings of his horse,
with gems and pearls ;   their value was estimated at more
than a hundred gold shillings.   The Duke and his consort
were differently attired on each successive day, as were
also their pages, and their example was followed by the
nobles who vied with each other in ostentatious display.

The curious and striking combinations of colours, which
were a feature of the celebrations, were frequently intended
as tributes to particular ladies.   Indeed clever people versed
in colour lore were hard put to it to puzzle out the significance
of some of the dresses, for every variation of temper and
fancy was symbolized.   Some lords wore *mantelines* of white
satin over black damask pourpoints, others green velvet
over scarlet, or green satin over violet damask, or pink silk
taffeta over black satin.   In addition to blue velvet *journades*,
coats of crimson satin were to be seen, and some of the
lords wore green satin *chapelets* with white feathers.   All had
assumed the much-favoured gold chains which were wound
several times around the neck.

Nor were the pages less gorgeously attired than their
lords.   The boys of Lord Scales strutted about in white
hoseaux and body-coats of black satin;   the green-velvet
surtout was studded with silver blossoms.   Yellow feathers
waved on the black velvet *berets*, which were lined with
crimson gold brocade.

Harlequin material was also much affected.   For instance,
the front of a robe would be made of green satin, and the
back of violet.   Pages appeared in velvet dresses, half
tawny, half blue.   Many of the jousters wore also distinctive
badges.   Thus a large green sash with white fringe fluttered
from the helmet of the Bastard Baldwin of Burgundy ;
from that of the Count of Salm depended a lady's headdress.

Great luxury was displayed in the decoration of the

horses. A single horse did not suffice and the knights brought with them, in addition to their friends and servants, a number of parade horses with which to make their progress round the arena. These were all decked out in different colours, and on each was a page as rider magnificently attired. The Lord of Fiennes, having chosen to appear with seven state horses, a lord of Ferrara, who held the post of a chamberlain at Court, appeared with twelve, as if striving to outrival the Duke himself.

As each combatant conceived it his duty to outdo his fellows, the costliest materials had been requisitioned. Gold and silver brocades in all colours, velvet, silk, satin, taffeta, damask, serge, the rarest furs, gold and silver embroideries and feathers had all been employed in every possible combination for the trappings of the horses. The bells which were very popular in Germany at that time were everywhere displayed. Some were of gold or silver, others of silver gilt. Some were as large as children's heads, others were shaped like cow-bells. The most original were modelled after fruits, such as pears, and others were fashioned like flowers. Flowers were also used as decorations on the horse-trappings. Silver gilt rings hung from silver roses on violet velvet, and irises and marguerites were freely employed. Oak leaves figured on the embroideries or were displayed with other emblems, in relief or imitated plastically. A golden branch or flower rested beside an apple on the horse's crupper. Amidst a profusion of other ornaments were artichokes, leopards' heads with a ring in the jaws, shells, clouds, crescents, sun-rays, tears, sparks, baskets, doublets, shields, fiery brasiers and barbicans with blazing flames. These barbicans had been chosen by the Bastard Anthony in addition to the cross of St. Andrew and the carpenter's plane, which recalled the party disputes between the Burgundians and the Orleanists.

Letters, initials of names, mottoes, perhaps the name of some adored lady, cyphers, and Greek letters, especially Y were very popular. In one case the entire alphabet in gold embroidery was displayed on the edge of a blue velvet cloth. Pierre de Bourbon, Lord of Carency, showed his device, the letter O twice, embroidered in curious fashion in gold on crimson gold brocade : " *l'un estoit un O d'une*

lettre et l'aultre l'os d'un cheval."   The Lord of Ternant appeared
with trappings of crimson-gold brocade, whereon large silver
bells were scattered.   After the third round, he caused them
to be removed, alleging that they disturbed him.   Whereupon
other equally splendid trappings were disclosed beneath the
bell-trappings.

But this costly and extravagant parade was still too
commonplace for some.   Philippe de Poitiers, Lord de la
Ferté, had himself led to the barriers by a beautiful maiden,
the Dame Blanche, who read aloud verses of welcome.   Jean
de Chassa, Lord of Monnet, made his appearance as *chevalier
esclave.*   A letter addressed to the ladies supplied the
necessary explanation.   Having spent all his life in the
service of a *dame d'Esclavonie* who was too full of pride to
obey the dictates of love, he, in desperation, at last withdrew
into a lonely wilderness, where he lived on sorrow, sighs, and
tears for nine full moons.   At length his lady, repenting of her
cruelty, sent him a maiden, who to heal him of that most
terrible disease of love, despair, was to go wandering with
him for a year.   He had left Slavonia with a heavy heart,
but as many an infidel, even the brave Saladin himself, had
come to France in search of adventure, so he too dared to
present himself at the hospitable Court of Burgundy, craving
leave to try conclusions with the Knight of the Golden Tree.
The ladies having graciously given their consent, the coat
of arms of the stranger was hung up on the tree.   A pack-
horse now appeared carrying two large baskets, elaborately
decorated, in which two Moors and a fool made music.   The
maiden followed leading the knight, with whom were four
noblemen with long beards, all dressed in luxurious Turkish
costume, and armed ; on their attire could be read in great
golden letters the words, *Le Chevalier Esclave.*

Anthony of Luxembourg, Count de Roussy and Brienne,
on his part had also prepared an unusual entry.   A dwarf
from Constantinople, belonging to the English King, rode in
behind trumpeters.   In his right hand he held a paper
after the fashion of a petition ; a key was tied to his arm
as if to add a suggestion of mystery.   A stately counterfeit
citadel was then rolled in, the walls being of black stone,
having four towers at the corners, and one in the centre.
Within the citadel, by command of an unknown lady, the

Count of Roussy was held a captive. Having reached the
ladies' presence, the dwarf read his petition aloud. *Danger*,
it ran, possessed the key to this prison and had entrusted
it to him, *Petit Espoir*, his servant. The knight would
only gain his liberty and take part in the *Pas* by the intercession of the noble ladies assembled here, for not even *Danger*
could refuse such a request. The ladies having signified their
approval, the dwarf flung open the great gate and out
sprang the Count of Roussy in armour. His motto was
inscribed in gold letters on his horses' trappings, which were
of white satin. Six state horses concluded the procession.
They had little to do with the story of the citadel, but the
desire for magnificence was once more suffered to destroy
the unities.

There was no lack of small mishaps to hinder the gentlemen
from tilting. A visor did not fit, the clasp of the armour broke,
or a horse was unruly. On the other hand, serious wounds
were not infrequent. The Bastard Anthony was particularly
unfortunate. He did not fight with Lord Scales in accordance
with the arrangement, but allowed Adolph of Cleves to
represent him, and remained in the lists as a spectator.
While there, he was kicked by a horse on the knee, so badly
that he could not continue to joust. He did not, however,
break off the *Pas*, and various noble lords took his place,
but he bore the whole expense of contests and supplied the
horse-trappings. On the ninth day, when the spectacles
were even more numerous and costly than before, he was
carried into the lists in a splendid litter. " One would
have supposed him to be not a Bastard of Burgundy, but the
heir of one of the greatest rulers in the world."

Duke Charles himself desired to take part in the final
display, and entered amidst extraordinary pomp. First
came the trumpeters and musicians, then the Toison d'Or
King-at-Arms, officers-at-arms, heralds, and noblemen,
pages, servants, and state-horses, and finally the Duke
appeared in armour. Rhenish gulden jingled on his shield
and gold pennies on his crimson velvet trappings. On the
garments and trappings the emblems of his Order, flint,
steel, and sparks shone out.

His opponent Adolph of Cleves now appeared, magnificently
preceded and arrayed. He took his place in a pavilion of

white and violet damask, and some twenty trappings which
hitherto had been used only by the Bastard, were once more
displayed on his horses.

The dwarf turned the sand-glass for the last time.   When
it had run out and the trumpet sounded, it was discovered
that the Duke had broken eight lances while his cousin had
broken eleven, so that the latter and not the Duke received
the golden ring.   Now, too, the question had to be decided
as to who was to be declared the victor in the *Pas*.   This
placed the judges and the ladies, who had been asked for a
decision, in a great dilemma.   Finally the prize was awarded
to Jehan de Chalons, Lord of Arquel, who had broken thirteen
lances in accordance with the regulations.   Amidst the blasts
of many trumpets the pursuivant *Arbre d'Or* accompanied
by the dwarf and the giant brought in a battle-steed,
caparisoned in black satin with silver armour, to which had
been added the magnificent trappings of the Bastard.   The
horse was paraded up and down before the admiring
spectators and finally presented to the lucky knight.

The jousts were thus at an end and the tourney was
to begin, in which all the jousters had to take part.   The
barriers and the judges' box were hastily removed, and the
arena was levelled.   The jousters, whose opponents in the
meantime had brought in their coats of arms to be hung
on the Golden Tree, were all of them arrayed on this occasion
in violet velvet cloth.   Even Duke Charles made no exception,
but he was accompanied by ten pages who wore collars of
golden roses, which fell down at the back of their gold-
embroidered crimson velvet dresses in the shape of a
St. Andrew's cross.   On each horse, which was caparisoned
in the same material, a hundred bells of fine gold tinkled
gaily.   Each jouster received a sword and a lance, both
blunted, which were first examined by the judges.

It was a glorious sight, the chronicler tells us, to see these
fifty nobles, in gleaming armour, mounted on their horses
with their gaily-coloured trappings fighting stoutly with each
other.   A similar tourney may once have inspired Chaucer
when he wrote his vivid lines :—

" The heraudes lefte hir priking up and down ;
  Now ringen trompes loude and clarioun ;
  Ther is namore to seyn, but west and est
  In goon the speres ful sadly in arest ;
  In goth the sharpe spore in-to the syde.
  Ther seen men who can juste, and who can ryde ;
  Ther shiveren shaftes up-on sheeldes thikke ;
  He feleth thurgh the herte-spoon the prikke.
  Up springen speres twenty foot on highte ;
  Out goon the swerdes as the silver brighte.
  The helmes they to-hewen and to-shrede ;
  Out brest the blood, with sterne stremes rode.
  With mighty maces the bones they to-breste.
  He thurgh the thikkeste of the throng gan threste.
  Ther stromblen stedes stronge, and down goth al.
  He rolleth under foot as dooth a bal."

The sword contest was fought so bitterly that the Duchess, fearing for her husband's safety, gave the signal to stop ; the ladies waved their veils, the dwarf sounded his trumpet, but in vain. Those zealous champions did not cease their contest, until the Duke rode in himself among them. Even then it was only by showing his face that he succeeded in parting the combatants, for many here and there had come to blows again. " And therefore he spared none, whether he were cousin, Englishman or Burgundian." After the tourney, by special request, single combats took place, one against one, and two or three against two or three. But here again the Duke had in every case to call a halt.

When at length even the most ardent jouster had had his fill, an end was made, and Duke Charles and the Bastard returned in great state to their palaces. After the banquet, before the dancing commenced, John Wydeville, younger brother of the English Queen, was declared the victor in the tourney, in the first place to honour the foreign guest and secondly to incite all youths to glorious deeds. The dancing then continued until early morning.

On the following day, Tuesday, 12th July, 1468, a State dinner was served after mass, at which the Papal Legate sat at the Duke's right. Towards the end of the meal the kings-at-arms and heralds rose from the table : two of the former placed a staff across their shoulders, from which they hung a sack with money. They then proceeded to the Duke's place and afterwards to the other tables. Amidst cries of " largesse, largesse ", and the deafening blast of trumpets, six hundred francs were distributed among the officers-at-arms, trumpeters, and musicians. The English herald, Chester, received a long robe of green and gold brocade, lined with ermine.

When grace had been said and the spices handed round, the officers-at-arms took up their positions before the Duke. In the presence of all he made promotions, appointed heralds to be kings-at-arms and marshals, pursuivants to be heralds, and baptised in the customary manner new pursuivants.

With this ceremony the wedding celebrations ended. Affairs of State summoned the Duke to Holland.

CHAPTER VIII

FEASTS

And as for the Dwyks coort, as of lords, ladys and gentylwomen, knyts, sqwyers and gentylmen, I hert never of non lyek to it, save kyng Artourys cort.—JOHN PASTON.

THE fall of Constantinople made a very deep impression in Burgundian Court circles. The rulers regarded it as of paramount importance that they should devote all their energies to the defence of the Cross in the East. Duke Philip, although fully occupied with the foundation of the new Burgundian State, desired with all his heart to take up arms against the infidel. He sent his eldest son John, Count of Nevers, with numerous knights and gentlemen to the assistance of King Sigismund of Hungary in his expedition against the Sultan. Even the complete failure of this crusade, the terrible defeat at Nicopolis, at which the future Duke was captured by the Turks, and the heavy financial burdens entailed by the levy of the immense ransom which had to be paid, did not cool the ardour of the Burgundians. On the contrary, the sovereign and his nobles, diplomats, scholars, and artists were inspired to further efforts, and devoted even more attention to the Eastern question. Philip the Good was in active correspondence with the Christians in Palestine. He provided for the preservation of the Holy Places and had wood sent from Venice for the rebuilding of the Church at Bethlehem. A hospice for pilgrims was erected at his expense at Ramlah. By his order, Ghillibert de Lannoy and Bertrandon de La Broquière undertook voyages of inquiry to Palestine and Syria. One of the travellers visited Poland, Russia, Hungary, Wallachia, and Moldavia, the other went to Constantinople and was able in Adrianople to gain detailed information concerning the Turks and their military strength. A miniature of the period displays de La Broquière on his return presenting Philip the Good with a Koran. These and other records were placed in the ducal library which was also splendidly provided with literature concerning the Turks.

135

Bishop Jean Germain, Chancellor of the Golden Fleece, strove indefatigably with speech and pen for the cause. In his remarkable work, *Deux Pans de la Tapisserie chrétienne,* he instructed artists how best to decorate their tapestries in order to strengthen the religious ardour of Christian knights.

The support given to the Christians in the East was active and energetic. Geoffroy de Toisy appeared with Burgundian galleys off Rhodes at a moment of the greatest peril, while Walerand de Wavrin carried the fame of the Burgundian flag to the Black Sea and the Danube. Jean Wauquelin sings as follows :—

> Sa bannière par tous pays
> Est cogneute très grandement,
> Car par elle sont envays
> Et Turcs et Sarrasins souvent :
> Sa valeur plus rade que vent
> Vole par tout en grand crémeur :
> Renommer se fait vaillamment
> Phelippe de Bourgoingne seigneur.

Duke Philip was thoroughly alive to the terrible and ever increasing dangers which threatened the Greek empire, and begged the French King to undertake a Crusade, offering him his support. The victor, he urged, would thus earn a reputation second only to that of David, Constantine and Charlemagne. But all the arts of persuasion displayed by the Burgundian orator, Bishop Jean Germain of Chalon, were in vain. Charles VII could not leave his country, and Philip himself was entirely occupied with the rebellion of the people of Ghent. In 1453 Constantinople fell to the Turks, and the banner of the Prophet waved in triumph over the church of St. Sophia.

The triumph of the infidel was regarded by Duke Philip as a personal insult. He still determined to draw the sword personally against the enemies of the Cross, as soon as political conditions permitted. In any event it was Burgundy which must play the chief part in the recovery of Constantinople. With feverish haste he set to work upon his plans. The East as well as the West was to learn that the *Grand Duc d'Occident* would bring deliverance from captivity and wipe out the disgrace to Holy Church. The world of chivalry was to be assembled at a sumptuous feast which posterity would not

PLATE 16

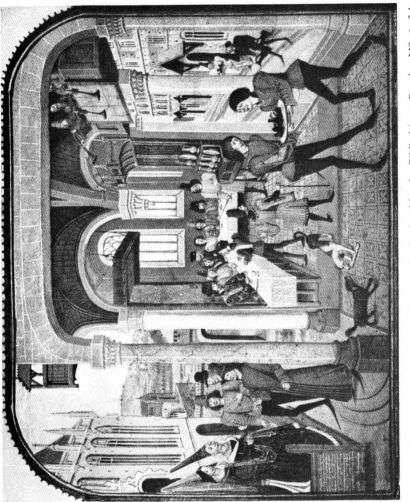

Loyset Liédet : Banquet. Miniature : Histoire de Charles Martel. Bibliothèque Royale MS. 8, fol. 33v., Brussels.

[face p. 136

soon forget, and which was to win over knights and nobles to his project.

In preparation for this festival the Duke appointed a committee to which he summoned Jean de Lannoy, the esquire Jean Boudault, and finally Olivier de La Marche, who might well find here abundant scope for his talents. Numerous preliminary meetings were held. Nicolas Rolin, the chancellor, Antoine de Croy, Count of Porcien, the first chamberlain, and other office-holders at Court, the " highest gentlemen and the most privy of the councillors " were summoned to the deliberations.

How were the celebrations to be organized so as to make a lasting impression on knights and gentlemen and spur them on to noble enthusiasm ? They were used to luxurious displays and extravagant feasts and tourneys. Duke Philip had seen to that. But after much deliberation it was determined, first of all, to humour the knights with two minor feasts, then to hold a joust, and finally to prepare a magnificent banquet with elaborate stage representations.

The greatest interest was taken in the theatre, that is, in the theatre as understood by the age. Performances were not expected to stimulate and encourage the intellects of the spectators, nor even to educate them. People of all ranks desired to be amused, to see a pleasant spectacle, to hear sweet music. Much importance was attached to decoration and scenery. Gradually a Court theatre was evolved in addition to the clerical and popular stage, and it was not tied down to any special place or building. During banquets the company delighted to be entertained by players and dancers, acrobats and fools, jesters and comedians. Life in a princely house must have been pleasantly varied when a troup of vagrant performers presented themselves to rehearse in word and play some popular story or important event.

Accounts have been preserved of actual stage pieces, of a few secular dramas which are closely allied to the Mysteries of the period. The *Mystère de la Pucelle ou du siège d'Orléans*, the sole surviving contemporary Mystery, brings Philip the Good himself upon the stage. At Amiens the *Spectacle de la Passion*, at Bruges *certain jeu, histoire et moralité sur le fait de la danse macabre* were performed in the presence of the Duke. George Chastellain

wrote *La Paix de Péronne,* a piece which is said to have
been played in the presence of King Louis XI and Charles
the Bold after their reconciliation. The Dukes, however,
did not specially care for performances of this nature, and
the representations offered at their most brilliant feasts
for the entertainment of their guests were of a very
different kind.

In accordance with the prevailing taste at Court, the committee relied chiefly on the extravagant exhibitions or
entremets which allowed the imagination the widest scope
and seemed never to lose their fascination, but huge table
decorations were also provided with living people acting as
automatons.   For the stage play, " Jason at Colchis," a
Mystery in glorification of the Golden Fleece, was proposed.
In addition to recitations and pantomimes, jugglers, trained
animals, and trapeze artists were hired to amuse the less
seriously-minded guests.   There were to be songs and music
from a great variety of instruments, and at the conclusion
a State ball was to be held for the guests and such of the
performers as could be properly admitted to Court functions.

The distress into which the Church had fallen by the
conquest of Constantinople naturally formed the central
theme of the performances.   The sad story was to be presented
very forcibly, since it was to be followed by the solemn oaths
of the Paladins who obeyed the Duke's summons to give their
life's blood for the delivery of the Cross of Christ.

Here the festival committee made use of an old custom.
When knights and gentlemen pledged themselves to special
deeds and desired to give their oaths a special significance,
they swore preferably by some noble bird, such as the
peacock, which was held in peculiar estimation. The ducal
library contained a number of romances which were founded
on this curious ritual, such as the *Vœu du Héron,* the *Vœux
du Paon,* the *Restor du Paon,* the *Parfait du Paon,* and the
Alexander the Great by Jean Wauquelin.

At solemn banquets the roasted bird was usually brought
in ornamented with its own feathers. A knight carved and
was specially applauded if he cut the bird so that each of
those taking the oath received a small portion. It may be
that this partaking of the same food was intended to create
a mysterious tie between the oath-takers, and that a memory

of the Holy Communion survived in the custom. The committee on this occasion, however, deviated from the common practice in so far as the peacock " that food of the brave and amorous ", was supplanted by a pheasant, and, moreover, by a living bird.

As soon as all details of the programme had been settled, the work of preparation began. There was scarcely a craft that was not employed. Once again an excellent opportunity was offered to skilful craftsmen and artists to earn good money, and possibly to attract the notice of the Duke and obtain that most coveted of all posts, the office of ducal groom of the chamber. Jacques Daret, a pupil of Robert Campin, was among the scene painters, and to judge by his wages, his work was very highly esteemed.

A stream of gold poured forth anew from the audit office at Lille ; its officials must often have asked themselves how the huge sums, which were swallowed up by festivals of this kind, were to be raised. But here as in everything the Duke's word was law. He tolerated no contradiction : " *car ainsi nous plaist-il estre fait.*"

After weeks of laborious activity, the long looked for days arrived. The festivities began with a banquet given on 20th January, 1454, in the palace of Lord Valeran des Aubeaux, at Lille, by Duke John of Cleves, a nephew of Philip the Good, in honour of his uncle and the Court.

On the principal table a splendid show piece, which recalled the family legend, attracted universal attention. A knight bearing the Cleves colours was represented on a beautifully-made sailing boat ; a silver swan appeared to pull the craft by a golden chain, which was fixed to the bird's golden collar. At the end of the table was the stately castle of Cleves : in front of it a ship rocked on the Rhine.

In the course of the banquet Lord Adolph of Ravenstein, Duke John's brother, caused this pronouncement to be made : The Knight of the Swan would be present in tourney armour on the day on which Duke Philip gave his banquet at Lille, and challenged all comers to a joust on war saddles with tilt poles over barriers. The ladies would present the victor with a golden swan on a golden chain.

At the conclusion of the banquet, John of Burgundy, Count of Étampes, the Duke's cousin, received the chaplet which intimated to him that it was now his turn to furnish the next entertainment, and he acquitted himself magnificently.   At this banquet on 5th February, 1454, a number of striking novelties were introduced.   The most interesting event, however, was the presentation of the chaplet to Duke Philip. Torch-bearers accompanied Dourdain, an officer of the Court, who appeared in his herald's coat. He was followed by two chamberlains, Robert de Miraumont and Gauvain Quiéret, Lord of Drueil, bare-headed and clad in long black velvet robes lined with marten, with a wreath of flowers in their hands. Behind them, a charming twelve-year-old girl rode on a palfrey which was caparisoned in blue silk.   This Princess of Joy was dressed in violet silk with rich gold trimmings, and her sleeves displayed Greek letters. Her beautiful fair hair was artistically braided, and jewels shone in her veil.   Three men walked beside the palfrey, wearing mantles of red and chaperons of green silk. Singing, they proceeded slowly towards the Duke's seat.

After low obeisances the officer presented the Princess of Joy to the Duke. Her escort then lifted the maiden from her palfrey, she bowed low, mounted the table by means of steps, knelt down and put the chaplet which the chamberlain had handed to her to her lips, and then placed it on the Duke's head, who thanked her with a kiss.

With this ceremony the banquet came to an end ; all minds were now concentrated on the third banquet, the last and greatest. Sunday the 17th February, 1454, brought with it the long awaited Feast of the Pheasant.

The celebrations began with a joust. Immediately after the midday meal, Adolph of Cleves, the Knight of the Swan, proceeded to the jousting place, accompanied by a stately train. Duke Philip with his two sons, Charles, Count of Charolais, and Anthony the Great Bastard, were also present. The princes wore black velvet, with diamonds, rubies and pearls on golden collars. Philip's chaperon shone with costly stones.

In this procession, which included also the Count of Étampes, all the gentlemen of Adolph's suite, dressed in his livery, marched first ; then came the tambourine-players, next a pursuivant in coat of arms ornamented with swans, and finally a great counterfeit swan made its appearance with a golden crown bearing the Cleves banner about its neck. Two crossbowmen marched to right and left of the swan, threatening the spectators with their bows if they dared to approach too near. At last came the Knight of the Swan himself riding in full armour ; his shield and horse covered with white damask and edged with golden fringes. On both sides of him and behind were small pages, dressed in white, " like angels," and mounted on fine horses with white trappings. An equerry, dressed also in white and mounted on a small horse, led the tourney steed which was covered by a white damask cloth. Its border was hung with golden fringes and showed the letters of the motto. John of Coïmbra, grandson of the King of Portugal, with numerous knights and noblemen, all dressed in white, brought up the rear.

In the market-place, Jean le Févre, Lord of Saint Remy, King-at-Arms of the Golden Fleece, presented the Knight of the Swan to the Duchess Isabella, to the princesses and the noble ladies and maidens. The swan with the crossbow-men was placed on a small stage, and the joust began. The Count of Charolais and the Great Bastard broke a few tilting-poles. They had armed themselves in the meanwhile and now wore violet velvet which was trimmed with silver bells and fringes of gold and silk. The Knight of the Swan and his opponent fought at close quarters ; both fell beneath their horses, and were so severely bruised that they could take no further part in the joust, whereupon a knight disguised as a hermit then appeared in the lists and cried the battle-cry *peine pour joie.*

In spite of the splendour of the knights' accoutrements and the singularity of their equipment, no special attention was paid on this ocasion to the joust, for the thought of the mysterious banquet filled all minds. Those who were fortunate enought to have been granted permission to view the dining hall before arrival of the Court, left the tourney field early in order to proceed to the Hotel de la Salle.

Five doors, all strictly guarded by crossbowmen and noblemen, barred the approach to the hall, and each door had to be passed. The officials wore liveries of grey and black, the new ducal colours.   These liveries were made of silk damask, satin, or wool, according as the wearer was knight, esquire, or servant.

It is a matter for lasting regret that not a single one of all the splendid palaces of the Burgundian dukes has withstood the ravages of time, whether in Paris, the Netherlands, Burgundy, in Brussels or Bruges, in Arras and Hesdin, in Argilly and Germolles.   From the meagre remains in Paris, Lille and Dijon, we have in imagination to recreate these stately palaces, astir with life, with their innumerable apartments, large and small, their nooks and corners, their long galleries and wide staircases, and their lovely chapels and oratories.   At that time a palace still wore the aspect of a fortress, ready at any moment with its battlements, towers, portals and ditches to withstand attack.   Nothing resembling an economical distribution of space was to be found within. Apartments were still arranged in a most unpractical manner. New things in a new fashion were quickly added to old ; and what was superfluous was removed at once.   But the richly decorated banqueting halls must have made a lasting impression on all beholders.   Here the very pick of the aristocracy was assembled beneath the glare of countless candles and torches, the magnificent robes shining and glittering in the light, taking fresh colours from the costly furniture and hangings with which the hall was filled.   It is a thousand pities that no painter or miniaturist should have taken the Pheasant Banquet as his subject.

The walls in the great hall, which contained a window forty-six feet wide, were hung with tapestries depicting the labours of Hercules.   This most popular hero, who on his journey into Spain is said to have tarried in Burgundy, was glorified as the founder of the ducal house.   Three tables had been set up.   The Duke's seat was at the cross table beneath a canopy of golden material, with velvet trimmings adorned with crests and devices.   A cushion of similar material and trimmings lay on the seat.   A buffet was close by, the six shelves of which were loaded with gold and silver services and crystal and glass of all colours and shapes, studded with pearls and jewels.   Only the cup-bearers were allowed to approach this buffet through wooden barriers. On the tables lay cloths of silk damask reaching to the floor, and on the benches were cushions with embroidered coats of arms. The figure of a naked woman leant against a column on the long side of the hall opposite the great table ; a veil inscribed with violet Greek letters was twisted round her hips, and her loosened hair fell down to her feet. Her hat of gold was ornamented with precious stones and crowned with a second hat of flowers ; during the banquet, spiced wine flowed from her right breast. On a lower pedestal was chained a live lion as her guardian. " Do not touch my mistress," was to be read in gold letters on a blue ground. It is not clear what this spectacle was intended to represent, but possibly the figure symbolized the city of Constantinople with the Flanders Lion as protector and guardian.

Four further representations were exhibited at the Duke's table. At the one end was a church with belfry and stained glass windows. Four musicians sat within and entertained the company with the organ and with songs. From a rock a naked boy spurted rose-water in the most natural manner in the world. Farther on a heavily-laden carrack was anchored, which in regard to sails, tackle and crew was not inferior to any real ship. It swarmed with sailors who climbed to the masthead, busied themselves with the yards, and dragged the bales and casks hither and thither.

At the extreme end of the table was the wonderful fountain, which the groom of the chamber, Jehan Scalkin, and Gossuin de Vieuglise had constructed out of lead and glass. A meadow with blossoming bushes figured in glass formed the ground-work of the basin, which was surrounded by rocks of sapphire and finished off with other rare stones. In the centre rose a statuette of St. Andrew, the patron saint of the ducal family, from one arm of whose cross a jet of water a foot high gushed out to trickle mysteriously away into the meadow.

No less than twelve pieces were exhibited on the other two tables. The rare, the droll, the exciting, the familiar and the strange were here in gay confusion. Twenty-eight musicians were seated in a huge pasty. An imitation castle Lusignan had been erected. On its principal tower Melusine with her fish tail was to be seen ; from the two side towers orange water ran down into the moat. A well-found ship sailed on a lake between towns and castles. A fool rode on a bear through the wintry landscape. Here in a desert tigers

and serpents engaged in furious combat ; there a savage
passed up and down through the land seated on a camel.
A pedlar wandered through a village hawking his wares.
Now the scene was transported to India where in a forest
wild animals, moved by clockwork, sought their prey.

Some of these *entremets* had a special meaning, hinting
at some topic of the day, or illustrating some well-known
proverb.   In one of them a windmill stood on a height,
with a tall mast fixed to its longest sail on which a magpie
was perched.   People were seen shooting at the bird with
bow and crossbow " in order to indicate that it was the
common occupation of all men to shoot at magpies ".

In a vineyard lay a cask containing good and mellow, as
well as bad and sour wine.   A splendidly dressed man held a
placard aloft on which could be read " Who wants, let him
help himself ".

In another a man was seen striking a bush full of little
birds with a pole.   A knight and a lady sat near in an
orchard enclosed by a trellis of roses, eating heartily of the
birds, the lady pointing with her finger at the man, who was
working away and wasting his time.   The key to this was
doubtless the French proverb :   " *Vous batés les buissons,
dont un autre prend les oysillons* " or " *Qui va coyment,
prendra le merle au nid* ".

Finally a lion was seen fastened to a tree in the centre of
a meadow.   In front of him a man was beating a dog.   This
recalled the saying :   " *battre le chien devant le lion,*" or in
the Flemish :   " *Om den leeuw te dwinghen, slaet men dat
hondeken cleyn.*"

There was indeed enough to examine and admire before the
banquet commenced.   Those favoured ones who were permitted to enter the palace had scarcely finished their survey
before the Court arrived.   There was much crowding.   So
great was the multitude of ladies and gentlemen that movement was almost impossible, and the servants had great
difficulty in discharging their duties.

Not all the guests took part in the banquet.   Many people
of note, for the most part masked, were content to watch
the proceedings from the galleries.   They had come from
far and near, some even from across the sea.   A few citizens,
too, were to be seen.

Having inspected the *entremets,* the ducal pair and their guests were ushered to their seats by marshals of the Court. Marie, Lady of Charny, a natural daughter of the Duke, sat next to the Duchess. Marie de la Viéville, wife of the Great Bastard, and *madame la chancelière,* Guigone de Salins, the wife of Nicolas Rolin, the chancellor, were also at the high table. Charles of Charolais and his half-brother Anthony were seated at the second table. The esquires were placed at the third. So great was the company that both sides of the tables were needed.

At last the banquet began. The chroniclers had so many other things to note and remember on this memorable day that they did not trouble about the dishes and beverages. Carriages and litters covered with golden and blue material and ornamented with the Burgundian arms were let down from the roof of the hall by cranes. These contained the food. Each meat course had over forty different dishes, and each carriage contained eighty-two pieces of meat.

When the noise had somewhat abated, the peal of church bells was heard announcing the first interlude. Then the choir boys sang and a tenor chanted a lovely Benedicite ; after this a shepherd played a new air on the bagpipes.

And so it continued almost without end. Each new interlude was introduced by music. The artists in the church and among the guests changed places with each another. The most varied kinds of instruments were heard, both alone and accompanied by the choristers, who sang amongst other pieces the chanson "*La Saulvegarde de ma vie*" and a motet.

Eight interludes then followed under the direction of sixteen nobles in ducal uniform.

First of all a trained horse appeared, caparisoned in pink silk. It entered the hall backwards and paced through it in the same manner. Two trumpeters, back to back, rode it astride. They wore grey and black *journades* and curious hats, their faces being disguised by masks. A monster in green and white striped silk, the upper part man, the lower part a griffin, with an extraordinary face and beard, rode past the tables on a wild boar, which was also decorated with green silk. He juggled with two daggers and a sword, and on his shoulders was an acrobat balanced head downwards. A beautiful white stag with gilt antlers then appeared. With the stag was a twelve-year-old boy in a short crimson velvet coat, small black hat, and pointed shoes, who was presented sitting on a pink silk rug.   He sang with pure voice the chanson " *Je ne vis onques la pareille* " and the stag played the accompaniment.   A fiery dragon flew through the hall and disappeared again as mysteriously as it had come.   A heron was let loose high up in the roof.   Men dressed as falconers drove it off, and two falcons pursued it, one of which pressed the bird so hard that it fell to the floor between the tables.

Between these curious representations, the three acts of the Mystery, the Adventures of Jason at Colchis, obviously split up on account of the change of scenery, were interpolated. A large stage, with a green silk front curtain, had been erected near the door.

After a fanfare of trumpets Jason entered, attired as a Burgundian knight, his sword at his side, his spear in his hand, and his shield, after the Spanish fashion, about his neck.   After he had gazed around like a stranger in an unknown country, he knelt down, looked up to heaven and read the letter he had received from Medea when setting out to obtain the Fleece.   Scarcely had he finished when two wild bulls fell upon him, spitting fire and flame from their jaws and nostrils.   A tremendous combat ensued, Jason plying lance and sword without success.   Then he bethought him of the phial given to him by Medea.   He hurled the miraculous liquid at the bulls.   The fire was extinguished, and the beasts became tame at once.

In the second part, which likewise was introduced by the trumpets, Jason was attacked by a horrible dragon, whose jaws gaped mightily beneath its large green eyes.   From distended nostrils a sheet of fire and malodorous poison poured forth, and so fierce was the combat that it seemed to be a struggle for life and death rather than a theatre play.   This time again both spear and sword failed, and Jason was only rescued by the magic ring placed on his finger by Medea. The victor then cut off the dragon's head and pulled out its teeth.

The trumpets sounded for the third and last time.   Jason, armed as before, was seen ploughing with the two bulls which he had tamed and sowing the dragon's teeth in the furrows,

as directed by Medea. He had hardly proceeded any distance
before the crop sprang up, and armed men grew out of the
ground. They attacked one another so ferociously that the
blood poured in torrents, and not one of them escaped with
his life, while Jason stood by and beheld the massacre.

The green curtain was then lowered : the pantomime was
over. Once again the organ in the church resounded, and once
again the musicians were heard from inside the pasty. The
music was intended to present a hunt. The hounds were
heard baying, as the huntsmen halloed and blew their
horns.

These diversions served as a kind of prologue to the
evening's entertainment, and were followed by the great
performance which was to announce to the guests the real
purpose of the feast.

A huge giant, dressed in green and striped silk, now
appeared who represented a Saracen. In his left hand he
held an ancient battle-axe, and with his right hand he led
an elephant. On its back it carried a tower resting on a
silken saddle-cloth, and in the tower a personage was seated
wearing female attire. Her modest dress of white satin
betrayed her distinguished birth, the black mantle falling
over it her mourning and sorrow. A Béguine's white coif
was her only head covering. She came representing Holy
Church, begging in her distress for succour at the Court of
the *Grand Duc d'Occident*.

The elephant recalled distant lands, the giant the Saracens,
by whom she would be enslaved and extirpated from the
world, unless her loyal children, good and true catholics,
came forward to take her under their protection. The solid
tower represented the faith which lives ever in the hearts
of mankind.

Many crowded forward to see who played the part of the
woman. It was none other than Olivier de La Marche himself,
who uttered the complaints in a high falsetto voice. The
four-part "*Lamentatio Sanctae matris ecclesiae Constanti-
nopolitanae*", probably composed by Master Binchois,
was declaimed. The tenor part was taken from the Lamentations of Jeremiah : "*Onmes amici ejus spreverunt eam,
non est qui consoletur eam ex omnibus caris ejus*". The
other voices sang French verses, La Marche probably taking

the alto part in which the well-known melody of the Lamentations of the Church resounded.

When the dirge was finished, the feast had reached its
culminating point.   Numerous heralds-at-arms now appeared
and with them the Golden Fleece King-at-arms, Jean le
Févre.   He carried in his hands a live pheasant, having round
its neck a collar of gold, richly garnished with precious stones
and pearls.   He was followed by two ladies, Iolanthe, a
natural daughter of Philip, and Isabeau de Neufchatel,
accompanied by two knights of the Fleece, the Lords of
Créquy and Lalaing.   Golden Fleece made a low obeisance
before the Duke, and spoke as follows: "Highest and Mightiest
Prince, my most revered Lord, behold these ladies who
humbly commend themselves to you.   Since it is and was
ever customary to present a peacock or other noble bird at
great feasts before the illustrious princes, lords and nobles,
to the end they might swear expedient and binding oaths,
now I, with these two ladies, am here to offer to you this
noble pheasant ; may its memory be preserved ! "

At the conclusion of this speech, the Duke rose and handed
Golden Fleece a parchment.   He looked at the " Church "
as if sorrowing for her, and then placing his right hand on
his breast, he declaimed as follows : " I swear before God
my creator, the glorious Virgin Mary, the ladies and the
Pheasant, that I will do and perform diligently what I have
set down in this writing."

Thereupon Golden Fleece read the oath aloud : Should
the most Christian and victorious King his master take the
Cross, Philip will accompany him, so long as he is not prevented
by illness.   Should the King be obliged to appoint a deputy,
he will render him obedience.   Should the King be prevented
and should other princes of sufficient power be prepared to
take his place, he will, with the King's consent, accompany
them, provided that the country of Burgundy is then in a
state of peace.   Should the Sultan desire it, he is ready, with
the help of Almighty God and His gracious Virgin Mother,
whose aid he implores, to engage with him in single combat.

Thereupon the " Church " returned thanks to the Duke in
stirring verses, and after inviting those present to follow their
Duke's example quitted the hall on her elephant.   Charles of
Charolais, the Duke of Cleves, the Great Bastard and others

took the oath. In order, however, not to prolong the ceremony, the Duke commanded that the remainder should hand their oaths in writing to the King-at-Arms on the following day. But the programme was still not at an end. A final act remained to be performed.

Through the great doors of the hall torch-bearers now appeared, and with them were musicians with tambourines, harps and lutes. They were followed by a lady clad in a very simple dress of white satin, like a nun, over which was a cloak of white damask. The head covering also was white and modest. On a roll on her left shoulder was to be read in golden letters, " God's Grace." She was accompanied by twelve knights, each of whom led a lady by the hand. The knights wore crimson doublets, black tights and grey-black satin tunics with sleeves, which like their black velvet hats were richly embroidered with leaf and other gold work. They had golden masks and carried torches. The twelve ladies appeared in crimson satin petticoats lined and edged with fur. Over these was a robe of finest linen with golden fringes in Brabant fashion, through which the satin gleamed. The round white head decoration was worked in the Portuguese mode ; roses ornamented the hair cushion, a diaphanous veil, strewn with gold, fell down the back in folds and also covered the face. Each lady had a collar studded with jewels about the neck and a leaf on the left shoulder with her designation. These were the twelve virtues. " God's Grace " led the twelve virtues through the hall to the Duke. She introduced herself in a few verses as the Almoner of Heaven and handed him a letter.

By command of the Duke, the Lord of Créquy read it aloud. As the sworn oaths had pleased God and the Holy Virgin well, they sent " God's Grace " together with the twelve virtues, whom all were to obey, so that they might bring their project to a happy end and gain glory here below and Paradise above.

The virtues then presented their letters to " God's Grace " who read them aloud. Thus Faith, Love and Hope, Truth and Justice, Understanding and Prudence, Courage, Temperance, Strength, Ardour and Generosity were introduced to the Duke and his guests. Whereupon " God's Grace ", with a few parting words, quitted the hall, whilst the virtues,

having taken off their badges, remained for the ball and
entertainments.   Mademoiselle de Bourbon, Mademoiselle
d'Étampes, the Duke's illegitimate daughter Margarete,
had taken part in the Epilogue, and Charolais, the Bastard
Anthony, John and Adolph of Cleves were among their escort.

The kings-at-arms, the heralds, and the noblemen appeared
during the dance and inquired of the ladies and noble maidens
which champion had been the best jouster that day.   The
prize was awarded to Charolais ; two princesses, Mademoiselle
de Bourbon and Mademoiselle d'Étampes, presented it to the
Count.   In return, conforming to custom, he kissed them,
while those standing round broke out into the cry of
Montjoie.

Wine and spices were once again handed round in bowls
gleaming with precious stones.   Charolais announced a joust
for the following day, at which he would appear with a black
violet shield, accompanied by two companions as adven-
turers.   It being now almost three o'clock, the Duke and the
Court withdrew.   The feast was at an end.

In accordance with the Duke's command, the oaths were
handed to the King-at-Arms, in writing, and later enrolled
in the Court records.   Of these there are over a hundred.
The gist is the same, the form, however, varies very considerably.   Some are short and terse, others are full of detail
and extravagant.   Some make conditions, others use the
opportunity to show their adored lady their boldness and
to boast of their prowess.

Duke Philip, however, was still not satisfied with what he
had accomplished at Lille.   The invitation to participate
in the Crusade was sent also to those knights and gentlemen
who had not been present.   The Count d'Étampes and the
Bishop of Arras received at Arras on 15th March the oaths
of the nobles of Picardy, Artois, and the Boulonnais.   The
Count of Charolais assembled the notables of Flanders at
Bruges.   Holland also was recruited, and at Mons on
21st April, 1454, a summons was issued to the nobility of
Hainault.   Though the latter could not avoid the pressing
exhortation, it is evident that their feelings were much more
sober and restrained.   The Duke was far away, and the
ravishing presence of the admired and admiring lady was
wanting, as was also the rosy mood engendered by the wine

PLATE 17

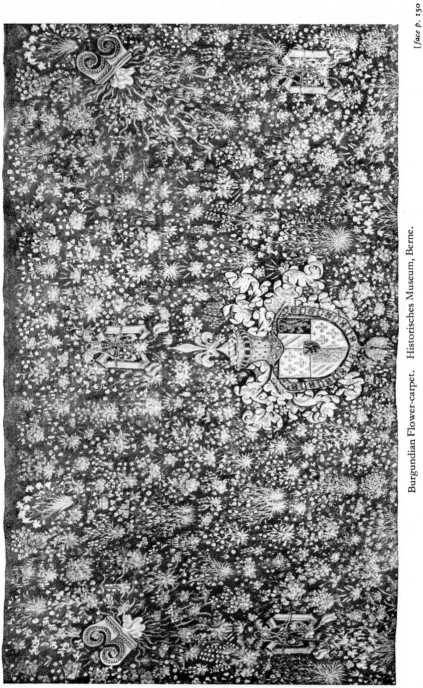

[face p. 150

Burgundian Flower-carpet.   Historisches Museum, Berne.

and good food at the banquet at Lille. There it was much easier to promise to leave wife and child, house and home, to expend huge sums, and to risk one's life, than here in the cold reality of everyday life. All kinds of scruples obtruded themselves. One nobleman of Hainault declared roundly that it was madness to undertake such a journey unless Duke Philip bore the cost, and many others shared his opinion.

The Pheasant banquet was over, but criticism was rife. The festive day was now only a memory for the numerous guests, actors, artists and craftsmen, officials and servants. Heavy demands had been made on eye and ear. The presentations had been almost oppressive in their abundance, the programme much too profuse. The cunningly contrived mechanical devices had seemed rather childish and naive. Christian virtue had hidden itself in shame in the presence of unveiled pagan beauty. Holy Church had been obliged to tolerate the company of Hercules, and even of the perjured rascal Jason. There had been a good deal of emotional excitement and the guests must have been conscious that they had been carried away by their feelings.

Considered as a whole, the Feast of the Pheasant left behind it the impression of a carefully contrived theatrical performance at which the most splendid scenery and costumes, the most wonderful and ingenious machinery had been employed. It was not by chance that spectators were admitted to the galleries, and to them, as they looked down, the lords and ladies at the tables must have seemed very much like actors. The Duke himself had not shrunk from taking part in the play and participating in the pantomime.

The allegory which the custom of the period demanded was not always easy to interpret, and the interlude of the "Church" was therefore explained in the official report of the feast. The "Virtues" were given a badge so that their names might be clear to all. On the other hand, the figure of the woman guarded by a lion and some of the other items lent themselves to various interpretations. One thing at least was clear. The Duke's subjects, accustomed as they were to the parade and flourish of the Court, had never imagined such a riot of extravagance and splendour as was exhibited at the Feast of the Pheasant at Lille.

"*En conclusion ce a esté la plus haulte et pompeuse*

besongne et la plus riche et la plus grande magnifisance que l'on veit oncques faire."   So writes a ducal secretary to Dijon, and Georges Chastellain in his *Epistre* dedicated to the *bon duc* thought Lille very highly favoured to have been chosen as the scene for such a feast :—

Quant le rapport te fut fait par exprès
De la grant perte et du mortel comprès
De Constantin, la noble sainte ville :
Certes bien digne et bien heurée Lille
D'en avoir pris les vœux de mainte clause
Que tu y fis à celle seule cause.

Doubtless, however, depreciatory judgments were associated with praise and approval. Many must have asked themselves : Was this sumptuousness justified ? Had the mighty plan any prospect of success ?

That Duke Philip and his intimates expected awkward questions such as these, is proved by a passage in the official record of the feast. Already before the conclusion, even before the last interlude, the writer begins to doubt. Everything appears to him as in a dream ; had he really seen what had passed before his eyes ? He continues to reflect and criticize. Certain things do not please him at all, as for instance, the custom of handing the chaplet of flowers as a challenge to a tournament.   He considers this an onerous constraint ; it only incites the knights to outrival one another. Altogether the Feast of the Pheasant had caused a "*fort oultrageuse et desraisonable despense*" such as had scarcely been seen on the occasion of a princely wedding or the visits of illustrious strangers. The interlude of the Church and the oath alone meet with his approval. Moreover, in his opinion, the difficulties of the crusade had not been sufficiently weighed and considered.

He finally communicates his doubts to a councillor and chamberlain, with whom he is well acquainted, and who enjoys the Duke's confidence. The courtier's answer is intended to disperse his misgivings. Duke Philip was obliged to organize these banquets and festivities in such resplendent fashion in order to attract notice to his proposals, for the rebellion of the people of Ghent had disturbed men's thoughts. In the meanwhile the Turks had captured Constantinople. The welfare of Christendom had left the Duke no alternative but to announce to the world his determination to subdue the enemies of the Cross.

We may well ask whether the answer gave general satisfaction. The reminiscences of paganism, the fusion of the noble idea of the Crusade with the romanticism of chivalry, which stood entirely under the banner of the service of love, displeased many and those not the most ill-disposed. The Crusade was to be no artificial enterprise of adventurous knights and nobles. No one was likely to forget the disgrace of Nicopolis. Those who had gone forth on that occasion were not soldiers strictly disciplined, or even suitably equipped but cavaliers glistening with jewels, resplendent in their costumes and trappings, consumed with the idea of re-enacting the romances of chivalry and out-doing each other in feats of heroism. After the terrible defeat, in which the flower of French nobility had been cut off, Philippe de Mézières, the untiring herald of the Crusades, called attention to the errors into which the knights had been drawn by " vain Madame Ambition, one of the mightiest Ladies in the world ". He criticized severely the false atmosphere created by the romances, as for instance, the Vœu du Paon. His voice, however, resounded unheeded. The *Grand Duc d'Occident* went his own way. Like Godefroy de Bouillon, another duke of Brabant, whose name still lived on everybody's lips, he summoned his knights and vassals to follow him and take the Cross. In spite of repeated discouragements he pursued the great object of his ambition for many years, and only relinquished it when political conditions became still more complicated, and the quarrel with France threatened to develop into open warfare. But the Feast of the Pheasant remained a lasting testimony to his crusading zeal, for then Philip had uttered the magic spell, which for centuries was to bind the hearts of men.

" The most Christian princes . . . have set up chapels for the glorification of the service of God, after the example of David ; in these they kept various singers at great expense in order to praise God pleasantly and fittingly with harmonious voices. And because the princely singers win honour, renown and wealth, many have taken up this calling with ardour.

Therefore music has made such wonderful progress in these days that a new art appears to have arisen."

Thus justly does John Tinctoris, the eminent theorist and conductor of the orchestra of King Ferdinand of Aragon, emphasize the efforts of the princes of that age on behalf of music. But, nevertheless, in those very circles where dissent might least be expected, many-voiced and formal singing and organ playing encountered violent opposition. Strict monasteries like the one at Windesheim would have nothing to do with it. For them the words of Thomas à Kempis were sufficient : " If ye cannot sing like the lark and the nightingale, then sing like the ravens and frogs in the puddle, who sing as God made them."

Musical feeling was deeply rooted in the people of the Netherlands. The citizens were wont to make music at social gatherings, and organized the most elaborate and artistic performances. "The Belgians," says Lodovico Guicciardini, at a later period, " are true masters of the art of music, which they have restored and developed to the highest perfection. For it comes to them so naturally, being born in them, that men and women sing without effort most graciously, rhythmically and harmoniously, and having added to their innate ability all the developments of art, they have achieved great success in vocal and instrumental music, of which we see examples every day, and are rightly to be met with in all the courts of Christian princes."

By the genius of Dufay and Binchois, Busnois, Okeghem and Josquin, music attained a new organic development, with a new style and new rules and laws. The combination with instruments was new and characteristic, the scoring well thought out, the counterpoint artistic. As tapestry weavers subdued and incorporated each single thread into their masterpieces, so composers wove the voices into one perfect harmony. Precedence was given to none, all were of equal importance. And it is a remarkable fact that this music, in which, regardless of the principles of the Renaissance the individual submitted to the mass, should have met with special recognition in Italy. Singers and composers from the Netherlands were greatly sought after not only at the Vatican, but also at the courts of Italian princes.

The Burgundian Dukes shared their Netherland subjects'

predilection for music. There is evidence that Philip the Bold sent musicians to German schools to be trained. Philip the Good, too, was always graciously inclined to the *ménestrels* and all other musicians. He ordered a splendid instrument from the distinguished Janne van Steenreen, "*geheeten van Aren, in Aerschot, meester van orgelen spelende by henselven*", and sent it to Dijon. Music played also an important part in the Feast of the Pheasant. It was, in fact, the only art which received unstinted praise on that memorable occasion.

It is a pity that so little of the music which resounded at those festivals has survived. Many details of the *entremets* seem to us gaudy and in bad taste, but we might understand them better if we could hear the music which accompanied them, now flowing sweetly with artificial flourishes, now idealistically lovely, now realistically descriptive. Although the *Chanson " Je ne vis onques la pareille "* is extant, we can only guess from the other works of Burgundian masters of that period how lovely a " charming Benedicite " must have been, and with what delight the listeners may have heard the *Chanson " La Saulvegarde de ma vie "*, or a hunting piece with sounds of horns and baying of hounds.

The great Dufay, too, *luna totius musicae atque lumen cantorum*, the founder of the first Netherlands school, was, it appears, a member of Philip the Good's chapel orchestra. Dufay was *Baccalaureus in decretis*, choir-boy and later canon of Notre Dame de Cambrai and occupied also a prebendal stall in St. Waudru at Mons. His music has an air of solemn peace and intimacy, which reminds one of the early Cologne school of painting. His mass *L'Homme armé* gives the impression of a smile amidst tears, and is born of the same spirit that inspired the verses of Charles of Orleans.

> Mais ma bouche fait semblant que je rie
> Quant maintes fois je sens mon cuer pleurer.

Guillaume Dufay, who seems to have been a teacher of the Count Charolais and was remembered by him in his will, was by birth a native of Hainault, as was also Gilles de Binche, called Binchois, who exchanged his soldier's uniform for the robes of a priest. Philip the Good appointed him his chaplain, and procured him a prebendal stall in St. Waudru at Mons. Binchois does not appear to have been to Italy, but his fame reached across the Alps. *Chansons* and *Motets* by him are still to be found to-day in the Vatican, and exhibit genial grace. Binchois and Dufay were great men in their own way. Binchois, the old *soudard*, and after him Obrecht laboured to spiritualize the popular wordly music; Dufay and Okeghem after him, laboured equally to secularize the music of liturgy and the Church.

Martin Le Franc speaks highly of Dufay and Binchois, and prefers them to the famous artists of Paris, now entirely forgotten.

> Tapissier, Carmen, Cesaris
> N'a pas long temps sy bien chantèrent
> Qu'ilz esbahirent tout Paris
> Et tous ceulx qui les fréquentèrent.
> Mais onques jour ne deschantèrent
> En mélodie de tel chois—
> Ce m'ont dit ceulx qui les hantèrent—
> Que G. du Fay et Binchois.
> Car ilz ont nouvelle pratique
> De faire frisque concordance
> En haulte et en basse musique,
> En fainte, en pause et en muance ;
> Et ont pris de la contenance
> Angloise et ensuy Domp Stable,
> Pour quoy merveilleuse plaisance
> Rend leur chant joyeux et notable.

Jean de Cordonval and Jehan Ferrandes, blind musicians, who like many others were hospitably received at the Court of Burgundy, played the viol so beautifully that Dufay and Binchois could not conceal their jealousy.

> J'ay veu Binchois avoir vergongne
> Et soy taire emprez leur rebelle
> Et Du Fay despité et frongne
> Qu'il n'a mélodye si belle.

Nicholas Dupuis and the English chaplain Robert Morton were attached to Philip the Good's chapel, and Charles of Charolais begged the Englishman from his father for his own service. In the chapel all kinds of instruments were heard. Organ, harp, flute, German horn, trumpet, oboe, bagpipe, tambourine, lute, viol and fiddle : all these are mentioned on the occasion of the Feast of the Pheasant alone.

The chapel of Charles the Bold comprised twenty-four singers, singing boys, and organist, a flute-player, several viol players and oboists as well. The singers received special attention. Like the heralds, they received raw meat at table.

"*Et comme le roi Charlemaigne avoit honoré ceste science en son temps, lorsqu'il avoit mandé les expers musiciens de Rome pour enseigner ceux de France en vraie modulation, le duc Charles recueilloit les plus fameux chantres du monde et entretenoit une chapelle estoffée de voix tant armonieuses et délectables que après la gloire céleste il n'estoit aultre liesse,*" says Molinet. Antoine Busnois was appointed singer in the chapel and received the dignity of dean. He was one of the most important composers of his age. His art is bolder and more virile than that of Dufay. Contemporary with him was the *chantre* Heyne van Ghizeghem. Pierre Beurse was employed as organist, and later gave lessons to the Duchess Marie on the clavichord.

Charles the Bold took such pleasure in music that he had a contrapuntal mass sung every day. His orchestra had to accompany him on his expedition to Neuss, and at his wedding celebrations many of the chief attractions were musical in character.

Shortly after his accession Charles the Bold resolved to marry for the third time, and to offer his hand on this occasion to Margaret of York, sister of the English King. This highly significant event was to be celebrated with royal pomp. Once more a festival committee was appointed and, as in the case at the Feast of the Pheasant, the management was again in the skilful hands of Olivier de La Marche. He was assisted by Jacques de Villers, the Duchess's cup-bearer and an esquire, by Jehan Hennekart and Pierre Coustain, both painters and ducal grooms of the chamber, and finally by Master Jehan Scalkin, who was without doubt the contriver of the wonderful fountain which had attracted so much attention at the Feast of the Pheasant. The services of skilled craftsmen and artists were now again in demand. Among the countless names which are to be found in the account books of the period, that of Hugo van der Goes appears without any special distinction or comment. Just as the name of Jan Van Eyck is for ever inseparable from that of Philip the Good and his Portuguese bride whose portrait he painted, so the unhappy Hugo van der Goes will always be remembered in connection with the wedding festivities of Charles the Bold.

The festival committee had again a very difficult task, for there were bound to be comparisons, and the celebrations on the occasion of the marriage of Philip the Good to Isabella of Portugal, to say nothing of the famous Feast of the Pheasant at Lille were not easily to be surpassed or even equalled. Nevertheless, the command of the sovereign once more removed all difficulties and spurred on the workers to tremendous efforts. It was decided to hold a joust, arranged by Anthony, Charles' half-brother, and to give numerous theatrical performances of which the principal feature was to be the labours of Hercules. Duke Charles evinced a distinct preference for antiquity. It is unfortunately not known on what works the leading part was based and worked out. There was indeed no lack of mythological literature in the ducal library. The *Recueil des histoires de Troie*, the popular work of Raoul Lefèvre, was concerned with Hercules, and must have been familiar to all. But the ancient fable was considerably altered. The twelve labours presented do not agree with those of tradition. It is remarkable that Theseus also is frequently mentioned, although the glory always devolves on Hercules. Moreover, in sympathy with the prevailing taste a Christian interpretation was tacked on to the pagan material. At the conclusion of each act a placard with French verses was affixed to the lowered curtain in order to explain the drama and to drive home the moral. The poet, who may have been Olivier de La Marche, also seized the opportunity to praise the Duke, naturally without mentioning his name, and to indulge in pious exhortations. Pagan Hercules appeared as God's messenger combating evil and aiding virtue ; and a morality play concluded the entertainment.

Miming alone, however, was not considered sufficient. A few details were added which aimed at acoustic effects. For instance, the muses awoke crying out loudly ; the clash of armour resounded at the liberation of Proserpine. Great stress was again laid on realism. The muses had to do everything for the children, " just as nurses are wont to do." The fight with the serpents drew from Olivier de La Marche these words of recognition, " *Et fut la contenance si bien tenue,*

PLATE 18

Unknown Master : Charles the Bold.   Musée, Avignon.

tant des serpents comme de Hercùles, que ce sembloit chose vive, sans mistaire."

Bruges, in those days still a flourishing commercial city, with its stately buildings, was chosen as the scene of the festivities. The most important business was to prepare the princely quarters. This work was undertaken by the master mason Mikiel Goetghebeur and the master carpenter Anthoine Gossins. The ducal residence did not suffice, and great alterations were necessary in the living apartments, as well as in the household rooms. The rain came through into the old hall and the roof had to be mended. Floors were repaired, windows and doors broken through, and the various apartments entirely refurnished. Adjoining houses and cellars were requisitioned. A large wooden hall was erected on the tennis court which was to be used for the banquets and theatrical performances. This building was constructed in Brussels and brought by ship to Bruges. It was 140 feet long, 70 feet wide and about 62 feet high. Glass windows and wooden shutters, which could be opened for ventilation, were placed in the two turrets and at the sides. A staircase led to the Duke's apartments, and numerous additional rooms were built close at hand. The ceiling of the hall was covered with blue and white woollen material. Tapestries glorifying Gideon and the Golden Fleece hung on the walls. Wooden candelabra, which were painted blue and white, stood in the hall. Among the chandeliers two works of Master Jehan Scalkin were particularly admired. Huge castles, in which a man could be hidden to work the machinery, arose from shining rock and glittering stone. Men and animals scaled the mountain amidst trees and shrubs and bushes and flowers. The base was formed by rosettes made of seven large mirrors wherein all that took place in the hall was plainly reflected. " It seemed as if one beheld there ten thousand people."

The high table had been placed on a platform on the north side of the hall. This was fifty feet long and five feet wide ; above it was a rich canopy, the backcloth of gold material falling over the benches. Along the long walls two slightly narrower tables, likewise raised, had been set with benches on both sides. Three galleries were visible on the north side, and from them the ladies who desired to remain unrecognized could view the proceedings beside the trumpeters and musicians. A lozenge-shaped buffet stood in the centre of the hall, on which the finest State gold and silver services were placed. The other apartments were also furnished in the most costly fashion and decorated with tapestries.

At length the wedding day arrived. The princess landed at Sluis on 25th June, 1468, and remained there a week, being frequently visited by the Duke. She resided at a merchant's house in the market-place. Opposite the house a stage with curtain and tapestries had been erected. The inhabitants of the port could not deprive themselves of the pleasure of presenting the new Duchess with the story of Jason and the Golden Fleece and the Queens Esther and Vashti, consorts of Ahasuerus. And what Sluis offered on a small scale was magnificently re-enacted at Bruges.

In the early hours of Sunday morning, 3rd July, the wedding was solemnized at Damme by the Bishop of Salisbury. Charles then returned to Bruges secretly. All the honours of the entry were to be reserved for his bride alone.

The reception was extraordinary, even for Bruges. Clergy, nobility, foreign merchants, Venetians, Florentines, Spaniards and Osterlings vied with each other in the splendour of their welcome. The Genoese presented a knight on horseback, St. George, together with a noble maiden, the King's daughter, whom he had rescued from the dragon. Thommaso Portinari rode at the head of the Florentines, "the chief of their nation", the art-loving representative of the Medici, clad in the robes of a ducal councillor. Hundreds upon hundreds wended their way through the streets which had been decorated with carpets, costly stuffs, and branches and flowers. Margaret herself was borne in a richly-gilded litter, wearing a robe of gold brocade with her crown upon her head, and round her on all sides were grouped Burgundian and English bowmen, officers-at-arms, heralds, trumpeters and musicians. At the Gate of Holy Cross and other prominent buildings, pageants and " histories " were presented on trestle platforms, all of which had reference to the marriage. The subjects were for the most part biblical, and texts inscribed on banners served as explanations. Adam, to whom the Lord God was

presenting Eve, was seen in Paradise ; here was the marriage
of King Alexander to Cleopatra, daughter of King Ptolemy
of Egypt, and there Joseph and Mary with a bridal couple
and a crowd of youths and maidens, who glorified love in
texts from the Song of Songs ; now the scene was the marriage
at Cana with Jesus turning water into wine ; then again a
bridal couple ; the crucifixion of Christ ; the marriage of
Moses to Tarbis, daughter of the Egyptian king ; Ahasuerus
placing the crown on Esther's head ; and Tobias receiving
the blessing. The final tableau presented a virgin with the
Burgundian coat of arms, seated beneath a lily, with a lion and
leopard on either hand. The inscription read : " *Leo et
pardus se mutuo invenerunt et amplexi sunt se invicem sub
lilio* " : the Flanders lion and the English leopard were now
united.

The young duchess entered the ducal residence at noon ;
the midday meal followed, which, in accordance with
ceremonial, the newly-married couple took apart. They
showed themselves together, however, at the *Pas de l'Arbre
d'Or*, which followed. In the evening the first great banquet
was held. Among the illustrious guests were the papal
legate, two brothers of the Queen of England, numerous
bishops and envoys of princes, the Duchess of Norfolk and
other English ladies.

The *entremets* standing on the table were once again
very varied and splendid. The meat dishes, to the number of
thirty, resembled ships, and each bore the name of one of the
ducal dominions. Five duchies and fourteen countships
could be enumerated. A standard of violet and black silk
with the golden flint and steel and initial letters of Charles'
motto " *Je l'ay emprins* " fluttered from the tallest mast.
The arms of each territory and the ducal colours were utilized,
the cordage was covered with fine gold. Knights and sailors
were to be seen everywhere on the vessels which were attended
by small boats and laden with fruit and spices. Beside the
ships stood thirty large pasties from which rose lofty towers
proclaiming the glory of the Duke's cities " which had not their
equal in the world ".

The first evening was devoted entirely to pantomime.
First of all a unicorn made its appearance, a creature
specially favoured at the Burgundian Court, whose symbolical

significance, however, had been somewhat overlooked, seeing that two of the bishops present were illegitimate children of deceased dukes. It entered amidst trumpet blasts. On its back was a leopard holding the banner of England in its left paw and a marguerite in its right. When the unicorn had reached the Duke's seat, a marshal of the Court took the flower and handed it to the prince, offering also a greeting in the name of the leopard.

A lion, entirely gilded, as big as a battle charger, entered next. On a silk covering bearing the ducal arms was mounted Madame de Beaugrant, the dwarf of the Duchess Marie, attired as a shepherdess. Pacing through the hall, the lion began to sing, opening and closing its jaws most skilfully. A marshal of the Court lifted up the dwarf, and placing her on the table in front of the duchess, requested the latter to accept her as the country's gift.

Finally a third animal appeared, a stately dromedary, caparisoned in the Saracen fashion, upon which was mounted a wild man who threw gaily coloured birds into the hall.

There was no dancing that night, for the third hour after midnight had struck when the guests rose from table. The exertions of the wedding day must have tried even the strongest constitutions. The Duke had returned to Bruges immediately after the wedding ceremony, and had retired to his apartments in order, as the chronicler thinks, to sleep a little. He was very wise, for on the Monday the festivities began in earnest.

On that night the company was regaled with the story of Hercules, and after the performance a griffin entered the hall, beating its wings and moving its head amidst a fanfare of trumpets. A blue and white silk trapping bore the initials of the newly-married couple, and when the griffin opened its jaws live birds fluttered out and flew to and fro in the hall.

The festivities were continued for a week and on almost every evening there were feasts and interludes in the banqueting hall, followed by dancing. The *entremets* continued to be varied and surprising. The guests were entertained by piping goats, musical wolves, and singing asses. A group of monkeys plundered a pedlar and distributed his goods as presents to the guests. There were counterfeit elephants, camels, unicorns and deer, to say nothing of a dragon belching forth flames. Finally some giants brought in an enormous whale, from whose jaws emerged sirens and knights who sang and danced and quarrelled until the giants drove them back again into the whale's belly.

Thus excitement and entertainments succeeded each other without cessation, feasts, interludes and dancing by night, and the exertion of joust and tourney by day. When we recall the splendour and extravagance which marked every item of the programme, the variety of incident, and the never-ending round of pleasure and pastime, we are not surprised to find John Paston writing to his mother that nowhere save at King Arthur's Court could the like have been seen before.

CHAPTER IX

The Library

Philippe duc de Bourgogne . . . aujourd'hui c'est le prince de la chrestienté, sans réservation aulcune, qui est le mieux garni de autentique et riche librairie.—David Aubert.

THE founder of the Burgundian State was also the founder of the Burgundian Library. The Duke brought the idea with him from France. King John, his father, had grown up among splendid manuscripts. Important literary undertakings such as a translation of the Bible, and of Livy, owed their inspiration to him. He did his utmost to attract Petrarch to his Court. It was his custom to take books with him among his field-baggage.

His successor, King Charles V, Philip's brother, went still further. He had pronounced scientific interests and a special predilection for instructive literature. He liked to associate with the men of learning, and it was his habit to invite the Rector and Master of Paris University to converse with him on literary matters. A large part of his collection of codices was deposited by his orders in the Louvre, where the Tour de la Fauconnerie was set aside for the collection. The walls and vaulting on the first floor were timbered with bogwood and cypress ; strong, solid doors enclosed the room, and close gratings were fixed in front of the windows " to keep away birds and other animals ". The King entrusted the care of his books to Gilles Malet, one of his " varlets ", and ordered him to take an inventory of them. He personally wrote his name in his favourite works. He was a great reader, he liked to have books read aloud to him, and instigated numerous translations. The other brothers of Duke Philip, especially the Duke de Berry, were also distinguished bibliophiles.

Encouraged and supported by his relatives, Duke Philip began to survey the works he found in the princely residences of Burgundy and Flanders, had them repaired, and supplemented them by new purchases. Writers and miniaturists commenced to work for him. He ordered a splendid Bible from the Limburg brothers. Professional booksellers, or merchants who negotiated the sale of books, soon began to look on the Duke as a notable patron. Presents were received not only from princes or noblemen and friends, who gave for the sake of giving, but from writers and other personages who gave in the hope of receiving notice and reward. A request for a yearly salary or a sum of money was apt to be modestly clothed in the guise of a literary offering. Writers of the rank and fame of Eustache Deschamps or Christine de Pisan devoted their attention to this gifted statesman who was always ready to promote their interests. They worked for Burgundy and proclaimed its glory to the world.

The inventory taken after Philip's death enumerated seventy works. Many of them were theological, but didactic and historical writings were also largely represented.

John the Fearless continued his father's artistic and literary work. In this sphere, at least, he was no destroyer. He allowed the works started in Dijon to continue, and did not close his hand to those authors and writers who had already received commissions from Duke Philip. Many new works were acquired under his rule; the library grew considerably, especially in the domain of theology and learning. The preparation of the ducal breviary was entrusted to distinguished artists. Laurent de Premierfait translated Boccaccio's *Decameron*, the work being profusely illustrated. Guillebert de Mets, an alderman and tavern-keeper of Geraardsbergen, the author of an interesting description of Paris, was responsible later for another copy of Boccaccio's masterpiece.

At John's bidding, likewise, a historical work, " The Justification of Master Jean Petit," came into being, although it cannot have been said to merit a place of honour in the library. Here again is an example of how evil as well as good may leave its mark on the art of historiography. Writers troubled themselves more about Duke John than about his more remarkable father. The author of the *Bataille de Liège* and Pierre Salmon wrote much concerning John the Fearless, and shortly after his death unknown writers glorified him in the *Geste*, in the *Livre des Trahisons de France* and in the *Pastoralet*. The author of the *Geste* desired to present

his readers with an epic, but gave them a rhymed chronicle.
The externals he acquired from his originals, but he could not
make himself master of their spirit.

The conception of the *Pastoralet* is very bizarre. A noble
shepherd Florentine (King Charles VI), in splendid Pourpris
(France), rules a happy pastoral people. Belligère (Isabeau)
his " *drue* " burns, however, with a sinful love for Tristifer
(Louis of Orleans), who desires to remove the irksome husband
by poison and magic. Léonet (John) appears as the avenger
and liberates the earth from the monster. The poet required
more than nine thousand verses for his bucolic idylls, his
dainty ballads, his *pastourelles*, and lays and rondeaux
which contrasted oddly with the tale of murderous deeds and
devastating wars.

Christine de Pisan, too, even though her most sacred feelings
were wounded by the cowardly assassination of Louis of
Orleans, could not deny her sympathy to the son of a prince
whom she had so deeply honoured. A prayer for Duke John
rises to heaven in the " *Sept Psaumes* ".

With Duke Philip the Good, the golden age of Burgundian
literature dawned. The tree extended its branches and
blossomed forth in all directions. Works of the greatest
diversity were produced. Ballads and unpretentious occasional poems, dedicated to the joys and sorrows of every day,
chronicles and memoirs, theological tracts, and books of
devotion, geographical, military and pedagogic writings,
literature on the Turks, descriptions of voyages, statutes and
works concerning the Golden Fleece ; romances, like that
of Jehan de Saintré, and highly-polished short stories glittering
with erotic brilliance, like the *Cent Nouvelles Nouvelles* ;
encyclopaedias in which the collected knowledge of the age
was laboriously assembled, translations and revisions of
earlier works, endless romances and mighty epics which
filled several folios : all these began to take their places in the
ducal collection, which was soon celebrated as " the best
equipped library in Christendom ". The French king's collection was no longer a rival. The " King of Bourges " was
unable to preserve his grandfather's books, which passed
into the hands of the Duke of Bedford and were dispersed

after his death. An inventory of the Burgundian library dating from the year 1420 already comprises 248 works ; Duke Philip left behind him nearly nine hundred codices. Besides French and Latin, a certain number of works in Flemish and High German, English, Portuguese, and Italian had begun to appear, but works in the Greek language were entirely absent.

Philip the Bold had his successor taught Flemish, the Dukes John and Philip the Good did likewise. Charles grew up in the Netherlands, and was thirty years of age when he returned to Burgundy, which he had not seen since his birth. Duke Philip was never completely a master of Latin, but his son Charles knew English and Latin as well as he knew French.

Most of the works, however, were in French. If a book such as the *Minnenloop* by the Dutch nobleman Dirk Potter did not find its way to the ducal library, the failure can have been due solely to the fact that it was written in Flemish ; for the entertaining discussions concerning lawful and illicit love, and the descriptions of the innumerable affairs of the heart which characterize the work would soon have found other readers besides the Duke.

Scribes, calligraphists, and miniaturists were now employed about the Court in considerable numbers, but no special workshops, similar to those erected at Dijon for the building and equipment of the Carthusian monastery, seem to have been provided. The codices were produced under great difficulties and amidst considerable confusion. They were carried from town to town : composed in one place, written down in another, illuminated in a third, and finally bound elsewhere. It is not surprising, therefore, that the production of a book took at times ten, fifteen, and even twenty years.

Of individual works there exists often a copy on paper, as well as one on parchment. Most of the books, however, were written on parchment, and ornamented with little drawings in the margins, with delicate initials and lovely pictures. For the writing the pretentious and nobly flowing *bastarda* was used ; this was employed very spaciously, as if conscious of its own beauty. Dainty stems and innumerable small flowers and blossons lie on the parchment pages, embracing here the miniature, there the lines of the text. They are very beautiful and true to nature, and often remarkably small, but there was no attempt at shading and the effect is somewhat flat.

In the last years of Charles the Bold's reign other settings came into vogue. Flowers, fruit, insects, birds, medals and ornaments begin to take their places on golden or gaily-tinted parchment. They are frequently life-size, and present us with the most charming little still-life studies. In the same way recourse was had to architectural embellishment, the influence of Gothic prevailing everywhere until the changes brought about by the Renaissance began to make themselves felt.

Among the most noted miniaturists were Jehan de Pestivien, who came from the Paris school and who, like Dreux, was employed as *varlet de chambre* and *enlumineur*; Willem Vrelant, who worked in Bruges; Jehan Tavernier, the creator of splendid work for the *Conquêtes de Charlemagne* and for Philip's breviary, as well as of beautiful *Grisailles* with mystic letters. The most prolific *historieur* was Loyset Liédet, a member of the Gilds of St. John and St. Luke in Bruges, who worked on the *Histoire d'Alexandre* for Duke Charles and subsequently for the Lord of Gruuthuuse. He was attracted above everything else by the business of composition. His pictures are well constructed, but the execution leaves something to be desired in the matter of detail. His faces are unreal; his figures and animals often wooden. Jehan Hennecart and Simon Marmion, whose pictures were in considerable demand, were also successful miniaturists.

Duke Charles gave commissions to Nicolas Spierinc, and had a special fondness for the works of the Frenchman Philippe de Mazerolles, in whose bookshop at Bruges a woman was employed. Mazerolles contributed some splendid pages to the great edition of Froissart.

The fame of these miniaturists, who found worthy successors in Sanders Benning and his sons, Paul and the renowned Simon, and in other masters of the Ghent-Bruges school, penetrated far abroad. King Edward IV, Duke Charles' brother-in-law, whom the inconstant fortunes of war led to the Netherlands, knew how to appreciate costly works, and many a beautiful volume found its way across the Channel. Nor did the miniaturists abandon their calling when the new mysterious art of printing took root in the Netherlands. As had earlier been the case with the caligraphists, they worked now in conjunction with the type-setters and inserted beautiful initials or dainty little pictures in the spaces left on the printed page. Moreover, there were always book-lovers, true to the old fashions, to whom the expenditure of a few pieces of gold more or less made no difference. Books of Hours were specially executed for these connoisseurs, in which the portraits of the owners and their coats of arms could easily be inserted.

Among the printers who flourished at that period Colard Mansion stands first. He was a member and later president of the gild of Sint Jan Evangelista at Bruges, the gild to which booksellers and authors, schoolmasters and mistresses, scribes and parchment-makers, miniaturists and painters, bookbinders and printers all belonged. Mansion, who had already executed manuscripts for Philip the Good, set up later, perhaps with the support of Lord of Gruuthuuse, a printing press at Bruges and published some beautifully printed works on various subjects for which he employed a handsome *bastarda*. He translated the texts, some personally, from Latin into French. William Caxton, who had played a considerable part among the English merchants at Bruges, worked for a time in conjunction with him. Under commission from the Duchess Margaret, Caxton translated the compilation of *Raoul Lefèvre* and printed *The Recuyell of the Histories of Troye* in Flanders, thus publishing the first printed work in the English language. His translation may possibly have given Shakespeare the inspiration for *Troilus and Cressida*.

Great value was attached to the external appearance of the codices. As the inventories show, almost all the manu-scripts were bound ; the remark *non couvert* is seldom met with. Beautiful material was often employed for the bindings and the finely worked locks harmonized well with the splendid covers. The *Champion des Dames*, with which Martin Le Franc had such poor success, is still resplendent to-day in blue velvet. Specially treasured books were kept in wrappings or in small silver chests or miniature cupboards.

The costliest bindings were bestowed on the books of the

Church, bibles and psalters, books of hours and prayers, breviaries and missals. Here there was no sparing of gold and silver, pearls and sapphires, and other gems.

Our sources of information are unfortunately silent on the subject of the building and rooms in which the books were housed. A *Tour de la Librairie* in the castle of Dijon is mentioned. Was it equipped like the *Tour de la Fauconnerie*? We can probably answer that in this case also the French example was followed. It is surprising to learn that no scholar was in charge of the library as librarian. Under Philip the Bold the books were entrusted to the *varlet de chambre* Richard Le Comte, who was at the same time employed as principal barber. We find, too, *gardes-joyaux* cited as librarians. Scholarship and learning were kept in the background ; the codices in the first place were looked upon as valuables, as literary treasures in the truest sense of the word.

Philip the Good is extolled as *père des escripvains . . . qui toute sa vie a esté nourry en histoires pour son singulier passetemps.* Bishop Guillaume Fillastre refers to his versatility and indefatigable activity : " *je l'ay souvent veu (si ont plusieurs) coucher à deux heures après mynuit et estre levé à six heures au matin et jamois n'estoit oyseux qu'il ne s'occupast ou en estudes de livres ou de tirer de l'arc ou pour exercice en quelque esbatement honneste ou au conseil de haultes choses, quant le cas le requéroit.*"

Apparently Duke Philip did not meet in this sphere with any profound understanding on the part of his wife Isabella, although the consorts of the first two dukes had set her an excellent example. It was Margaret of York, the patroness of Caxton, who first extensively promoted literary efforts at Court. Agnes, Duchess of Bourbon, Philip's sister, is also credited with intellectual interests.

Frequent evidence exists of Philip's personal tastes. Writers sent him the original manuscripts of their works ; if they met with his approval, he ordered them to be copied on parchment and illustrated with pictures. The same thing was done with romances and epics or other writings which were extant in faulty and antiquated editions ; they were given the honour of translation and revision. Philip generously supplied the necessary funds and made his library accessible to writers, so that they might have the requisite literature at hand.

There existed, doubtless, a pedagogic intention in the commissioning of translations. What Raoul de Presles wrote of King Charles V, that he had translations made for the advantage and profit of the kingdom, can be said also of Philip the Good. The author of the *Histoire de Charles Martel* makes the significant remark that he translates old histories into verse, and recasts them in prose, as the nobles prefer prose to verse, the former requiring less restraint. Wauquelin indicates in his *Belle Hélène* that he has suppressed tedious passages and useless words. Martin Le Franc, it is true, expresses the ironic opinion that so much learned work had been done that only glosses were left for scholars :—

> On a fait textes, or à gloses
> Composer fault le temps user.

Authors belonged to the most various ranks and professions. Aristocrats and citizens wielded the pen, as did also knights, esquires, and heralds, bishops and other ecclesiastics. Many a poor scribbler, who composed verses for his daily bread, tried his luck at Court. One wonders how it was that François Villon is not to be found among the court poets harnessed to the Burgundian chariot.

The miniatures give us vivid pictures of Duke Philip and later of his son visiting their scholars and graciously accepting their work, which had cost them countless weeks of industry and exertion. Loyset Liédet, with some humour, shows us Charles the Bold hiding behind a pillar in order to surprise David Aubert, who is seen hard at work at his desk.

Writers and scholars were greatly respected at Court. Knightly society could not express its regard better than by the recognition that learning was equal to knighthood. The two pillars of the world, according to the Book of the Deeds of Marshal Boucicaut, are knighthood and learning, which agree excellently with each other. The doctor could claim equal rights with the knight.

Jean Wauquelin, David Aubert, Jehan Miélot, were all distinguished for their great versatility. Jean Wauquelin, a native of Picardy and a *varlet de chambre* of Duke Philip, was active as a writer of romances, translator and calligraphist. At one time the Hainault Year-Books of Jacques de Guyse or the Chronicles of Dynter, lay on his desk, at another works on Alexander the Great, the Romance *La Belle Hélène de Constantinoble*, or *The History of Girard de Roussillon*, whose insurrection against his suzerain Charles the Bold must have been followed with real interest.   David Aubert, too, a native of Hesdin, the favourite ducal residence, could show an imposing list of transcriptions.   Some historical like Charles Martel, some ecclesiastical, and some romantic, and he compiled a library catalogue as well.   Jehan Miélot, a native of Gueschard, half-way between Hesdin and Abbeville, translated the *Miroir de la Salvation Humaine* and transcribed the important Travels of Bertrandon de La Broquière.   He was rewarded with a canonry at Lille, and continued to work under Charles the Bold.   As one page proves, he was able to provide sketches for the miniatures and to jot down suggestions for their subject and arrangement.

Duke Charles the Bold must always occupy a special place.   The world in which he was born and grew up, the world of Lancelot and Gawain, became strange and displeased him, and was too narrow for him.   He aspired to the distant, unknown, desiring a more beautiful, a gayer, a braver, a more heroic world.   " *Tournoit toutes ses manières et ses mœurs à sens une part du jour ; et avecques jeux et ris entremeslés se délitoit en beau parler et en amonester ses nobles à vertu comme un orateur.   Et en cestuy regard plusieurs fois s'est trouvé assis en un hautdos paré et ses nobles devant luy, là où il leur fit diverses remontrances selon les divers temps et causes.   Et tousjours comme prince et chef sur tous fut richement et magnifiquement habitué sur tous les autres.* "

Molinet supplements these words of Chastellain by saying : " *Après la réfection du corps donnoit la réfection à l'âme et employoit ses jours non pas en folle vanité, en mondain spectacle, mais en sainctes escriptures, histoires approuvées et de haultes recommandations.* "

Seeking the land of the Greeks and Romans with the eyes of his mind, Charles had need of companions for this journey and found them in the writings of antiquity.   It is said that he never went to bed without first having some story of ancient deeds read aloud to him by the Lord de Humbercourt who

PLATE 19

[face p. 172

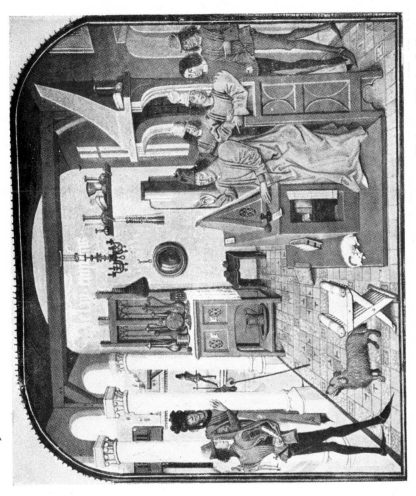

Loyset Liédet : Charles the Bold surprises David Aubert at work. Miniature : Histoire de Charles Martel. Bibliothèque Royale MS. 8, fol. 7, Brussels.

recited excellently. Charles was so absorbed in his favourite subject that he felt himself at home in the ancient world. Once when he appeared before the States General at Salines, he referred in his speech to Rome and Livy.

It is very characteristic that King Louis XI, desiring on one occasion to pay his opponent a compliment, did not send him one of the usual royal presents such as a *canis sagax*, but " a work written in the Italian tongue and character which contained the life and deeds of Charlemagne and some other French kings, as he knows that the Duke has made a perfect study of the customs and genius of the Italians ".

The choice of tapestries in his apartments is also significant. When, as Count of Charolais, he received at Brussels the delegates from Ghent who had come to him to implore forgiveness, the deeds of Hannibal and Alexander the Great were to be seen displayed on the walls. At his request the town of Bruges and the Franc procured for him some very beautiful tapestries depicting the destruction of Troy.

Charles was particularly interested in Julius Caesar and Pompey, in Hannibal and Alexander the Great, whom he wished to imitate and equal. He laid great stress on reading and made himself acquainted with the deeds of these heroes in the best texts that could be found.

A fantastic production, the endless *Perceforest*, was read with constant attention, and regarded as the veritable encyclopaedia of chivalry. In this romance an anonymous writer attempted to amalgamate the story of Alexander with the legends of the Round Table, the Holy Grail, and King Arthur.

Charles took little interest in the works which David Aubert had so carefully transcribed for Duke Philip on splendid parchment sheets. Charles Soillot, his secretary, whose father had already served the house of Burgundy, translated Xenophon for him, and Jehan Hennecart illuminated the manuscript with miniatures. Jean du Chesne made a copy of Caesar's Commentaries. Vasco de Lucena, who was probably in close touch with the Italians, transcribed the Cyropaedia of Xenophon from Poggio's Latin text.

In these works, the authors did not hesitate to draw parallels between past and present to the glorification of their

master. Most interesting of all are the remarks which
Vasco de Lucena makes in the *Faictz et Gestes d'Alexandre*.
The learned Portuguese had been occupied for seven long
years on Quintus Curtius, whose work he had completed,
revised, and translated. "Alexander does not surpass you,
most illustrious sovereign, but you surpass him in piety,
chastity and wise moderation. Already there are extant
about him many rhymed and unrhymed histories in French,
but they are full of lies. You receive here an authentic text ;
you behold here his true life, how he conquered the whole
Orient, "*et comment un autre prince le peut arrière conquester,
sans voler en l'air, sans aler soubs mer, sans enchantements,
sans gayans, et sans estre si fort comme Regnauld de Montalban,
comme Lanselot, comme Tristan, comme Raynoard qui tuait
cinquante hommes cop-à-cop.*" The toil and trouble would be
equally great for heathen and Christian, and equally great
would be the earthly profit and glory. Alexander did not
escape eternal damnation ; the Christian warrior would gain
for himself eternal glory.

The old gods had been dethroned ; new divinities made
their entry into the Court of Burgundy.

The steps of the French scholars who entered on the paths
of Humanism are mostly very tentative and uncertain.
Interest in the subject matter preponderates. We watch
them adopt with almost childish zeal the forms and formulas
of the learned epistolary style. Gontier Col begged Christine
de Pisan to excuse him for addressing her as "thou". Scholars
at times made bad slips. Montreuil apologized, perhaps with
well-feigned indignation, for having written *proximior* instead
of *proprior*. The name of the Church of Sophia in Constantinople was explained in such a way that St. Sophia was
regarded as its patron saint. The author of a work on
Hercules confused Proteus with Pirithous. But the essential
thing was that a breach had been made in the old building,
and new structures were being raised in a new spirit.

Duke Charles did not stand alone in his preference for the
antique. Many a bibliophile and Maecenas at his court had
the same interests, as, for instance, John of Anjou, Duke of
Calabria, and Jean de Créquy who had drawn the attention
of Vasco de Lucena to Quintus Curtius Rufus ; Anthony the
Grand Bastard, whose proud devise, the Barbican with

the motto " Nul ne s'y frote ", may be seen to-day decorating many splendid manuscripts; and the Bastard Jean de Wavrin. The influence of the Renaissance was furthered also by Jean Jouffroy, that ambitious prince of the Church who frequently travelled to the Curia on diplomatic missions, and as an elegant orator was only too ready to display his Ciceronian eloquence.

> Tantum alios homines anteis virtute Joannes
> Joffredi, quantum rosa formosissima vernos
> Excedit flores ac virtus imminet auro,

enthusiastically exclaims Lionardo Dati, the papal Scriptor who cultivated the muses.

Many other book lovers might be mentioned such as Louis of Bruges, Lord of Gruuthuuse, who could offer worthy hospitality to a King of England in his palace at Bruges; Philip of Horn; Philip de Croy, who appears as the narrator in the *Cent Nouvelles Nouvelles* and was painted by Roger van der Weyden; Raphael de Mercatel, a natural son of Duke Philip who was provided for by the Abbey of St. Bavo in Ghent.

The services of Duke Charles to humanism did not remain unknown even to distant poets and scholars.

Stephanus Surigonus, a *Poeta laureatus*, sent the Duke in the midst of the clash of arms a copy of some enthusiastic verses, from which it is true he promised himself material advantages.

> Salve caesarea Princeps ornande corona
> Cum sis cunctorum gloria magna ducum.
> Quis posset tantam dux inclite Carole famam
> Qua fulges, verbis enumerare suis !
> Meonia sunt digna tuba versuque Maronis,
> Si tua cantanda carmine facta forent.
> In te dignus honos est et sanctissima virtus
> Et specimen vere nobilitatis habens.

Burgundian literature has a strong didactic tendency. It strives to awaken the slumbering, to form, to instruct, it endeavours to lead its readers, as Charles Soillot did Duke Charles, to happiness and reputation. The authors of the *Enseignements paternels* and of the *Instruction d'un jeune prince* sought to show esquires how to become knights without fear and without reproach. Books instruct but do not yet bemuse their readers. There is scarcely as yet any question of purely aesthetic enjoyment such as the Renaissance offered its disciples across the Alps. Charles the Bold was one of the exceptions.

Like the work of sculptors, literature consented to be veiled in a splendid mantle. When we listen to such verses as

> Souffle, Triton, en ta bucce argentine ;
> Muse, en musant en ta doulce musette,
> Donne louange et gloire célestine
> Au dieu Phébus à la barbe roussette

the works of art with which the park of Versailles was adorned in the *Grand Siècle* rise before our eyes. Simple lines are lacking, the draperies are too rich and complicated ; the style, overloaded with similes, is too stilted and laboured.

Literature had a distinct Court tendency. Philip the Good, *un soleil d'homme*, was born to be loved, exclaims Chastellian with glowing enthusiasm. Would a courtier have expressed himself differently in lauding *Le Roi Soleil* ? To David Aubert it seemed a not unlikely thing that Duke Philip would one day be received into the assembly of the Saints. La Marche in his *Chevalier Délibéré*, placed Duke Charles among the great heroes of history. Whoever, like Martin Le Franc, displayed a critical tendency or a too imprudent candour, ran the risk of neglect, his sole consolation being to appeal to a juster posterity. Very sadly the poet says of one of his books :—

> Pour plaire à chacun n'es tu fait.

As the Dukes withdrew from France which was their native country, so literature, which was cultivated at their court and magnanimously promoted by them, became separated from the French, and took its place side by side with it, as with its neighbours, the English and German. Party passions exhibited their reaction even in literary work.

This is most noticeable in the case of historiography. It is true the dukes were interested in the past, in Villehardouin, in Froissart, in old annals and chronicles, above all when they dealt with the *Regnum Lotharii*, but the claims of the moment were never forgotten. In those times of irreconcilable political differences, the dukes required unconditional partisanship. They demanded unquestioning support for their policy, coupled with the aggrandizement of their House and the glorification of their personal achievements. In these circumstances literature was bound to be tainted by officialdom.

Sire Georges Chastellain stands at the head of Burgundian historians and rhetoricians, *homme très éloquent, cler d'esprit, très aigu d'engin, prompt en trois langages, très expert orateur et le non pareil en son temps*, as he is eulogized by Molinet. In his numerous prose works and poems especially in the chronicles (unfortunately incomplete), Chastellain proclaimed the glory and greatness of the House of Burgundy. Not that he was a blind admirer of his masters. Even with Duke Philip, who occupies the foreground of his narrative, he is not sparing either of censure or criticism. But his sympathies were with the *Grand Duc*, and he was always ready to see the faults of the French Kings.

" *Qui Anglois ne suis, mais François, qui Espagnol, ne Italien ne suis, mais François, de deux François, l'un roy, l'autre duc, j'ay escript leurs œuvres et contentions*," he says on one occasion. He felt called upon to bring about a reconciliation of the contending parties. The longing for agreement between the quarrelling mother and daughter runs like a red thread through his stately works with their detailed descriptions and melancholy reflections. The French Burgundian problem weighed on his mind and frequently robbed him of his rest. Chastellain expected nothing but good from Louis XI to whom, whilst still Dauphin, and in spite of King Charles, Duke Philip had given protection and aid. The events of the first years of the King's reign greatly disappointed him. With a lack of consideration which was certainly deliberate Louis XI commenced the struggle against his vassal, with whose overwhelming power he was only too well acquainted.

If Commines, who may well be named with Chastellain, devoted himself entirely to politics, Chastellain was always ready to play the philosopher and moralist and to seek anxiously for causes. Highly gifted as a writer, he knew how to approach princes and office-holders confidentially, and to describe all sorts and conditions of men. He could reproduce dramatic episodes convincingly and in attractive style : we seem actually to hear the passionate outbursts of Duke Philip, who was at times impotent with rage. Nor was Chastellain blind to the charms of landscape ; he has described with grace and feeling how Duke Philip took his way through the lonely woods at the approach of night.

The Fleming in him, which could not be easily veiled in elegant French attire, emerges frequently in his partiality for a piquant popular expression and a pithy and vigorous proverb.

It was once said that the pen is mightier than whole armies. Charles the Bold, who showed little understanding in his treatment of his followers, could thoroughly appreciate Chastellain, the writer.   He conferred upon this loyal servant and friend of his House the highest distinction which the chronicler of the splendour of chivalry could desire by bestowing on him, as Court historiographer, the golden spurs.   By a merciful fate Chastellain died in 1475, before the collapse of the Burgundian State, which was brought to ruin by his beloved master.

Jean Molinet, who lived for many years in Valenciennes, the *val fleuri*, considered that the best tribute of admiration he could pay to the esteemed master was to beg Charles the Bold's permission to continue Chastellain's chronicles. Thus he in his turn became the Burgundian historiographer, and enjoyed a very great reputation in wide circles as a zealous chronicler and a prolific poet.   " *Molinet qui moulinoit doulx mots en molinet* " with his elaborate grandiloquent style met with great approval.   A poet bitterly deplores the loss which the " Gallic tongue " has suffered by the disappearance of the brilliant twin stars :

> L'un pour Virgile et l'autre est pour Ovide pris.
> L'un donques fut plus grave et l'autre plus facile.
> Plus humain fut Ovide et plus divin Virgile.

Olivier de La Marche devoted his whole life to the Burgundian House, which he did not forsake even after its fall.   His memoirs and occasional writings, like the Chronicles of Jean Le Févre, Lord of Saint-Remy, Toison d'Or King-at-Arms, are not the equal of Chastellain's chronicles.   The point of view of the Court official, punctiliously concerned with ceremonial, never fails to show itself.   But as an eye-witness he was able to narrate many important matters, and to preserve many personal details concerning the Dukes, whom he was able to observe at important moments.   The

PLATE 20

Unknown Master : Disputation.   Miniature : Martin Le Franc, Le Champion des Dames.   Bibliothèque Nationale, MS. franç. 841, fol. 31v., Paris.

Lord of Saint-Remy, too, was never really at home except in the splendid world of chivalry. He could not easily avert his gaze from jousts, tourneys, and the chapters and feasts of the Golden Fleece. Nevertheless he has supplied much useful material for the diplomatic and political history of his period.

Pierre de Fenin frankly acknowledged himself a Burgundian party follower, whereas Enguerrand de Monstrelet attempted to preserve a semblance of impartiality, although in his inmost heart he was devoted to the Burgundian cause. Monstrelet bestowed particular attention upon the conflicts which beset France in the dissensions between the Armagnacs and Bourguignons and has preserved valuable documents.

Monstrelet, who cannot be proved to have had any relations with the Burgundian Court, always observed the conventions. Pierre Cochon, on the other hand, apostolic notary at Rouen, attacked Duke Louis of Orleans, whom he regarded as the source of all evil for France, in immoderate and undignified language. Yet another step and the chronicler becomes a pamphleteer, such as the writer of the *Songe Véritable,* and the authors of the *Geste,* of the *Pastoralet,* and of the *Livre des Trahisons,* who aimed their poisoned arrows from the safe shelter of anonymity.

The *Bourgeois de Paris* in his *Journal* reproduces the temper of the citizens of the French capital which had for a time become a second London. This temper was one of disgust at the extravagance and arrogance of the aristocracy, coupled with a determination to take no part in the revolutionary activities of the masses. Their balance upset by economic distress, frequently engrossed by petty worries over their money-bags, the citizens, after long hesitation, joined the Bourguignons, without, however, regaining their peace of mind. They were incapable of adapting themselves to the hardness of the times and the heavy burden of taxation. The exaggerated price of an egg was quite sufficient to rob the anonymous Bourgeois of his night's rest.

Mathieu d'Escouchy, possibly for the very reason that his life had been a stirring one, toned down his chronicles and excluded all semblance of colour. Jacques Du Clercq, who greatly loved his native city, concerned himself less with petty details than with the events of the great world. He was stirred to the depths of his soul by the awful drama of the Vauderie which was enacted before his eyes. In the background of his narrative loom the towers and battlements of that flourishing industrial centre, the *Cité* and *Ville d'Arras*.

Municipal freedom and independence in Flanders found enthusiastic supporters in Olivier van Dixmude, the so-called Jan van Dixmude and other anonymous writers, who wrote at a time when the proud *Lede* had ventured on their unequal contest with princely absolutism. They described the communes' struggle of despair, and the internal discords which facilitated their opponent's victory. Although these Flemings wrote for their fellow-countrymen in Flemish, there were other Netherlanders who could not forbear to use the Latin language ; Edmundus de Dynter, the weighty chronicler of Brabant, whose work was translated into French by Jean Wauquelin by command of Philip the Good ; Adrianus de But, and Johannes Brando, the learned monk of Dunes.

They make an imposing array, these chroniclers who wrote the records of the Burgundian House, some of them officially, others without any connection with the Court. The French monarchy had every reason to be grateful to that stroke of fate which detached Philippe de Commines from the Court of Charles the Bold, and brought his skilful pen to France.

CHAPTER X

La Vauderie d'Arras

Maleficos non patieris vivere.—Exodus xxii, 18.

CONTEMPORARIES of the dukes of Burgundy looked back upon terrible decades, while decades full of alarming problems lay wrapped in obscurity before them. In addition to political confusion and the desperate conflict between France and England, which might rob a man in a day of all his goods and chattels and even of his life, there were the ecclesiastical conflicts during the schism which might deprive him also of his salvation. Here again was the torture of uncertainty as to who was in the right. If venerable prelates and learned masters could not agree amongst themselves, how then were simple ignorant people to be saved?

The Council of Constance made an end of the schism, but the fundamental reforms within the Church were still delayed. Would the Gallican Church maintain her freedom in opposition to the papacy and gain a foothold in France? Would she give France peace within the Church and purified religious conviction? The faithful saw with sorrow how ugly and destitute, how poor and weak, how downtrodden the Church had become. Would she free herself from her fetters and again shine forth arrayed in stainless purity and beauty as Dionysius van Ryckel had once beheld her in a vision?

The contests for the papacy, waged often with violence and complete absence of dignity, had undermined all sense of respect for the Church and her representatives. Wyclif had already likened the dissensions of the two Popes to a couple of dogs scuffling for a bone. The most blasphemous abuse was hurled by clerics against the antipope in the heat of the dispute; and the jests concerning Pope John XXIII and the *Pape de la Lune*, were malicious in the extreme.

Secularization, which had spread among the clergy, and the shameless immorality which was everywhere displayed aroused the most hostile criticism. A church was never better filled than when a monk pilloried the sins of the secular clergy. Many prelates were priests only in name, and like Bishop David of Utrecht, who at his entry into Utrecht *estoit armé tout au blanc comme seroit un conquéreur de païs, prince séculier* would have cut a better figure in armour, while the letters of legitimization which the Duke was called upon to issue for their children tell a significant story. Gerson complains bitterly of the ignorance of the priests who were the laughing-stock of the laity, of their unworthy behaviour and superstitions. Very few of them could possess or be acquainted with the books which Dionysius van Ryckel so thoughtfully recommended for their use.

The inferior clergy participated only too willingly in the dissolute pleasures of the masses. Wild orgies took place in the immediate neighbourhood of the altar. On the vigils of the feasts people danced and sang in churches to secular tunes. This was indeed a revenge for the frequent theatrical performances in the churches in which hilarity and coarseness were the most prominent features.

The priests often set a bad example by cursing and diceplaying. A canon of Notre-Dame not only played publicly, but turned his house into a gambling hell. The sodomites who were burned at Arras included a priest among their number. In order to be revenged on his opponent in a law-suit, a village priest prepared a magic charm; it was concocted from poisons and from a toad which he had christened with the name of John, like a Christian child, and nourished with a holy wafer.

Priests regarded it as their prescriptive right to keep concubines. If they were deprived of them they threatened to take vengeance upon the women and girls among their congregation.

The established type in literature of the dissipated prelate, the lascivious monk, and the wanton nun acquired through the incidents of everyday life fresh justification and further development. The author of the *Cent Nouvelles Nouvelles* delights in scandalous stories concerning clerics. Priests were made the butt of scurrilous burlesques, and not even the highest were spared. When Cardinal Jouffroy on one occasion came to Paris, the members of the university ridiculed him in a most impudent piece. Rats coming on the stage gnawed the seals from a document of the Pragmatic Sanction. Suddenly, after devouring some of the seals, they acquired red heads—an allusion to the reward which the ambitious prelate had received. Having induced Louis XI to abrogate the sanction, he was decorated with a cardinal's hat by the Pope.

The Church had succeeded in gaining entire mastery over the masses. Man belonged to her; his existence was filled with her teaching. Religious ideas had penetrated everywhere and permeated everything. The Trinity had descended to man. Faith became more direct, but brought with it at the same time the danger of profanation. Divinity itself became secularized and was dragged in the dust of everyday life; all reverence was lost in the common round. The hair-splitting methods of scholasticism gave rise to inquisitive and wanton inquiries. The ever-recurring controversy as to the Immaculate Conception of the Virgin Mary emphasized the distinction between the natural and the supernatural and the mysterious divisions of which theology was capable.

The saints fared no better. Each man had his saint, his friend, and guardian, who belonged to his family and was dressed in the latest fashion. The lives of the saints were known to all; images in churches and on buildings proclaimed their deeds and miracles, instructed the ignorant, and showed the simple what they had to believe. The adoration paid to the saints at times exceeded all bounds. But woe to the saint whose protégé was disappointed in his expectations, for adoration soon changed to cursing.

The house of God belonged to all. It was the one public place where the poor felt at home. The rich and well-born possessed their private chapels in which to serve God in company only with their families and servants, but the poor had their favourite spots in the churches where they could offer flowers and blossoms to their saints, and burn candles to them in times of peril.

The church was open at all hours of the day. There the pious man prayed to his God, and met his friends and neighbours with whom he had to discuss pressing business. The lover sought to snatch there at least a glance, if not a word from his lady, and endeavoured to stand beside her, if possible, when the Pax was handed round.

> Se souvent vais au moustier,
> C'est tout pour veoir la belle
> Fresche com rose nouvelle,

sings Christine de Pisan.

But it must be admitted that churchgoers showed little respect for their surroundings. Men paid no attention to the words of the priest, but inspected the gravestones and monuments, while the women displayed their new clothes, often very *décolletées*, and flaunted their high head-dresses. Courtesans, who had but just bemoaned their sorrows to the Holy Virgin, brazenly returned the expectant glances of men, while pedlars offered the young people immoral pictures. Nor was church or altar safe from deeds of violence. One priest who knew himself to be threatened, actually kept arms beside the altar.

Pilgrimages were only too willingly used for secular purposes, since a pilgrim on the road was freed from the supervision of his acquaintances. Processions became part of the common passion for pleasure. The wildest excesses and orgies disgraced the procession which accompanied the relics of St. Livinus, when they were borne year by year from Ghent to Hauthem, the scene of his martyrdom, and back again. Drunken vagabonds bawled and made game of everything; and Chastellain asks what had become of the members of the upper classes.

Loose scoffers, sceptics, and free thinkers expressed their opinions openly and mostly without opposition. Blasphemous cursing became fashionable, and sectarians and heretics raised their heads boldly. Under Duke Philip the Good the Church had repeatedly to invoke the secular arm and to proceed very rigorously against heretics as, for example, against the *faulx hérétiques Praguois*. At Douai sixteen heretics, including four women, were brought to trial. They were accused of denying the Trinity, of spreading wicked heresies by means of evil books which affirmed that the sacrament was nothing, and that the saints had no power in Paradise. The Church, they said, was only a " bordel ", holy water was an abuse, the sign of the cross deserved no respect, requiem masses were of no value for the dead, and Saturday should be the Sabbath.

Unbelief, like superstition, flourished greatly. Men and women were repeatedly accused of being in league with the devil, or of having injured their kinsmen by his aid. This was particularly the case with women. Carried away by sensual passion, practically without rights, they frequently took refuge in magic arts. Charms must help to win a husband and ensure his love. Charms must remove the consequences of illicit intercourse. Charms could punish the faithless lover and bring about his impotence or the sterility of the hated rival. Dante had already consigned to hell all women who made disreputable wax images and caused other mischiefs.

> . . . le triste che . . .
> Fecer malie con erbe e con imago.

It is remarkable that in contrast to many other *coutumes* the *Somme rurale* of Jehan Boutillier, which originated about the year 1380, and which reproduces the law then current in Northern France and the neighbouring Netherlands, contains special regulations dealing with magicians and the harm done by them.

In vain the urgent command resounded time after time from the pulpit to refrain from every kind of magic ; in vain the pastor from the confessional exhorted the keeping of the first commandment. The book of Guido de Mont-Rocher, widely circulated in France, clearly shows that the efficacy of magic was assumed, and that, being a sinful action, it was strictly forbidden.

Zealous to preserve the purity of the faith, the Inquisition assumed the right to deal with magicians, male and female, and with wizards and witches, who had previously come within the jurisdiction of the secular and episcopal courts. Those accused of *sorcheries* were dragged to the stake, as happened on one occasion at Douai. The Inquisition had frequently to proceed even against priests for practising magic and thus setting a fatal example to the people. The theoretical cult of demonology, found especially among the Dominicans, led naturally to practical experiments. The use of magic books, and all meddling with alchemy and other secret arts was prohibited.

Under the Emperor Constantine in the ancient Roman empire, heathens and heretics were branded as magicians ;

now the position was reversed.   Magicians were declared to
be heretics ; as such they were criminals, whether ecclesiastic
or secular, and worthy of death.

The interest in magic among the circles of the Inquisition
and in the schools was constantly increasing.   Under the
presidency of Gerson, the Sorbonne explicitly declared
that devil worship had a real efficacy, and that all relationship between men and demons, brought about by invocation
of the devil, was idolatry and apostasy.   In the view of the
Inquisition, however, apostasy and idolatry savoured of
heresy, and in the fusion of heresy with magic ingenuity
and fantasy found ample scope.   All opposition, even that
of the Franciscans, was silenced.   Just as once upon a time
the poor of Lyons, the Waldensians and the Knight Templars
had been accused of Satan-worship, so now participation
in the heretical sabbath and synagogue of Satan was ascribed
to those devoted to magic.   Heretics had held their secret
assemblies in order to elude the Church's avenging arm,
and now magicians and witches were accused of similar
practices.   In these assemblies they met their lord and master,
giving him as the sign of their complete submission the
obscene kiss of homage, for the idea of vassalage penetrated
even into these circles.   The incidents of the sabbath were
depicted with the greatest vividness.   A special part in this
was played by the blasphemous abuse of the sacraments,
by illicit intercourse with devils, which came under the head
of bestiality, and by homosexual immorality, all of them
crimina laesae majestatis divinae, and like sodomy, punishable
at the stake.

Consistently with the development of the notion of the
devil's sabbath went that of flight through the air.   The
belief in night-riding women existed from of old in the popular
mind ; the *tabula fortunae* was still laid for them even though
the *Canon episcopi* forbade these superstitions, and confessors uttered warnings against the belief in demons.
Caesarius of Heisterbach, who was much read, could tell
many wonderful tales in this connection, as could also Thomas
of Cantimpré, in his Book of Miracles.   If the magicians
of Pharaoh had been able to change their staffs into serpents,
to bring forth frogs and turn water into blood, why should
not demons, who were much mightier, have the power of

removing men ?   When, after the battle of Mons-en-Pévèle the corpse of Count William of Jülich could not be found, many believed that, thanks to those magic arts which he had cultivated, he had vanished from the earth.   Theologians, even, occupied themselves with these mysteries, and solemn disputations concerning magic were held at Paris.   In time nocturnal levitation was ascribed to the magicians, just as in earlier days it had been ascribed to heretics.   In the fifteenth century canonists were found, who, taking their stand upon trials, confessions, and evidence of witnesses, declared that the witches' sabbath-ride was an established fact, and tracts were written whose sole object was to turn delusive visions into scientific truths.

The age, which regarded the non-virginal woman who led a sexual life as the immoral seductress of men and an altogether inferior being, was content naturally to draw the vilest deductions ; while men as a whole still offered successful resistance to the powers of evil, women were always to be found ready and willing to serve the devil as concubines. The authors of the *Malleus maleficarum*, which in its deprecia-tion of woman outdistanced even Jean de Meung, had the hardihood to declare later that the name alone revealed woman's true character since *femina* was derived from *fe* and *minus* and women had and kept inferior faith.

Nicolas Jacquier the Dominican, a native of Burgundy, and inquisitor in Northern France, published in 1458 his *Flagellum haereticorum fascinariorum* with the special intention of proving the reality of the witches' sabbath-ride against all attacks.   Demons, the founders of all abominable sects, seduced the weaker brethren and led them to regard every-thing practised by magicians as a dreamer's illusion. Jacquier, however, has much to say concerning the infamous crimes of heretics, of their wicked sabbath practices, how they profaned the Holy Sacrament, and brought bad weather and sickness to their fellows.

Superstition was by no means confined to the lower classes.   Pope John XXII and Benedict XII, both natives of southern France, the promised land of witchcraft, had an extraordinary faith in magic.   They proceeded very vigorously against magicians and smoothed the path for the Inquisition.   Pope John pledged all his wealth to the Countess de Foix for a marvellous serpent's horn, with the aid of which food and drink could be very thoroughly tested for poison, and sent the bishop of his native town to the stake on a charge of attempting his life by diabolical means.

The witchcraft trials at the French Royal Court offer a counterpart to those at the Curia. France, and with it the famous University of Paris, the dictator of the world of learning, had fallen a victim to the witchcraft delusion, and cultivated scholastic demonology with avidity. The trial of Enguerrand de Marigny under King Louis X created a very painful sensation, and the fearful charge was hurled later against a princess of the blood. When King Charles VI became insane, it was commonly believed that magical plots had caused his derangement. His brother, Louis of Orleans, was conversant with wizards, and did not desist, in spite of serious exhortations, from occupying himself with secret arts. Thus, unconsciously, he provided material for the accusations brought against him after his murder, and Jean Petit in his Justification made the most of these magical dealings. In contrast with Duke Philip the Good, his son Charles the Bold believed in the efficacy of magic, resembling in this respect the French King Louis XI, who was altogether sunk in superstition. Charles was convinced that his foes desired to *envouter* him, to kill him with one of those small diabolical wax figures christened with his name. When the Count of Nevers was expelled from the Order of the Golden Fleece, it was said that his expulsion was due to heresy and witchcraft.

There was of course a certain amount of opposition, but no one paid much attention to it. Martin Le Franc in his *Champion des Dames* makes mention of sorcery; the *Adversaire* presents the accusations, the *Champion* the defence. The *Adversaire* gives a vivid description of the sabbath.

> Dis mille vielles en ung fouch
> Y avoit-il communément,
> En fourme de chat ou de bouch
> Veans le dyable proprement,
> Auquel baisoient franchement
> Le cul en signe d'obéissance,
> Renyans Dieu tout plainement
> Et toute sa haulte puissance.
> Là faisoient choses diverses :
> Les unes du dyable aprenoient

Arts et sorceryes perverses,
Dont plusieurs maulx elles faisoient.
Aux aultres les danses plaisoient
Et aux plusieurs mengier et boire ;
Là en habondance trouvoient
De tout plus qu'on ne porroit croire.
Le dyable souvent les preschoit,
Et qui se vouloit repentir,
Trop durement il le tenchoit
Ou le batoit sans alentir.
Mais à tous ceulx, qui consentir
Vouloient à tous ses plaisirs,
Il promettoit sans rient mentir
Le comble de tous leurs désirs.

  .   .   .   .

Chacun tel honneur lui faisoit
Comme à Dieu ; aussy le faulx gars
Ungs et aultres resjouissoit
Par paroles et par regars.
Et sachiez qu'en la départye
Chacun sa chascune prenoit,
Et s'aucune n'estoit lotye
D'homme, ung dyable luy sourvenoit.
Puis ung chascun s'en revenoit
Comme vent sur son bastonchel . . .
. . . O Dieu quel horreur !
Vray Dieu, que la coulpe est notable !
O Vray Dieu Jhésus quel erreur !
La femme est mariée au dyable !

The *Champion*, however, does not allow himself to be led
astray and declares all bedevilment to be a figment of the
imagination ; it is not possible to fly on a stick.

Ja ne croiray tant que je vive
Que femme corporellement
Voit par l'air comme merle ou grive !

The poet dedicated his work to Philip the Good, but he had
no luck with it. It was not even read to the Duke, for the
courtiers took exception to its bitterness and critical atmosphere.
But it was a brave start, for as a rule the doubter who went
his own way did so at his own peril. We need only take the
case of Guillaume Edeline, Doctor of Theology and Prior of
Clairvaux in Franche-Comté. He had supported the Papacy
at the Council of Basle and had taught for a time at the
University of Paris, but had so far forgotten himself as to
declare that the witches' sabbath existed only in the imagination. Brought before the court of the Inquisition, he
confessed that he himself was a Vaudois, and that he had

made the shameless allegation at the instigation of the devil. Only this complete confession saved him from the stake; but he had to rue his words in close imprisonment on a diet of bread and water.

Upheld by decrees of the Curia, by Pope Eugenius IV, and by imperial and royal enactments, the Inquisition raised its head more proudly and relentlessly than before. Its measures against its opponents became ever stricter. Even secular jurisdiction had to give place to it, until finally the edict went forth that whoever did not submit unreservedly to the principle and rules of the Inquisition was a suborner of heresy and himself a heretic.

Mankind, stirred to its depth by the horrors of the Hundred Years War, was peculiarly apt to be deluded by the devil. This, at least, was the opinion of a contemporary, the learned professor Peter Mamoris of Poitiers. How had Joan of Arc fared ? She had suffered at the stake as a witch, her crime being that she had fought for her King with unshakable trust in God. The re-examination of her case had, indeed, restored her honour; but for many she still remained the devil's concubine.

A few years after her rehabilitation, a terrible rumour became current in French and Burgundian territories that the Vaudois, a new sect, were practising their devilish activities in the province of Artois. As to the name itself, contemporaries were already asking themselves how it arose. One chronicler remarks, " *ne sçay à quel propos.*" The " *Vodeis* " are first met with in Alpine lands. A variety of circumstances contributed to the formation of the name: there were the accusations that the older Waldensians, the poor of Lyons, likewise, had already celebrated the nocturnal devils' sabbath; secondly, the custom in Swiss territory of describing those men who gave themselves up to unnatural practices, as " *Vodois* "; and finally, the recollection that in the Pays de Vaud, in the Waadt, the summit of a mountain was selected for the assembly of the communes, a preference said to be shared also by heretics. After 1440, in which year Pope Eugenius IV in a Bull against heresy, makes mention of the " *Waudenses* ", the name quickly penetrated into French-speaking territory.

The process which brought about this result was lengthy

PLATE 21

Unknown Master: Witches' Sabbath. Miniature: Traittié du crisme de vaulderie.
Bibliothèque Nationale MS. franç. 961, Paris.

and involved. A variety of circumstances contributed, some advancing, others retarding and obstructing the movement. Old superstitions and popular delusions were revived, and to these were added religious mania, fantastic investigations into metaphysics, the speculations of theoretical theologians, the weight of secular and canon law, the decisions of the episcopal and synodal courts, and the relentless procedure of the Inquisition.

It was romanticism which aroused the enthusiasm for the golden age of knighthood and castles, but when it dragged forth from the chronicles all the old tales of ghastliness and horror, the Vauderie of Arras was reborn. Tieck founded his tale " The Witches' Sabbath " upon it.

In the Chapel *degli Spagnuoli* in Santa Maria Novella in Florence, a picture can still be seen which has for its basis the teachings of St. Thomas Aquinas. The *ecclesia militans* and the *ecclesia triumphans* are both represented. One detail attracts the visitor's special attention. Black and white spotted dogs are seen rushing about in all directions in pursuit of wolves. These are the *domini canes,* whose duty it was to track heretics. The citizens of Arras might well have hung a similar picture in any one of their churches.

At a chapter of Dominicans held at Langres in 1459, a hermit was condemned to the stake for heresy. Before his death he accused certain people living in Arras of *Vauderie.* Scarcely had he returned to his jurisdiction when the Inquisitor of Arras, Pierre Le Broussard, a Dominican and doctor of divinity, procured the arrest of the accused, a prostitute Deniselle, and Jehan Lavite, a man in the sixties, known far and wide as the Abbé de Peu-de-Sens.

The question was disputed as to whether the testimony of a magician could be accepted as proof, but in general practice, as in this case, the evidence was admitted, since how otherwise in the interests of the Faith could guilt be detected ? Deniselle and Lavite were both brought to the episcopal prison. The former demanded to know why she was deprived of her liberty. She was mocked and asked whether she knew the hermit. " *Et que chechy ? cuide-t-on que je sois vauldoise ?* " Torture soon showed what was required from her. The man, too, knew well what was in store for him.

Jehan Lavite, painter and rhetorician, had travelled far and wide : he wrote poetry and sang his own songs and ballads in honour of God and the saints, especially in honour of the Holy Virgin, thereby winning much favour. His friends esteemed him highly ; in their circle in one of the numerous societies founded for mirth and entertainment, he occupied the fool's post as " *Abbé de Peu-de-Sens* ", which allowed him a good deal of licence and a certain liberty of speech. It was his custom when he finished his performance to take off his hat and say : " *Ne déplaise à mon maître,*" and these words were his ruin. When he realized that he was looked upon as the Chief Rabbi of the Vaudois, he attempted to cut off his tongue, lest he should condemn himself out of his own mouth, but he only succeeded in wounding himself so severely that for a considerable time he was unable to speak. As he could use a pen he was forced to put down his statements in writing.

The bishop was then Jean Jouffroy, who was shortly afterwards raised to be cardinal, but as he was frequently entrusted with diplomatic tasks he happened to be in Rome at this time. His suffragan was a Minorite, the titular bishop John of Beyrout.

The vicars and the secretary of the bishop, as well as the archdeacon and the official and another canon acted as examining judges. The greatest interest centred, however, around the dean of the Chapter, Master Jacques Dubois, doctor of divinity, a young man whose excitability might well be calculated to lead him astray.

The usual procedure of the Inquisition was employed and officially instituted. The old accusatory methods of the canon law were relinquished. The trial took place " *summarie, simpliciter et de plano absque advocatorum et judiciorum strepitu et figura* ". Suspicion justified the arrest. The names of the witnesses were not given to the accused ; no evidence was excluded, whether from the lips of a relative, an accomplice, or a person who in the eye of the law was incapable of testifying. It was essential that a confession should be procured, since without it no condemnation could take place. The judges were provided with practical hints as to the methods to be adopted. The *Directorium inquisitorum* of Nicolaus Eymericus, the Dominican and Inquisitor General of Aragon, was the standard text-book, and was in almost universal use. This work, known as " the golden book ", assisted in making the inventive theories of the schoolmen intelligible to practitioners, and its principal thesis that witchcraft was to be pursued as heresy secured for it a first place in the inquisitorial library. Eymericus advocated the most questionable methods ; lying and threats, promises and misrepresentations, were all to be resorted to in order to extort a confession. It followed as a matter of precedent that everybody suspected of heresy was asked the same questions, with the extraordinary result that the confessions obtained in the most diverse places and countries were almost identical in form, a condition of things which was easily explainable, but which greatly astounded the inquisitors who were driven to the false conclusion that a new sect had sprung up and had spread throughout the world.

It was under these conditions that Arras witnessed a very grotesque and amazing manifestation, an affair, the details of which are known to us not only from Martin Le Franc but from other sources as well.

The rack was employed as the principal means of making the accused condemn himself. Just as Roman law had tolerated the torture of those accused of *lèse majesté*, so torture was employed unmercifully and arbitrarily against high and low, rich and poor, old and young in all cases of heresy, an offence which was regarded everywhere as *crimen laesae majestatis*. The claims of the Faith were supreme and knew no exceptions. Pope Innocent IV in his time had permitted torture. It was finally introduced into heresy trials through the Clementines. Confessions extorted on the rack were considered as providing new and important facts. The torture could not be repeated ; but if obstinacy on the part of the accused made necessary a second or third application, this was considered as a continuation of the original torment and in no sense a fresh proceeding. For sensitive natures imprisonment before trial, frequently of very long duration, was torture in itself. Hunger in a dark cell loosens the tongue, was the opinion of one inquisitor. Special torments designed

for the prison were added to those inflicted by the apparitors
and executioner's assistants. The sufferings reserved for
women were peculiarly revolting, for in the search for the
witches' mark every particle of hair had to be removed from
the body.

Punishment increased in severity according to the crime.
If the victims appeared for the first time before the Inquisition, showed repentance and abjured their errors, they were
dealt with by the Church and sentenced to pilgrimage, to
wear a penitential crucifix, or to imprisonment, which might
be for life :—mercy which was no mercy, for the " waters of
sorrow " were bitter enough and the " bread of affliction "
exceedingly hard. If, however, the heretics remained
obstinate and unrepentant, the Church handed them over to
the secular arm for punishment : *ecclesia non sitit sanguinem*.
This punishment was invariably death : in France, from
the very beginning, death at the stake. If the secular judges
attempted a show of independence they could be coerced
into submission by excommunication and interdict.

In an age accustomed to severe and merciless laws men
watched with dread and apprehension the development of
a system which left the accused scarcely any hope of escape.
Over the door of the tribunal of Arras, Dante's words
might have been inscribed in letters of fire : *Lasciate ogni
speranza voi ch'entrate*.

Deniselle and Lavite could not face their torture. They
confessed their misdeeds and admitted having been present
at the witches' sabbath. Deniselle remembered seeing
the Abbé de Peu-de-Sens at the place of meeting. The old
man collapsed and made accusations against all kinds of
people, from honourable folk to prostitutes.

The prisons now commenced to be filled. The affair
assumed such dimensions that the vicars became frightened.
They wanted to abandon the matter and to release the
prisoners. The dean, however, convinced of the reality of
witches' rides and sabbaths violently opposed such a step,
and found in the suffragan, an ardent smeller-out of heretics,
a most passionate supporter. These two vied with each
other in zeal and orthodoxy.

The suffragan John of Beyrout was a very notable man. In Rome in 1450, the Jubilee year, he had filled the post of papal penitentiary. He claimed to possess an infallible eye for heretics. He needed to look at a man once only to discover whether he had been at a *Vauderie*, that is, at a witches' sabbath or not. He showed himself here the docile pupil of Eymericus, who in his study of external characteristics had discovered that a pale complexion disclosed a heretic and that a wild glance was the certain token of a magician.

Like the dean he scented heretics everywhere. Bishops, prelates, even cardinals, were heretics. There were so many that if they could but agree to appoint a king or prince over them, they would certainly usurp the government and oppress the world. The dean for his part told anyone who would listen that a third part of Christianity was heretical; such terrible happenings had he encountered that he could not relate them. Whoever was accused of heresy was by that accusation a heretic; heretics could accuse no one who was not so. Recantation under torture before death was valueless. The devil compelled his servants to act thus, for he desired at any price to send them to hell. It was very significant that the Vaudois, even when they knew they were to be accused as such, lacked the power to escape. No one could help a suspect, neither relative nor friend, unless he himself desired to be accused. If anybody, even a cleric, raised a voice in protest, the dean would prosecute him at once as a Vaudois.

In order to encourage the vicars, the bishop and dean summoned the secular power to their aid. At their instigation, Count John of Etampes, Captain General of Philip the Good in Picardy, issued the strictest injunctions to the vicars that they were to proceed against all heretics, failing which he would hold them personally responsible.

The vicars still hesitated. They laid the matter before two highly respected clerics at Cambrai, the aged dean and the official of Notre-Dame. These were of opinion, it was rumoured, that if the prisoners, being innocent of murder and not having abused the Holy Sacrament, would retract, their lives, in the first place at least, should be spared. But the bishop of Beyrout and dean Dubois would have none of this. They demanded unconditionally that sentence of

death should be pronounced not only on Deniselle and
Lavite, but also on those whom they had denounced, provided
that three or four witnesses could be found to testify against
them.

The vicars, to whom fresh orders had been sent by the
Count of Etampes to advance the trial, now summoned
all the clergy of the city, the canons and chaplains,
Dominicans, Minorites, and Carmelites, secular priests,
as well as two advocates from Beauquesne. Documents
were produced ; not a voice was raised in protest, and destiny
took its course.

On 9th May, 1460, a lofty scaffold was erected in the
courtyard of the episcopal palace. It was visible from afar,
and crowds hastened thither from town and country for the
last act in the terrible drama. Deniselle, Lavite, and the
others were dragged to the place of execution, accompanied
by a corpse which was carried by the executioner's assistants,
for the sergeant of the aldermen had hanged himself in
prison by the strap of his chaperon, or had been hanged
there lest he should accuse others.

The dreadful business then began. Mitres were clapped
on to the heads of Deniselle, the Abbé de Peu-de-Sens and
the other victims. On them were pictures representing
the crimes to which they had confessed : abandoned by God,
a man was seen kneeling before the devil, paying him homage.

The inquisitor then commenced his speech and reported
the disclosures made during the trial. First of all, to
accomplish their diabolical work, the criminals had used
a salve of supernatural power. In order to concoct this, they
recoiled from no enormity. They laid hands on the consecrated wafer and gave the Holiest of Holies to toads as
nourishment. The toads were then burned, and powder
distilled from the bones of persons who had been hanged,
as well as herbs and the blood of innocent young children
were added to the ashes. For this purpose Lavite had killed
two children and Deniselle her own child. Only a small
staff and the hands and soles of the feet needed to be smeared
with this salve, whereupon the staff placed between its
owner's legs, would go galloping away over towns and woods
and waters to the sabbath. The meeting was held at three
fixed spots, in the light of day, after the midday meal. They

could be reached comfortably on foot. At the *Vauderie*, the devil, in the shape of a goat, of a dog, of a monkey, at times even of a man, awaited his lieges. Homage and adoration took place under the leadership of Abbé de Peu-de-Sens. Each one knelt down before the Prince of Hell and gave him his soul and presented him with a portion of his body, a finger-nail at least, or a few hairs. Thereupon he gave expression to his subjection by solemnly kissing, burning candles in hand, the posterior of the diabolical animal. Finally, as proof that he had fallen away from the faith, he trampled and spat upon the Cross and made an obscene gesture accompanied by blasphemous words. Shameful orgies followed, sexual intercourse with the devil, who appeared at one time as a man, at another as a woman. Abominable and infamous crimes were committed, of such a character that the inquisitor dared not name them for fear of leading the innocent astray.

In a telling sermon the devil then summed up his teaching : prohibition of church attendance, of the sacrifice of the Holy Mass, of confession, and of Holy Water. If his listeners were obliged to enter a house of God to avoid becoming conspicuous they were to utter the words : " *Ne déplaise à mon maître.*" Man had no soul ; only on this earth was there life. Woe to him who desired to break with the devil. He would be flogged with an ox-hide so unmercifully that the memory of it would be with him to his dying day.

The inquisitor had now finished ; he had dispensed with all attempts at scholastic ingenuity ; his simple unlearned words were comprehensible to everyone. One more question followed. Each heretic was asked if the inquisitor had spoken justly ; and each one answered : " Yes."

Amidst breathless silence judgment was then read out in Latin and in French. The infamous heretics were to be handed over to the temporal jurisdiction as foul creatures unworthy of living in company with the members of Holy Church. Their inheritance was seized in favour of God, and their chattels in favour of the bishop.

The constables of the various jurisdictions at once seized the accused. Deniselle was carried to Douai for execution, Lavite and the others were brought before the judges in Arras itself ; all were condemned to be burnt at the stake.

These sentences must have occasioned a good deal of surprise. A certain degree of mercy had generally been shown to repentant sinners, but in the course of time the methods had become increasingly severe. In order to avoid any question of pardon it had been laid down that persons found guilty were not in fact repentant; alternatively, that their repentance was assumed or had been made only in fear of punishment and not with any serious desire for improvement. The judges' discretion was entirely unrestricted, and in Arras full use was made of their powers.

The despairing women broke out into screams and lamentations. They heaped accusation after accusation upon the advocate, who had taken part in their cross-examination, and was supposed to give them legal aid if necessary. " Base traitor, you counselled us to confess what we were told to say, for then we were to be freed and only punished by being sentenced to undertake a short pilgrimage a few miles from the city." Never had they been at a *Vauderie* ; all their confessions had been extorted solely by torture and under threat of the stake, or by the tricks and promises of the advocate and priests. But nothing could save them, and the executioner seized his prey. The women protested their innocence to the end ; they confessed their sins and begged the populace to have masses said for their salvation. The Abbé de Peu-de-Sens retracted everything, alleging that cruel wrong was being done to him. As the flames enveloped him he broke out into the words :—*Jesus autem transiens per medium illorum ibat.*

The people were wholly unconvinced of the guilt of the victims and became restless and began to murmur. The judges considered it advisable to publish their justification : the " *Recollectio casus, status et condictionis Valdensium ydolatrarum* ". The author of this work is unnamed, but he was probably in close touch with the inquisitor Pierre Le Broussard, if the inquisitor himself was not the writer. The reasoning follows the same line of thought as was taken by the inquisitor in his sermon. But everything is treated in much greater detail and attempts are made to prove the reality of the witches' ride and of the incidents at the sabbath.

Full details are given of the misdeeds of the Vaudois ; arson, damage to vineyards, fields and meadows by hailstorm, the poisoning of streams and wells, acts of vengeance on their enemies, infanticide, concoction of love-potions, and so on.

The use of torture is defended on the ground that the accused had obstinately refused to confess or to name their accomplices. It was the devil who supported them and closed their mouths so that he should not be deprived of his prey. Thus the devil rather than the human being was at fault, and consequently the rack was fully justified. It was also at the devil's instigation that the accused retracted their confessions at the stake. From many details it is obvious that the author was present at the examination. " *Va de par le dyable, va* " or " *Sathan n'oublye pas ta mamye* ", exclaimed the Vaudois at the beginning of the nocturnal ride. The devil, being the father of arrogance, received the lower classes unwillingly into his sect, but was greatly concerned to win over those of high rank. He is described in great detail, with large fearful eyes, darting fire, a voice like the sound of a trumpet. His speech was the speech of a drunken man. No warm blood coursed through his veins, and his body being soft and cold was generated from evil-smelling vapours.

Finally the condemnation of the guilty is emphasized and justified. Deniselle had murdered a child, and the Abbé de Peu-de-Sens had committed several murders. The judges are earnestly exhorted to remember the transitoriness of earthly joys, and to show honour to the eternal and true God by waging relentless war against the devil.

Master Jehan Taincture of Tournai, a very celebrated man of learning, who had at one time taught at Cologne, also took part in the controversy and in a sermon scourged the crimes of the Vaudois. He calls upon Christian princes and judges, and admonishes them to gather in the tares and burn them. " Remember that it is not for nothing that you wear a sword." Would Charlemagne, the unconquerable prince of the Franks, be held in such honoured memory beyond all other rulers of the earth, if he had not with God's help made safe the boundaries of Christianity and overthrown and destroyed her enemies ?

There is a very impressive passage in a French revision of the sermon : " If *Vauderie,* which is worse than the idol worship of pagans, more infamous than the sin of heresy and the unbelief of the Saracens, should take root, State and society would collapse, the wicked would triumphantly usurp all sovereign power, and godly, humble people might go begging in despair. Men would murder one another in terrible wars, friends attack one another, children resist the old and wise, the *vilains* would band together against the nobility, and the abominations of Sodom would be revived. Then would come the days foretold by the prophet Daniel : Antichrist would draw near. Therefore must the whole world combine for the destruction of the Vaudois ; prelates and priests and all princes must fight against them."

A reign of terror now broke out in Arras. One imprisonment followed another. Wealthy citizens, magistrates, even a nobleman and knight, Payen de Beauffort, who belonged to one of the oldest and most distinguished families of the countship, were thrown into the episcopal prison. Beauffort as well as Master Antoine Sacquespée, a municipal magistrate, had been warned, but remained in Arras, protesting their innocence. Beauffort, who in his pious zeal had founded three cloisters, declared that if he were a thousand miles away he would return to Arras to meet his accusers. Others behaved in a more practical manner. When soon afterwards, before the magistrates had passed the death sentence, the stake blazed for a second time, two wealthy men fled to Paris, which was somewhat remarkable, since the Dean had expressly declared that anyone conscious of being a Vaudois was deprived of the power to escape.

The tribunal was now enlarged still further. Duke Philip appointed his confessor, the aged Dominican and titular bishop of Siliwri (Selimbria), the Count d'Etampes and among others, the knight Philippe de Saveuses, a great zealot. The inquisitor of Tournai was added to them. The Curia observed restraint. Politics and the private and selfish motives of individuals were exploited to fan the flames of fanaticism and superstition.

A terrible oppression weighed down the whole city. Many

did not dare to leave it even for a few days for fear of being suspected of trying to avoid pursuit. Paris and the whole of France became attentive. While the Vaudois who had been arrested in other towns were set free again, the prisons in Arras continued to be filled. Its inhabitants were regarded with distrust. No one cared to have anything to do with them. Merchants lost their credits and nobody would lend them money, for if they were unmasked as heretics, their wealth was confiscated and their creditors received nothing.

The vicars recognized the danger. As they had sought to influence public opinion by writings, so they now attempted to justify their procedure by sermons. No one, they said, would be imprisoned without cause ; and there must be at least eight, even ten witnesses to secure a conviction. But their utterances were unheeded. It was well known that frequently only one or two, or at the most three witnesses, sufficed to bring citizens under the most terrible suspicion.

The vicars therefore were constrained to act with violence. On one occasion the son of a fugitive appeared with a Parisian notary at Matins in Notre-Dame, and handed the vicars an appeal to the *Parlement* of Paris. The couple escaped from the city, but were caught on the way, thrown into prison, and shamefully treated ; nor were they liberated until the appeal had been withdrawn. It was clear that the vicars would not countenance any appeal from the combined court of the bishop and the Inquisition.

The most exquisite and illegal tortures were employed. An accused when handed to the executioner might appear to have his eyes covered, but he could see enough to frighten him into confession. Huguet Aubry, who languished for eleven months in prison, was tortured fifteen times at intervals. He was thrown into the river as if he were to be drowned. On another occasion he was hung from a tree with his eyes bandaged. The limbs of the unfortunate man were dislocated, his soles burned with candles, and water and even oil and vinegar were poured down his throat.

The vicars recognized, however, that the trial of the knight would have to be conducted with prudence ; it was too dangerous to incur the hatred of aristocratic society. As fit priests for various reasons, which were probably excuses, refused their invitation to come to Arras, they sent envoys

to Duke Philip.   This placed the Duke in a delicate position.
As champion of the Faith he neither desired nor dared
to spare heretics.   On the other hand, the rumours that the
persecutions were being conducted in order to secure for him
the estates of the victims were distasteful to the Duke.
He had to reckon with the possibility that the *Parlement*
of Paris might intervene on political grounds at any time,
and he determined to leave the matter to the scholars.
He invited the most famous professors of the university
of Louvain and other well-known personages to a session at
Brussels, but the old proverb " so many men, so many
counsels " upset their deliberations.   " Some said that
Vauderie did not exist : others that it was imagined, as might
be read in the *Canon episcopi*.   It was conceded that if by
the will of God a certain amount of reality was extant, there
was too much scope for the imagination ; the accused could
not have done everything they believed themselves to have
done.   Others again were of opinion that *Vauderie* was real ;
and that if anybody dedicated himself to the devil, God
permitted that the prince of hell should obtain such power
over him that he could lead him to *Vauderie* or anywhere
else."

The final decision of the learned gentlemen is unknown.
It appears that the sceptics gained the upper hand, for it
was noticed shortly afterwards in Arras that, in spite of
fresh accusations, no more arrests were made, and that
prisoners were treated less rigorously.

In order to obtain a trustworthy report on the whole matter
Duke Philip dispatched his confidant, Toison d'Or, the Lord
of Saint-Remy, to Arras.   The vicars were enjoined to send
the documents of the pending trial to Brussels.   When these
were returned the president of the Parliament of Ypres
appeared at Arras.   Politics were interposed, lest *Vauderie*
should develop into an important affair of State.

On 22nd October, 1460, the third Auto-da-fé took place.
Once again a huge crowd was present, since it was known
that the knight was to be sentenced.   He appeared with
three others on the scaffold.   The inquisitor of Cambrai
preached the sermon on this occasion.   The unfortunate
words " *Ne déplaise à mon maître* " again played a part ;
the devil had ordered one of the accused to use them each

time he went to church. Great astonishment was displayed at hearing that Beauffort, who had always insisted upon his innocence, had confessed everything voluntarily, without torture. No mitre was therefore placed on his head, as with the others.

The judgment was comparatively merciful. As a heretic, apostate and worshipper of idols, the knight was sentenced to be whipped on his shoulders, not, however, bared, to be imprisoned for seven years, and in addition he was heavily fined. The fines ran into thousands, whereas the knight's revenues were only estimated at five hundred pounds yearly. Huguet Aubry, a wealthy magistrate, who in spite of all the torments of the rack had confessed nothing, escaped, as did the third Vaudois, with imprisonment. The fourth victim alone, since he showed no repentance, was handed over to secular jurisdiction and suffered at the stake.

He was the fourteenth and last victim. The sequel showed that a complete change of outlook was approaching. The prisoners were gradually released on condition that they bore the expenses of their imprisonment and paid the costs of the proceedings. An exception was made only in the case of those entirely without means. The prostitute Belotte owed her life entirely to chance, or to the intervention of a protector. She would have been burned, but her mitre was not ready in time and she was returned to prison. A few of the accused were required to bring witnesses to prove their honourable lives, and no notice was taken of the fact that these witnesses included men who had themselves been suspected of *Vauderie*. Others were banished from the city ; a woman had to undertake a short pilgrimage ; one man, the soles of whose feet had been burned during torture and who had languished in a dungeon seven months, had to make good all the expenses of his imprisonment and pay the costs of the Inquisition in spite of the sufferings he had endured. Even a rich timber merchant, a *mangeur de pauvres gens* whose death would have been regretted by few, escaped with his life, ill-famed as he was. The opponents of the Inquisition now ventured out into the open and ridiculed the witches' sabbath and ride as nonsense. Strips of paper were to be found in the streets bearing audacious and satirical verses :—

Les traitons remplis de grande envie,
De convoitise et de venin couvers,
Ont fait regner ne sçay quelle vaulderie,
Pour cuider prendre à tort et à travers
Les biens d'aulcuns notables et expers
Avec leur corps, leurs femmes et chevanche,
Et mettre à mort des gens d'estat divers.
Hach, noble Arras, tu as bien eu l'advanche.

The dean had to listen to this :—

Mais garde toy avec tes compagnons,
Je te promets, nous d'Arras te ferons
Et à Barut dansser si belle danse.

Nor were the bishop of Siliwri and Pierre Le Broussard
to be spared. Rigorous punishment of the guilty was
demanded :

Et vous avez touts la puche en l'oreille . . .
Que maudit soit le cœur qui vous traveille ! . . .
Mais vous serez touts pugnis en ung tas,
Et sçaurons touts qui esmeut la merveille
De mettre sus les vauldois en Arras.

The inquisitor, vicars and bishop's secretary had been
concerned alone in these final measures. Neither the bishop
of Beyrout, nor the dean, nor the Lord de Saveuses was
called in : they kept themselves in fact sedulously in the
background. Possibly a higher authority had bestowed
a hint that they would do well to keep silent.

Possibly, too, the powerful Lords de Croy, the opponents
of Saveuses, succeeded in preventing further inquiries in
which they too might also be implicated. Again, in view of
their good relations with the French King, the intervention
of the *Parlement* of Paris, the supreme court of appeal in
France, may have been their work. For the *Parlement*
was only too ready to remind the Duke of Burgundy that
in spite of the plenitude of his power, the King of France was
his overlord. By the King's order an apparitor arrived at
Arras, forcibly liberated the Lord de Beauffort on the strength
of his appeal, and summoned the vicars to Paris. When the
case came before the court there in June, 1461, the advocate
Jehan de Popincourt launched the most violent accusations
against the inquisitors. It was now revealed that Beauffort's
confession, which had caused such universal surprise, had

been extorted by a trick. The teachings of the *Directorium* of Eymericus had in no sense been forgotten.

Popincourt alleged that in order to induce the Lord of Beauffort to confess, the dean, falling on his knees before him, implored him to acknowledge everything, for only thus could he save him. He would be liberated in four days without the indignity of the mitre or suffering the shame of a public sermon. When the Lord of Beauffort objected that to admit his guilt would be to commit perjury the dean promised him absolution and finally succeeded in making the knight forswear himself and declare that he was guilty. By what right, asked the advocate, could the judges demand from Beauffort four thousand francs for the Duke, two thousand francs for the Count d'Etampes or any other sums whatsoever ?

The Lord of Beauffort received his freedom and together with his fellow victims brought an action against the inquisitor, the vicars, and the other judges. Upon this the dean, Jacques Dubois, collapsed, and losing his reason, died shortly afterwards in great torment. Many regarded this as a punishment of God, while others spoke of poison. The bishop of Beyrout, too, fared badly at first. As one of the principal parties in the proceedings he was thrown into prison, but he contrived to escape and later to procure a privileged position at Court as confessor to the Queen Mother of France.

When at length bishop Jean Jouffroy returned to Arras he censured the proceedings of the Inquisition and dismissed Pierre du Hamel from the office of vicar. He received in the presence of the latter, the complaints of one of the accused, who alleged that he had been forced to denounce even him, the bishop, together with other honourable persons, as Vaudois.

The investigations of the *Parlement* of Paris proceeded very slowly, probably from political reasons, since it was a delicate business to bring an inquisitor to account for his official actions before a secular court. It was only after thirty years, on 21st May, 1491, that judgment was pronounced. The Lord of Beauffort and the majority of the other complainants had died in the meantime ; Huguet Aubry alone survived to see the day which restored his

honour.   All the judgments of the Inquisition were quashed,
the documents were ordered to be destroyed, all confiscations
were annulled, and the condemned were rehabilitated.   The
Duke of Burgundy and the other defendants, the bishop of
Arras and the clerical judges were ordered to pay com-
pensation and costs.   All clerical and secular judges were
strictly forbidden to employ illegal tortures in future.   From
the fines there was instituted in Arras Cathedral, in expiation
of the past, a daily requiem which was always heralded by
three times eleven peals.   A stone crucifix fifteen feet high
was to be erected to perpetuate the judgment of the
Parlement.

The expiation was as sensational as the deed.   The
proclamation of the judgment was fixed for the middle of
a popular festival.   Upon the arrival of the royal commissary, the population was summoned by heralds to cease
all work under threats of severe punishment, and to appear
punctually at the ceremony which took place on Monday,
18th July, 1491.

In solemn procession the commissary, a counsellor of the
Parlement of Paris, attended by royal and municipal
officials, together with the grandson of the Lord of Beauffort,
Huguet Aubry, and others concerned, proceeded to the
courtyard of the episcopal palace.   A scaffolding was erected
on the very spot where once the unfortunates had been
pilloried as heretics with the hat of shame upon their heads.
In a sermon of several hours' duration the Paris professor
Broussard preached on the text : " *Erudimini qui judicatis
terram.*"   The judgment was read aloud in the presence of
many thousands who had streamed thither from far and wide.
After the midday meal morality plays were performed in
front of the " Scales " where the officials had gathered.
Prizes, amongst others a silver lily, were presented to the best
players in a *follie moralisée* and in a *pure follie.*

Thus this terrible ordeal was brought to its conclusion
amidst the jubilation and the joyous uproar of the crowd.

Jacques Du Clercq narrated these events in his diary
with touching simplicity.   He declined to pass judgment ;
" *je m'en attens à Dieu qui tout sçait.*"

CHAPTER XI

Se tu parles d'art de paintrye,
D'istoriens, d'enlumineurs,
D'entailleurs par grande maistrye,
En fut il oncques de meilleurs ?

MARTIN LE FRANC.

THE revolt of Ghent, the proud and arrogant, had been suppressed ; the rebels were laid low. Once again absolute sovereignity had conquered that communal particularism which presumed on ancient and obsolete privileges. The dawning era forced its way into every phase of life. Both sides had fought with the utmost bitterness. Lust of blood and obstinacy had driven the insurgents to grave excesses. Both sides had incurred severe losses ; Duke Philip mourned the loss of a son, the bastard Corneille, and Jacques de Lalaing, the ideal Burgundian knight. The people of Ghent mourned not only the citizens who had died on the field of battle, but also many who had fallen victims to popular tyranny. The peace of Gavere put an end to the bloodshed, but the severest terms were imposed by the Duke. The men who now held the reins of power at Ghent left no stone unturned to restore friendly relations with their ruler, and finally succeeded in inducing Duke Philip in April, 1458, to honour with his presence the town which he had not entered for the last ten years. A royal reception was prepared for him, a reception which was to surpass everything of its kind.

In order still further to stimulate the citizens' ardour, costly prizes were offered to the chambers of rhetoricians, the gilds, and the city districts and wards for the finest achievement and the best reproduction of a *battement*. No expense was spared ; towers and gates, houses and streets were splendidly decorated in black, grey and red, the ducal colours, and the Duke's coat of arms with his device and watchword were present everywhere. There were to be pageants, shows, and allegories to soften the ruler's heart, and at night torches and candles were displayed in their thousands. A glorification, an apotheosis of the ruler, took place, to which the Court of Burgundy was not altogether unaccustomed. Duke Philip was greeted as the Messiah with texts from the Old Testament, while prophets jubilantly announced the delight of a people whose tears were scarcely dry.

Repentance and submission were emphasized again and again : the prodigal son prostrated himself in penitence before his father ; at the feet of King David, angered by Nabal, knelt Abigail, in all her charm, imploring pardon for her husband. Humble devotion was thus openly expressed, but with it was the hope of mercy. On his knees a senator paid homage to Julius Caesar, the traditional founder of the city of Ghent ; again, Pompey was seen magnanimously pardoning the King of Armenia who had revolted against the Romans. But these tableaux from ancient history, beautiful as they were, were overshadowed by a magnificent production showing the redemption of mankind by the Saviour, the Lamb of God, who bore the sins of the world.

The chamber of rhetoricians had erected a large three-storied tribune, 50 feet long and 28 feet deep, hung with blue cloth. When, on the arrival of the Duke-Count, the white curtains were drawn back God the Father was seen on high with the triple crown and sceptre, the imperial crown at his feet, on his right hand the Virgin with glittering diadem, on his left John the Baptist. At the two ends choirs of angels sang and played.

A costly altar with the Lamb of God stood in the centre of the stage over which hovered the dove : *Ecce agnus Dei, ecce qui tollit peccata mundi.* From a wound in the Lamb's breast blood poured into a chalice. Angels surrounded the altar ; some carried instruments of torture, others swung censers with incense.

From both sides the blessed approached the altar in five choirs, at times in six, all of them splendidly arrayed. On the right were the confessors in blue canonicals, the patriarchs and prophets in red robes, the Fathers of the Church in blue and black, the knights of Christ, St. George and St. Victor, St. Maurice and St. Sebastian, St. Quirinus and St. Gandolph, " once upon a time Duke of Burgundy," each

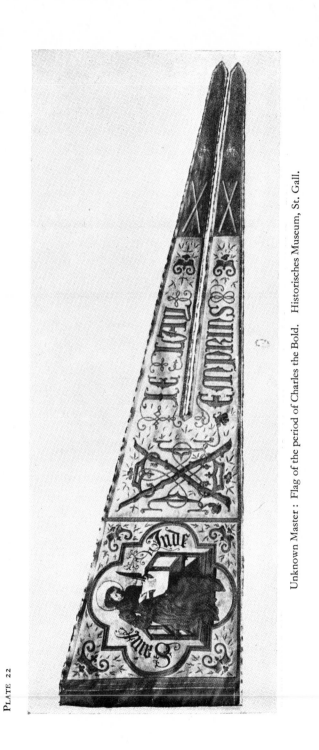

PLATE 22

Unknown Master : Flag of the period of Charles the Bold.   Historisches Museum, St. Gall.

[face p. 208

one with his standard; and behind them were the Just Judges in long flowing green robes.

On the left side were seen six virgins with flowing hair; then came the apostles and hermits, with Mary Magdalen and Mary of Egypt, the martyrs in red priestly vestments, and finally the pilgrims led by St. Christopher, a tall striking figure which commanded attention.

In front of the stage in white and green marble the fountain of life had been erected, and from it in three jets wine fell splashing into a basin.

Numerous inscriptions explained the tableau which was intended to represent the *Chorus beatorum in sacrificium agni pascalis*. But the natives of Ghent scarcely needed these explanations, for they were all familar with the mighty altar piece in St. Jan's Church which was here freely reproduced, the gift of their fellow-citizen, the wealthy patrician Josse Vyt, and the work of the brothers Van Eyck. Many of them indeed had known the younger of the two brothers who had died in 1441.

Thus did the people of Ghent pay grateful tribute to their two great masters.

Hubert and Jan were named after the small town of Eyck near Maastricht in the Meuse valley, where they were probably born or where their family lived. Destiny was very kind to them. In Liège, the city of St. Lambert, with its many churches and mansions, they found a wealth of suggestion and became familiar with the charm of landscape beauty. If their gaze travelled eastward, the highly developed culture and aspirations of Cologne streamed towards them. Did they turn their eyes towards Flanders " the richest county ship in the world ", towards Brabant or Holland, everywhere artistic aims and sympathies were astir. If in their craving for knowledge they inquired of widely-travelled gildsmen, or of mendicant friars, they would hear stories of the wonders of the land of sunshine, of the palace of Avignon which the artistic taste of the popes had so luxuriously equipped, of the royal Court at Paris which offered the muses hospitality. However much reports might vary in detail, the name of the pioneer master who had thrown even the glory of a Cimabue into the shade, was constantly recurring. Dante's words were still remembered :—

ed ora ha Giotto il grido.

The reports from Paris, however, would have interested them most of all, for many Netherlanders had wandered thither and had sought their fortunes in the service of the King or the princes of the blood.   Some had acquired citizenship on the Seine, while others had come back rich in knowledge and with well-filled purses.

King Charles V understood well how to honour an artist. To Jehan d'Orleans he presented the House of the Swan in Paris, allowed him a yearly salary and permitted him to reside in the Louvre.   The King's brothers, too, were great patrons of art.   Indeed, at that period, there was scarcely a celebrated artist who had not some kind of relations with Duke John de Berry, whose passion for art knew no bounds.   It is greatly to be regretted that so much has perished, for the Castle of Bicêtre, with its hall of state, must have been a very splendid place.   Philip the Bold of Burgundy, the Duke's younger brother, by the foundation of the Carthusian monastery of Champmol, had perpetuated not only his own name but those of the artists employed on it, and above all the name of Claus Sluter.

It was a good thing that these princes were open-handed in their treatment of artists, for soon after the death of Charles V of France, when his son had fallen sick beyond hope of recovery, the Court became more and more desolate. As learning commenced to decay at the university and became the plaything of political parties, so the Court, and with the court Paris itself, ceased to be an artistic and aesthetic centre.

The eyes of artists were now directed to the Duke de Berry, for, after the death of his brother Philip of Burgundy, the latter's son John was entirely absorbed in political conflicts and troubles.   The Duke de Berry had vast revenues at his disposal, the provinces under his administration were taxed with relentless severity, and the Duke denied himself nothing to satisfy his artistic tastes.   These were the days when illuminated manuscripts were greatly sought after and treasured.   The art of decorating manuscripts with dainty pictures had long flourished in France, and in the fourteenth century, when Italian and Netherland influences made themselves felt, it received fresh inspiration and stimulus.

In this department of art the versatile André Beauneveu had made successful experiments. Other Netherlanders, Jan or Hennequin of Bruges, Jacques Coene, Jacquemart de Hesdin distinguished themselves as miniaturists. Charles V of France, who shrank from no expense for his library in the Louvre, was a generous patron of artists, and set his sons an excellent example. No money was spared by the Duke de Berry in order to acquire the costliest works, particularly the splendid *Livres d'heures* which were then extremely popular. Fashion demanded of every lady that on her way to church she should display a beautifully ornamented book of devotions. Eustache Deschamps put these swords into the mouth of a church-going lady :—

> Heures me fault de Nostre Dame . . .
> Qui soient de soutil ouvraige,
> D'or et d'azur, riches et cointes,
> Bien ordonnées et bien pointes,
> De fin drap d'or très bien couvertes ;
> Et quant elles seront ouvertes
> Deux fermaulx d'or qui fermeront.

If ladies shrank from no expense in the adornment of their devotional works, it was natural that a prince such as the Duke de Berry should possess the finest to be obtained. One of his greatest treasures was the *Très Riches Heures de Chantilly*, on which his eyes must have rested with special pleasure. In the pictures of the month we are struck by the appreciation of landscape beauty and by the technical understanding of architecture. Paul of Limburg, whom the duke had attached to himself as *varlet de chambre*, and his brother are believed to have been the creators of this exquisite masterpiece.

The *Heures de Milan* and *Heures de Turin*, which together originally formed one work, compete successfully with the *Heures de Chantilly*. Various masters worked upon these manuscripts. A few leaves which may be ascribed to the same hand have attracted particular notice. An acute and delicate feeling for nature is betrayed in the sea voyage of St. Julian ; on the page presenting Count William of Holland and his daughter Jacqueline on the seashore a distinct gift for historical painting is shown, while the picture of the

Nativity of St. John and the solemn requiem, exhibit considerable talent for *genre* painting.

With Dante we could eulogize the painter.

> . . . l'onor di quell'arte
> che " alluminare " chiamata è in Parisi,

for it was a heaven-sent master who created these pages. He shows a complete understanding of space and lighting. In his treatment of the small and minute he never loses sight of the complete work, and his pictures may indeed be classed among the first of the modern school. He seems to have been one of those fortunate beings who could utter the unspeakable. He composed a Song of Songs of beauty, the music of which came to him from Nature as well as from the masterpieces of art and architecture.

Who then was the painter of these miniatures ? They have been ascribed on weighty grounds to Hubert as well as to Jan Van Eyck. We shall not enter into this controversial question. In any case one fact is clear, that having regard to the work of Jan in his authentic paintings, the ascription to him of the authorship of these pages is perfectly justified.

Unfortunately very little unequivocal and reliable information is available concerning Hubert and Jan Van Eyck. Almost everything is uncertain, hypothetical, and disputed, even in the case of Jan, where indeed the sources are slightly more copious. If we desire to know something of his origin and school, his tendency and aims, we must imagine that an artist of the 13th century, or earlier, is before our eyes; the man's work is our only clue to his life. Beyond this we have a few notices in the archives, a spoiled and hazy inscription beneath his masterpiece, a few artists' signs mostly on old frames: and that is all.

A few years after the production of those miniatures Jan was employed at the castle of the Hague in the service of Count John of Holland. The decisive factor, however, for his whole life, was the fact that after the death of this Wittelsbacher who maintained close relations with the Burgundian dukes, his star led him to the Court of Philip the Good. It was fitting that these two men should meet.

Like his grandfather and his royal great-grandfather, Philip always found time and leisure to employ himself with art and artists, even when the assassination at Montereau had clouded the political sky. The Duke gave with open hand and approached artists as man to man : when he so desired the laws of etiquette did not exist. Jan became *son peintre et varlet de chambre aux honneurs, prérogatives, libertés, droits et prouffis et émoluments accoustumez.* Thereupon Jan, like the other *varlets* was assigned first of all the task of painting coats of arms, standards, and shields. He succeeded, how ever, in executing his commissions so splendidly that he attracted special notice. He gained the Duke's confidence and was frequently sent on missions connected with the Court. We are reminded of Rubens, whom the Archduke Albrecht and his wife Isabella employed on diplomatic business.

The grant of a yearly salary for life removed the artist from the anxieties and struggles of daily life. When on one occasion the Chamber of Accounts raised difficulties about paying the appointed sum, the Duke expressly commanded them to do so, lest Jan should leave his service, for, said he, " *nous trouverions point le pareil à nostre gré ne si excellent en son art et science.*" The Duke stood godfather to one of the artist's children, and made him and his wife Margaret a present of six silver cups. As with his favourite writers, he visited Jan in his studio. It is fascinating to dwell in imagination upon the intercourse between the *Grand Duc du Ponant* and the "king of painters". Philip certainly profited by such opportunities to gain information on matters in which his courtiers took little interest. These informal conversations were a thorn in the side of the nobles who reproached the Duke with being on too familiar terms with persons of the lower orders.

It seems that Philip succumbed entirely to the charm of Van Eyck's art. The artists working in Dijon, also Netherlanders, were gradually forgotten. It is true that the Duke and his consort had fixed on the Carthusian monastery as their burial-place and made gifts to it, but no real interest was taken in the men who trod in the footsteps of Sluter and Maelweel. Claus van Werve, who was to execute the tomb of the Duke's parents and his own, was constantly

oppressed with money troubles and had to take private work
in order to earn his daily bread. Henri de Bellechose of
Brabant, who had been promoted to be Court painter in
place of Maelweel, fared no better. In the end his salary
was stopped and he fell into the direst distress, his wife having
to retail salt in order to support their family. After the
death of these artists the ducal workshops were closed,
and the title and privileges of *varlet* were no longer
bestowed on those working in Dijon.

What objection could there be against summoning Claus
van Werve and Henri de Bellechose to the Netherlands ?
Distance and external difficulties were not likely to delay
Duke Philip. The greater the hindrances, the greater
the ardour to remove them ; while the desire for travel
was ever present.

Under these circumstances it is not surprising that the
Duke did not object more strongly to the extraordinary
delay in the completion of his parents' sarcophagus. After
the death of Claus van Werve the work was entrusted in
1442 to an Aragonese, Juan de la Huerta of Daroca, who
had been employed by the Carmelites in Chalon-sur-Saône.
This was, however, an unhappy choice, for the Aragonese
was as frivolous and deceitful as he was gifted. He was
completely successful in outwitting the officials of the Chamber
of Accounts, who as a rule were not easily deceived, and
in gradually extorting almost the whole of the agreed
honorarium. He boasted to the Duke that he could procure
rich returns from the Burgundian gold, silver, cobalt, and
lead mines, and he contrived to defraud even the *receveur
général*. The work, however, drew no nearer to completion.
When the artist at last deemed it advisable to vanish
mysteriously, the alabaster figures—one of the Duke and two
of the Duchess—were unusable owing to cracks. A sister
of the Duke, Agnes, Duchess of Bourbon, now recommended
to her brother Antoine Le Moiturier of Avignon, who had
erected the mausoleum in Souvigny for her deceased husband
after the pattern of Champmol. Le Moiturier received the
commission, and Duke Philip himself made improvements
in the plans but did not live to see the completion of the
work. The memorial was only put up in the Carthusian
monastery three years after his death and is executed entirely

in the style of the tomb of Philip the Bold. Nothing more was heard of a tomb for Philip the Good.

The centre of art at this period had thus been moved from Burgundy to the Netherlands. Just as once Dijon had eclipsed Paris, so Dijon was now to recede in favour of Bruges, Ghent and Brussels. This was a calamity for those artists who were working in Burgundy, especially since the Carthusian monastery was still influencing both French and foreign art, and many tombs were being executed with Pleurants after the Burgundian manner. When the council of the town of Basle in 1418 entrusted the decoration of the Elenden Kreuz Chapel to Hans Tieffenthal of Schlettstadt, it was laid down in the contract that the painting should be done after the model of the Carthusian monastery of Champmol.

The political neglect of Burgundy set in also at that time, and was bitterly revenged later under Charles the Bold. " *Puyssance suyt la cour du prince et se tint en Flandre, en Brabant, à Bruges, à Gand, en Hollande, en Zélande et à Namur, et est trop plus flamengue que wallonne,*" says Molinet. The prince and his relatives showed themselves even less frequently than before in the land of their race. Isabella, Philip's consort, was there only for a short time ; Charles the Bold came there no more after his accession, his consorts, Isabella and Margaret, never. The Netherlands exercised a wonderful power of attraction over Philip the Good ; possibly the blood of his mother, the Countess Margaret of Holland and Hainault, was making itself felt.

Through the Duke's favour Jan Van Eyck as Court painter was freed from all gild restrictions. In the execution of his missions, protected by the authority of his prince, he was free to trust his eyes everywhere in France and in the new Burgundian State. A lucky stroke of fortune came to him in 1428, when he was sent to Portugal by Duke Philip with the diplomatic mission which was to negotiate for the hand of the Infanta. In the suite of Jean, Seigneur de Roubaix, and other lords of high rank, he was to become acquainted with all the miseries and perils of a sea voyage in stormy weather, with forced landings, with withdrawals and long delays due to unfavourable winds. But he found a wealth of experience when at last, after eight weeks, the mission reached Cascaës and proceeded by way of Lisbon to Aviz, where King John held his Court. While there Van Eyck painted the Infanta's portrait. In the course of the negotiations it was found necessary to obtain instructions from Duke Philip and months elapsed before the messengers could return. The lords, and Van Eyck with them we may be sure, employed the interval in performing their devotions at the shrine of Santiago di Compostela, and in visits to the King of Castile and the Moorish King of Granada. It was a splendid opportunity to learn something of the country and people, of the southern flora and fauna. When the envoys again reached Lisbon they arrived in time for the celebrations attending a royal marriage. At the entry of the bride, the Infanta of Aragon, the Jews and Saracens with their curious dances and songs, attracted particular attention. There were strange happenings also at the great banquet held in the Hall of Galleys, where the *chalenges* took place. Mounted nobles and knights, fantastically arrayed, appeared at the table before the host, offering in a romantically worded letter, to joust with all and sundry. One lord came studded with quills like a porcupine ; another brought in the seven planets ; and on the following day the jousts were held in the " New Street ".

Van Eyck's picture of the Infanta Elizabeth, afterwards the Duchess Isabella of Burgundy, has unfortunately been lost. Nor is there any mention or trace of the portraits which the artist must have executed of his ducal master. Apart from the miniaturists, it was left to Rogier van der Weyden to transmit the features of Philip the Good to posterity.

Enriched by his impressions and experiences, supported by the confidence of his art-loving sovereign and in the full consciousness of his power. Jan on his return undertook the mighty task laid on him by the death of his brother— the completion of the altar-piece at Ghent.

Of Hubert we know very little. Shortly before his death he was engaged on work in Ghent ; that is all we can learn from the archives. There is no authority for the statement contained in the inscription on the picture that Hubertus, "than whom none was more skilful," began the "difficult work" of the Ghent altar, and that Johannes, "the second brother, completed it."

Hitherto Jan had been principally employed by his sovereign, but now a patrician made his appearance as patron. At this time not only rulers but progressive cities and rich merchants took increasing delight in patronizing the arts. Wealthy citizens had their private chapels built or ornamented at great expense; they dedicated altar-pieces to the Holy Virgin or their patron saints, it being a term of the contract that the donor should appear in the finished work together with his wife and children. At the annual Halfvasten fair at Ghent, which always attracted strangers, native and foreign artists could exhibit their works in churches or in secular buildings, and it was on these occasions that the contracts were concluded.

Josse or Jodocus Vyt and his wife are known far and wide as the donors of the Ghent altar piece. Had they not spent a part of their handsome fortune in the completion of a great work of art their names would have been completely forgotten, for there is nothing remarkable in their lives. Josse Vyt, Lord of Pamele, came of a rich family in Waesland. His father had gained his spurs in the service of the Count of Flanders, and, like the majority of the capitalists of Flanders of that period, he amassed a large fortune by the construction of dykes and the reclamation of broad tracts of land from the sea. Having married the daughter of a Ghent patrician, he obtained admission to the Poortery, the patriciate of Ghent.

The son Josse remained in his native town. He married into an influential patrician family, and as representative of the Poorter he was from time to time both alderman and burgomaster. When the fullers made preparations for a rebellion he proceeded against them with great severity and caused a number of the rebels to be beheaded. Looking at the picture of the donor and concentrating our attention upon his features, we gather the impression that Vyt was a man who understood how to conceal a wide knowledge of affairs and great vitality under a cloak of indifference. We can well imagine that no scruples would restrain him from taking full advantage of an adversary. A few years after the tenth chapel of Sint Jan had been ornamented with their coats of arms and ciphers and a splendid screen, Vyt and his wife commissioned an altar-piece from the brothers Van Eyck.

The altar was completed in 1432. The conflict of opinions, the attempt to apportion each brother's share, cannot be entered into here. This mighty work presents many difficulties. The interpretation is still obscure, the literary source of the painters' inspiration being even now undetermined. The rhetoricians of Ghent called their tableau after the picture, the choir of the Blessed at the sacrifice of the Easter Lamb. They presented God the Father, the Virgin, St. John and the angel choirs, but Adam and Eve in their sinful nakedness and the two pictures in the lunettes, the sacrifice of Cain and Abel, and the fratricide, are omitted, probably with the idea of simplification. It is certainly an All Saints' picture. The solemn and mysterious words of the Apocalypse upon which it is based were subsequently explained and developed by liturgic and other ecclesiastical texts, by hymns, sermons, and legends.

In his widely-known sermon *De omnibus sanctis*, Honorius of Autun strikingly described the heavenly Jerusalem and the heavenly Garden, which holy men and women adorn as flowers, the patriarchs and prophets who are companioned by Adam and Eve as progenitors, the Apostles and Evangelists, the martyrs and confessors, the virgins, the penitents and believers. John the Baptist shines in the brightest light, for it is he who foretold the Lamb of God. Adoration of the Trinity and the Virgin resounds. Angel choirs behold in unceasing ecstasy the countenance of the Father. " Call upon all the saints with heart and tongue ; with praise and thanksgiving commend yourselves to them, so that by their intercession Christ, the Holiest of the Holy, may forgive you all the sins you have committed during the whole year against the Christian religion."

Jacobus de Varagine made clear to the world the significance of the Feast of All Saints in his *Golden Legend* which contains a chapter on the institution of the festival. The sexton of St. Peter beheld in a vision the King of Kings on a high throne and all his angels about Him. The Mother of God came crowned, and there followed her a multitude of virgins and chaste women. John the Baptist and St. Peter advanced with patriarchs and prophets, apostles and martyrs, and honourable knights and aged men. All came to adore the King and to pray for the sins of mankind.

In contrast to the interior of the altar-piece, the exterior pictures present no problems. The Annunciation of Mary points to the coming of the Saviour whose appearance the Prophets Zachariah and Micah, the Erythrean and Cumaean Sibyls have foretold. John the Baptist and John the Evangelist are the patron saints of the church; it was only dedicated to St. Bavo at a later period. Next to them kneel the donor and his wife.

The Last Judgment was depicted on the Predella which has been lost.

The two brothers created an amazing work which up till then had no equal; amazing not only in its greatness, in the diversity of its scheme, in the number of figures, in technique, in its subject, which later attracted Dürer and Raphael, but above all in its conception and execution. When the physician and humanist Joachim Münzer in the course of his journey in the Netherlands, visited Ghent in the year 1495, he summed up the glory of the altar: " Everything is painted in a wonderful and artistic spirit. Not one picture but the whole art of painting is seen here. . . . How wonderful are the pictures of Adam and Eve; everything seems to be alive ! "

Dürer, too, was unrestrained in his praise; he entered in the diary of his travels: " Then I saw Jan Van Eyck's picture, which is a most precious painting, full of thought: especially noteworthy are the Eve, Mary, and God the Father."

So much for the judgment of experts and art-lovers. The living picture which the rhetoricians of Ghent produced in honour of their sovereign shows best of all how this work had already influenced and was still influencing the general public. The unnamed multitude must have experienced much the same sensations as Villon's mother, whose book of pictures was the church with its drawings and statues:

Femme je suis povrette et ancienne,
Qui riens ne sçay ; oncques lettres ne leuz ;
Au moustier voy dont suis paroissienne,
Paradis paint, où sont harpes et luz,
Et ung enfer où dampnez sont boulluz :
L'ung me fait paour, l'autre joye et liesse.

One thing, however, the rhetoricians did not reproduce and perhaps did not attempt, was the wonderful landscape through which the choirs of the Blessed wind their way. What magic, what festive mood, lies in these heavenly regions ! Flowers are growing in the verdant grass, lilies of the valley and violets and yellow blossoms of celandine ; dandelions and clover show their dainty leaves ; watercress and cuckoo flowers deck the edge of the little brook which runs through the meadow. Stately bushes surround the landscape. Natives of the rugged north are to be seen side by side with children of the south. Did Jan by chance thus perpetuate his memories of his Iberian journey ? Beside the delicate rose blooms the startling red of the pomegranate. A vine entwines a fig with its leaves. Protected by sturdier growths, small shrubs are to be seen, irises, lilies, and peonies in their noisy splendour, as if proclaiming to the world their medicinal virtues ; modest tansy and swallow-wort, proud of their delicate foliage. Beneath its protecting leaves depend the white tubular blossoms of Solomon's seal. Woodruff lies hidden in the shade of the bushes.

The ground rises gradually. On the edge of wooded slopes gleam the silver blossoms and golden fruit of lemon-trees. Beside a spreading pine a cypress raises its slender shape, a date-palm waves its fruit-laden branches. Proudly and majestically rise the towers of the heavenly Jerusalem ; where the eye loses itself in immensity eternal snows shimmer on the mountains.

Unlike Giotto, Hubert and Jan missed the good fortune of being praised by Dante. For a long period Hubert disappeared from the memory of men. It was only, more than a hundred years after his death, that the inscription, which recalls him was discovered. Jan fared somewhat better. About fifteen years after his death he was mentioned in the *Liber de viris illustribus* by the Italian Humanist,

Bartolomeo Fazio, as *Johannes Gallicus nostri saeculi pictorum princeps*, and in time other writers added their praise. But the information is meagre, and we know very little about him. Whatever Jan's share in the altar-piece may have been, his collaboration had familiarized him with every kind of problem and trained him in the creation of those works which can with certainty be ascribed to him.

About the year 1431 he moved to Bruges and bought a house in Sint Gillis Nieustraet. He was naturally attracted by the luxurious town, which Philip the Good had chosen as his residence, a town which was always pulsing with life, and crowded with strangers from every part of the world, with merchants, envoys, couriers, diplomats, and princes. As Court painter and confidant of the Duke, Jan had no difficulty in establishing contact with officials and officers, and even with the more illustrious guests, several of whom he has immortalized.

When Nicolaus Albergati, cardinal of Santa Croce, arrived at Court in order to negotiate peace between France and Burgundy, Jan received orders to paint his portrait. As the cardinal had little time, it seems, for sittings, Jan was obliged to make a hasty drawing from which he afterwards painted the picture. The drawing has been preserved, and the detailed notes on the back of it, recording even the sitter's stubbly beard, reveal the keenness of the artist's powers of observation.

In praising the clever and distinguished Cardinal, Pope Eugenius IV said that he was a stranger to every passion, his thoughts and counsel being solely directed to the preservation of unity and peace. These words can be readily appreciated when we look at Jan's picture and especially at his sketch. Here is a man whose eyes speak of his kindheartedness. As a legate, widely travelled and entrusted with many delicate tasks, Albergati had special opportunities for marking the world's ways and acquainting himself with all sorts and conditions of men—with popes, kings, statesmen, and prelates. A slight melancholy is noticeable which suggests that he was not without his disappointments. But they do not seem to have affected his character, nor to have destroyed his faith in mankind.

Jan was evidently engrossed by his model : with great

pains he sought for his most conspicuous characteristics and reproduced them with the same faithfulness with which he portrayed even the smallest external peculiarity which attracted his notice. We do not know what he thought about his models in general; the artist retires modestly into the background when his work is finished. He does not emphasize the features of his sitters, nor does he tone them down. The artist is content to show us the people of his age and to present them in their full vitality and with amazing truthfulness.

It would be interesting to know what attracted the master to " Jehan Arnolfin " of whom he did not only a half-length picture, but a full length portrait also, showing Arnolfini with his wife, a bold attempt, unusual in those times. By placing the couple in their own room he has shown us at the same time a charming interior.

The man is presented with a curiously-shaped head; dull, tired eyes, a large ugly nose, large mouth and large ears. Is he a member of a family whose strength is exhausted and is in need of fresh blood? Giovanni Arnolfini, who seems to accept his destiny with imperturbable serenity, overcame every obstacle which nature had placed in his cradle. He came from Lucca to Brussels a poor man, amassed a large fortune by the importation of silks, and grew to be honoured and respected.

It is curious that although we see at once that Giovanni Arnolfini was a remarkable man, his wife Giovanna Cenani shows no very striking characteristics. We can understand how the master contrived to adapt, without much alteration, this comely figure to that of St. Catherine in one of his devotional pictures. Even if we take the Flanders coif from the head with the dreamy face, there is nothing of the Italian woman about her. There is also a mystery surrounding this picture. What did Jan really mean by the inscription: " *Johannes de Eyck fuit hic?* " Was he a witness of the marriage, and did he desire to perpetuate the moment when the young couple entered the wealthy patrician home, the husband asking for confidence and protesting his goodwill with his raised right hand, while Giovanna, with bashful and chaste reserve, offers him her hand softly and delicately?

PLATE 23

Jan van Eyck : Giovanni Arnolfini and his wife. National Gallery, London.

In contrast to Giovanna Cenani, the artist's wife, Margaret, appears full of energy and purpose ; he painted her in her thirty-third year, five years after the birth of their child. The tightly closed mouth gives evidence of will power. With her quiet, clear glance, not quite so critical as the Man in the Turban, she gazes searchingly at the spectator.

Jan honoured Giovanna Cenani, Arnolfini's wife, by enrolling her among his saints. Unfortunately we know little of the women whose faces were present to him when he painted the Virgin Mary. He must have heard from his scholar friends a great deal about the theological controversies connected with Mariolatry. Unbelievers were constantly to the fore. In the immediate neighbourhood, in Arras, a woman was condemned by the Inquisition for alleging that Mary had borne other children before Jesus Christ, and prudence was everywhere necessary. The Inquisition was busy in the Netherlands and at Lille the stake blazed. Moreover, during Jan's creative period the decision of the Council of Basle on the doctrine of the Immaculate Conception was pronounced. As Martin Le Franc wrote subsequently :—

> Maistre Jan de Segobia
> Très solennel docteur, qui a
> Par dix mille raisons prouvé
> Que nostre Vierge Maria
> Ne fut conchue au mortel vé.

But the Church's attitude did not divert Jan from his realistic conception : the Virgin Mary whom he represents with the Infant Christ is not transcendental. Mary is no dream shape, no supernatural being, no budding tender virgin, but a wife and mother in full maturity, such as he saw daily in the streets of Bruges, a large, sound, healthy, and rather big-boned Flemish woman with engaging, friendly, but not over-delicate features. The Child, too, is by no means idealized.

This is the conception of Mother and Child which appears in the devotional picture which the Canon George van der Paele commissioned the artist to paint for the church of St. Donatian in Bruges, where he had founded two chapels.

Mary sits with Christ on an exquisite throne, richly decorated with sculptured ornaments. The space is enclosed by a semi-circle of splendid columns. A carpet of Oriental colouring lies on the blue and white Spanish tiles, adding new tones to the colour of the robes.   On the left stands St. Donatian, a dignified figure, the wheel with burning candles in his hand.   On the right the donor is seen kneeling, clad in a surplice, a grey fur over his arm.   He has just been reading from the opened book, and his right hand still holds his spectacles.   The figures are solemn and silent.   St. George in shining armour stands behind his protégé.   As if to interrupt this quietude, he raises his helmet, and seems with an embarrassed smile, to be introducing the Canon, but neither saint nor donor looks towards the Christ Child whose face is turned towards them.

The aged Canon, on whose intellectual features illness has left its traces, may possibly be numbered among the learned patrons of the artist and his brother.   In any case it is noteworthy that the inscription which proclaims the glory of the Virgin on the altar-piece at Ghent is identical with that on this devotional picture ; both originating in the Breviary according to the use of the church of St. Donatian.

If in this solemn work the artist's aim was to be monumental, in the picture which the Chancellor Rolin caused to be painted for Notre-Dame in Autun, the artist has emphasized the *genre* style of painting.   It seems as if in remembrance of his native Meuse valley he has tried to sing a hymn in praise of the beauty of the landscape.   Through the wide windows of the apartment the eye roams over a garden of roses, lilies, and peonies.   Two peacocks, a bird much favoured by knighthood, display their plumage.   From the balcony two spectators are looking out upon the beauty of the scene.   The background is formed by lofty, snow-capped mountains ;   beneath them stretch the verdant hillsides. A broad river with many windings flows through a peaceful, fertile plain.   On an island a castle is seen.   Houses and churches emerge, battlements and towers glisten in the light, while men and women pass busily to and fro.   A fortified bridge leads from the prosperous city to its less pretentious suburb.

In a state department rich with Renaissance luxury the Queen of Heaven is seated with her Child on her knee.   A shining crown is held over her head by an angel.   In spite of her lovely robes, her figure is lowly and modest.   She

PLATE 24

Jan van Eyck: The Madonna of the Chancellor Rolin. Louvre, Paris.

smiles serenely in maternal happiness and dignity, yet not without a touch of solemnity as she looks down at the Christ Child.

The picture is full of light, but there is no lack of deep shadows ; before the Mother with her divine Child the Duke's all-powerful Chancellor is presented kneeling.

His immobile, rigid features testify to his inflexible will-power and unscrupulous determination. The gloomy eye glows with an ardent consuming ambition. A man of high gifts, Nicholas Rolin was untiring in his zeal for the greatness of the House of Burgundy, of whom he deserved extra-ordinarily well. He contrived to make himself indispensable to his sovereign ; for many years nothing could be done in that mighty State without his knowledge and approval. Rolin knew well how insecure was his grip on fortune. Threatened daily by intrigues and cabals, even by the assassin's dagger, he pursued his path with something of the recklessness of a gambler, but he was shrewd enough to attend to his own and his family's interests in a thoroughly practical fashion. He amassed untold wealth : possessions were added to possessions. Even the Curia was anxious to oblige so powerful a man, and invested his son with the cardinal's hat. As was customary at Court, the Chancellor was a strict churchman. In Beaune he founded a large hospital and commissioned the portrait by Jan Van Eyck in which he is shown paying homage to the Virgin. It is possible that Rolin, to whom nothing human was strange, was anxious to square his account with heaven. The master with his penetrating eye seems to have doubted whether he had succeeded : another doubter was Jacques Du Clercq, who wrote :—" *ledit chancellier fust réputé ung des sages hommes du royaume à parler temporellement ; car au regard de l'espirituel, je m'en tais.*"

Unfortunately many of the master's works have been lost. Duke Philip had a *mundi comprehensio orbiculari forma*, a kind of map, made by Jan, which not only showed districts and places but exact distances as well. Still more important would it be to have the picture of women bathing which was in the keeping of an Italian cardinal, How was the feminine nude treated ? Bartolomeo Fazio, to whom we owe the description, especially emphasizes a light as being

" extremely like a burning one ", and praises above all a mirror, which was painted so splendidly that everything could be seen in it as in a real one.

Jan was probably dependent on the public baths for his studies of the female nude. The *étuves* played a great part in the daily life of the period and had already acquired the character of the brothel. The age regarded the arrangement as natural and necessary ; any evil was better than incest, rape and crimes against nature. A chronicler relates as a matter of course, that when English envoys arrived at the Burgundian courts, *bains estorés de tout ce qu'il faut au mestier de Vénus, à prendre par choix et par élection ce que on désiroit mieux, et tout aux frais du duc*, were placed at their disposal. The bathing cabinets knew no restraint. Fights, murders and assassinations, were common happenings. Jacques Du Clercq tells a tale of what took place in the *étuves* at Arras. Scenes were enacted there which only a Jan Steen or a van Vliet could have depicted.

Jan Van Eyck was gifted with great versatility. Heaven and earth, fire and water, with their marvels and riddles, occupied him incessantly. His keen eye was always open, and his hand seems never to have been still. He studied atmospheric problems ; light in all its aspects interested him continuously. He followed the sun's rays to the remotest corner and gloried in light and shade. He laid great stress upon atmosphere and light in painting, and at the same time reduced the materiality of space.

In the same way in which he observed every wrinkle in the human skin, so he explored the earth's surface and paced the hills and valleys. He had a thorough knowledge of stones and rocks, and some perception of plant life. This " natural philosopher " would have made an excellent goldsmith or architect. If we consider the jewels which he chased, the crown with which he ornaments God and his Madonnas, we can see at once that he was no stranger to the goldsmith's workshops. One of the cleverest of them, Jan de Leeuw of Bruges, sat to him.

His buildings, his splendid apartments and churches, all reveal a technical understanding which is most remarkable.

We can imagine that Jan was quite capable of designing and executing an actual building. The means of expression which he took over from his fellow-craftsmen did not suffice for his methods of painting, and he discovered, surely only after countless experiments, the rich, full, gleaming, shining colours afforded by the technique of oils.

The artistic fire which burned in Jan transformed every fibre in his being and made of him one of the greatest of painters the world has ever seen. He was the creator of modern panel painting; he was an active *genre* painter, and was far ahead of his age in the presentation of landscape and still-life. Of strong and original character he knew how to resist and, when necessary, to adapt foreign influences. He became acquainted with the *Rinascimento*, from which he borrowed materials and forms of ornamentation, but he remained at the same time true to himself. Healthy and vigorous, full of the joy of life, he was not given to brooding and does not seem to have exhausted himself in fruitless endeavours to give expression to his genius. Even though his ardent craving for realism caused him to burden with earthly heaviness the divinity of the saints whom he painted for the edification and elevation of his fellow-men, he yet remained a good son of the Church and kept himself aloof from dangerous theological controversies and metaphysical speculations. Skilful and conciliatory, he was able to order his life without arousing useless opposition; nor does he seem to have shared his contemporaries' craving for gold. After his death his widow was obliged to invoke his prince's favour. Jan, moreover, never lost himself in the unclean atmosphere of Court life. Like all men ahead of their age, he must have remained something of a solitary, but there is nothing to show that he suffered from his isolation. The favour of his prince and the confidence of his fellow-citizens must have eased his path through life. Posterity has placed a wreath of immortality on his brow

> . . . le roy des peintres Johannes,
> du quel les faits parfaits et mignonnetz,
> ne tomberont jamais en oubly vain.

Thus exclaimed Jean Lemaire at the dawn of the sixteenth century.

Craftsmen's workshops were passed on from father to son or son-in-law ; they remained sometimes for generations in the same family.   The studio of Jehan d'Orleans can be traced from the time of King Louis IX to that of Charles VI. If there were no descendants, the workshops were leased. Did Petrus Christus conclude such an agreement with Jan's widow, by which he was given disposal of the shop and workroom " with its decorative materials, models and splendid armour " ?

We should like to know definitely that Petrus Christus, or Christi, as he signed himself, laboured in Jan's studio, and that the master in his lifetime influenced him not only by his works.   Petrus learned a very great deal from Jan : indeed he succumbed so completely to his spell that he lost his own soul ; he does not succeed in adding anything personal to the achievements of Van Eyck which he had adapted to his use.   And yet he may well have had the qualifications necessary to create something original.   Let us look more closely at the landscape background of his pictures, or consider the zeal with which he has transformed the utensils and trinkets in the picture of St. Eligius into a still-life.   Thus Petrus painted his portraits and devotional pictures, walking in Jan's footsteps.   But, however much the brilliant pitchers and chalices on the shelf, the rings and chains in the picture of St. Eligius may please the eye, the constrained attitude of the figures is very noticeable : they have the appearance of being posed.   Nor is the significance of the picture itself quite clear.   Does Petrus Christus intend to convey that the bridal couple desired to invoke special divine protection on their walk through life by procuring a ring of indissoluble unity from the goldsmith who was honoured as a saint ?   In any case it is important for subsequent development that an artisan should have been portrayed here, even though he wore a saint's halo.

At a period when Jan Van Eyck's creative power was at its highest, an illustrious master was working in Tournai or Doornik, the French enclave in the Netherlands.   In that flourishing city celebrated for its glorious cathedral, miniaturists, sculptors, and tapestry weavers were busy, whose masterpieces spread their renown far and wide. There was thus no lack of stimulation for those who aspired to higher things. Robert Campin, who has latterly been identified with the Master of Flémalle, or, as he has also been called, the master of the Mérode altar, brought painting into fame as the creator of immortal works and as the teacher of Rogier van der Weyden.

Like all great masters Jan Van Eyck had exercised both a fascinating and a repelling influence. Robert Campin learnt much from him, how to poise a head gracefully, how to arrange an interior with taste or make a landscape-background charming. But Robert Campin added new features to *genre* painting. With easy discursiveness, like one who has travelled far, he relates all that he has seen and studied. He, too, is a friend of light and chiaroscuro; he shows the Virgin reading by the light of a candle as the angel enters her apartment. In the chamber of St. Barbara, a merry fire is crackling on the hearth. Dainty figures in stone decorate the walls. In the workshop of St. Joseph, all kinds of tools, indispensable to a carpenter, are lying about, and on the table stands a mouse-trap. In order to give external expression to the interest of the donors in the Annunciation, Campin leaves half open the door leading to the room in which the Virgin is seen. The enjoyment of these novel features at times impairs their full effect. Did the master recognize this himself and therefore abandon the method in his Descent from the Cross ? The emotion of the human soul alone attracts him in this dramatic scene. Overcome by pain, Mary swoons. The falling body is unskilfully depicted, but the *mater dolorosa* produces a thoroughly convincing effect ; we feel the agonies she must be suffering. How deep are the furrows which sorrow has drawn in the face of St. Monica ! Distracted, she seeks in vain for consolation. In contrast to Jan Van Eyck, who gives his figures a serenity and dignity alien to the age, Robert Campin instils his figures with a passionate emotion which knows no bounds. He thus connects, independent as he is, with the idealistic mode of thought of the past, and bridges the Gothic to Rogier van der Weyden by way of the Van Eycks.

Rogier van der Weyden—Rogier de la Pasture, exists too,

in a kind of mysterious twilight.   Not even a signature of the
artist can be proved with certainty on any picture of his.
One of his chief works, the pictures of Justice in the Town
Hall of Brussels, is destroyed and can no longer testify
for him.

Like his teacher Campin, " Rogelet " was a native of
Tournai.   Sculpture must have exercised a deep influence
on him.   The sculptor repeatedly emerges behind the painter
Rogier.   He introduced the painted portal sculpture as a
border in the altar-piece.   He was likewise interested in
architecture.   He attempted to reproduce the rock tomb
of the Holy Land, which pilgrims may have described to him,
and he places the birth of Christ not in a manger, but in a
ruin.   On the other hand fidelity to nature has less weight
with him.   Woodruff, which thrives only in a wood, and
wall-lettuce, which flourishes on rock and stone, he depicts
as growing in a meadow.

In Brussels, that bright and wealthy city where Philip
the Good was always glad to reside, Rogier took up his abode
and filled the office of town painter.   This would have
been sufficient for Jan Van Eyck, but it was not enough for
Rogier.   Jan went joyously through the world ; he accepted
with pleasure whatever was beautiful and marvellous as it
came in his way and transferred it to his pictures.   In his
naive piety he thus proclaimed the glory and honour of God,
whose world was so full of beauty and wonder.   But Rogier
amid all the distractions which surrounded him in Brussels,
remained serious and melancholy.   Even the sun of Italy
did not enliven his spirits.   For him the earth was the vale
of tears such as the priests in their fervent sermons were
wont to describe to their congregations.   Rogier would never
have ventured to remove God and the Saints from the
heavenly sphere.   His St. Luke Madonna shows that he
was acquainted with Jan's picture of the Chancellor Rolin.
Rogier learnt from the great master, but the latter's style and
conception did not meet with his approval.   Fidelity to
nature was not of the greatest importance to him.   His ideas
and attempts were centred in giving expression to the divine
in the Virgin Mary and depicting her heavenly grace.   He was
content to ignore the fact that the head which St. Luke had
begun to draw is not that of his model, and that the drawing-

paper is not large enough to add the figures of Mary and the Child Jesus.

Still under the spell of ecclesiastical authority, he fell back on the honoured conception of earlier days, thus bringing his work much closer to the hearts of the ecclesiastically-minded than Jan's Madonnas with their worldly joyousness could ever be. He became the favourite painter of pictures of the Virgin. How often did he vary his theme ; how often have his paintings been copied ! He could, in fact, abandon all detailed *genre* work, and still be successful. He introduced into the Netherlands a new method of portraying the Mother of God, the idea of which he had probably acquired in Italy. He frequently depicted the Madonna in semi-figure, thus abandoning the stately splendour of her chamber and the charm of a smiling landscape. But the halo in its glory raises Mother and Child far above the things of earth.

His Descent from the Cross in the Escorial shows how deeply and earnestly the Passion of our Lord had influenced Rogier. A passionate symphony of sorrow reverberates through the picture. Even though Nicodemus and Joseph of Arimathea have contrived to control their emotions, the women are entirely beyond restraint. Mary Magadalene is actually writhing in pain ; Mary falls senseless to the ground.

The artist must have been carried away by his feelings, as Jacopone da Todi expresses it in his touching verses :

Stabat mater dolorosa
Juxta crucem lacrimosa
Dum pendebat filius.
Cuius animam gementem,
Contristatam et dolentem
Pertransivit gladius.

Quis est homo, qui non fleret
Matrem Christi si videret
In tanto supplicio ?
Quis non posset contristari
Christi matrem contemplari
Dolentem cum filio ?

Plastically, like coloured wooden figures, the shapes show up against the golden background. The scene does not take place in the foreground of a landscape ; Cross, ladder and a skull alone indicate Golgotha. Here was no lyric poet with the cheerful disposition of Jan Van Eyck, but a dramatist whose soul was stirred to its depths by the solemn and the

gloomy. But the artist who clings to tradition and regards
the new with critical eye runs the risk of becoming lifeless.
This Descent from the Cross is not surpassed by any of
Rogier's later works of a similar character.

It is curious that this master who took life so seriously,
should have been for a long period the most favoured portrait
painter at the Burgundian Court. Although not a ducal
varlet, he was closely in touch with the Court, and soon
attained favour and distinction. The Chancellor Rolin
commissioned from him the Last Judgment for his hospital
at Beaune and had himself perpetuated once more as donor.

Unfortunately no original portrait of Duke Philip has
survived. It is not clear whether the old copies which have
been preserved are taken from two originals or from one
original, the copies having suffered alteration in the process.
Duke Philip is presented in a stately black robe, such as he
was accustomed to wear and which he abandoned for the
first time at the Feast of the Pheasant. He appears at
one time wearing his chaperon, at another bareheaded, with
his hair cut short and combed down on his forehead, in
accordance with the fashion of the time. The chain of the
Golden Fleece is seen in his chaperon or at his neck ; a gem
gives lustre to the painting. The pictures date from the
period when the Duke was afflicted with ague ; the sunken
cheeks give evidence of his disease. It is interesting to
compare these portraits with the detailed description of
Philip's person given by Chastellain. His body was of
medium stature, the upper part beautiful, slim as a reed ;
the neck well proportioned, back and arms powerful ; hand
and foot lean, the veins full of blood ; hair smooth, between
blond and black ; his face, like his father's, of sufficient
length ; the forehead high and broad, not bald ; glittering
blue eyes whose expression was proud at times, but as a rule
friendly ; a long nose but not aquiline ; a well-formed
mouth ; red, fleshy lips, brownish, dull complexion ; beard
and eyebrows like the hair ; the eyebrows very strong and
bushy, " which in anger bristled like horns."

One detail is brilliantly expressed by the master, a detail
authenticated by the chroniclers :—something uncanny lies
in the eyes. They give the idea that behind this unruffled
serenity and this intentional self-control, there were forces

slumbering which could break out like a tornado when the curbing restraints were torn away from the tumultuous temperament. Chastellain eulogizes Philip's forbearance, which in the case of disloyal officials could change into inexcusable weakness, but he remarks that the man who offended him had an implacable enemy. His sorrow and boundless rage when the news of his father's murder reached the twenty-three-year-old prince was typical of the man. Philip lay senseless on the bed in a state of utter collapse with glassy eyes and black lips, his arms and legs quivering convulsively; the whole house " *emmeublé de hélas* " resounded with weeping, sobbing, and clamour. And this paroxysm was the result of shock not on an old man but on a youth. Later in life, after a dispute with his son, Philip threw himself speechless with rage on to his horse and rode away at random without escort of any kind. He lost himself in a wood, and spent the night in a charcoal-burner's cottage, while his terrified courtiers searched for him and knew not what to do.

Charles as Count of Charolais was also painted by Rogier. The portrait is strangely touched with melancholy. Charles owed his tendency to sadness, as well as his obstinacy, to his Portuguese mother. According to Chastellain he was not so tall as his father, nor did he carry himself so erect, but he also was of imposing appearance. His gleaming, laughing eyes, clear as an angel's when he was sunk in thought, are strongly reminiscent of Duke Philip. His body was vigorous, agile and muscular, capable of any work or exertion. Charles had strong shoulders, a fine leg and powerful thighs, a long hand and a beautiful foot. His face was rounder and the complexion fairer than his father's; the mouth, however, was identical. He possessed a well-shaped nose, noble brow, and plenty of thick black hair. In walking he leant forward looking to the ground.

These portraits of Philip and Charles show that Rogier aimed at psychological analysis. He is not content with an unprejudiced and incisive reproduction of external features, his desire is to force his way into the interior and seize the spiritual man. There is nothing glad or positive in his portraits. They seem to have been executed under some kind of constraint, as if the artist were tortured and unable to control himself, and this, whether the portrait was that of a knight of the Golden Fleece, or Philippe de Croy, or an aged princess.

Possibly Rogier transmitted to some of his sitters a tincture of his own melancholy. But this was not always necessary. The aristocracy had a streak of weariness which they did not attempt to conceal, and even emphasized in order to be in the fashion :

> Je suis celluy au cueur vestu de noir,

as Charles d'Orleans once complained. Even Villon, the plebeian and homeless vagrant, was tinged with melancholy. It was, while at Blois, that a like temper gave birth to the beautiful verses :—

> Je meurs de seuf auprès de la fontaine . . .
> Je riz en pleurs, et attens sans espoir . . .
> Je m'esjouys et n'ay plaisir aucun.

Very different are the verses of Lorenzo de' Medici, deeply as they too are plunged in melancholy.

> Quant'è bella giovinezza,
> Che si fugge tuttavia !
> Chi vuol esser lieto, sia :
> Di doman non c'è certezza.

Rogier's fame spread quickly, even beyond the Alps. Italians celebrated him principally as a pupil of Jan Van Eyck. He himself must have made many friends during his stay in Italy and particularly at Ferrara, where he gave lessons in painting. In the course of his journey he painted the portrait of Lionello d'Este, as well as two devotional pictures, of which one passed into the possession of the Medici, while in the other, the Bewailing of Christ, the influence of Fra Angelico can be clearly traced. This work, it appears, met later with the full approval of Michaelangelo. It is pleasant to observe this exchange of ideas among artists, who had so much to tell and give to one another ; the intercourse between them may well have been far more active than we are tempted to think. With their lively interest in everything that was new, Italian artists were only too willing to go to the Netherlands : "*fu una bellissima invenzione ed una gran comodità all'arte della pittura il trovare il colorito a olio,*" as Vasari wrote subsequently. Francesco Sforza sent the Milanese painter Zanetto Bugatto to Brussels where he worked for several years in Rogier's

PLATE 25

Rogier van der Weyden : Charles, Count of Charolais.   Kaiser-Friedrich Museum, Berlin.

[face p. 234

studio. Justus of Ghent left his home to settle down in Urbino. Bishop Guillaume Fillastre of Tournai, whose business often led him to Italy, had his tomb executed in the workshop of della Robbia.

The *Medailleurs* followed the painters' example. Nicolo Spinelli, who was painted by Memling, and Giovanni Candida were both employed about the Burgundian Court. Candida, a skilful diplomatist, made medals as a hobby, and his beautiful productions may well have helped him to success in his diplomatic missions.

Countless orders for pictures, miniatures, carpets, stuffs, armour, and jewellery were given on both sides of the Alps to celebrated masters. The great Italian houses had their representatives in Bruges who drew their attention to anything noteworthy. Princes took pleasure in sending one another their portraits, and political relations were frequently opened up and cemented by costly presents. Jan Maelweel painted Duke John for the King of Portugal.

Tapestry weaving was much in favour at Court. Duke Philip the Bold liked to adorn his castles with bright-coloured tapestries and gave large orders to the *tapissiers*. He favoured specially the workshops of Arras, but took pleasure also in those of Tournai; the work of Pasquier Grenier excited his particular approval. The tapestries of Tournai soon dominated the market, and there were in addition smaller manufactories at Ypres and Oudenaarde, as well as at Paris.

The dukes took their tapestries with them from one residence to another, and even on their journeys abroad. Great admiration was aroused by the splendid pieces displayed by Charles the Bold at Trèves, and costly tapestries were among the spoils captured by the Swiss after the battle of Grandson.

Tapestries had to be very carefully selected to suit the occasion. Great value was attached to symbolical significance. Upon one occasion when some French and English lords were negotiating an armistice, the Duke of Lancaster required the removal of the tapestries which presented battle scenes, saying, " He who is striving after peace, should not be reminded of war and destruction ! "

The diversity of subjects is surprising; mythology,

history, literature, biblical stories provided an absolutely inexhaustible source. Allegories were greatly in fashion. Incidents were taken from the life of the upper classes ; the activities of shepherds and the people were also reproduced, and flower pieces, with highly coloured blooms, and richly blazoned coats of arms were freely employed. Scenes from the lives of the Saviour and the Virgin, incidents from the Romance of the Rose and the Trojan wars were always popular. Trajan and Caesar, Alexander the Great and Charlemagne, Hercules and Jason, King Arthur, Godefroy de Bouillon, the Neuf Preux, and the Neuf Preuses all had their share of triumphs, and to them were added Popes and Cardinals, Emperors and members of the nobility. *Honneur* summoned her knights with warning voice. Virtue proclaimed to the world her victory over sin. Bear and stag hunts, falconry, the pursuit of wild swans and duck brought fresh pleasures to the beholders, while fashionably attired lords and ladies were introduced to show that affairs of the heart were not to be forgotten.

A considerable rivalry arose between painters, sculptors, miniaturists, *medailleurs*, and cartoonists, a rivalry which raised the standard of production and gave rise to a fruitful interchange of ideas between artists, scholars, and writers.

Jean Wauquelin in his history of Alexander the Great, supplied the tapestry-weavers with a whole series of episodes suitable for reproduction. Bishop Jehan Germain in his work *Deux Pans de la Tapisserie chrétienne* actually prescribed to artists the choice of their subjects. The pictures of Justice by Rogier van der Weyden, which were destroyed by fire, still live in the Berne tapestries.

The notes struck by two masters such as Jan Van Eyck and Rogier van der Weyden did not quickly die away. They are constantly to be heard again, sometimes loudly, sometimes softly, sometimes with greater purity, sometimes mingled with the new.

Hans Memling came from the Middle Rhine to Rogier's studio. His Last Judgment shows distinctly the influence of the painting of the same subject at Beaune. Memling moved later to Bruges and there developed his productive genius. How splendidly he has succeeded in depicting the incidents from the lives of the Saints !

Dirk Bouts went from Haarlem, where Albert van Ouwater worked, to Louvain, and there became the town painter. Though he was clearly influenced by the achievements of the two great masters, he pursued his own course. Two of his works are of particular interest, the great Last Supper altar-piece for the church of St. Peter, and the pictures of Justice.

Somewhat shyly and embarrassed, Bouts approached his task of grouping the Saviour and his twelve disciples in the chamber. The arrangement is a little constrained, but the artist has succeeded in creating an atmosphere which is perfectly in harmony with the scene. The Apostles listen to their Master's words with emotion. The servant pauses in the midst of his work, and standing still, overcome by his feelings, folds his hands in prayer. The steward by the dresser and the two listeners at the serving hatch recognize that something unusual is taking place, something which lies far outside the life of every day.

Though well acquainted with the splendour of the Burgundian Court, Bouts in this picture has avoided depicting fashionable costumes and gives the Saviour and the Apostles very simple garments. The table, too, is plainly laid, and shows no useless accessories. Only the hall where the celebration takes place, the hall of a Gothic castle, has any claim to magnificence. The stewards and servants provide additional evidence of the owner's wealth, a contrast introduced possibly with intention, as if to emphasize the poverty of the Saviour.

In his pictures for the Louvain town hall, on the other hand, Bouts took as his models for the spectators, courtiers, worshipful personages and burgesses of the town, all revelling in the richness and splendid colours of the costumes of the age. In addition to the long ceremonial *Houppelande*, as worn by the Emperor Otto, we see displayed the short fashionable coat, drawn in tightly at the waist, which constantly aroused the anger of moralists. Bouts kept closely to his subject which concerned the life of the Emperor Otto III. According to a legend, Otto's wife had made charges concerning an illustrious count who had rejected

her advances.   The first picture represents the execution
of the innocent man.   The second shows the divine punishment : the wife of the count appears before the Emperor's
court of justice with her husband's head demanding justice,
and substantiates her assertions by the ordeal of fire.   The
Emperor orders the slanderess to be executed.   Could the
demand for absolute justice, without regard to persons, be
better represented than here, where the Emperor refuses
to spare the Empress, his own wife ?

Bouts paid more heed than his contemporaries to the
drawing of children.   In his devotional pictures which
consequently acquired a *genre* touch, he gives the Infant
Christ very varied positions and movements.   In one, he is
lying contentedly at his Mother's breast, in another he is
romping in her lap ; in yet another, he is fondling her, or
tries to seize a flower or plays delightedly with his big toe.

This interest is all the more surprising, for children still
played a wholly subordinate rôle in art and were but little
heeded in literature.   It is a matter for comment that
a monument was erected in the Church of Halle to the child
of the Dauphin who had died during his stay at the Burgundian
Court.

Dirk Bouts and Memling, like so many others, borrowed
what they needed from Jan Van Eyck and Rogier van der
Weyden, and were satisfied with their own creations.   Hugo
van der Goes alone seems to have felt the burden of his
inheritance of genius.   He was tortured by doubts as to whether
he had administered properly the heritage of Jan Van Eyck,
which had been entrusted to him as to all gifted artists.

Hugo van der Goes was a restless innovator full of glowing
ambition, sensitive and hypercritical.   He worked in Ghent
and had already acquired a considerable reputation when
he was invited to take part in the preparations for the wedding
celebrations of Charles the Bold in Bruges.   Tommaso Portinari, the representative of the Medici in Flanders, conceived
the idea of presenting a devotional picture to the Hospital
of Santa Maria Nuova, which his ancestor Folco, father of
Dante's Beatrice, had founded, and he approached the Ghent
painter.   This was the origin of the Adoration of the Infant
Christ, the remarkable work of a great genius.   Goes depicts
the incident with an unparalleled power of illusion.   In their

passionate excitement lest the divine message should be lost, the shepherds are seen rushing along;—powerful, healthy, strong men of the people. Joseph lacks entirely that comical pathetic touch, which was so often given him at that period. Bare trees, on which daws are perched, show clearly the winter season. The fresh flowers are painted with delicate understanding; there are violets strewn on the ground; lilies and irises in an earthenware pot and glass mug, and columbine.

We see the same love of nature again in The Fall. Among the flowers appear pansies, wormwood, and pennyroyal. The mussel-like snail-shell of the sea-ear incited Goes to reproduce it. He devoted, however, his special attention to the serpent. In the records of old commentators he found that, like other animals before the Fall, it had walked on two legs. Consequently Goes gave it the legs of a frog; for its head he chose that of a woman, for its body that of an otter which tapered into the tail of a lizard. This fantastic, yet not ridiculous shape, heightens the picture's romantic attraction. A melancholy charm rests on the blossoming landscape. Nature, and with her the master, mourns the victory of evil, the fate that has befallen the whole of mankind.

Like the shepherds, overcome by the glad tidings of the angels, so also are the men and women in the Bewailing of Christ, and the apostles in the Death of Mary. The disciples are as different from one another as their attitudes, but all display the same elemental outburst of sorrow. He, who could feel thus for those who had died so long ago and inspire them afresh with newly pulsating life, was possessed of an abundant and deep inner feeling. But this over-sensitive man had not sufficient power of resistance in that harsh age full of glaring contrasts in which his fate had placed him, and fate overtook him in the prime of life.

Having moved from Ghent to Brussels, he lived as lay brother in the priory of Rouge-Cloître (Roo-Clooster) near that city. The stately buildings of the cloister were situated amidst pleasant but somewhat melancholy scenery in the heart of a wood, where giant trees raised their heads in monastic splendour, where flower-bedecked meadows shimmered in the dew, and a delicate veil of mist lay lightly over the peaceful fishponds.

Highly honoured by his contemporaries, distinguished by princely favour, and treated with benevolent indulgence by the Prior, the soul of the master was still without the peace he needed for his work. He despaired of his art and his capacity. He was " seriously alarmed as to how he was to finish all the pictures he had still to paint ". That mighty pioneer, Jan Van Eyck, to whom he owed so much, became his curse; the desire of surpassing him deprived him of his reason.

He collapsed during a journey to Cologne ; in the malignant burning fever which attacked him he wailed incessantly that he was a lost soul, condemned to eternal perdition, and tried to make away with himself. He was brought back to Brussels, and the Prior, in remembrance of the sufferings of King Saul, ordered him to be soothed by sweet music. He provided other distractions as well, to dispel, if possible, the clouds which obscured the patient's mind, and in time he recovered and his reason was restored to him. In deepest humility he renounced all worldy joys, but his creative powers were exhausted. Goes died in 1482, a broken man. He was buried in the courtyard of the cloister under the open sky.

Had his brooding brought him to the perception that the art of the Netherlands, once so famous, had now again reached a turning point and must seek for new ideals ?

Pictor Hugo Van der Goes humatus hic quiescit.
Dolet ars cum similem sibi modo nescit.

CONCLUSION

Rien ne m'est seur que la chose incertaine.—VILLON.

THE storms of the Hundred Years War witnessed the birth of the New Burgundian State and even during periods of temporary peace the fury of war was lurking in the background. It was in battle that Duke Philip the Bold accomplished the feat which brought him fame and wealth :—it was on the field of battle that his great-grandson met his death.

So, heavily and harshly, amidst the clash of arms, the age passed on. The gold, the pomp and splendour to be met with on all sides, only superficially concealed the misery which lay beneath. Hardly was the thunder of the battle silenced before society was seized by a perfect frenzy of pleasure. The bitter dregs, however, were not spared to those lords and ladies who yearned for the cup of rejoicing. No cry of joy, as of an *aurea ætas*, resounded through the world.

Philip the Good on one occasion cursed the day of his birth. On the death of his one-year-old son, he cried out in his grief : " *Pleust à Dieu que je fusse mort aussi josne, je me tenroie bien heurés.*" Others, too, might have echoed this sentiment. What value had human life in an age in which the best might fall a victim to every clumsy chance, in which hundreds, without choice or alternative, were swept away in incessant warfare, leaving no trace behind ; in which hundreds met their death by plague and famine.

The wild, stormy age could not leave the world in peace. " *Rien ne m'est seur que la chose incertaine,*" says Villon. The incessant uncertainty must have been unbearable. None ever knew what the morrow would bring forth. Suicides increased. No crime seemed impossible. Rumours throve and prospered as never before. When the great and powerful died the thought of poison was in everybody's mind. The violence of the times favoured one class only, the newly rich. These upstarts knew how to turn the

changed conditions to their profit, which they did with
impudent boldness. But their prosperity was brief, and
they vanished as speedily as they arose. It was an age of
destruction and dissolution, which played havoc with every
aspiration and emotion, and above all an age of glaring
contrasts. We are faced with acts of the deepest piety,
with entire renunciation of the world, as, for example, in the
Windesheim houses, then with a purely superficial and
conventional religion which dragged down holy things into
the dust and turmoil of daily life. Fervent belief, sincere
resignation to God, and crude superstition and heretical
unbelief ; strict ecclesiasticism and thoughtless scoffing ;
ascetic denials, mortification of the flesh and a luxurious,
sensual mode of life on the part of the princes of the Church,
who regarded their sacred office solely as an inexhaustible
source of wealth. Complete indifference towards the idea
of an after-life went hand in hand with a miserable fear of
magic, with wizardry and devilry. Subtle learning was
allied to the basest superstition ; the most horrible crimes
gave rise to a system of justice which seems to us inhumanly
severe. Wild orgies of immorality and gluttony were
followed by spontaneous acts of penitence : exultant hymns
in praise of the rose-garlanded goddess of Love, by stammering
prayers to the gracious image of the Virgin ; untamed and
boundless arrogance and aggression, by acts of the deepest
humility and contrition. Unbridled passions were concealed
beneath a rigid ceremonial. At one moment we have an
apotheosis of the ruler, and the next a riot of criticism which
makes an end of all reverence. Noble chivalry based on
honour was stained with cowardly violence against the weak.
While a rigid code of rules controlled the jousts and tourneys
we find an utter failure of knightly ideals in battle. Glorification of the lady and the tenderest service of love ended
too often in marriages of convenience and in the sexual
degradation of woman. It was an age of fiery enthusiasm
and weary nonchalance ; of senseless waste on the one hand
and grinding poverty on the other ; of childish naiveté
and sophistical cunning ; of noisy and flamboyant achievement, contrasted with a simple and genuine striving after
beauty which trembled in the presence of the wonders
of creation.

In the general resignation of despair there was no longer any belief, no longer any loyalty and honour upon earth. *Taire, souffrir, faindre et dissimuler* was the common watchword. Was not the world ripe for the advent of the Anti-Christ? There were conflicts in the domain of the Church, in politics and economics; conflicts in the domain of art and science, intellectual conflicts and a new conception of life. Humanism and the Renaissance were pressing forward from Italy. The attitude towards them was still in doubt. Scholastics and craftsmen striving to become artists preserved their own outlook, but none could ignore the signs of the times. The conflict of two worlds was beginning. Charles the Bold turned aside from the chivalry in which Philip the Good had seen salvation. He revelled in the antique, filling his mind and imagination with pictures of the great conquerors and intoxicating himself with the stories of their deeds. Charles was willing to welcome the Renaissance, but in attempting to liberate himself from the fetters of tradition, he nevertheless remained its prisoner. In his adventurous policy of conquest he still clung to the ideas of knighthood and romance. What a contrast is here between Charles' ambitions, and the cool, calculating methods of Louis XI, to whom honour itself was little but a hollow mockery.

Charles was carried off by death in the midst of the fiercest intellectual and political conflicts. The Burgundian State had still to prove its capacity and justify its existence, while society parleyed with the Renaissance knocking at its gates.

NOTES

IN these notes I mention only the most important works which will introduce the reader to the literature of the subject. I have avoided all controversy. The knowing reader will appreciate at once to what extent I have followed the earlier writers on Burgundian history and again to what extent I have exercised my own judgment. As I have dealt in detail in the past with certain important points which have arisen, so I hope in the future to employ myself with other questions which are equally important. There is no up-to-date bibliography of Burgundian history. The following works, however, are important.

H. Pirenne, Bibliographie de l'histoire de Belgique. Bruxelles, Gand 1902[2].

A. Kleinclausz, La Bourgogne. Les régions de la France III. Paris 1905.

L. Febvre, La Franche-Comté. Les régions de la France IV. Paris 1905.

V. Fris, Bibliographie de l'histoire de Gand depuis les origines jusqu'à la fin du XVe siècle, Société d'histoire et d'archéologie de Gand, Publication extraordinaire no. 2, Gand 1907.

A. Molinier, Les sources de l'histoire de France des origines aux guerres d'Italie (1494). T. 1–6 Paris 1901–1906.

* * * * *

Of importance for the whole work are :—

H. Pirenne, Histoire de Belgique II[3], Bruxelles 1922.

H. Pirenne, Les anciennes démocraties des Pays-Bas. Paris 1910. [English translation by J. L. Saunders. Manchester 1915.]

P. Fredericq, Essai sur le rôle politique et social des ducs de Bourgogne dans les Pays-Bas. Gand 1875.

H. Pirenne, The formation and constitution of the Burgundian state ; American Historical Review XIV (1909) 477 ff. (Die Entstehung und die Verfassung des burgundischen Reiches im 15. und 16. Jahrhundert ; Jahrbuch für Gesetzgebung . . . im deutschen Reich 33 (1909) 895 ff.)

L. Febvre, Les ducs Valois de Bourgogne et les idées politiques de leur temps, Revue Bourguignonne . . . 23 (1913).

J. Huizinga, Herfsttij der middeleeuwen. Studie over levens- en gedachtenvormen der veertiende en vijftiende eeuw in Frankrijk en de Nederlanden. Haarlem 1921[2].

J. Huizinga, The Waning of the Middle Ages [English translation]. London, 1924.

A. Kleinclausz, Histoire de Bourgogne, Paris 1909.

Histoire de France p. p. E. Lavisse : IV, 1 A. Coville, Les premiers Valois et la guerre de Cent ans (1328–1422), Paris 1902 ; IV, 2 Ch. Petit-Dutaillis, Charles VII, Louis XI et les premières années de Charles VIII (1422–1492), Paris 1902.

J. H. Wylie, History of England under Henry the Fourth. 4 vols. London 1884 ff.

J. H. Wylie, The reign of Henry V. I 1413–1415, Cambridge 1914.

James H. Ramsay. Lancaster and York. Oxford 1892.

G.-P. de Barante, Histoire des ducs de Bourgogne de la maison de Valois 1364–1477 has now only a literary value, but the notes contain much that is valuable. See the edition with notes by M. Gachard, vols. 1 and 2. Brussels 1838.

CHAPTER I
INTRODUCTORY

Page 1   O. Cartellieri, Geschichte der Herzöge von Burgund 1363–1477. Bd. 1 Philipp der Kühne, Herzog von Burgund. Leipzig 1910. See the bibliography pp. 163 ff. ; E. Petit, Ducs de Bourgogne de la maison de Valois d'après des documents inédits. T. Ier Philippe le Hardi. Ière partie. 1363–1380. Paris 1909.

Page 1   Praise of Flanders in Christine de Pisan, Le livre des faits . . . du sage roy Charles VI. Michaud et Poujoulat, Nouvelle collection des mémoires . . . II (Paris 1857) 19.

Page 3   M. Chaume, Les origines du duché de Bourgogne. Ière partie. Histoire politique. Dijon 1925. Also W. M. Crowdy, Burgundy and Morvan. London 1925.

Page 3   On the purchase of the County of Charolais in 1390 : Cartellieri, Philipp der Kühne 111. Note 3.

Page 3   Wilhelm Brito, Philippis lib. I v. 568 ff. ; see also lib. X v. 501 ff. : Œuvres de Rigord et de Guillaume le Breton vol. II Paris 1885. Soc. de l'hist. de France.

Page 3   Gregorii Turonensis historia Francorum l. III c. 19, Opera I 129. SS. Rerum Merovingicarum I. Hannoverae 1885.

Page 3   Francisci Petrarchae opera quae extant omnia, Basileae 1554, Litterae seniles l. VII ep. I S. 909 ; compare l. IX ep. I.

Page 4   J. Michelet, Histoire de France. Nouv. éd. II (Paris s. d.) 160 : " La France n'a pas d'élément plus liant que la Bourgogne, plus capable de réconcilier le nord et le midi."

Page 4   J. Froissart, Chroniques. P. ed. S. Luce et G. Raynaud Paris 1869 ff. IX 161 (compare IX 158).

Page 4   Bartholomaeus Anglicus, called de Glanville, Liber de proprietatibus rerum ; Praise of Flanders, see Laude, Catalogue des manuscrits de la bibliothèque de Bruges. Bruges 1859.

Page 4   On the " drie lede van Vlaenderen ", to which the Franc of Bruges was added later as fourth member, see Pirenne, Hist. de Belg. II 165.

Page 4   On Froissart compare Kervyn de Lettenhove, Froissart. Etudes littéraires sur le XIVe siècle I (Bruxelles 1857) 145.—V. Fris, Histoire de Gand. Bruxelles et Paris 1913.

Page 4   R. Häpke, Brügges Entwicklung zum mittelalterlichen Weltmarkt. Berlin 1908. Abhandlungen zur Verkehrs- und Seegeschichte I. Bd. ; G. Eckhout, Le port de Bruges au moyen-âge : Rev. des Quest. Scientifiques 60 (1906) 110 ff. Malcolm Letts, Bruges and its Past, 2nd ed. Bruges and London, 1926. According to the much-travelled Pero Tafur, Bruges was a more important mercantile centre than Venice. Pero Tafur, Travels and Adventures (1435–1439), translated by M. Letts, London, 1926, p. 198, and Otto Cartellieri, Pero Tafur, ein spanischer Weltreisender, in Festschrift Alexander Cartellieri, Weimar 1927 1 ff.

Page 5   Olivier van Dixmude, Merkwaerdige gebeurtenissen, ed. J. J. Lambin Ypre 1835, p. 32, laments in 1405 the growing poverty of Ypres which was once so flourishing, " dat mense compareerde tjeghen Paris."

Page 6   On the regency, see R. Holtzmann, Französische Verfassungsgeschichte . . . Handbuch der mittelalterl. u. neueren Gesch . . . München und Berlin 1910 S. 189 f.

Page 6   On the illness of Charles VI see A. Brachet, Pathologie mentale des rois de France. Louis XI et ses ascendants (Paris 1903) 621 ff. J. Saltel, La folie du roi Charles VI. Thèse. Toulouse 1907.

Page 7   N. Valois, La France et le grand schisme d'occident. 4 vols. Paris 1896 ff. ; J. Haller, Papsttum und Kirchenreform. Vier Kapitel zur Geschichte des ausgehenden Mittelalters, vol. I Berlin 1903.

Page 7   O. Cartellieri, König Heinrich V. von England und Herzog Johann von Burgund im J. 1414, Beiträge zur Geschichte der Herzöge von Burgund IV. Sitzungsberichte der Heidelberger Akademie der

Wissenschaften. Philos-hist. Klasse. Jahrgang 1913, 9. Abhandlung. W. Söchting, Die Beziehungen zwischen Flandern und
England am Ende des 14 JH. Hist. Vierteljahrsschrift 32 (1928)
182 ff.

Page 7 On the paix fourrées : Jean Jouvenel in Jean Juvenal des Ursins,
Histoire de Charles VI, roi de France augmentée . . . par Denys
Godefroy. Paris 1653. S. 198 (after the Peace of Chartres 1409) :
" Et avoit (le duc de Bourgogne) un très bon fol en sa compagnée
qu'on disoit estre fol sage, lequel tantost alla acheter une paix
d'église et la fit fourrer et disoit que c'estoit une paix fourrée.
Et ainsi advint depuis."

Page 8 P. Durrieu, Jean Sans Peur, duc de Bourgogne, lieutenant et
procureur général du diable ès parties d'occident. Annuaire-
bulletin de la soc. de l'hist. de France 24 (1887) 193 ff.

Page 8 Jouvencel 351.

Page 8 Henry V. : Chronique de Jean Le Févre, seigneur de Saint-Remy.
ed. F. Morand 2 vols. Paris 1876, 1881. Société de l'histoire de
France.—I 261. Vgl. Œuvres de Georges Chastellain ed. by baron
Kervyn de Lettenhove. 8 vols. Bruxelles 1863–1866. I. 309.

Page 8 Chastellain (Le Miroer de nobles hommes de France) VI 215.

Page 9 Murder at Montereau : G. Du Fresne de Beaucourt, Histoire de
Charles VII vol. I (Paris 1881) 128 ff. does not persuade me of
the innocence of the Dauphin (Charles VII).

Page 9 On the general demand for revenge, Olivier de La Marche. Mémoires
ed. H. Beaune et J. d'Arbaumont. 4 vols. Paris 1883/88. Soc.
de l'histoire de France. I 201. See also I 89, Chastellain I 79 ff.

Page 10 Philip the Good and England : Chastellain I 332, II 9.

Page 10 caudati : compare F. Liebermann in Mon. Germ. SS. XXVII
77 note 2 ; also Etienne de Bourbon, Anecdotes . . . ed. A.
Lecoy de La Marche (Paris 1877) S. 234. Société de l'histoire
de France.

Page 10 F. Schneider, Der europäische Friedenskongress von Arras (1435)
und die Friedenspolitik Papst Eugens IV. und des Basler Konzils.
Greiz 1919.

Page 10 Philip the Good : Grand duc du ponant, Chastellain II 150.

Page 11 On the Burgundian demands, La Marche I 207 ; Chastellain I 196.

Page 11 Philip's complaint : Chastellain III 419.

Page 12 Chastellain II 151 ff.

Page 12 Death of Henry V. : Chastellain I 331.

Page 12 F. v. Löher, Kaiser Sigmund und der Herzog von Burgund. Münch-
ner Historisches Jahrbuch 1866.

Page 12 Otto Cartellieri, Wie das Deutsche Reich die Niederlande verlor.
Die Grenzboten 74 (1915) Heft 44–46.

Page 13 On the Hanse, beside the works of Daenell, see W. Stein, Die
Burgunderherzöge und die Hanse. Hansische Geschichtsblätter
XXV (1901) 7 ff. W. Vogel, Kurze Geschichte der deutschen
Hanse : Pfingstblätter des hansischen Geschichtsvereins. 11.
Blatt 1915.

Page 16 On the Burgundian treasure, see a characteristic passage from
Chastellain III 92, printed in the original German edition p. 262.

Page 16 Chastellain (Déclaration) VII 222 : la perle des vaillans et l'estoile
de chevalerie.

Page 16 Court of Horn : Mathieu d'Escouchy, Chronique, ed. G. du
Fresne de Beaucourt. Soc. de l'hist. de France 3 vols. Paris 1863
f. II 169.

Page 16 Count Eberhard II of Würtemberg was trained at the Court of
Philip the Good. C. F. v. Stälin, Wirtembergische Geschichte
III (Stuttgart 1856) 555 ; also Chastellain IV, 60. 76. 429.

Page 18 On Georges Chastellain : A. Pinchart, Archives des arts, sciences et
lettres, Documents inédits. Première série I. II. III. Gand 1860–
1881. II 277.

Page 18 It was only with great difficulty that the Brussels Amman and the other Flemish lords understood the "gros haut allemand" spoken by the envoys of the Emperor Frederick III, Chastellain 423 f.

Page 19 Philip's care for his people. After his 60th birthday he said to Chastellain : qu'il ne désiroit point que Dieu lui donnast ceste grâce de tant vivre . . . , car savoit bien que l'eage en celuy temps est tout décrépite et confusible à la propre personne et à tout autre ; par quoy il ne désiroit point les longs jours, ce dist, sinon en tant que nature le pourroit entretenir estre utile à quelconque bien et donner fruit à son peuple ; Chastellain III 134.

Page 19 Abbeville. Philip's illness in 1462. Chastellain IV, 201 f.

Page 19 On death of Philip the Good, Chastellain V 228 (also IV 210). E. Clerc, Essai sur l'histoire de la Franche-Comté II (Besançon 1870²) 544 Note 2. E. Clerc, Histoire des états-généraux . . . en Franche-Comté I (Besançon 1882) 130 Note 1.

Page 19 J. Huizinga, Uit de voorgeschiedenis van ons nationaal besef. De Gids 76, 1 (1912) 432 ff.

Page 19 L. Febvre, Philippe II et la Franche-Comté . . . Thèse . . . Paris (Paris 1911) 50 f.

Page 19 Molinet, Le throsne d'honneur, Les Faictz et dictz (Paris 1537) fol. 61. On the verse, Par trois fois fut requis pour gouverner l'empire compare Chastellain (Déclaration) VII 216, Guill. Fillastre, below p. 252. Le premier volume de la Toison d'Or fol. 129ᵛ: The most important passages need explanation.

Page 20 John F. Kirk, History of Charles the Bold, Duke of Burgundy. 3 vols. 1863 ff. R. Putnam, Charles the Bold, the last Duke of Burgundy, New York 1908.

Page 20 La Marche I 89 : " Phelippe . . . eut deux noms acquis et donnez. Le premier fut Phelippe l'Asseuré et en longhe continuance d'expéri-ment de ses meurs et vertus il fut nommé le bon duc Phelippe, en nom et tiltre, et luy est ce tiltre demouré." Compare III 315.

Page 20 President Philippe Wielant († 1520) says " Le ducq Philippe aymoit la maison de France et se tenoit fort heureux et bien honnoré d'en estre venu et sorty ", but " le ducq Charles ne hayssoit rien tant que la maison de France. Depuis la paix d'Arras le ducq Philippe portoit tousjours grand honneur à la personne du roy de France, ostant tousjours son chaperon, quant on parloit de lui, et le ducq Charles se tenoit esgal au roy de France et en tous traittez et actes vouloit user d'égalité ". Recueil des Antiquités de Flandre, Corpus Chronicorum Flandriae p. p. J. J. De Smet IV (1865) 52 f.

Page 20 Charles the Bold's speech in 1473 : Monget II 162.

Page 21 Mémoires de Philippe de Commynes. Nouvelle édition ed. B. de Mandrot. Collection de textes pour servir à l'étude et à l'enseigne-ment de l'histoire 2 vols. Paris 1901, 1903.—I 390.

Page 22 H. Delbrück, Geschichte der Kriegskunst . . . III² Das Mittelalter (Berlin 1923) 629 ff.

CHAPTER II

The Carthusian Monastery of Champmol

Page 24 Social position of artists : H. Bouchot, La condition sociale des peintres du XIIIᵉ au XVᵉ siècle. Revue des Deux Mondes 5ᵉ période 43 (1908) 153 ff. H. Huth, Künstler und Werkstatt der Spätgotik. Augsburg 1923.

Page 24 On Colart de Laon : Bouchot 163.

Page 25 The Maillotins who in 1391 caused an insurrection in Paris were named from their weapon, maillot, a hammer.

Page 25 Christine de Pisan, Cité des dames lib. I c. XLI.

Page 25   The position of the " varlets de chambre " is not clear in spite of the important and somewhat neglected passage in La Marche (Estat) IV, 18. There seem to have been many gradations in rank.

Page 25   On the right of using seals : J. Simonnet, Le tabellionage en Bourgogne (XIVe et XVe siècles) in Mémoires de l'académie impériale des sciences, arts et belles-lettres de Dijon IIe série t. XII (Lettres 1864) 11 ff., also Mémoires pour servir à l'histoire de France et de Bourgogne . . . II (Paris 1729) 314 f.

Page 26   Complaints of taxation : B. Prost, Une nouvelle source de documents sur les artistes dijonnais du XVe siècle, Gazette des Beaux-Arts 3e période IV (1890) V, VI (1891). Claus van Werve IV 352, and Monget (s. below) II 102.

Page 27   A. Kleinclausz, Les peintres des ducs de Bourgogne, Revue de l'art ancien et moderne 20 (1906) 161 ff.

Page 27   Bellechose painted in 1427 de blanc et de rouge den jaquemart of Notre-Dame, sculpté par " Pierre l'Alement tailleur d'ymages ". This notice, from the Bibl. Nat. Coll. Bourg. vol. XXI fol. 66 (Monget II 108) seems to have escaped P. Fredericq, in Le vieux Courtraisien de Dijon, Bulletins de la classe des lettres et des sciences morales et politiques et de la classe des beaux-arts de l'académie royale de Belgique 1909 S. 379 ff. compare Cartellieri, Philipp der Kühne 21.

Page 28   Vagabondage : P. Champion, François Villon. Sa vie et son temps. 2 vols. Paris 1913. II 82 ff.

Page 28   Inns at Dijon : H. Chabeuf, Charles Le Téméraire à Dijon en janvier 1474. Mémoires de la soc. Bourguignonne . . . 18 (1902) 106.

Page 29   The standard work is C. Monget, La Chartreuse de Dijon d'après les documents des archives de Bourgogne 3 vols. Montreuil-sur-Mer 1898 ff. Compare A. Kleinclausz, Claus Sluter et la sculpture bourguignonne au XVe siècle Paris s. d. Les Maîtres de l'art (Bibliographie p. 169 ff.) ; A. Germain, Les Néerlandais en Bourgogne, Bruxelles 1909 ; A. Humbert, La sculpture sous les ducs de Bourgogne (1361–1483) Paris 1913. Also J. Casier, Les imagiers de la chartreuse de Champmol à Dijon (Gand) 1909.

Page 29   Maelweel : " un tableaux à plusieurs ymages d'apostres et de Saint Anthoine qu'il fait mettre tous les jours devant lui en son oratoire " ; Monget I 287. Carved altars, Monget I 201 ff.

Page 29   The foundations were laid in 1383.

Page 30   Jean de Marville died before 1 July 1388. He was probably a Fleming and came perhaps from Merville (Dép. Nord) ; Monget I 65. He was helped by the gilder Herman de Couloigne, Monget I 345. See E. Firmenich-Richartz, Wilhelm van Herle und Hermann Wynrich van Wesel . . . Düsseldorf 1896.

Page 30   Sluter's appointment dated 23 July 1389 ; see V. Habicht, Claus Sluter, ein Niedersachse ? Rep. für Kunstwissenschaft 44 (1924) 154 ff. Monget I 406 nr. 29.

Page 30   Sluters seal, Monget I 181. Illustration p. 76.

Page 30   André Beauneveu : Froissart (ed. Kervyn de Lettenhove, Bruxelles 1872) XIV 197.

Page 31   The figures of the two saints were set up in 1391, those of the Duchess Margaret and the Duke in 1393 and 1396–7 respectively. See illustration p. 30.

Page 31   On the Duchess Margaret, see Cartellieri, Philipp der Kühne 13 f.

Page 31   It is not possible to fix from the accounts the date when the Madonna was set up.

Page 31   Illustration p. 24.

Page 31   Jean de Beaumez, or Biaumes (Monget I 113.286), came probably from Beaumetz-les-Loges (Arr. Arras) and died 16 Oct. 1396. Ledit feu Maulouel, qui estoit du païs d'Alemaigne, Monget I 286 Note 2.

Page 32   The works are in the Louvre except the carved altar which is in the Museum at Dijon.

Page 32   Jacques de Bars (Baers) from Dendermonde : Monget I 201.
Page 32   Melchior Broederlam, seal and signature : Monget I 205.
Page 32   Dispensation : Monget I S. VIII.
Page 32   Illustration of the Fountain, p. 32.
Page 34   On the part played by Jean de Marville in connection with Philip's monument, see Monget I 181.
Page 34   Sluters contract with Saint-Etienne in Dijon. 7. April 1404 : Monget I 371.
Page 34   On death of Philip the Bold, see Cartellieri, Philipp der Kühne 108 ff. ; On his debts, see 109.
Page 34   Dino Rapondi : Monget I 47 f. ; Le Roux de Lincy et L. M. Tisserand, Paris et ses historiens au XIVe et au XVe siècles (Paris 1867) 335 ff. ; Doutrepont 13 Note 2.
Page 35   An account for mourning amounts to 1304 escus 2 sols 9 deniers parisis for 2011¼ ells of cloth.
Page 35   On the grant of monachatus the 9 Juli 1404 : Monget I 368 ff.
Page 35   Skins were spread over the marble slab " pour que les chiens ne montassent dessus ".
Page 35   Only two Pleurants were finished at Philip's death. Monget II 16.
Page 35   Sluter died between 24 Sept 1405 and 31 Jan. 1406. Monget I 373. See H. Drouot, La mort de Claus Sluter et la fin de sa carrière. Bulletin monumental 75 (1911) 277 ff.
Page 35   On the completion of the monument in January 1411 : Monget I 374 II 17. S. Mâle, L'art religieux de la fin du moyen âge en France 415 ff. The pleurants are no longer in their original places and some originals are missing. On their fate see Monget III 175. 184 f. ; Ch. Oursel, Les " pleurants " disparus des tombeaux des ducs de Bourgogne au musée de Dijon, Bulletin archéologique du comité des traveaux historiques et scientifiques 1909 S. 14 ff. ; H. Drouot, Le nombre des " pleurants " aux tombeaux des ducs de Bourgogne, Revue de l'art chrétien 61 (1911) 135 ff. ; H. Drouot, De quelques dessins du XVIIIe siècle représentant les tombeaux des ducs de Bourgogne, Revue de l'art chrétien 61 (1911) 486 f. Philip's wife Margaret was buried at the church of St. Pierre in Lille. See illustration p. 34.

CHAPTER III
THE GLORIFICATION OF TYRANNICIDE

Page 36   O. Cartellieri, Die Ermordung des Herzogs Ludwig von Orléans (23 November 1407). Beiträge zur Geschichte der Herzöge von Burgund (I). Sitzungsberichte der Heid.Ak. der Wiss. Philos.-Hist. Kl. Jgg. 1912 Abh. 11. See also Chroniques de France (Ms. de Lille nr. 26) printed by de la Fons-Melicocq in Bulletin de la soc. de l'hist. de France 2e sér. I (1857/58) 181 f. See illustration p. 38.
Page 36   Louis of Orléans : E. Jarry, La vie politique de Louis de France, duc d'Orléans 1372-1407. Paris, Orléans 1889. Cartellieri, Philipp der Kühne 59 f.
Page 36   Chastellain I 17 : Johann " ayant fait faire (the murder) sans conseil que de lui-mesmes ".
Page 37   Chronique normande de Pierre Cochon . . . p. p. Ch. de Robilla d de Beaurepaire (Rouen 1870) 222 : " Beneët soit qui tel coup y rua ! Car, s'il eust plus vesqui, il eust destruit tout le royaume."
Page 37   Among the chroniclers it is enough to mention Enguerrand de Monstrelet, Chronique . . . 1400-1444 . . . p. par L. Douët d'Arcq 6 vols. Paris 1857 ff. Société de l'histoire de France Bd. I 167 ff. Chronique du Religieux de Saint-Denis . . . p. p. L. Bellaguet 6 vols. Paris 1839 ff. Collection de documents inédits sur l'histoire de France. III 748 ff.

Page 38   On this interesting but sadly damaged Manifesto, until now unknown, datum in villa nostra Actrabatensi XVII febr. anno domini M⁰ CCCC⁰ septimo : see Lille, Arch. du Nord B 1460 nr. 15124, copy or draft on paper.

Page 40   Jean Petit : L. Puiseux, Les docteurs normands du XVe siècle . . . Mémoires lus à la Sorbonne dans les séances . . . tenues 1863. Histoire . . . (Paris 1864) 363 ff. ; Valois, La France et le grand schisme d'occident und im Chartularium universitatis Parisiensis . . . collegit et . . . contulit H. Denifle O. P. auxiliante A. Chatelain vol. IV Parisiis 1897, Monstrelet I 183. 208.

Page 40   A. Coville, Le véritable texte de la justification du duc de Bourgogne par Jean Petit (8 mars 1408). Bibliothèque de l'école des chartes 72 (1911) 57 ff. See Doutrepont 283 ff. A faulty text in Monstrelet I 178 ff.

Page 41   1. Tim. 6, 10.

Page 43   The fifth and sixth " Truths " are given by Monstrelet I 215 f., but incomplete. In the MSS. at Brussels is a long addition (printed in the original German ed. at p. 268). Bibliothèque Royale nr. 12881 fol. 17ᵛ sqq. saec. XVII und nr. 4374 fol. 173ᵛ sqq. saec. XV.

Page 46   Monstrelet I 242 : " après dist icellui proposant que icellui duc de Bourgogne retenoit et réservoit encores aucunes autres choses plus grandes à dire au roy quant lieu et temps seroit ".

Page 46   Religieux de Saint-Denis III 764.

Page 47   On the pardon dated 9 March 1408, see O. Cartellieri, Zum Frieden von Chartres (9. März 1409). Beiträge zur Geschichte der Herzöge von Burgund (II). Sitzungsberichte der Heidelberger Akademie der Wissenschaften. Philos.-hist. Klasse. Jahrgang 1912. 11. Abhandlung. p. 10, note 23.

Page 47   Disorders at Liège, see F. Schneider, Herzog Johann von Baiern . . . Historische Studien Heft 104. Berlin 1913.

Page 48   Thomas von Cerisi's speech, see Monstrelet I 269 ff.

Page 49   O. Cartellieri, Fragmente aus der zweiten " Justification du duc de Bourgogne " des Magisters Johann Petit. Herausgegeben unter Mitwirkung von W. Holtzmann. Beiträge zur Gesch. der Herzöge von Burgund V. Sitzungsberichte der Heid. Ak. der Wiss. Philos.-hist. Kl. Jahrgang 1914. 6. Abhandlung.

Page 50   J. B. Schwab, Johannes Gerson . . . Würzburg 1858. B. Bess, Zur Geschichte des Konstanzer Konzils I : Frankreichs Kirchenpolitik und der Process des Jean Petit über die Lehre vom Tyrannenmord bis zur Reise König Sigismunds (Marburg 1891) ; C. Kamm, Der Process gegen die " Justificatio ducis Burgundiae auf der Parifer Synode 1413–1414. Diss. Freiburg i/Br., Rom 1911 (Separatabzug aus der Römischen Quartalschrift 1912). B. Bess, Die Lehre vom Tyrannenmord auf dem Konstanzer Konzil, Zeitschr. für Kirchengesch. 36 (1915/16).

Page 51   On a plan to murder Duke John in 1408, see the assertion by Jaquemin d'Oylin, Dijon, Arch. Côte d'Or nr. 11892, draft on paper Paris, Bibl. Nat. Coll. Bourgogne 54 fol. 167.

CHAPTER IV
THE RULER AND HIS COURT

Page 52   A. Coville, Les Cabochiens et l'ordonnance de 1413 (Thèse . . . Paris ; Paris 1888).

Page 53   Karl Wenck, Philipp der Schöne von Frankreich, seine Persönlichkeit und das Urteil der Zeitgenossen (Marburg 1905) 54 ff. L. v. Ranke, Weltgeschichte IX 238.

Page 54   Entry into Ghent, see below p. 207. Sy fut le duc celle première nuyt si asseuré et si à sa paix d'estre là que lui troisième ou quatrième alla voir et visiter les feux et les festes tout partout, dont le peuple

se laissa cheoir en terre de joie et baisoit les marches de ses piés . . .
Chastellain III 416.

Page 54   Jacques Du Clercq, Mémoires (1448–1467), éd. F. de Reiffenberg.
Bruxelles 1823. 4 vols. II, 205.

Page 54   A. de Lalaing, Voyage de Philippe le Beau en Espagne, p. p. Gachard,
Coll. des voyages des souverains des Pays-Bas I (Bruxelles 1876)
297, 301.

Page 54   One example will suffice : ung curedent, ouquel est mis en œuvre
ung diamant nommé la Lozenge et une grosse pointe de diamant
et une grosse perle. The manners of the time are well illustrated
in the account books. See Le comte de Laborde, Les ducs de
Bourgogne. Etudes sur les lettres, les arts et l'industrie pendant
le XVe siècle. Seconde partie t. 1–3 preuves Paris 1849/52. B.
et H. Prost, Inventaires mobiliers et extraits des comptes des ducs
de Bourgogne de la maison de Valois 1363–1477, vol. I Philippe
le Hardi 1363–77. Vol. II, Philippe le Hardi 1378–1390. Paris
1902/4. 1908/13 ; also M. Quantin, Les ducs de Bourgogne . . .
mœurs et usages (1384–1477). Paris 1882 (Extrait de la Revue
catholique de Louvain).

Page 55   Chastellain (Déclaration) VII 224 : avoit aussi en luy le vice de la
chair ; estoit durement lubrique et fraisle en cest endroit. Guillaume
Fillastre, Le premier volume de la Toison d'Or. Le second volume
de la Toison d'Or. Paris 1516 I fol. C XXXIv : de la fragilité
de la chair ne le vueil je excuser, car on me tiendroit flateur, mais
je vueil dire comme Saint Pol que la vertu de chasteté est donnée à si
peu de vivans sur la terre que qui la peult avoir, la tiegne ; car
il se pourra dire plus angélique que humain ; mais Dieu mercy
par luy ne fut oncques commis rapt ne violence ne chose faicte dont
nulle esclande soit advenue.

Page 55   de Reiffenberg, Enfants naturels du duc Philippe-le-Bon, Bulletins
de l'académie roy . . . de Belgique XIII, 1 (1846) 172 ff. XIV,
1 (1847) 585 ff. F. B., La fin d'une maîtresse de Philippe le Bon.
Nicolle la Chastellaine, dite du Bosquet. Souvenirs de la Flandre
Wallone 14 (1847) 186 ff. ; also H. Nélis in Revue Belge I (1922)
337 ff.

I give here some of the better-known Burgundian bastards :

Bastard of John the Fearless : John, Bishop of Cambrai † 1479,
son of Agnès de Croy.

Bastards of Philip the Good : Anthony, after Corneille's death :
le grand bâtard, seigneur de Beures etc. † 1504, son of Jeanne de
Presles.

Baudoin, † 1505, son of Catherine de Tiesferies.

Corneille, le grand bâtard, seigneur de Beures, † 1452, son of
Catherine Scaers.

David, Bishop of Thérouanne, afterwards of Utrecht † 1496,
son of Nicolle (Colette) la Chastellaine, dite du Bosquet (de Bosquiel).

Raphaël, Abbot of St. Bavo † 1508 ; son of the lady de
Mercatel, born de Belleval.

Anne, † 1505 married 1. Adriaan van Borselen † 1468 2. Adolph
of Cleves, Lord of Ravenstein † 1492.

Marguerite † 1454, daughter of Isabelle de la Vigne.

Marie, married Pierre de Bauffremont, sire de Charny ; daughter
of Nicolle la Chastellaine, dite du Bosquet.

Yolande, married Jean d'Ailly, baron de Picquigny.

Page 55   La Marche I 110 ff. ; also Des böhmischen Herrn Leo's von Rožmital
Ritter-, Hof- und Pilgerreife durch die Abendlande 1465–1467 . . .
Bibliothek des literarischen Vereins VII (Stuttgart 1844) 28 f.

Page 55   On the christening of Marie of Burgundy, see Aliénor de Poitiers,
Les honneurs de la cour : La Curne de Sainte-Palaye, Mémoires sur
l'ancienne chevalerie avec une introduction . . . par Ch. Nodier.
Nouv. éd. II (Paris 1826) 133 ff. p. 180 ff.

Page 55 On the Duchess Isabella, see Duclercq III 205 : la duchesse . . . se tenoit au bois de Nieppe, ainsy comme en dévotion, sans porter d'habit de religieuse. Compare also II 240 f. 286 f. IV 213. Chastellain III 443. VII (Advertissement) 331. Molinet, Faictz fol. XLIV.

Page 55 Charles the Bold : Jean Molinet, Chroniques, 5 vols. Collection des chroniques nationales françaises p. p. J.-A. Buchon 43–47 Paris 1827 f. I 72. Th. Basin, Histoire des règnes de Charles VII et de Louis XI p. p. J. Quicherat. 4 vols. Paris 1855 ff. Société de l'histoire de France II 224. Duclercq IV 212. On the slanders, see above, p. 80.

Page 56 On the quarrel between Philip the Good and Charles see Chastellain III and IV, and Du Clercq IV 95 ff.

Page 56 Chastellain (IV, 427) reports with pride that envoys from seven kingdoms were at Philip's Court at one time. Du Clercq (IV, 80) makes Philip say to the French Chancellor : Je veulx bien que chacun sçache que sy j'euisse voullu, je feusse roy.

Page 57 On the founding of the Order of the Golden Fleece in January, 1430, see Chastellain II 5 ff. ; Le Févre II 172 ff. Chastellain VII (Déclaration) 216 : " Pour évader des Anglois et de leur ordre, mit sus le sien propre, la Toison d'Or." Baron de Reiffenberg, Histoire de l'ordre de la Toison d'Or . . . Bruxelles 1830. Baron H. Kervyn de Lettenhove, La Toison d'Or. Notes sur l'institution et l'histoire de l'ordre . . . Bruxelles 1907. Les chefs-d'œuvre d'art ancien à l'exposition de la Toison d'Or à Bruges en 1907, Bruxelles 1908. Bibliography in Vicomte de Ghellinck Vaernewyck, L'Ordre de la Toison d'or et l'exposition de Bruges : Bulletin de l'Académie royale d'archéologie de Belgique 1907 (Anvers) 212 ff.— On the Livre des ordonnances de la Toison d'Or, 1518 to cc. 1565 with numerous miniatures, preserved at Vienna, see Th. Frimmel und F. Klemme, Ein Statutenbuch des Ordens vom Goldenen Vliesse : Jahrbuch der kunsthistor. Sammlungen des allerhöchsten Kaiserhauses V, 1 (Wien 1887) 263 ff.

Page 57 La Marche IV (Espitre) 161 ff. deals in detail on the difference between Device and Order and is of opinion that the French Order of St. Michael is not a duly constituted Order.

Page 57 On the articles of foundation, 27 November 1431 : Le Févre II 210 ff.

Page 57 Charles made alterations in the dress : velour cramoisy an Stelle von escarlate, and increased the number of church services ; La Marche IV (Espitre) 167.

Page 57 Failure to wear the chain entailed, peine de faire dire une messe de quatre solz et quatre solz donner pour Dieu.

Page 57 On the number of knights (gentilz hommes de nom et d'armes et sans reproche) : La Marche IV (Espitre) 160 f.

Page 58 On the 11th and 12th chapters in 1468 and 1473, see de Reiffenberg 54. 71. See illustration p. 58.

Page 58 On the judgment of John of Burgundy Count of Nevers in 1468, see de Reiffenberg 47 f. Chastellain V 376 f., also Ducange, Glossarium sub arma reversata.

Page 58 Pope Eugenius' letter 4 Nov. 1432 : de Reiffenberg 10, also Chastellain IV 233 : ordre de la Thoyson d'Or, en quelle religion . . . and VI (Epistre) 154.

Page 59 Jason and Gideon : La Marche IV (Espitre) 163 ff. G. Doutrepont, La littérature française à la cour des ducs de Bourgogne. Paris 1909. Bibliothèque du XVe siècle Bd. VIII. S. 159 ff., also the noteworthy but inexact passage in Du Clercq III 172 : Philippe le Bon avoit prins son ordre sur la bible et ne l'avoit voullu prendre sur la Toison que Jason conquesta en l'isle de Colchos, pour ce que Jason mentit sa foy.—G. Doutrepont, Jason et Gédéon, patrons de la Toison d'Or. Mélanges Godefroy Kurth II (Liège, Paris 1908) 191 ff. Bibl. de la fac. de philos. et lettres de . . . Liège fasc. 2.

Page 59 Only the first two books of Fillastre's works are printed, see p. 252, Chastellain III, 333 describes Fillastre : agréable homme, doux parlier, affable.

Page 59 Chastellain VII (Déclaration) 217.

Page 60 On the Pragmatic Sanction: Histoire de France IV, 2,268 note 1. On the relations with the Curia, N. Valois, La crise religieuse du XV siècle. Le pape et le concile (1418–1450) 2 vols. Paris 1909.

Page 60 Chastellain III 69 ff., also Bishop David van Bourgondië en zijn stad. Utrechtsch-Hollandsche Jaarboeken 1481–1483 van de hand van een onbekenden, gelijktijdigen schrijver . . . uitgegeven . . . door N. B. Tenhaeff. Utrecht 1920. Herdrukken van de Maatschappij der Nederlandsche Letterkunde nr. 2.

Page 60 Fillastre and the bishopric of Tournai : Chastellain IV 172. Chastellain V 55 criticises ces grans théologiens et ces gens dévots qui riens ne savent des affaires du monde, ne sont experts des humaines convenabletés, but who still concern themselves with politics.

Page 60 Guillaume Fillastre, Le premier volume de la toison d'or fol. CXXXI praises Philip the Good : quant aucuns de ses serviteurs mouroient fust par maladie ou autrement, il faisoit secrèttement célébrer messes pour leurs âmes ; pour ung baron quatre ou cinq cens messes : pour ung chevalier trois cens ; pour ung gentil homme deux cens et pour ung varlet cent. Et n'estoit si petit ne si grant qu'il n'eust sa porcion, dont le moindre et fust varlet ou gallopin de sa cuisine avoit cent messes. Philip the Bold : see the letter of brother Boniface, humilis prior maioris domus Cartusie, Monget I 368.

Page 60 On Philip the Good's piety see Chastellain II 300. VII (Déclaration) 222. 225 ; La Marche II 40 ; Jean Germain, Liber de virtutibus . . . Philippi . . . Chroniques relatives à l'histoire de la Belgique sous la domination des ducs de Bourgogne III (Bruxelles 1876) 10 f. ; Jean Jouffroy, Ad Pium papam II. de Philippo duce Burgundiae oratio ebenda S. 118.

Page 60 J. v. Schlosser, Der burgundische Paramentenschatz des Ordens vom Goldenen Vliesse. Wien 1912.

Page 60 A. Piaget, Martin Le Franc, prévot de Lausanne, Thèse . . . Genève. Lausanne 1888, to which I add : Martin Le Franc, Champion des dames 91.

Page 61 Martin Le Franc, Champion des dames 90 ; Journal d'un Bourgeois de Paris 1405–1449, p. P. A. Tuetey. Documents de la société de l'histoire de Paris, Paris 1881, p. 289.

Page 61 On Beatrice of Portugal, Chastellain IV 217 f.

Page 61 Retirements: La Marche II 398.

Page 61 On devotion in general, La Marche I 49 f. ; Chastellain III 451 ; Doutrepont 223 ff. ; Laborde I 499 nr. 1942. On St. Andrew's cross, La Marche I 85 ; de Reiffenberg S. XXX.—Jost Trier, Der Heilige Jodocus. Sein Leben und seine Verehrung . . . germanistische Abh. 56 (1924).

Page 62 On St. Colette : J.-Th. Bizouard, Sainte Colette à Auxonne (1412–1417). Lyon 1879. P. Bergmans, Marguerite d'York et les pauvres Claires de Gand. Notice sur un manuscrit enluminé de la Vie de sainte Colette. Bulletin de la soc. d'hist. et d'arch. de Gand 1910. B. Prost, Documents inédits sur Sainte-Colette, Archives historiques, littéraires I (1889/90) 112 ff.

Page 62 On Denis van Ryckel : A. Mougel ; Denys le Chartreux, Montreuil-sur-Mer. W. Moll, Johannes Brugmann en het godsdienstig leven onzer vaderen in de vystiende eeuw. Amsterdam 1854. 2 vols. I 70. Johannes Schäfer, Die kirchlichen Zustände des XV. Jahrhunderts nach Dionysius Carthusianus. 1. Teil Tübinger Diss. Schkeuditz 1904. See also Doutrepont 250, note 3.

Page 62 On the coronation banquet of Charles VI, Cartellieri, Philipp der Kühne 15 f.—At the banquet in honour of the English the guests came to blows. See letters of Pardon issued to Guillaume de Fontenay, Paris, Arch. Nat. JJ 149 nr. 169.

Page 63 Numerous examples of the Pax were to be found in the Burgundian treasury. See Laborde II nr. 2043. 44. 45. 75. 2126. 2140. 5293.

Page 63 On the constable of St. Pol at Bruges, see Chastellain V 395 f., compare Chastellain III 208.

Page 63 Aliénor de Poitiers, Les honneurs de la cour 167. 187. Reception in Bruges, Chastellain III 301.

Page 63 Franz Lindner, Die Zusammenkunst Kaiser Friedrichs III. mit Karl dem Kühnen von Burgund im Jahre 1472 zu Trier : Greifswalder Diss. 1867.

Page 64 Die Geschichten und Taten Wilwolts von Schaumburg ed. by A. v. Keller, Bibl. des Lit. Vereins in Stuttgart 50 (Stuttgart 1859) 14.

Page 64 On the execution of the Bastard de la Hamayde, see below p. 81. On the execution of the Constable, de Saint-Pol, Molinet I 184 : Basin II 375 f.

Page 64 On the burial of John the Fearless, Lefévre II 11 ; Monstrelet III 347 ; Pierre de Fenin, Mémoires . . . 1407–1427. Nouv. éd. par Mlle Dupont. Paris 1837. Société de l'histoire de France. p.   115. 140.

Page 64 The miniature has been attributed to Rogier van der Weyden. See P. Post, Die Darbringungsminiatur der Hennegauchronik in der Bibliothek zu Brüssel. Jahrbuch für Kunstwissenschaft hrg. von E. Gall (Leipzig 1923) 171 ff., also Comte P. Durrieu, La miniature flamande au temps de la cour de Bourgogne (Bruxelles et Paris 1921) 51 f. See illustration, p. 64.

Page 64 La Marche IV 1 ff. ; L'estat de la maison du duc Charles de Bourgogne.

Page 65 La Marche : compare H. Stein, Etude . . . sur Olivier de La Marche, Mémoires couronnés . . . p. p. l'Académie Royale . . . de Belgique 49 (1888), and H. Stein, Nouveaux documents sur Olivier de La Marche et sa famille, Ac. Roy. de Belg., Classe des lettres et des sciences morales et politiques, Mémoires, 2e sér. IX (1922) fasc. 1. (Coll. in 4°).

Page 66 On these audiences see Chastellain V, 370.

Page 68 On the regulations against poisoning, see H. Pogatscher, Von Schlangenhörnern und Schlangenzungen vornehmlich im 14. Jahrhundert. Römische Quartalschrift 12 (1899) 162 ff.—S. 188 ff.

Page 68 On the Ordonnance touchant la conduite du premier escuier d'escuerie . . . see Th. Frimmel, Urkunden . . . Jahrbuch der kunsthist. Sammlungen . . . V, 2 (Vienna 1887) V nr. 4004.

Page 70 La Marche (L'estat) IV 83. p. 88 (1474) there were 20,000 men including footmen, English archers and artillery. On the army organization, Pirenne, Hist. de Belg. II³ 411. Molinier, Sources de l'histoire de France nr. 4755. On the Ordonnances du duc Charles de Bourgogne pour la tuicion et deffense de ses pays . . . Doutrepont 328 ; Molinier, nr. 4756.

Page 70 Aliénor wrote at the time of Philip the Fair and Charles VIII. She married Guillaume, seigneur de Stavelo, vicomte de Furnes.

Page 71 See especially, Les honneurs de la cour 211 ff. 172 ff. 188 ff.

Page 72 La Marche II 421 f. ; Philip " se fit resre la teste et oster ses cheveulx, et pour n'estre seul rez et desnué de ses cheveulx, il fit un édit que tous les nobles hommes se feroient resre leurs testes comme luy . . . aussi fut ordonné messire Pierre Vacquembac et aultres qui prestement qu'ilz veoient ung noble homme, luy ostoient ses cheveulx ". There seems to be some exaggeration here.

Page 72 Duclercq IV 300 f. and the chronicle cited by La Marche II 422. Although the Haller Dissertation, P. Post, Die französischniederländische Männertracht einschliesslich der Ritterrüstung im Zeitalter der Spätgotik 1350–1475, Diss. Halle a. S. 1910, is important, it is to be regretted that he did not give the costumes the names which are found in the contemporary chronicles. See also C. Enlart, Manuel d'archéologie française III Le costume. Paris 1916, J. Quicherat, Histoire du costume en France . . . (Paris 1875) 277 ff. and Comte A. de Bastard, Costumes de la cour de Bourgogne sous le règne de Philippe le Bon (1455–1460). Paris 1881, Die Moden der Renaissance, ed. by Hans Floerke. München 1924.

Page 72 On the chlamys . . . adeo curta, por more Burgundorum, ut nec femora nec pudenda contegeret at the court of the Palsgrave, see H. C. von Byler, Libellorum rariorum . . . fasciculus (Groningae 1733) 188 ; compare F. Schmidt, Gesch. der Erziehung der pfälzischen Wittelsbacher, Monumenta Germaniae paedagogica 19 (1899) p. LVI.

Page 73 On the envoy of the Infanta Isabella. Le Févre II 153.

Page 73 Martin le Franc, Champion des dames, Piaget 119. (vous soliez-aviez l'habitude : ne faictes mye-ne le faites vous pas). Illustration, p. 178.

Page 73 Jean Meschinot : P. Champion, Histoire poétique du quinzième siècle II (Paris 1923) 219 (gittent-jettent).

CHAPTER V

The Knight

This chapter appeared in a slightly different form in the Hist. Zeitschrift, vol. 132 (1925) with the title : Die ritterliche Gesellschaft am burgundischen Hofe.

Page 75 Chastellain (Le Miroer de nobles hommes de France) VI 213 : Mais vous, seigneurs, extraits d'autre semence . . .

Page 75 Olivier de La Marche, Le livre de l'advis gaige de bataille, Traités du duel judiciaire, relations de pas d'armes et tournois . . . p. p. Bernard Prost (Paris 1872) 45.

Page 75 On evidence of ancestry, see Le Livre des faits du bon chevalier messire Jacques de Lalaing in Œuvres de Chastellain VIII, p. 96, 184.

Page 76 Chastellain (Exposition sur vérité mal prise) VI 416 f. ; L'entrée du roy Loys VII 13, compare p. 10.

Page 76 Molinet III 99 ff.

Page 77 L'Instruction d'un jeune prince : Œuvres de Ghillebert de Lannoy . . . p. p. Ch. Potvin . . . Louvain 1878. S. 289 ff. S. 412. 404.

Page 77 On this affair at Arras : Duclercq II 245 ; at Lille : Chastellain III 82 ff., without a word of criticism on Philip's action.

Page 78 The verses are from Le Mirouer de la Mort, London, Brit. Mus. ms. Lansdowne 380 fol. 95, after Champion, Villon II, 214, note I.

Page 78 On the curses of the common people, see Joannis Gersonii . . . opera omnia. . . opera et studio M. Lud. Ellies du Pin. Editio secunda. Hagae Comitum 1728. Centilogium de impulsibus III col. 154.

Page 78 Molinet, I, 83 f.

Page 78 Instruction d'un jeune prince 361 : " Gardez vous . . . de vous esseuler avec varlez ne gens de basse condition."

Page 79 Philip " en chambre se tenoit clos souvent avec valets et s'en indignoient nobles hommes " ; Chastellain (Déclaration) VII 224.

Page 79 Le Rozier des Guerres composé par le feu roy Lois XI de ce nom pour monseigneur le daulphin Charles son fils. Mis en lumière . . . par le sieur d'Espagnet. Paris 1616, compare Molinier, Les sources de l'histoire de France nr. 4665. On the author, see Ch. Sameran, Pierre Choisnet, Le Rosier des guerres, in Bib. de l'Ecole des Chartes, 87 (1926) 372 ff.

Page 80 Chastellain VII (Advertissement) 310, Chastellain VII 458, note 4.

Page 80 Commynes says of the family of Lelaing : " une rasse dont peu s'en est trouvé qui n'ayent estez vaillans et courageux, et presque tous morts en servant leurs seigneurs à la guerre." Compare F. Brassart, Le Pas du Perron Fée tenu à Bruges en 1463 par le chevalier Philippe de Lalaing . . . (Douai 1874) 24, note 2.

Page 80 Letter of the Lord de Chassa : Duclos, Histoire de Louis XI. Bd. III La Haye 1746) 368 f. compare Chastellain V 469 ff.

Page 80 Chastellain V 473

Page 80 On the audiences, see Chastellain V 370.

Page 80 Chastellain V, 397 ff. (1468).

Page 81 On Charles' violence, Duclercq IV 239, 262.

Page 82 Les Enseignements paternels. Œuvres de Ghillebert de Lannoy . . . p. p. Ch. Potvin . . . Louvain 1878. S. 441 ff. — S. 456 f. ; also S. 460. Potvin sees in Ghillebert de Lannoy the author of the Enseignements and of the Instruction d'un jeune prince, but I subscribe to Doutrepont's views.

Page 82 On treatment of opponents, see Enseignements paternels 457 f. Chastellain II 134 f.

Page 82 Richard II : Rymer, Foedera . . . III 3 158 (VII 407).

Page 82 On the challenge by Louis of Orleans, 14. October 1403 : Paris, Bibl. Nat. Brienne 34 fol. 239 ff. and Gent, Univ. Bibl. Hs. 434 fol. 79 ff. ; compare Cartellieri, Philipp der Kühne 106.

Page 82 On Philip's challenge, Monstrelet IV 219.

Page 83 On the proposed duel with William of Saxony, see La Marche, Livre de l'advis de gaige de bataille 22.

Page 83 Preparations for a duel, Monstrelet IV 244 ; Lefévre II 106 f. ; Jean Germain, Liber de virtutibus 27.

Page 83 Instruction d'un jeune prince 416.

Page 83 John of Salisbury, Policraticus 1. VI c. 8.

Page 83 Instruction d'un jeune prince 421 f.

Page 84 Chastellain VII 10.

Page 84 On the impulse for renown, see Huizinga 86 against Jakob Burckhardt.

Page 84 Neuf preuses : Deschamps III 192 nr. 403, compare M. Kastenberg, Die Stellung der Frau in den Dichtungen der Christine de Pisan (Heid. Diss. 1909) 27. 29.

Page 84 Quenson, La Croix Pèlerine. Notice historique sur un monument des environs de Saint-Omer. Mémoires de la Société . . . d'agriculture, des sciences . . . du département du Nord V (1833/4) 307 ff., with illustration and plan.

Page 85 Du Guesclin : Religieux de Saint-Denis 1 598 f. compare Deschamps X S. XXXV nr. XXVIII. S. LXXIX nr. LXXI.

Page 85 On swords, etc., in the Burgundian treasury, see Laborde II 146 nr. 3343 ; 138 nr. 3342 ; 242 nr. 4091 ; 260 nr. 4220.

Page 85 Hercules : La Marche I 42 f.

Page 85 On the burial of Henry V, Chastellain I 333.

Page 85 On Duke René, Journal de Jean de Roye connu sous le nom de chronique scandaleuse . . . p. p. B. de Mandrot. Société de l'histoire de France II (Paris 1896) 42 ; Mémoires de messire Philippe de Commines ed. Lenglet du Fresnois II (Paris 1747) 249.

Page 85 Le livre des faicts du mareschal de Boucicaut, Petitot, Collection complète des mémoires . . . VI and VII.—VI 393.

Page 86 L'Hystoire et plaisante cronicque du Petit Jehan de Saintré et de la jeune Dame des Belles Cousines . . . p. p. J.-Marie Guichard. Paris 1843.

Page 86 Chronique de l'abbaye de Floreffe : Philip the Good

> Aveucque ce est si libouraulx
> Qu'il passe Alexandre en largesse.
> Roy Octovian en richesse.

Page 86 Triomphe des Dames : Doutrepont 310 f.

Page 87 The verse from Livre du Cuer d'amours espris in Chastellain II 161, note 2.

Page 87 On the Duchess of Orleans, Chastellain IV 136.

Page 87   Chastellain III 149.
Page 87   Letter of Philippe de Croy : Chastellain VIII 266.
Page 87   Livre . . . Boucicaut VI 398 f. for the passage see the German
           edition, p. 279.
Page 88   Le blason des couleurs en armes, livrées et devises par Sicille,
           hérault d'Alphonse V, roi d'Aragon, publié et annoté par H. Cochéris.
           Paris 1860 ; W. Gloth, Das Spiel von den sieben Farben. Teutonia
           I, Königsberg i. P. 1902.
Page 88   N. Jorga, Philippe de Mézières . . . et la croisade au XIVe siècle.
           Bibliothèque de l'école des hautes études. Sciences philol. et hist.
           fasc. 110. Paris 1896. p. 348.
Page 89   Les Cent Nouvelles Nouvelles . . . Nouv. éd. par P. L. Jacob.
           Paris 1858.
Page 89   Deschamps, IV 289 nr. 785.
Page 89   Enseignements paternels 471.
Page 89   Ransom of prisoners, Champion, Charles d'Orléans 158 ff.,
           Chastellain I 272.
Page 89   Coville in Lavisse, Hist. de France IV, 1 154 ; la rançon du roi Jean
           est fixée à trois millions d'écus d'or, soit près de quarante millions de
           francs, valeur intrinsèque.
Page 90   povre aventurier : Chastellain III 354 ff.
Page 90   On Philip the Good, Chastellain II 140. I 260.
Page 90   On Nicopolis, J. Delaville le Roulx, La France en Orient au XIVe
           siècle 2 vols. Paris 1886. Bibliothèque des Ecoles d'Athènes et de
           Rome. Cartellieri, Philipp der Kühne 77 ff.
Page 91   Deschamps IX 80 :

                    Car à piet se fait la bataille,
                    Afin que nulz homs ne s'en aille.

Page 91   For the oaths, see D'Escouchy II.
Page 92   Epitre de Jean Le Févre, seigneur de Saint-Remy . . . publiée . . . par
           feu F. Morand. Annuaire bulletin de la société d'histoire de France
           1884 S. 177 ff.   On the authorship of the Livre des faits de Jacques
           de Lalaing : Molinier, Sources de l'histoire de France nr. 3941 ;
           Doutrepont 99 ff. ; P. Rudnitzky, Der Turnierroman " Livre des
           faits du bon chevalier messire Jacques de Lalaing " in Fors-
           chungen und Funde IV, 1. München i. W. 1915.
Page 94   Jean de Bueil, Le Jouvencel p. p. C. Favre et L. Lecestre. 2 vols.
           Paris 1887. 1889. Société de l'histoire de France.
Page 95   Recollection des merveilleuses advenues en nostre temps . . .
           Chronique métrique de Chastellain et de Molinet . . . par le baron de
           Reiffenberg. Bruxelles 1836. p. 58. Sans foulle . . . =sans lésion et
           sans difficulté.
Page 95   According to Du Fresne de Beaucourt IV 99 ff. 439 the Pas d'Armes
           did not take place at Nancy as reported in the Livre des faits, and
           in La Marche, but at Châlons. Compare D'Escouchy 1 50.
Page 96   La Marche II 309 f.

CHAPTER VI

THE LADY

Page 97   Petrarch : Piaget, Martin Le Franc 58 f.
Page 97   Guillaume de Lorris et Jean de Meun, Le roman de la rose. p. p.
           E. Langlois, Paris, 1914, v. 9415 ff., 13886 ff., 2115 (iii, 120 f. ;
           iv, 39 : ii, 109).

Martin Le Franc 39 adds :

> Toutes pour tous ! Vierge royne !
> C'est parlé amoureusement.
> Dames, escoutez la doctrine,
> Retenez cest ensengnement !
> Ha ! Jan de Meun grandement
> Tu as failly, ce m'est advis . . .

Page 98

v. 9147 f. (iii, 109).

> Car leur nature leur comande
> Que chascune au pis faire entende.

v. 9155 ff. (iii, 110).

> Toustes estes, sereiz ou fustes
> De fait ou de volenté putes.

Page 98   Les lamentations de Matheolus et le livre de Leesce de Jehan Le Fèvre, de Resson, p. p. A.-G. Van Hamel : Bibl. de l'Ecole des Hautes Etudes fasc. 95. 96 (Paris 1892, 1905)

Page 98   The verses Livre de Leesce or Le Rebours de Matheolus, fasc. 96 p. 137.

Page 99   The verses : Lamentations III v. 2164 ff. : fasc. 95 p. 218 f. Adam and Eve : Lamentations III v. 1427 ff. ; fasc. 95 p. 199.

Page 99   Verse : Lamentations II v. 90 ff. ; fasc. 95 p. 49. Lamentations II v. 2777 f. 2787 f. ; fasc. 95 p. 121.

Page 99   Le Livre du Voir-Dit p. p. G. Paris, Société des bibliophiles français 1875.

Page 99   F. Koch, Leben und Werke der Christine de Pizan. Goslar 1885. Œuvres poétiques de Christine de Pisan p. p. M. Roy. 3 vols. 1886 ff. Société des anciens textes français. See illustration, p. 100.

Page 100   Verse : Rondeaux nr. 1, Œuvres I 147 ; " Mutacion de Fortune," Koch 20 ; " La vision," Koch 32.

Page 100   A. Farinelli, Dante nell' opere di Christine de Pisan. Aus romanischen Sprachen und Literaturen. Festschrift Heinrich Morf . . . dargebracht. Halle a/S. 1905 p. 121.

Page 100   Christine de Pisan, Le livre des fais et bonnes meurs du sage roy Charles VI. Michaud et Poujoulat, Nouvelle collection de mémoires . . . vol. I and II. Paris 1857.

Page 100   Works of C. de Pisan in possession of Philip the Good, see Doutrepont 292.

Page 100   Christine on France : " Livre du corps de Policie," Bibl. Nat. ms. franç. 12439 fol. 210v, ebenda fol. 211, in S. Solente, Un traité inédit de Christine de Pisan. L'épistre de la prison de vie humaine. Bibliothèque de l'école des chartes 85 (1924) 264, also R. Thomassy, Essai sur les écrits politiques de Christine de Pisan (Paris 1838).

Page 100   Saint-Pol : Chastellain II 172.

Page 100   On the Madonna : Laborde II 264 nr. 4238 ; also II 10 nr 77.

Page 100   Chastellain II 79.

Page 101   Martin Le Franc : Kastenberg 30. Le Franc says of Christine :

> De laquelle à trompe et à cor
> Le nom par tout va et ne fine.

Page 101   On the nuptials of Charles and Isabeau, see Cartellieri, Philipp der Kühne 30 f.

Page 101   On the bridal night : Cent Nouvelles Nouvelles 148.

Page 102   Tertullianus, De cultu feminarum 1, I c. 1, Migne, Patrol. Lat. I col. 1417 ff.

Page 102   Innocentius III., De contemptu mundi sive de miseria conditionis humanae libri tres, Migne Patrol. Lat. t. 217 col. 705.

Page 102   Jean de Varennes, see Schwab, Gerson 672 f.
Page 102   Die Epistre au dieu d'amours, Dit de la Rose, Epistres sur le Roman de la Rose may be specially mentioned. For what follows, see M. Kastenberg, Die Stellung der Frau in den Dichtungen der Christine de Pisan. Heidelberger Diss. 1909.
Page 103   Cité des Dames, see Piaget, Martin Le Franc, 75 ff.
Page 103   Purgatoire des mauvais marys : Piaget, Martin Le Franc 51, note 3.
Page 103   J. Kalbfleisch geb. Benas, Le Triomphe des Dames von Olivier de La Marche. Diss. Bern, Rostock 1901 p. 55.
Page 104   Verse : Les Enseignements moraux, Œuvres III 41 nr. 94. 91.
Page 104   On the literary squabbles see A. Piaget, Chronologie des Epistres sur le Roman de la Rose : Etudes romanes dédiées à Gaston Paris . . . (Paris 1891) 113 ff. (unfortunately without the Latin letters). K. F. Schmid, Jean de Montreuil als Kirchenpolitiker, Staatsmann und Humanist. Diss. Freiburg i. Br. 1904. A. Thomas, De Joannis de Monsterolio vita et operibus . . . Pariser Diss. Parisiis 1883. Schwab, Gerson 697 ff. F. Beck, Les epistres sur le Roman de la Rose von Christine de Pizan, Progr. der K. B. Studienanstalt Neuburg a. D. 1887/8. Jean de Montreuil's tract on the Roman de la Rose is unfortunately not preserved.
Page 104   Jean de Montreuil on Christine : Thomas 79.
Page 104   Gerson's Tractatus contra Romantium de Rosa, Opera III col. 297 ff., 18 May 1402, his Responsio III col. 293 ff.
Page 105   Livre des faicts . . . Boucicaut VI 507 ff.
Page 105   The anecdote in Antoine de la Salle La Salade chap. 3 (Paris, M. le Noir 1521) f. 4v.
Page 105   Christine de Pisan, Le Débat de deux amants, Œuvres II 96 :

> Et le bon Bouccicaut
> Le mareschal qui fu preux, saige et cault
> Tout pour amours fu vaillant, large et bault . . .

compare Œuvres I 211 Balades nr. 4. On the emprise of the Duke de Bourbon on 1. Januar 1415, see Choix de pièces inédites relatives au règne de Charles VI p. p. L. Douet d'Arcq 2 Bände. Société de l'histoire de France. I (Paris 1863) 370 nr. 166.
Page 105   For the deed of foundation, see Ch. Potvin, La charte de la cour d'amour de l'année 1401 in Bulletins de l'ac. roy. des sciences, des lettres et des beaux-arts de Belg. 3e série t. 12 (1886) 191 ff. Compare A. Piaget, La cour amoureuse dite de Charles VI, Romania 20 (1891) 417 ff. ; A. Piaget, Un manuscrit de la cour amoureuse de Charles VI, Romania 31 (1902) 597 ff. ; F. Diez, Beiträge zur Kenntnis der romantischen Poesie. 1. Heft. Berlin 1825 ; Doutrepont 366 ff.
Page 106   For an attractive account of a festival at Tournai (1455) at which patriotic and love songs were presented, see Chronique des Pays-Bas, de France, d'Angleterre et de Tournay. Corpus chronicorum Flandriae ed. J.-J. de Smet III (Bruxelles 1856 ; Collection de chroniques belges inédites) 529 ff.
Page 106   Le Roman de la Rose, v. 10439 ff. ed. Langlois iii, 161.
Page 107   Charles d'Orléans, Poésies complètes revues sur les manuscrits . . . p. Ch. d'Héricault. 2 vols. Paris 1874. I, 12.
Page 108   Les Cents Ballades. Poème du XIVe siècle composé par Jean le Seneschal . . . p. p. Gaston Raynaud. Paris 1905. Société des anciens textes français. (cc. 1390). Compare Doutrepont 373 f.
Page 108   Alfred de Musset, Idylle : Poésies Nouvelles (Paris 1865) 127.
Page 109   Roblot-Delondre sees in the picture No. 4021 at Versailles : Un jardin d'amour de Philippe le Bon ; Revue archéologique IVe sér. 17 (1911) 420 ff.—On the MS. from which the illustration at p. 106 is taken, see Durrieu, La miniature flamande 62 nr. 72.

Page 109   Guillebert de Metz, La description de la ville de Paris et de l'excellence du royaume de France in Le Roux de Lincy et L. M. Tisserand, Paris et ses historiens au XIVe et XVe siècles 234.

Page 109   Abductions : A. Piaget in Romania XX 447.

Page 110   M. Thibault, Isabeau de Bavière, reine de France. La jeunesse. 1370–1405. Paris 1903. Cartellieri, Philipp der Kühne 29 ff. In the documents she is described as Ysabel and she so signs herself.

Page 110   Religieux de Saint-Denis III 348. 290. 266.

Page 111   Odette : E. Fyot, La petite reine en Bourgogne, Revue de Bourgogne 1913. S. 37. On the insinuations against Isabeau, see Le Pastoralet (Chroniques rel. à l' hist. de Belgique II (Brussels, 1873 : Coll. de chron. belges inédites) 585, 605) ; Le Songe Véritable p. p. H. Moranvillé. Mémoires de la société de l'histoire de Paris 17 (1891) 276. 296 v. 1740 ff. 2837 ff.

Page 111   Le Songe Véritable 296 v. 2838 f. : Ysabeau, enveloppée en laide peau ; compare Le Pastoralet 578 v. 151 ff.

Page 111   Deschamps, Le Miroir du mariage, Œuvres, IX 50.

Page 112   Legrand : Religieux III 268.

Page 112   M. Laigle, Le Livre des Trois Vertus de Christine de Pisan, Paris 1912, Bibliothèque du XVe siècle t. XVI Kastenberg 38 ff.

Page 112   F. v. Löher, Jakobäa von Bayern und ihre Zeit. 2 vols. Nördlingen 1862/9 in the absence of a critical biography can still be used. Compare K. H. Vickers, Humphrey, duke of Gloucester, London 1907.

Page 113   Monstrelet IV 388 : . . . ladicte pucelle. Laquelle ycelui duc alla veoir ou logis où elle estoit et parla avec elle aulcunes paroles, dont je ne suis mie bien record, jà soit chose que je y estoie présent.

Page 113   On the attitude of chivalry, see Chastellain II 49 ; 40 ff.

Page 114   The verses of Christine de Pisan : J. Quicherat, Procès . . . de Jeanne d'Arc V (Paris 1849) 13. 15 (chenin-lâche).

Page 114   Agnes Sorel : Du Fresne de Beaucourt, Histoire de Charles VII vol. IV 169 ff.

Page 114   The chronicle is cited in Chastellain IV 367, note 1.

Page 115   Martin Le Franc, Champion des dames 101.

Page 115   Chastellain IV 365 ff. (laquelle je vis et cognus) ; Duclercq III 141 f. La Marche II 55 : c'estoit une des plus belles femmes que je veiz oncques. He has a better opinion of her : et feit en sa qualité beaucop de biens au royaulme de France . .

Page 115   On this picture now at Antwerp : M. J. Friedländer. Die Votivtafel des Estienne Chevalier von Fouquet, Jahrbuch der kgl. preuss. Kunstsammlungen 17 (1896) 206 ff.

Page 115   Cent Nouvelles Nouvelles : Doutrepont 333 ff.

Page 116   On the exploit of Louis XI and Guillaume de Bische : Chastellain IV 115 f.

Page 116   Prostitutes in Paris : Champion, Villon I 87 ff.

Page 116   Prevôt luxurieux : Journal d'un Bourgeois de Paris 383.

Page 117   Christine de Pisan : Laigle 361 ff.

Page 117   The Italian was Antonio d'Asti :

> Miror et innumeras forma praestante puellas,
> Tam lascivo habitu cultas adeoque facetas,
> Ut Priamum aut veterem succendere Nestora possint.

Le Roux de Lincy et Tisserand, Paris et ses historiens 544.

Page 117   Œuvres de maître François Villon p. p. F. Ed. Schneegans. Bibliotheca Romanica 35. 36. Le (Grant) Testament v. 1699. 577 f. 1976 f. 325 ff. 712. 657 ff. 606 ff. 713 f. 958 ff. (souef-délicat ; je fus battu comme toiles au ruisseau ; despite-dédaigne).

Page 118   Lais v. 77 ff. Testament v. 985 (transy-glacé).

Page 118   Christine de Pisan, Dit de la Pastoure, Œuvres II 291 v. 2173 ff.

CHAPTER VII
JOUSTS AND TOURNEYS

Page 119 Chaucer, Canterbury Tales (The Knyghtes Tale), lines 2490–2512.
Page 119 Chastellain III 466.
Page 119–120 Pas de l'Arbre Charlemagne, 1443: Monstrelet VI 68 ff. ; La Marche I 290 ff.

Pas de la Belle Pèlerine, 1449 ; D'Escouchy I 244 ff. ; La Marche II 118 ff.

Pas du Perron Fée, 1463 ; F. Brassart (see above, p. 257) also Kervyn de Lettenhove, La joute de la dame inconnue à Bruxelles . . . Compte rendu des séances de la commission royale d'histoire 3e série XI 473 ff. R. C. Clephan. The tournament, its periods and phases. London s. a. (1919).

Page 120 Festival at Oudenaarde, 1408 ; D. J. vander Meersch, Kronyk der rederykkamers van Audenaerde : Belgisch Museum VI (1842) 380. B. Prost, Inventaires mobiliers et extraits des comptes des ducs de Bourgogne I 447 nr. 2363 : une queue de vin de Beaune que monseigneur fit acheter . . . et ycelle donner aus aubelestiers de Bruges la journée que monseigneur traia avec eulx au papegay ".

Page 120 Festival at Tournai, 1455 : Chronique des Pays-Bas 529 f.

Page 120 Jean Germain : Liber de virtutibus 100 f.

Page 121 Eustache Deschamps I 222 nr. 108 (folour-folie ; sotie-sottise ; chétis-malheureux ; malostrus-mal en point).

Page 121 Lalaing : Chastellain II 363.

Page 122 Pas de la Fontaine aux Pleurs : La Marche II 142 ff. and the Livre des faits de Jacques de Lalaing, Chastellain VIII 188 ff. D'Escouchy I 264 ff. See also extended note in German edition, p. 286.

Page 123 Traicté d'un tournoy tenu à Gand par Claude de Vauldray, seigneur de l'Aigle, l'an 1469 (vieux style) : Traités du duel judiciaire. Relations de pas d'armes et tournois . . . p. p. B. Prost (Paris 1872) 55 ff. O. Cartellieri, Der Pas de la Dame Sauvaige am Hofe Herzog Karls des Kühnen von Burgund. Historische Blätter I (1921) 47 ff. In 1494 Maximilian himself jousted with Claude de Vaudray.

Page 123 On the appearance of savage men and women, see F. v. d. Leyen (im Verein mit A. Spamer), Die altdeutschen Wandteppiche im Regensburger Rathause : Das Rathaus zu Regensburg 1910.

Page 123 On the numbers 17 and 7, see A. Rauschmaier. Über den figürlichen Gebrauch der Zahlen im Altfranzösischen. Münchener Beiträge zur roman. und engl. Philol. III 69 f.

Page 124 On the death of Philip's natural son Cornelius in 1452 Anthony was granted the right to call himself Bastard of Burgundy. La Marche II 270.

Page 124 Pas de l'Arbre d'Or : I refer to my essay : Ritterspiele am Hofe Karls des Kühnen von Burgund (1468). Tydschrift voor geschiedenis 1921 S. 14 ff., which is fully noted. La Marche III 101 ff. gives a detailed account. Compare Traictié des nopces de monseigneur le duc de Bourgoigne et de Brabant (La Marche IV 95 ff., vgl. I p. CXX f.) ; and an English account. Marriage of the princess Margaret, sister of Edward IV. A.D. 1468, Excerpta historica or illustrations of English history (London 1833) 227 ff. The authorities are considered in an extended note in the German edition, p. 287.

Page 124 On the number 100 + 1 see J. Grimm, Deutsche Rechtsaltertümer I⁴ 303 f. ; W. Knopf, Zur Gesch. der typischen Zahlen in der deutschen Litteratur des Mittelalters, Leipz. Diss. 1902.

Page 127   A note on the use of the colour green appears in the German edition, p. 287.

Page 127   Verses, see Chansons du XVe siècle p. p. Gaston Paris (Paris 1875, Soc. des anciens Textes) 50 nr. 49.

Page 128   Lord Scales : Anthony Wydeville, Earl Rivers, brother-in-law of Edward IV.

Page 130   Brocades : see especially Otto von Falke, Kunstgeschichte der Seidenweberei II (Berlin 1913) 81 ff., and note in German edition, p. 288.

Page 133   The Knyghtes Tale, lines 2599–2614.

CHAPTER VIII

FEASTS

Page 135   See my essay Das Fasanenfest. Am Hofe der Herzöge von Burgund (1454). Histor.-polit. Blätter 167 (1921). The authorities are considered in a long note in the German edition, p. 288.

Page 135   Miniature, see Durrieu, Miniature flamande pl. 17.

Page 136   A noteworthy MS. of the Deux Pans showing rough sketches intended no doubt for the weavers to copy is at Cheltenham (No. 219). See P. Durrieu, Les manuscrits de Sir Thomas Phillips à Cheltenham, Bibl. de l'école des chartes 50 (1889) 400 ; Doutrepont 252 f.

Page 136   Jean Wauquelin : Doutrepont 381. (rade-rapidement).

Page 137   Marriage of Philip the Good, see above, p. 56, and Le Févre, II, 168. Fools are frequently met with in Burgundian miniatures, see L'Ystoire de Helayne. Reproduction des 26 miniatures du ms. no 9967 de la Bibliothèque royale de Belgique par J. van den Gheyn S. J. (Bruxelles 1913), Plate I, also Le Bréviaire de Philippe le Bon. Reproduction des mss. nos 9511 et 9026 de la Bibliothèque royale de Belgique par J. van den Gheyn S. J. (Bruxelles 1909), Plates XV and XL.

Page 137   Theatre Doutrepont 345 ff. ; W. Creizenach, Geschichte des neueren Dramas I (Halle a. S. 1911) 373 ff.

Page 137   Plays : Creizenach 374. 489. L. Petit de Julleville, Répertoire du théâtre comique en France au moyen-âge (Paris 1886) 89.340.

Page 138   On oaths taken on a bird, see Doutrepont 106 ff., and his earlier work A la cour de Philippe le Bon. Le banquet du faisan et la littérature de Bourgogne. La Revue générale 70 (1899) 787 ff. 71 (1900) 99 ff., also La Curne de Sainte-Palaye, Mémoires sur l'ancienne chevalerie. Avec une introduction par Ch. Nodier. Nouvelle édition I (Paris 1826) 157 ff. ; P. J. Bapt. Le Grand d'Aussy, Histoire de la vie privée des Français I (Paris 1782) 299 ff. Oaths of this nature in general are considered in an extended note in the German edition, p. 290.

Page 139   Jacques Daret, a pupil of Roger Campin, worked at the marriage of Charles the Bold in 1468. Judging by his pay his work must have been valued highly : Friedländer II. plates 65–67, nr. 78/81. See also my essay mentioned above : Das Fasanenfest Beilage II " Verzeichnis der Maler, die an den ' Entremets ' des Fasanenfestes gearbeitet haben ".

Page 139   F. Lampp, Die Schwanenritterfage in der Litteratur. Ratibor 1914 Progr. It was possibly this feast which caused Philip to order from the " tapissier marchand " Pasquier Grenier of Tournai, three " goutières " with the history of the knight of the Swan (c. 1462).

Page 140   On Philip's Chaperon : Jehan de Molesmes 462 : On Philip's preference for precious stones as against gold and silver, see Chastellain (Déclaration) VII 223.

Page 141   On the Duke's colours, Du Clercq II 197.

Page 141   Hôtel de la Salle : A. de Saint-Léger, Lille sous la domination des ducs de Bourgogne (Lille 1909) 47 ff. Accounts in connection with the castle at Hesdin. Laborde I 268 f. nr. 944 ff. For a picture of the Tour de Bourgogne at Paris, Le Roux de Lincy et Tisserand, Paris et ses historiens 342.

Page 144   On proverbs and representations, see François Goedthals, Les proverbes anciens flamengs et français correspondants de sentence les uns aux autres (Anvers, Chr. Plantin 1668) 44 ; R. Riegler, Das Tier im Spiegel der Sprache (Dresden und Leipzig 1907, Neusprachliche Abhandlungen aus den Gebieten der Phraseologie, Realien, Stilistik und Synonymik Heft XV–XVI) 24 ; Ch. Rozan, Les animaux dans les proverbes I (Paris 1902) 237. (coyment-doucement).

Page 144   battre le chien devant le lion ; Chastellain IV 145.

Page 145   On the banquet : Chron. de Floreffe 170 : et se commencha ledit banket environ sept heures du soir et dura jusques à XI.—Vint petites charrettes estoffées de doubles fons, de tourelles et de proue, lesquelles ont servy à aporter les mets aux tables, Nord B 2017 ; Inv. Nord IV 196.—chariots . . . si plains de bien qu'il falloit de IIII homes à porter chascun chariot ; et y avoit divers mez jusques au nombre de chinquante-deux, Chron. de Floreffe 170.

Page 146   A miniature shows Jason's fight with the dragon : Bruxelles, Bibl. Roy. ms. 9392 fol. 57v : reproduced in Christine de Pisan, Epître d'Othéa, déesse de la prudence, à Hector, chef des Troyens . . . (Bruxelles 1913) pl. 54 ; compare plate 58 (f. 61v : amours de Jason et de Medée).

Page 148   On the oaths, see Doutrepont 112 note 1, also his treatise : Epitre à la maison de Bourgogne sur la croisade turque projetée par Philippe le Bon (1464) Analectes pour servir à l'histoire ecclésiastique de Belgique 3e série II 1906) Louvain 1906 p. 14 f. and Notice sur le manuscrit français 11594 de la Bibliothèque Nationale : La Croisade projetée par Philippe le Bon contre les Turcs, Notices et extraits des munuscrits de la Bibliothèque Nationale 41 (Paris 1923) 1 ff. To the 103 oaths at Lille must be added 27 at Arras, 54 (53) at Bruges (Louis of Gruthuse had already sworn at Lille. Doutrepont, 24, 10, note I), 4 in Holland, 27 in Hainault ; in all 214. Charles left Sluys for Seeland on 25 March, 1454. Inv. Nord viii, 27.

Page 151   Hainault nobleman, see Doutrepont, Notice 18. 22 f.

Page 152   Letter of the secretary, Jehan de Molesmes 462. Chastellain (Epistre au duc Philippe) VI 159 f. (comprès-oppression).

Page 152   Official record : D'Escouchy II 222 ff. With variations from the MS. franç. 5739. La Marche II 368 ff.

Page 153   Expedition to Nicopolis : Cartellieri, Philipp der Kühne 77 ff.

Page 153   Philippe de Mézières, Songe du vielz pelerin adreciant au blanc faulcon : Doutrepont 295 f.

Page 153   J. D. Hintzen, De Kruistochtplannen van Philips den Goede. Diss. Leyden. Rotterdam 1918.

Page 153   See generally. A. W. Ambros, Geschichte der Musik, especially II[3] (Leipzig 1891) 492 ff. ; III[3] (Leipzig 1891) 172 ff. ; Handbuch der Musikgeschichte hrg. von Guido Adler XI (Frankfurt a. Main 1924) 250 ff. ; 316 ; and especially R. Ficker, Die Musik des Mittelalters. Deutsche Vierteljahrschrift IV 1925, 501 ff. The note in the German edition p. 293 is extended.

Page 154   Tinctoris (cc. 1446–1511 ; Handbuch der Musikgeschichte 267.

Page 154   Windesheim : J. G. R. Acquoy, Het klooster te Windesheim en zijn invloed. Utrecht 1875 ff. 3 vols. II 246 ff.

Page 154   Guicciardini : Descrittione di tutti i paesi bassi (Anversa 1588) 42.

Page 154   Dufay † 1474: Ch. van der Borren. Guillaume Dufay, Brussels, 1926, Pinchart III 145 ff. ; Fr. X. Haberl, Wilhelm du Fay, Vierteljahrsschrift für Musikwissenschaft I (1885) 397 ff. Binchois † 1460 : Pinchart Archives III 143 ff. Jan Okeghem († 1495) and Jakob Obrecht († 1505), Ambros III 172 ff.

Page 155   Philip the Good and the German schools. Pinchart III 139.

Page 155   1410 : " Monseigneur de Charolais (Philip the Good) apprenoit à jouer de la harpe." E. Petit, Itinéraires de Philippe le Hardi et de Jean sans Peur, ducs de Bourgogne (1363–1419), Collection de documents inédits sur l'histoire de France (Paris 1888) 594.

Page 155   Chanson " Je ne vis onques la pareille " : Mscr. Trient Cod. 90 fol. 352[1], Gurlitt, Burgundische Chanson . . . Kunst 173.

Page 155   Les poésies de Charles d'Orléans p. . . . p. A. Champollion-Figeac (Paris 1842) 59 ballade XI.

Page 156   The blind musicians, Pinchart III 151. I give the verses according to the MS. For rebelle read rebec, Paris Bibl. Nat. franç. 12476 fol. 98.

Page 157   Molinet I 73.

Page 157   " Il (Charles) aimoit la musicque, combien qu'il eust mauvaise voix, mais toutesfois il avoit l'art et fist le chant de plusieurs chanssons bien faictes et bien notées " ; La Marche I 122 ; II 217. 334 ; Chastellain VII (Déclaration) 229 f. ; Basin II 425.

Page 157   On the marriage of Charles and Margaret of York : Cora L. Scofield, The life and reign of Edward the Fourth. 2 vols. London 1923.

Page 157   O. Cartellieri, Theaterspiele am Hofe Karls des Kühnen von Burgund. Germ.-romanische Monatsschrift 9 (1921) 168 ff., and the authorities quoted in the note in the German edition, p. 296.

Page 157   Jehan Scalkin : " maistre Jehan Scalkin, aussi varlet de chambre" La Marche III 119. 197; " maistre Jehan Stalkin, chanoine de Sainct Pierre de l'Isle." On the account book of Fastre Hollet, contreroleur de la despense ordinaire de l'ostel, see Laborde II 293 ff. A. Michiels, Hist. de la peinture flamande I (Paris 1866[2]) 422 ff.

Page 157   Hugo van der Goes : Laborde II 338 (Michiels I 427) : A Hugue van der Gous, paié pour X jours et demy qu'il a ouvré, à XIIII sols par jour. VII lib. VII solz.

Page 160   Tommaso Portinari : La Marche III 113. IV (Traictié) 104. Commynes, Mémoires II 140 f.

Page 161   The various stage representations are described in detail at pp. 173–178 of the German edition, but, owing to considerations of space have been omitted in the translation.

Page 163   John Paston the Younger 8. Juli 1468. The Paston Letters, edited by J. Gairdner II, 317 f.

CHAPTER IX

THE LIBRARY

Page 164   Léopold Delisle, Recherches sur la librairie de Charles V. Paris 1907, Bd. 1–2.

Page 164   Nine inventaries of Burgundian libraries exist : Doutrepont S. LIV :—

    1. 1404. Philip the Bold. Paris : Peignot 41–57 ; Barrois, nr. 605–637 ; Dehaisnes 839–40 ; 851–852.

    2. 1405 : Margaret of Flanders widow of Philip the Bold, Arras : Peignot 57–76 ; Barrois, nr. 638–663 ; Matter 19–39 ; Dehaisnes 879–81.

3. 7420. Philip the Good, Dijon ; G. Doutrepont, Inventaire (248 items).

4. 1424 (1423 Jan. 25). Margaret widow of John the Fearless. Dijon und Auxonne : Peignot 76–85 ; Barrois nr. 664–675.

5. 1467. Philip the Good, Bruges or Lille : Barrois nr. 705–1612.

6. 1477. Charles the Bold, Dijon : Peignot 85–98 ; Barrois, nr. 676–704.

7. Maximilian, Gent : Barrois nr. 1613–1634.

8. Maximilian, Brussels : Barrois nr. 1625–2180.

9. Maximilian, Bruges : Barrois nr. 2181–2211 (Appendix nr. 2212–2311). For the authorities see note at p. 298 of the German edition.

Page 165 G. Hulin, La bible de Philippe le Hardi, historiée par les frères de Limbourc : manuscrit français n° 166 de la Bibliothèque nationale à Paris. Bulletijn der maatschappy van geschied- en oudheidkunde te Gent 16 (1908) 183 ff., le comte P. Durrieu, Manuscrits de luxe exécutés pour des princes et des grands seigneurs français. IV. Les bibles français des ducs de Bourgogne. V. Sur quelques manuscrits Parisiens des ducs de Bourgogne Philippe le Hardi et Jean Sans Peur : Le manuscrit II (Paris 1895) 82 ff. 162 ff.

Page 165 Boccaccio's Decamerone : Durrieu, La miniature flamande 42 ff., H. Martin, Le Boccace de Jean Sans Peur. Des cas des nobles hommes et femmes. Reproduction . . . du ms. 5193 de la bibliothèque de l'Arsenal. Bruxelles 1911.

Page 165 Bataille du Liège : Mémoires pour servir à l'histoire de France et de Bourgogne I (Paris 1729) 373 ff.

Page 165 Les demandes faites par le roy Charles VI . . . avec les réponses de Pierre de Salmon . , . p. p. G.-A. Crapelet. Paris 1833. Doutrepont 412 f.

Page 165 La Geste des ducs Philippe et Jehan de Bourgogne, Le Livre des Trahisons de France envers la maison de Bourgogne are included with Le Pastorale : Chroniques relatives à l'histoire de la Belgique . . . II (Bruxelles 1873 ; Coll. de chroniques belges inédites).

Page 166 L. Delisle, Notice sur les sept psaumes allégorisés de Christine de Pisan : Notices et extraits des manuscrits de la Bibliothèque Nationale . . . 35 (1897) 555.

Page 167 Dirk Potter † 1428 : W. J. A. Jonckbloet, Gesch. der niederländischen Literatur. German edition by . . . W. Berg I (Leipzig 1870) 292 f. G. Kalff, Geschiedenis der nederlandsche letterkunde I (Groningen 1906) 553 ff.

Page 168 Jehan de Pestivien and other miniaturists, Durrieu, La miniature flamande 15 ff. ; E. Bacha, Les très belles miniatures de la Bibliothèque royale de Belgique (Bruxelles et Paris 1913). F. Winkler, Die flämische Buchmalerei des XV. und XVI. Jahrhunderts (Leipzig 1925).

Page 168 A. Lindner, Der Breslauer Froissart. Festschrift des Vereins für Geschichte der bildenden Künste zu Breslau. Berlin 1912. F. Winkler, Loyset Liedet, Der Meister des Goldenen Vliesses und der Breslauer Froissart, Repertorium für Kunstwissenschaft 34 (1911) 224 ff.

Page 169 Van Praet, Notice sur Colard Mansion, libraire et imprimeur de la ville de Bruges en Flandre dans le quinzième siècle, Paris 1829. H. Michel, L'imprimeur Colard Mansion et le Boccace de la Bibliothèque d'Amiens. Paris 1925. Publication de la Société française de bibliographie S. 4 ff.

Page 169 W. Blades, The life and typography of William Caxton, London 1861, 1863. K. Haebler, Die deutschen Buchdrucker des XV. Jahrhunderts im Auslande, München 1924. S. 273 ff. H. O. Sommer, The Recuyell of the Historyes of Troye written in French by Raoul Lefevre, translated and printed by William Caxton (about A.D. 1474). The first English printed book . . .

London 1894. Ch. Magnien, Une page de l'histoire anglo-belge (1441–1472 ?). Caxton à la cour de Charles-le-Téméraire à Bruges . . . : Annuaire de la société d'archéologie de Bruxelles 23 (1912) 49 ff.

Page 169   Martin Le Franc, Champion des Dames : Bruxelles, Bibl. Roy. nr. 9466.

Page 170   Guillaume Fillastre, Le premier volume de la toison d'or, fol. CXXXIv.

Page 170   On Margaret of Burgundy and literature, see L. Galesloot, Marguerite d'York, duchesse douairière de Bourgogne (1468–1503). Annales de la Société d'Emulation . . . de la Flandre. IVe série III (1879) 254 ff. Doutrepont 234, note 3.

Page 171   Prologue de Charles Martel : Doutrepont 505.

Page 171   Martin Le Franc, Champion des Dames 124.

Page 171   Livre des faicts . . . de Boucicaut VI 375 f.

Page 173   Louis XI : Letter from Christ. Bollato to Galeazzo Maria Sforza, Beauvais, 27. Januar 1474 : " Louis XI " manda de presente a donare uno bellissimo libro scritto in lingua et littera italiana continente la vita et gesti di Carlo Magno et de alcuni Regi de Franza al prefato Ducha de Brugogna : et mandagli a dire che glil dona intendendo essere in tuto dato alli costumi, modi, et governi italiani, acciò che anche più se ne possa delectare " ; Bern, Bundesarchiv copy : Mailand Arch. di Stato Potenze Estere Francia.

Page 173   Carpets : Doutrepont 186.

Page 173   Perceforest : Doutrepont 49 f.

Page 173   Charles Soillot, Jean du Chesne : Doutrepont 179 f.

Page 173   Vasco de Lucena : P. Meyer, Alexandre le Grand dans la littérature française du moyen-âge II (Paris 1886) 378 ff. ; Doutrepont 179, 183.

Page 174   Gontier Col. : Piaget 69, note 1.—Johannis de Monasterolo epistolae, Martène et Durand, Amplissima collectio II col. 1338 nr. 15. Du Clercq II 190 : " . . . prins la cité de Constantinople . . . le corps de madame Sainte Sophie ardse et bruslé ! "

Page 174   Bibliophile : A. Boinet, Un bibliophile du XVe siècle. Le grand bâtard de Bourgogne. Bibliothèque de l'école des chartes 67 (1906) 255 ff. Ph. Lauer, Déchiffrement de l'ex-libris du Grand Bâtard de Bourgogne. Bibl. de l'école des chartes 84 (1923) 298 ff. A. de Laborde, Les manuscrits à peinture de la cité de Dieu de Saint Augustin (Paris 1909) Plate XVIII. See also extended note in German edition, p. 302.

Page 175   From the unpublished verses of Stephanus Surigonus : London, British Museum, Arundel MSS. 249 fol. 101.

Page 176   Verses Chastellain VII 208, note 1.

Page 176   Chastellain IV 360.

Page 176   David Aubert : Doutrepont 221.

Page 176   Olivier de La Marche, Le chevalier délibéré . . . Collection de poésies, romans, chroniques publiée d'après d'anciens manuscrits et d'après des éditions des XVe et XVIe siècles 16 (Paris 1842).

Page 176   Piaget, Martin Le Franc 233 : p. 104, note 3.

Page 177   A satisfactory biography of Chastellain is still wanting. Much useful material in G. Pérouse, Georges Chastellain. Etude sur l'histoire politique et littéraire du XVe siècle. Mémoires p. p. la classe des lettres et des sciences morales . . . de l'Académie royale de Belgique. IIe série collection in 8o t. VII 1910 (see Mitt. d. Instituts f. österr. Geschsforsch. 33 (1912) 548 f.).

CHAPTER X

La Vauderie D'Arras

Page 181   Dionysii Cartusiani opera omnia . . . I (Monstrolii 1896) p. XLIII sqq.

Page 181   John Wiclif's polemical works in Latin II (London 1883) 591. Wyclif Society.

Page 182   Monstrelet IV 304 : sermon of Brother Thomas.

Page 182   David von Utrecht : Chastellain III 155. Gerson's complaint, De distinctione verarum visionum a falsis, Opera I col. 45, compare Du Clercq II 257 f. Mougel, Denys le Chartreux 60, note 1.

Page 182   Dice-playing : Journal d'un Bourgeois de Paris 242, note 6.— Sodomites in Arras : Du Clercq II 283 ; also 272. 282. 337 f. III 15.   Village priest, Du Clercq III 111. Concubines, Schwab, Gerson 697.

Page 182   Cardinal Jouffroy in Paris : Du Clercq IV 22.

Page 184   Christine de Pisan, Rondeaux I 172, nr. 46.

Page 184   Chastellain V 253 f.

Page 184   Philip the Good's orders to support the Inquisition : Corpus documentorum inquisitionis haereticae pravitatis Neerlandicae . . . uitgegeven door P. Fredericq, Gent, s'Gravenhage 1889 ff. I 305 nr. 268, 323 nr. 282.   On the faulx hérétiques Praguois : Corpus I 312 ff. nr. 276.   Heretics in Douai im J. 1420 : Corpus III 56 ff. nr. 48, 49.   Burning a magic book in Dijon, 1463 : J. Hansen, Zauberwahn, Inquisition und Hexenprozess im Mittelalter und die Entstehung der grossen Hexenverfolgung (Historische Bibliothek vol. 12, München and Leipzig 1900) 428, note 26. In March 1459 the heretical hermit Alfons of Portugal was burnt, Du Clercq II 339 f. ; Corpus I 341 nr. 300 ; III nr. 71. 72. 73.

Page 185   Somme rurale des Jehan Boutillier c. 1380 ; Hansen, Zauberwahn 352.

Page 185   Guido de Mont-Rocher : Hansen, Zauberwahn 403.

Page 185   Inquisition and sorcerers, Hansen, Zauberwahn of which I have made much use.   On burning of witches at Douai July, 1446, Corpus III 83 f. nr. 66. 67. (284[4]. 284[5]).

Page 186   Sorbonne : Hansen, Zauberwahn 283.

Page 187   William of Jülich : Hansen, Zauberwahn 393.

Page 187   Malleus maleficarum edition of 1486 fol. 19[a] ; Malleus Maleficarum. Der Hexenhammer.   Verfasst von . . . Jakob Sprenger und Heinrich Institoris . . . ins Deutsche übertragen und eingeleitet von J. W. R. Schmidt. I (Berlin 1906) 99. On the work and its author Hansen, Zauberwahn 473 ff.

Page 187   Nicolas Jacquier, Flagellum haereticorum fascinariorum 1458 ; Hansen, Zauberwahn 446. Compare Corpus III 115 f. nr. 84.

Page 188   Talisman of the Countess de Foix : K. Eubel, Vom Zaubereiunwesen anfangs des 14.   Jahrhunderts, Hist. Jahrbuch der Görres-Ges. 18 (1897) 627, also Champion, Charles d'Orléans 473 f.

Page 188   J. M. Vidal, Bullaire de l'inquisition française au XIVe siècle et jusqu'à la fin du grand schisme (Paris 1913).

Page 188   Louis of Orléans ; Jouvenel 88. 135 f.   Gersonii opera I col. 206 ; and col. 205 on the nobles sorciers. Charles Count Charolais ; Chastellain IV 323 f. ; also 314, note 1 ; Du Clercq III 236 f. Chastellain IV 475 f.

Page 188   Count of Nevers : see p. 58 ; also Commines ed. Lenglet du Fresnois (preuves) II 392. 210.

Page 188   Verse : F. Bourquelot, Les Vaudois du quinzième siècle.   Bibl. de l'école des chartes IIe série 3 (1846) 86 f. and J. Hansen, Quellen und Untersuchungen zur Geschichte des Hexenwahns und der Hexenverfolgung im Mittelalter (Bonn 1901) 102 nr. 20 ; the concluding verse in Martin Le Franc, Champion des dames 239. (fouch-troupeau : lotye-pourvue ; voit-aille).

Page 189   Guillaume Édeline (Adeline) : Hansen, Zauberwahn 422 ; Quellen, especially 467 ff. ; Roberti Gaguini epistolae et orationes. Texte p. p. L. Thuasne II (Paris 1904) 474 f.

Page 190   Bull Eugenius IV. : Hansen, Zauberwahn 412, 415.

Page 190   Petrus Mamoris : Hansen, Quellen 209 nr. 38.

Page 190   Chronicles : Jehan de Waurin, Recueil des croniques . . . edited by W. and E. Hardy V (London 1891) 393. On the name Vaudois : Hansen, Zauberwahn 413 ff. Vauderie can mean also witches' Sabbath.

Page 191   L. Tieck's Schriften vol. 20 -Novellen vol. 4. Berlin 1846 p. 189 ff.

Page 191   The description of Vauderie is based principally on Du Clercq, Mémoires III 10 ff.   See also D'Escouchy II 416 ff. ; Jehan de Waurin ; Zantfliet, Martène et Durand, Veterum scriptorum . . . amplissima collectio V col. 501 f.   The passages noted occur in Corpus I 345 ff. nr. 302 ff. ; II 263 ff. nr. 157 ff. ; III 89 ff. nr. 75 ff. On the older literature see A. Duverger, La Vauderie dans les états de Philippe le Bon (Arras 1885). Compare Hansen Zauberwahn 423 ; and " Quellen " 408 ff. ; H. C. Lea, Hist. of the Inquisition, 3 vols. 1888, passim.

Page 191   Jehan Lavite called also Jehan Tevoy, Tannoye ; Corpus I nr. 312. 384. On the position of an Abbé de Peu-de-Sens ; compare the Pape des folz en l'église Notre-Dame d'Amiens the Evêque des folz de l'église de Saint-Pierre à Lille, and an Abbé des sots and a Evêque des sots des Carmes de Bruxelles : Laborde I nr. 612. 652. 1217. 1218.

Page 192   Fierville, Le cardinal Jean Jouffroy 8 f. 27 ff.

Page 193   Nicolaus Eymericus, Directorium inquisitorum 1376 : Hansen, Zauberwahn 218 f. 270 ff.

Page 195   The answer of the clerics of Cambrai : Corpus I 348 ff. nr. 303.

Page 196   The judgment of 9 May 1460 in French : Corpus III 89 nr. 75.

Page 198   " Recollectio " : Paris Bibl. Nat. lat. 3446 ; Hansen, Quellen 149 nr. 31 : Corpus III 93 nr. 77.

Page 199   " Sermo " des Jehan Taincture : Brussels, Bibl. Royale nr. 2 296 ; Hansen, Quellen 183 nr. 32 ; Corpus I 357 nr. 305 ; compare Du Clercq III 31 f.

Page 200   De la secte qui s'appelle des Vaudois : Brussels Bibl. Royale nr. 11209 ; Hansen, Quellen 184 nr. 33 ; Corpus II 269 nr. 165 ; Doutrepont 307.

Page 201   On the seizure of the goods of Spanish merchants suspected of sorcery, see Corpus I 361 ff. nr. 308–10.

Page 204   Paris judgment of June 1461 : Corpus I 392 nr. 324. Two witches and one Vaudois were burnt at Dijon and Nuits in 1470 and 1471 : Hansen, Zauberwahn 423.

Page 205   Judgment of 1491 : copie de la sentence et arrest en latin . . . Du Clercq III 267 ff. ; Corpus I 462 nr. 384 ; also " extrait du papier mémorial de l'échevinage d'Arras " Du Clercq, III 250 ff., Corpus I 476 ff. nr. 385 ; III 116 ff. nr. 85 ; also the verses in the Chronique métrique de Chastellain et de Molinet 111.

CHAPTER XI

ART AND ARTISTS IN THE NETHERLANDS

Page 207   V. Fris, Histoire de Gand 125 ff.

Page 208   Official account in Kronijk van Vlaenderen, ed. Blommaert et Serrure II (1839) 212 ff., and P. Bergmans, Annales du XXe congrès de la fédération archéologique et historique de Belgique II (Gand 1907) 532 ff.   On the Ghent altar, Weale 206 ff.   Compare E. Varenbergh, Fêtes données à Philippe-le-Bon et Isabelle de Portugal à Gand en 1457 (sic).   Annales de la Société des Beaux

Arts 12 (1870) 1 ff., also Jean Chartier, Chronique de Charles VII. Nouvelle édition p. p. Vallet de Viriville III (Paris 1858) 84.

Page 208   On the chamber of rhetoric, L. Diericx, Mémoires sur la ville de Gand II (Gand 1815) 109 ; Ph. Blommaert, Tonneelgenootschappen te Gent. Belgisch Museum . . . 10 (Gent 1846) 379 ff.

Page 209   The church of St. Jan was later dedicated to St. Bavo.

Page 209   My studies are based on the comprehensive work of W. H. James Weale, Hubert and John van Eyck, Their life and work, London, 1908 : additions in the Van Eycks (with M. W. Brockwell) London, 1912. Compare Max Dvořák, Das Rätsel der Brüder van Eyck. München 1925 (Neudruck der Ausgabe von 1904 im Jahrbuch der Kunsthistor. Sammlungen des Allerhöchsten Kaiserhauses). E. Heidrich, Alt-niederländische Malerei. Die Kunst in Bildern. Jena 1910. M. J. Friedländer, Die altniederländische Malerei : vol. 1. Die van Eyck, Petrus Christus. Berlin 1924. According to J. Lyna in Paginae Bibliographicæ I Nr. 4 (1926) p. 114 ff., the Van Eycks came from Maastricht and not from Maseyck.

Page 210   Jehan d'Orléans : Bouchot, La condition sociale des peintres p. 168.

Page 210   On the castle of Bicêtre destroyed in 1411. Champion, Villon I 322.

Page 210   Durrieu, La miniature flamande 6.

Page 211   Deschamps IX 45 f. : Le miroir de mariage v. 1311 f.

Page 211   Comte Paul Durrieu, Chantilly, Les Très Riches Heures de Jean de France, duc de Berry Paris 1904. The lovely miniatures in the Turin Book of Hours perished in the fire in the Turin Library and can only be studied in reproductions. Comte P. Durrieu, Heures de Turin . . . Paris 1920. G. Hulin de Loo, Heures de Milan . . . Bruxelles, Paris 1911.

Page 213   For the accounts in which Van Eyck is mentioned : Weale, XXVIII nr. 3 dated 2. Aug. 1425 ff.

Page 213   On Philip's patronage and visits : Weale, XL. XXXIX nr. 22. 20.

Page 214   Juan de la Huerta : Monget II 113 ff.

Page 214   Le Moiturier " le meilleur ouvrier d'imaigerie du royaulme de France " ; Monget II 135.

Page 215   Mourners : Mâle, L'art religieux de la fin du moyen âge 417.

Page 215   Hans Tieffenthal : Ch. Gérard, Les artistes de l'Alsace pendant le moyen-age II (Colmar, Paris 1873) 151 ff. R. Wackernagel, Geschichte der Stadt Basel I (Basel 1907) 361 ; H. Wendland, Konrad Witz, Gemäldestudien. Basel 1924. S. 110.

Page 215   Molinet, Les faictz et dictz fol. 93.

Page 215   Neglect of Burgundy : Chabeuf, Charles le Téméraire à Dijon 116.

Page 216   Account of the journey (Oct. 1428 to Jan. 1430) : L. P. Gachard, Collection de documents inédits concernant l'histoire de la Belgique II (Bruxelles 1834) 63 ff. ; Weale LV ff. The name Elisabeth (Le Févre II 163) soon gave way to Isabelle.

Page 216   Le Févre II 151 ff.

Page 216   Hubert († 1426) : Weale, XXVIII ff. nr. 2. 4. 8.

Page 217   On the inscription : Friendländer I 45.

Page 217   Halfvasten : Ch.—L. Diericx, Mémoires sur la ville de Gand II (1815) 110 note 3 ; V. Van der Haeghen, La corporation des peintres et sculpteurs de Gand (Bruxelles 1906) 332 ; V. Fris, Bibliographie de Gand 214.

Page 217   Vyt : V. Fris, Contributions à la biographie Gantoise. Bulletijn der maatschappij van geschied-en oudheitkunde te Gent 1907 S. 84 ff. P. G. de Maesschalck, Josse Vijt, Annalen van den oudheidkundigen kring van het land van Waas 33 (1915/19) 13 ff. It seems that neither Josse nor Elizabeth was buried in St. John's church (St. Bavo).

Page 218   Rudolf Günther, Die Bilder des Genter und Isenheimer Altars I (Studien über christliche Denkmäler Heft 15, Leipzig 1923) ; I am not quite convinced by his attempt at interpretation.

Page 218   Honorius von Autun, De omnibus sanctis : Migne, Patrol. Lat. 172 col. 1013 ff.

Page 218   Jacobus de Voragine or Varagine (from Varazzo close to Genoa), Legenda Aurea, rec. Graesse (Lipsiae 1850²) 727.

Page 219   Münzer : K. Voll, Hieronymus Münzer und der Genter Altar. Beilage zur Allgemeinen Zeitung, 7. Sept. 1899 nr. 204 ; Weale, LXXIV.—Albrecht Dürer : Weale, LXXV.

Page 219   Villon, Testament v. 893 ff. Œuvres S. 62.

Page 220   Compare Felix Rosen, Die Natur in der Kunst (Leipzig 1903) 62 ff.

Page 220   Fazio, Liber de viris illustribus (written 1454–55, printed in Florenz 1745) p. 46 ; Weale, LXXIII.

Page 221   Weale, 18. For a plan of Bruges 1562 showing Eyck's house, Weale, p. 19 ; Letts, Bruges, and its past, p. 20.

Page 221   Cardinal of S. Croce, Dufresne de Beaucourt, Histoire de Charles VII vol. 2. Weale 58 ff. The picture is at Vienna. Kunsthistorisches Museum ; drawing at Dresden, Kupferstichkabinett.

Page 222   Giovanni Arnolfini is probably the same man as messire Jehan Arnolfin, of whom Chastellain speaks : IV 351. 356. Compare Weale 73. The picture of the two is in the National Gallery. The portrait of Giovanni Arnolfini is in Berlin, Kaiser-Friedrich-Museum.

Page 223   The portrait of Margaret Van Eyck is at Bruges. The Man with the Turban is in the National Gallery, London.

Page 223   The picture of the Virgin and St. Catherine (Giovanna Cenani) is at Dresden, Gemäldegalerie.

Page 223   Witch-executions at Arras, 1420, and Lille, 1430 : Corpus III 56 nr. 48 (260bis) ; I 315 nr. 278.

Page 223   Martin Le Franc, Champion des Dames 230 (vé-voie).

Page 223   Canon van der Paele. Weale 78 f. 39. The picture is at Bruges.

Page 224   There is no satisfactory study of the Chancellor Rolin, but see A. Perier, Un chancelier du XVᵉ siècle, N. Rolin, 1380–1461 Paris, 1904. La Marche, Livre de l'advis 21. The picture is in the Louvre.

Page 225   Du Clercq III 203 ; compare Chastellain III 330.

Page 225   Bartolomeo Fazio, see Weale, LXXIII, and p. 174 f.

Page 226   Chastellain IV 165 f., Du Clercq IV 36 f. 267. Baths and prostitutes at Gent : Fris, Bibliographie nr. 299.

Page 226   The portrait of Jan van Leeuw is at Vienna, Kunsthistorisches Museum ; Weale p. 86.

Page 226   Perspective : G. J. Kern, Die Grundzüge der linear-perspektivischen Darstellung in der Kunst der Gebrüder van Eyck und ihrer Schule. 1. Die perspektivische Projektion. Leipziger Diss. Leipzig 1904. Perspektive und Bildarchitektur bei Jan van Eyck. Repertorium für Kunstwissenschaft 35 (1912) 27 ff.

Page 227   John Van Eyck † June 1441. Philip's gift (1441) Weale, XLVII, nr. 31 ; Jean Lemaire's verses (1504) ebenda LXXV.

Page 228   Workshops : Bouchot, La condition sociale des peintres 173.

Page 228   St. Eligius, at Cologne in Sammlung Baron Oppenheim.

Page 229   F. Winkler, Der Meister von Flémalle und Rogier van der Weyden. Strassburg 1913. M. J. Friedländer, Die altniederländische Malerei. 2nd vol. Rogier van der Weyden und der Meister von Flémalle. Berlin 1924.

Page 232   F. de Mély, Le retable de Beaune. Paris 1906 (Gazette des beaux-arts).

Page 232   Philip the Good's portraits : 1. without Chaperon : in Madrid. Gotha, Antwerp. 2. with Chaperon : Lille, Antwerp, Paris, Bruges. A long note on the iconography of the Dukes of Burgundy is printed in the German edition, p. 310.

Page 232   On Philip's ague, see Chastellain I 237.

Page 233   Chastellain (Déclaration) VII 219.

Page 233   On the news of John's murder, Chastellain I 49 ff. : quarrel with Charles, Chastellain III 230 ff.

Page 233   Chastellain (Déclaration) VII 228 f. IV 345. V 381. 436 ; Basin II 419.

Page 234   Charles d'Orléans, Ballade XIX, Poésies I 34. Villon, Œuvres 105.

Page 234   D. Roggen, Rogier van der Weyden en Italie. Revue archéologique Ve série 19 (1924) 88 ff. K. W. Jähnig, Die Beweinung Christi vor dem Grabe von Rogier van der Weyden. Z. f. bildende Kunst 53 (1918) 171 ff. A. Goldschmidt, Sitzungsberichte der Kunstgesch. Gesellschaft Berlin 1903 nr. VIII S. 56 f. B. Haendcke, Der französisch-deutsch-niederländishe Einfluss auf die italienische kunst (Etudes sur l'art de tous les pays etc. fas. 4, Strasbourg, 1925).

Page 234   G. Vasari, Vite de' più eccelenti pittori . . . (Introduzione cap. XXI) I (Roma 1759) p. XLIX. Compare Vita d'Antonello da Messina p. 337 ff.—Bugatto : Friedländer, II 121.—Joseph du Teil. Un amateur d'art au XVe siècle. Guillaume Fillastre . . . Paris 1920.

Page 235   Niccolo di Forzore Spinelli and Giovanni Candida : G. Habich, Die Medaillen der italienischen Renaissance (Stuttgart und Berlin 1923) 67 ff., and 83 ff.

Page 235   Princely gifts, La Marche I 281. Maelweel's portrait of John the Fearless (1412) see Kleinclausz, Les Peintres des ducs de Bourgogne, Revue de l'art ancien et moderne 20 (1906), p. 166.

Page 236   Tapestries : B. Kurth, Die Blütezeit der Bildwirkerkunst zu Tournai und der burgundische Hof. Jahrbuch der kunsthistor. Sammlungen des allerhöchsten Kaiserhauses 34 (1917) 53 ff. ; Doutrepont 117 ff. 329. Compare A. Weese, Die Cäsar-Teppiche im historischen Museum in Bern. Bern 1911. M. Morelowski, Der Krakauer Schwanritterwandteppich und sein Verhältnis zu den französischen Teppichen des XV. Jahrhunderts. Kunsthist. Jahrbuch der K. K. Zentralkommission 6 (1912). A. Warburg, Arbeitende Bauern auf burgundischen Teppichen. Zeitschr. für bildende Kunst N. F. 18 (1907). On Jean Wauquelin : Kurth, 71.

Page 237   Dirk Bouts : Last Supper in St. Peter's Church, Liège. Compare Mâle, L'art religieux de la fin du moyen âge en France 60, and Mesnil, L'art au nord et au sud des Alpes à l'époque de la Renaissance, Etudes comparatives (Brussels, 1911) 101 f.

Page 237   Pictures of Justice, Brussels, Museum. On the story concerning Otto III : Grimm, Deutsche Sagen II (Berlin 1818) 171 ; X, Notice sur Thierry Stuerbout im Messager des Sciences et Arts de la Belgique I (Gand 1833) 17 ff. Der Kaiser und der Kunige buoch oder die sog. Kaiserchronik ; ed. by H. F. Massmann III (Quedlinburg und Leipzig 1854) 1084.

Page 238   Hugo van der Goes † 1482 : J. Destrée, Hugo van der Goes (Bruxelles et Paris 1914).

Page 238   Adoration : Portinari-altar, Florence, Uffizi (earlier Santa Maria Nuova). The Fall and Bewailing of Christ : Vienna, Kunsthistorisches Museum, Death of the Virgin at Bruges.

Page 239   Rouge Cloître, Roo Clooster, in the Forêt de Soignes, im Sonje Bosch, see Sander Pierron, Histoire de la Forêt de Soigne (Bruxelles 1905) 390 ff.

Page 240   See the chronicle of Gaspar Ofhuys (1456–1523), who was a novice with Hugo at Roo Clooster : Hjalmar G. Sander, Beiträge zur Biographie Hugos van der Goes und zur Chronologie seiner Werke, Repertorium für Kunstwissenschaft 35 (1912) 519 ff. Latin Text (also in Destrée 215 ff.) and German translation (also in K. Pfister, Hugo van der Goes (Basel 1923) 19 ff.). Voll, Hieronymus Münzer und der Genter Altar (p. 271 above).

Page 240   Epitaph : F. Sweertius, Monumenta sepulcralia et inscriptiones ducatus Brabantiae (Antverpiae 1613) 323.

CHAPTER XII

Conclusion

Page 241   Philip the Good : Monstrelet IV 430.
Page 241   Villon, Œuvres 105.
Page 243   Taire, souffrir . . . : Champion II 219 note 4 ; note 2.
Page 243   On the belief in the end of the world : Hansen, Zauberwahn 536.
Page 243   Anti-Christ in Paris in 1445 or 1446 : Journal d'un Bourgeois de Paris 381 f. ; D'Escouchy I 69 ff. Basin IV 102 ff. Recollection des merveilleuses, Chronique métrique 51 :

> J'ay veu par excellence
> Ung jeune de vingtz ans
> Avoir toute science
> Et les degrez montans.
> Soy vantant sçavoir dire
> Ce qu'oncques fut escript,
> Par seulle foiz le lire
> Comme ung jeune antécrist.

FRANCE, BURGUNDY, ORLEANS.

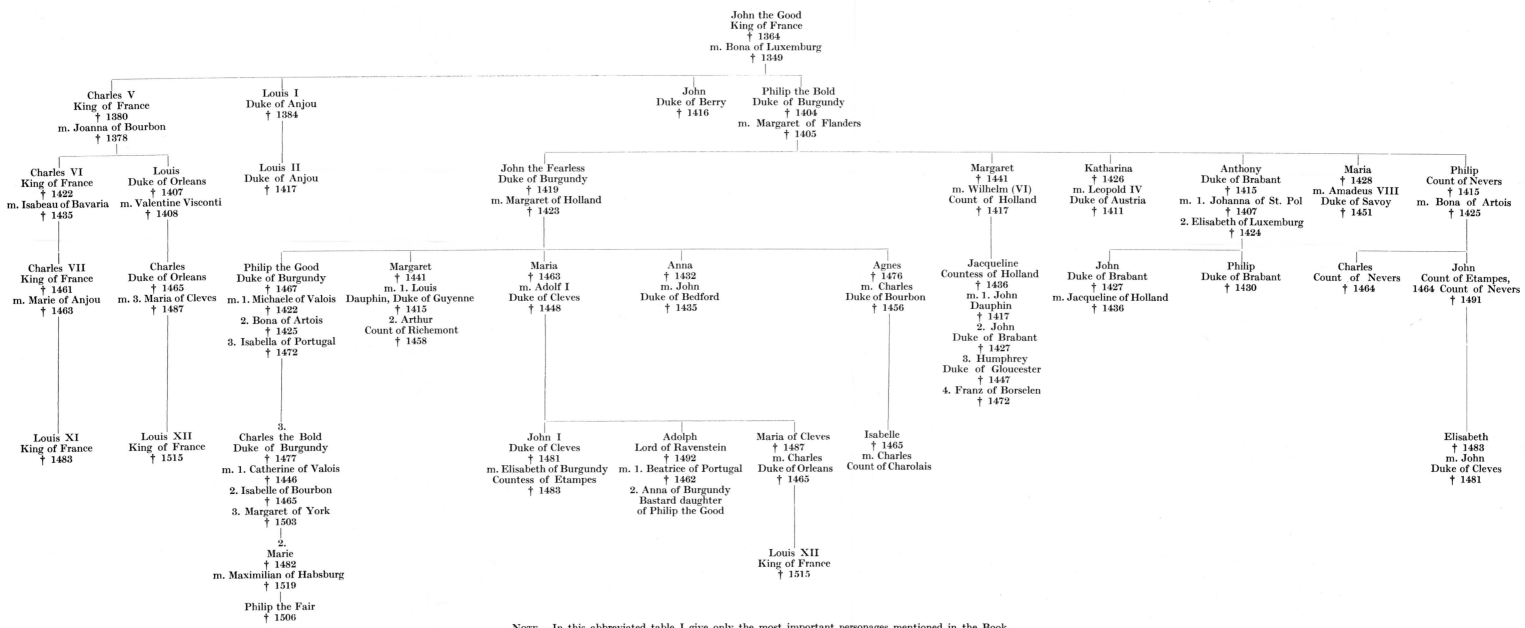

NOTE.—In this abbreviated table I give only the most important personages mentioned in the Book.

INDEX

Abbé de Peu-de-Sens, *see* Lavite

Abbeville, 19, 172.

Adolph of Cleves, Lord of, Ravenstein, Brother of Duke John, 61, 125 ff., 131

Agincourt, 8, 51, 79, 91

Agnes of Burgundy, daughter of Duke John the Fearless, wife of Duke Charles of Bourbon, 170, 214

Agnes, la Belle, *see* Sorel, 114 ff.

Albert II, King, 13

Aliénor de Poitiers, 70 f. ; her Mother, 70

Alix of France, wife of Count Thibaut V of Blois, 16

Amiens, 37, 106

Angelico, Fra, 234

Anne of Burgundy, Sister of Philip the Good, wife of Duke John of Bedford, 60

Antoine de Croy, Count of Porcien, 137

Anthony of Burgundy, Duke of Brabant, son of Philip the Bold, 35, 79

Anthony of Burgundy, the Great Bastard, son of Philip the Good, 120, 124, 127, 129, 131, 133, 140, 141, 145, 148, 156, 158, 174

Anthony of Luxemburg, Count of Roussy and Brienne, 130

Antwerp, 14

Aquinas, Thomas, 191

Aragon, 94, 214, 215

Arbre d'Or, Pursuivant, 124 ff., 132

Arc, *see* Joan of

Ardres, Lambert of, 55

Armagnacs, party of the, 7 ff., 51, 64, 179

Arnolfin, Jehan. Arnolfini, Giovanni, 222 ; his wife, 222 f.

Arras, treaty of, 10, 11, 21, 54, 77, 106, 180 ; Vauderie of, 181 ff., 200, 202 ff., 223, 235

Artevelde, James van, 76

Artois, Countship, 3, 4, 190

Aubert, David, 164, 171 f., 176

Aubry, Huguet, 201, 203, 206

Autun, 3, 224 ; Honorius of, 218

Avignon, 209, 214 ; Papacy at, 2, 37, 53 ; Cardinals of, 3

Aviz, Portugal, 216

Baldwin of Burgundy, bastard son of Philip the Good, 128

Bars, Baers, Jacques de, 32

Basle, Council of, 10, 189, 223

Bastard, the Great, *see* Anthony ; *also* Corneille

Bavo, Saint, Abbey of, 175, 219

Beatrice of Portugal, wife of Adolph of Cleves, 61

Beauffort, de, *see* Payen

Beaugrant, Madame de, Dwarf, 162

Beaumez, Biaumes, Jean de, 27, 31

Beaune, 3, 225, 232, 236

Beauneveu, André, Adryen, 30

Beauquesne, 196

Beauvais, 44

Bedford, Duke John of, 60, 166

Beirut, *see* John, titular Bishop of

Bellechose, Henri de, 27, 31, 214

Belligère (Isabeau, Queen of France), 166

Benedict XII, Pope, 187

Benedict XIII, Pope, Peter de Luna, 7, 45, 181

Benning, Sanders, sons Paul, Simon, 168

Bernabò, Visconti, 45

Bernard, Count of Armagnac, 7

Bernard, Abbot of Clairvaux, 3

Berry, Duke John, *see* John

Bertran de Born, 78

Bertrandon de La Broquière, 135, 172, 187

Beurse, Pierre, 157

Bicêtre, near Paris, 210

Binchois, Gilles de Binche, 147, 154, 155

Blois, 16

Boccaccio, 43, 102, 105, 165

Bologna, 99

Borluut, Elizabeth, wife of Jos Vyt, 217

Boucicaut, Jean le Meingre, called, Marshal, 85, 87, 93, 105, 108, 171

Boudault, Jean, 137

Bourgeois de Paris, 179

Bourges, King of, *see* Charles VII

Boutillier, Jean, 185

Bouts, Dirk, 237 f.

Bouvignes, 30

Brabant, Brabanters, Duchy of, 2, 12 f., 19, 180, 209, 215 ; Duke of, 14, 153

Brando, Johannes, 180
Brittany, Duke John VI of, 40
Brito, William, 3
Broederlam, Melchoir, 27, 32
Broussard, Geoffry, 206
Bruges, 4 f., 17, 23, 56 ff., 124 f., 137, 142, 150, 159 ff., 168, 169, 173, 175, 215, 221, 223, 235, 236, 238, 246
Bruges, Jan or Hennequin of, 211
Brussels, 14, 17, 34, 61, 63, 159, 202, 215, 230, 234, 240
Bugatto Zanetto, 234
Burgundian Party, 7, 36 f., 46, 52, 109, 114, 179
Burgundy, 1, 3 ff., 14, 23, 65, 166, 187, 215; see Agnes, Anna, Anthony, Corneille, David, John, Iolanthe, Isabella, Charles, Margaret, Marie, Philip, Raphael; Dukes, Philip the Bold, John the Fearless, Philip the Good, Charles the Bold.
Burgundy, New Burgundian State, 2, 6, 9, 12, 14, 17, 19, 20 f., 29, 35, 52, 54, 80, 135, 165, 178, 190, 215, 221, 241, 243
Busnois, Bugnoïs, Antoine, 154, 157
But, Adrianus of, 180

Caboche, Butcher, 52; Cabochiens, 52
Calais, 51
Cambrai, 195; Inquisitor, 202
Campin, Robert, 229
Candida, Giovanni, 235
Caesarius of Heisterbach, 186
Castile, 94, 216
Caxton, William, 169, 170
Cenani, Giovanna, wife of Giovanni Arnolfini, 223
Cent Nouvelles Nouvelles, 115, 166, 175, 182
Cervantes, Miguel de, 93
Chalon-sur-Saône, 3, 122, 214
Champmol, Carthusian Monastery near Dijon, 9, 24 ff., 210, 214 f.
Charles V, King of France, 29, 100, 164, 166, 171, 210; Brother, 210; sons, see Charles VI and Louis of Orleans
Charles VI, King of France, 6, 40, 43, 44, 45, 51, 53, 62, 79, 91, 100, 106, 110 f., 166, 188, 228; his children, 40, 45, 110; his wife, see Isabeau; brother, Louis of Orleans
Charles VII, Dauphin, later King of France (the king of Bourges), 9, 20, 51, 71, 115, 136, 166, 177, 190
Charles the Bald, 172

Charles the Bold, Count of Charolais, 140, 145, 150, 155, 156, 167, 233; Duke of Burgundy, 20 f., 54, 56, 58, 63, 64, 73, 80 f., 85, 118, 124 ff., 157 ff., 172 ff., 178, 180, 188, 215, 233, 235, 238, 243; his wives, see Michelle de Valois; Isabella de Bourbon; Margaret of York
Charles, Duke of Orleans, 8, 16, 89, 107, 234
Charolais, Countship of, 3; Counts of, see Philip the Good, Charles the Bold
Charolais, Herald, 122
Chartier, Alain, 8, 73
Chartres, Treaty of, 49
Chastellain, Georges, 8, 12, 18, 55, 60, 76, 80, 84, 87, 95, 101, 115, 137, 172, 177 f., 184, 232
Châtillon-sur-Seine, 3
Chaucer, 119, 133
Chesne, Jean du, 173
Chester, English Herald, 134
Christus, Peter, 228 f.
Cimabue, 210
Cîteaux, Abbey near Saint-Nicolas-lès-Cîteaux, 3
Clairvaux, 189
Claude de Vaudrey, 123
Cleves, see Duke Adolph
Cluny, Abbey of, 3
Cochon, Pierre, 179
Coene, Jacques, 211
Col, Gontier and Pierre, 104, 109, 174
Colette St., 62
Commines, Philippe de, 21, 177, 180
Constance, Council of, 50, 51, 180
Cordonval, Jehan de, 156
Corneille, Cornelius of Burgundy, the Great Bastard, son of Duke Philip the Good, 207
Courtrai, 6, 76.
Cousinot, Guillaume, 49
Coustain, Pierre, 157
Créquy, Lord of, see Jean
Crèvecœur, Sire de, 58
Croix Pèlerine, 84
Croy, Family, 56, 204

Dammartin, Drouet de, 29
Damme, near Bruges, 4, 160
Dante, 4, 100, 185, 194, 210, 212, 220, 238
Daret, Jacques, 139
Daroca, 214
David of Burgundy, illegitimate son of Duke Philip the Good, Bishop of Thérouanne, after of Utrecht, 60, 182
Deniselle, 191, 194, 196, 197, 199

Deschamps, Eustache, 18, 90, 111, 121, 165, 211.

Dijon, 3, 14, 20, 26, 29, 30; see Champmol

Dionysius van Ryckel, Carthusian, 62, 181

Dixmude, so-called Jan van, 180

Dixmude, Olivier van, 180

Donatello, 17

Donatian, Saint, 223

Douai, 184, 197

Dreux, Jehan, 169

Dubois, Jacques, 192, 195

Du Clercq, Jacques, 54, 179, 206

Dufay, Guillaume, 154 f.

Du Guesclin, Constable, 85

Dunes, Abbey of, 180

Dürer, Albert, 219

Dynter, Edmundus de, 172, 180

Edeline (Adeline), William, 189

Edward III, King of England, 1, 89

Edward IV, King of England, 20, 157, 168, 175

Eleanor, Queen of England, wife of Henry II, 16

Elizabeth of Portugal, see Isabella.

England, see Edward III, Edward IV, Henry V, Margaret

Enseignements paternals, Author of, 82, 89, 119, 175

Escouchy, Malthieu d', 179

Esterlings, 160

Eugenius IV, Pope, 58, 190, 221

Eyck, Jan van, 17, 78, 79, 209, 212 ff., 240; his wife, Margaret, 213, 223; Hubert, 209 ff., 212

Eymericus, Nicolaus, 193, 195

Feast of the Pheasant, 16, 17, 91, 92, 139 ff., 155, 157, 158, 232

Fazio, Bartolameo, 221, 225

Fenin, Pierre, 179

Ferdinand, King of Aragon, 154

Ferrandes, Jehan, 156

Fiennes, Lord of, 129

Fillastre, see Guillaume

Flanders, see Burgundy

Flémalle, Master of, 229

Flemish language, 18, 180

Florence, Florentines, 160, 191, 238

Foix, Countess Margaret of, 187 f.

Folco, see Portinari

Fouquet, Jehan, 115

France, see John: Charles V; Charles VI; Charles VII; Louis XI; Isabeau; Marie of Anjou

Francesco Sforza, 234

Franche-Comté, 3, 4, 19, 54, 189

Francis I, King of France, 9, 81

Franz of Borselen, 113

Frederick III, Emperor, 13, 15, 21, 63, 77

Frederick I, Elector of the Palatine, 72

Froissart, 4, 18, 30, 101, 168, 176

Fusil, Pursuivant, 69

Gandolph, St., 208

Garter, Order of, 10, 57, 82; King at Arms, 125

Gavere, Peace of, 207

Gelders, 21

Genoese, 160

Geoffroy de Toisy, 136

Geraardsbergen, 61

Germolles, 27

Gerson, Jean, Professor, 40, 50, 53, 102, 104, 186

Geste des Ducs de Bourgogne, author of, 9, 165, 179

Ghent, 4, 23, 37, 52, 54, 121, 136, 152, 168, 175, 184, 207 f., 216 ff., 224, 238, 239

Ghent, Justus of, 235

Ghiberti, 17

Ghillebert de Lannoy, 135

Ghizeghem, Heyne van, 157

Gian Galeazzo Visconti, Duke of Milan, 45, 89

Gideon, 59 f., 159

Gilles de Chin, 84

Gilles de Trazegnies, 84

Giotto, 210, 220

Gloucester, see Humphrey, Duke of

Godfroi de Bouillon, 84, 153, 236

Goes, Hugo van der, 17, 157, 238 ff.

Goetghebeur, Mikiel, 159

Golden Fleece, Order of, 11, 56 ff., 61, 136, 159, 179, 232; King-at-Arms, 69, 148; Fusil Pursuivant, 69

Gossins, Anthoine, 159

Granada, 5, 216

Grandson, 22, 235

Gregory of Tours, 3

Grenier Pasquier, 235

Gruuthuuse, Lord of, see Louis

Guicciardini, Lodovico, 154

Guillaume Fillastre, Bishop of Verdun, 60, 170, 235

Guillaume de Martigny, 91

Guines, Count of, 55

Guyse, Jacques de, 171 f.

Halle (Hal), 34

Hamayde, Bastard de la, 64, 81

Hamel, Pierre du, 205

Hanse, 5, 13

Hautem, 184

Hainault, Countship, 2, 4, 10, 13 30, 82

Hennecart, Hennekart, Jehan, 168, 173

Hennequin (of Liéges), 25

Henry IV, King of England, 7, 45, 82

Henry V, King of England, 8, 11, 51, 85, 90, 113

Henry VI, King of England, 10

Hesdin, Jacquemart de, 25

Histoire de Charles Martel, author, 171

Holland, see Jacqueline ; King William

Holland, Jan van, 25

Hue de Tabarie, 83

Huerta, Juan de la (Jehan de la Werta), 214

Huguenin, Companion to Marshall Boucicaut, 105

Humbercourt, Lord of, 172

Humphrey, Duke of Gloucester, 10, 82, 112

Hundred Years War, 1, 79, 120, 190

Hungary, 5, 135 ; see Sigismund

Innocent III, Pope (Lothar de Segni), 102

Innocent IV, Pope, 193

Instruction d'un Jeune Prince, author of, 183, 175

Iolanthe of Burgundy, natural daughter of Philip the Good, 148

Isabeau (Ysabeau, Ysabel), of France, Elizabeth of Bavaria, wife of King Charles VI, 36, 47, 49, 51, 101, 166

Isabella de Bourbon, 2nd wife of Charles de Charolais, 67, 71, 215

Isabella, Elizabeth, Infanta of Portugal, 3 ; wife of Duke Philip the Good, 55 f., 61, 63, 73, 141, 157, 158, 170, 215, 216, 233

Jacques de Lalaing, 75, 92 ff., 121, 148, 207

Jacqueline, Countess of Holland and Hainault, 9, 12, 13, 82, 112 f., 211

Jacquier, Nicolas, 187

James, Count of Horn, 16

Jan Evangelista, St., Gild of, 169

Jason, 59, 138, 146, 160, 166, 236

Jean de Beaumont, 91

Jean de Boniface, 122

Jehan de Chalon, Lord of Arguel, 132

Jean de Chassa, 86, 130

Jean, Lord of Créquy, 148, 149, 174

Jean Germain, Bishop of Chalon, Chancellor of the Golden Fleece, 59, 120, 136, 236

Jean Jouffroy, Bishop of Arras, Cardinal, 175, 192, 205

Jean (II) de Lannoy, Bailli of Amiens, 137

Jean Le Févre, Seigneur de Saint Remy, 92 f., 141, 150, 178 f.

Jean de Mailly, 108

Jean de Rebremettes, 91

Jean, seigneur de Roubaix, 215

Jehan de Saintré, 86

Jean le Senechal, 108

Jean de Varennes, 102

Jean de Wavrin, Bastard, 175

Jeanne de Harcourt, Countess of Namur, 170

Joan of Arc, 10, 12, 56, 113 f., 190

Jodocus, Saint, 61

John XXII, Pope, 187

John XXIII, Pope, 181

John the Good, King of France, 1, 81, 89, 164

John I, King of Portugal, 216

John of Anjou, Duke of Calabria, 174

John d'Avesnes, 2

John, Titular Bishop of Beirut, 192, 195, 205

John, Duke de Berry, 30, 37, 40, 47, 48, 100, 108, 109, 164, 210, 211

John the Fearless, Count of Nevers, 106, 134 ; Duke of Burgundy, 3, 6 f., 21, 26, 34 f., 36 ff., 52, 53, 64, 79, 120, 165 f., 210, 233, 235 ; his wife, see Margaret of Flanders ; son, Philip the Good ; bastard, John, Bishop of Cambrai

John of Burgundy, Duke of Brabant, son of Duke Anthony, 112

John of Burgundy, Bishop of Cambrai, bastard son of Duke John the Fearless, 55

John of Burgundy, son of Philip Count of Etampes, 150, 195 f., 200 ; Count of Nevers, 58, 188

John, Count of Holland, 211

John I, Duke of Cleves, 93, 150

Joan, Duchess of Brabant, and Limburg, 12

Josquin, Jossequin, musician, 154

Lalaing, Lord of, see Jacques

La Marche, Olivier de, 18, 55, 65 ff., 70, 75 f., 96, 103, 120, 122, 126, 137, 147, 157, 158, 176

Lannoy, see Ghillebert de

Laon, Colard de, 24

Lavite, Jehan (= Jehan Tannoye, Tevoy), Abbé de Peu-de-Sens, 191, 192, 194, 196, 198, 199

Le Broussard, Pierre, Inquisitor of Arras, 191, 198, 204

Le Comte, Richard, 170

Leeuw, Jan de, 226
Lefèvre, Raoul, 59, 158, 169
Le Fèvre, Jean of Ressons, 98
Le Franc, Martin, 52, 61, 73, 101,
    115, 156, 169, 171, 176, 188,
    193, 207, 223
Legois, Butcher, 52
Legrand, Jacques, Augustine, monk,
    112
Lemaire, Jean de Belges, 227
Le Moiturier, Antoine, 214
Liédet, Loyset, 168, 171
Liège, 20 f., 25, 209
Ligue du Bien Public, 20
Lille, 16, 17, 120, 139 ff., 172, 223
Limburg, Limbourg, Duchy, 2, 12 ;
    brothers of, 164, 211
Lionello d'Este, 234
Lipsius, Justus, 19
Lisbon, 216
Livre des Faits de Jacques de
    Lalaing, 93
Livres des Trahisons de France, 165,
    179
Lorenzo de' Medici, 234
Lorris, Guillaume de, 97
Louis de Chalon, Count of Tonnerre,
    110
Louis de Chevalart, 91
Louis VI, king of France, 53
Louis IX, St. Louis, king of France,
    53
Louis X, king of France, 188
Louis XI, Dauphin (son of Charles
    VII), 20, 63, 177, 238 ; king of
    France, 21, 22, 56, 63, 79, 116,
    138, 173, 177, 183, 188, 204,
    243
Louis I, Duke of Anjou, son of
    John the Good of France, 62, 81
Louis II, Duke of Anjou, king of
    Sicily, son of the last-named, 40,
    48
Louis, Duke of Bavaria, Ingoldstadt,
    106
Louis of Bruges, Lord of Gruuthuuse,
    169, 175
Louis, Duke of Guyenne, Dauphin,
    41, 47
Louis of Maele, Count of Flanders.
    1, 2
Louis, Duke of Touraine, 108 ; Duke
    of Orleans, 6, 7, 9, 36 ff., 41,
    43 ff., 82, 85, 100, 106, 109,
    111, 166, 179, 188 ; his sons,
    45, 47 ; his wife, see Valentine
    Visconti
Louvain, 237 f. ; University of, 202
Luna, Peter de, pape de la Lune :
    see Benedict XIII
Lusignan, Palace, 143
Luxemburg, Duchy of, 2, 13, 19, 83

Maastricht, 209
Machaut, Guillaume de, 99
Maelweel, Jan, 27, 29, 31, 35
Mahieu de Boulogne, Matheolus,
    98 f., 102, 104
Malet, Gilles, 165
Malleus maleficarum, 187
Malines, 3, 15, 30
Mamoris, Peter, Professor, 190
Mansion, Colard, 169
Margaret of Bavaria, Countess of
    Holland and Hainault, wife of
    John the Fearless, 215
Margarete of Burgundy, illegitimate
    daughter of Philip the Good, 150
Margaret, Countess of Flanders, wife
    of Duke Philip the Bold of
    Burgundy, 1, 3, 31
Margaret of York, third wife of Duke
    Charles the Bold, 73, 88, 124 f.,
    133, 157 f., 160 f., 161, 169, 170
Marie of Anjou, wife of King Charles
    VII of France, 71, 115, 205
Marie of Burgundy, daughter of
    Charles the Bold, 21 f., 63, 71,
    157, 162
Marie of Burgundy, illegitimate
    daughter of Philip the Good,
    Lady of Charny, 145
Marie of France, wife of Count
    Henry I of Champagne, 16
Mary of Cleves, wife of Duc Charles
    d'Orléans, 87, 85
Marie de la Viéville, wife of the Great
    Bastard, 145
Marigny, Enguerrand de, 188
Marmion, Simon, 168
Marville, Jean de, 30, 34
Maximilian, Archduke of Austria,
    King, 77
Mazerolles, Philippe de, 169
Mehun-sur-Yévre, 30
Melun, 90, 115
Memling, Hans, 17, 235, 236 f.
Mérode-Altar, Master of the, 229
Meschinot, Jean, 73
Mets, Guillebert de, 109, 165
Meung (Meun), Jean (Jan) de, 97 ff.,
    101 ff.
Mezières, see Philippe de
Michelle de Valois, 1st wife of Philip
    the Good, 41
Miélot, Jehan, 171
Molinet, Jean, 1, 19, 24, 76, 157, 172,
    178 f.
Mons-en-Pévèle, 6, 187
Monstrelet, Enguerrand de, 17, 113,
    179
Montereau-faut-Yonne, 9, 51, 213
Montfaucon, Gallows near Paris, 44
Montreuil, Jean de, 7, 104, 109,
    174

Mont-Rocher, Guido de, 185
Morton, Robert, 156
Münzer, Joachim, 219

Namur, Margravate, 12, 215 ; Countess of, 75
Nancy, 22
Navarre, 5, 94 ; king of, 100
Neuss (Nuys), 22, 87
Nevers, Countship, 3 ; see John the Fearless, John of Burgundy, Count of Etampes
Nicolas Albergati, Cardinal of Santa Croce, 221 f.
Nicolas of Cues, Cardinal, 62
Nikopolis, Bulgaria, 90, 135, 153
Norfolk, Duchess of, 161
Novare, Philippe de, 103
Nuremberg, 18

Odette de Champdivers, 111
Okegham, Jan, 154
Orgemont, Nicolas d', 117
Orléans, Jehan d', 210, 228
Orléans, Maid of, Pucelle d', see Joan
Orleans, party of, 5, 36, 46, 48 ; Dukes, see Louis, Charles ; Duchess, see Mary of Cleves
Othée, 49
Otto III, Emperor, 237 f. ; wife
Oudenarde, Prov. East Flanders, 120, 235
Ouwater, Albert of, 237

Paele, Georg van der, 233 f.
Paris, 5, 8 f., 24 f., 36 f., 39 f., 47 f., 60, 107 f., 114, 116, 165, 182, 201, 204, 206, 209,
Pas de l'Arbre Charlemagne, 119
Pas de l'Arbre d'Or, 86, 88, 120, 124 ff., 161
Pas de la Belle Pèlerine, 85, 119
Pas de la Dame Sauvage, 120
Pas de la Fontaine aux Pleurs, 94, 120
Pas du Perron Fée, 120
Paston, John the Younger, 135, 163
Pastoralet, Le, 9, 166, 179
Pasture, Rogier de la, see Weyden, Rogier van der
Paul of Limburg, 211 ; Brothers, 164
Payen de Beauffort, 200 ff., 206
Pepin, Jehan, 25
Perceforest, author of the, 173
Péronelle d'Armentières, 99
Pestivien, Jehan, 168
Peter, Pierre of Hagenbach, Vacquembach, 72
Peter de Luna, see Pope Benedict XIII

Peter de Luxemburg, 60
Peter, Master, Dwarf, 124, 125, 131
Petit, Jean, 36, 37, 40 ff., 50, 165, 188
Philip II Augustus, King of France, 51, 53
Philip IV the Fair, King of France, 53
Philip of Burgundy, Count of Nevers and Rethel, son of Duke Philip the Bold, 35
Philip the Bold, Duke of Burgundy, Count of Flanders, 1–4, 6, 12, 14, 19, 26, 29 f., 32, 34 f., 53 ff., 60, 100, 105, 135, 164, 167, 210, 215, 235, 241 ; wife, see Margaret of Flanders ; grandson, Philip the Good ; great-grandson, Charles the Bold
Philip the Fair, son of Maximilian and Marie of Burgundy, 54, 71
Philip the Good, Count of Charolais, Duke of Burgundy, Count of Flanders, 9 ff., 53 ff., 77, 79, 90 ff., 113, 119 ff., 166 ff., 175, 177, 212 f., 215 f., 233, 240, and passim ; his wives (1) Michelle of France, (3) Isabella of Portugal ; sons, Anthony, Charles the Bold ; bastard children, see p. 252 ; his father, John the Fearless mother, Margaret of Holland ; grandfather, Philip the Bold
Philippe de Croy, Count of Chimay, 87, 175, 234
Philip of Horn, 175
Philippe de Mézières, 45, 88, 153
Philippe de Poitiers, Lord of la Ferté, 130
Philippe Pot, 91
Philippe de Saveuses, 215, 204
Pierre de Bourbon, Lord of Carency, 129
Pierre de Hauteville, Lord of Ars, 106
Pisan, Christine de, 8, 18, 25, 88, 97, 99 f., 105, 110, 112, 114, 117, 118, 165, 166, 174, 184
Poggio, 173
Poitiers, 1, 190
Poitou, 5
Popincourt, Jehan de, 204 f.
Portinari (Portunay), Tommass (Thomas), 160, 238 ; Ancestor Folco, father of Beatrice
Portugal, see Isabella
Potter, Dirk, 167
Premierfait, Laurent de, 165
Presles, Raoul de, 171
Pucelle d'Orléans, see Joan

Raffael Sanzio, 219
Raphaël de Mercatel, bastard son of Duke Philip the Good, 175

Rapondi, Dino, 34
Ravenstein, *see* Adolph of Cleves
Ravenstein, Pursuivant, 125
Raynoard, Rainouart au Tinel, 174
Regnauld de Montalban, Renaud de Montauban, 174
Regnault d'Azincourt, 109
Religieux de St. Denis, 46, 110
René I of Anjou, Duke of Lorraine, King of Naples, 16, 85
René II of Vaudemont, Duke of Lorraine, 82
Rheims, 10, 53, 62, 113
Richard II, king of England, 82
Robbia, workshop of, della, 235
Rolin, Nicolas, Chancellor, 137, 224 f., 230 ; son, John, Bishop of Châlons-sur-Saône, Cardinal, 225
Roman de la Rose, 97 f., 105, 112, 121, 236
Rouen, 51
Rouge Cloître, Roo Clooster, near Brussels, 239
Roussillon, Girard de, 172
Rozier historial de France, author, 79
Rudolf of Habsburg, Emperor, 2
Rupert, King, 7
Ruysbroek, Johannes, 18
Ryckel, *see* Dionysius van

Sacquespée, Antoine, maître, 200
Saint-Bénigne, Abbey near Dijon, 3
Saint-Pol, Count of, Constable : Louis of Luxemburg, 63, 64, 101
Saint-Vaast, Abbey in Arras, 11, 21
Sale, Antoine de la, 115
Salisbury, John of, 43, 45
Salisbury, Bishop of, Richard Beauchamp, 160
Salm, Count of, 16, 128, 129
Salmon, Pierre, 165
Santa Croce, Cardinal of, *see* Nicolaus Albergati
Santiago di Compostela, 10, 216
Saveuses, *see* Philippe
Scales, Lord, 128, 131
Scalkin, Jehan, 143, 157, 159
Segobia-Segovia, Jan, Juan, de, 223
Sicily, King of, *see* Louis II of Anjou
Sigismund, King of Hungary, Emperor, 13, 19, 51, 90, 134
Sigismund, Duke of Austria, Count of Tyrol, 21
Silwri (Selimbria), Titular Bishop of, 200, 204
Sluis, Prov. Zeeland, 4, 29, 77, 160
Sluter, Claus, 17, 30 ff., 210, 213
Soillot, Charles, 173, 175
Songe Véritable, author of the, 179

Sorel, Agnès, demoiselle de Beauté, 114 ff.
Spierinc, Nicolas, 168
Spinelli, Niccolo di Foryore, 235
Steen, Jan, 226
Steenreen, Janne van, geheeten van Aren, 155
Stephan, Burgundian King, 61
Suger, Abbot of Saint-Denis, 53

Taincture, Jehan, Magister, 199
Tannoye, *see* Lavite
Tavernier, Jehan, 168
Ternant, Lord of, 130
Tevoy, Jehan, *see* Lavite
Thomas of Cantimpré, 186
Thomas, Abbot of Cerisi, 47 f., 52
Thomas a Kempis, 154
Tieffenthal, Hans, 215
Tinctoris, Johannes, 154
Todi, Jacopone da, 231
Toison d'Or, Lord of Saint-Remy, *see* Jean Le Févre
Toison d'Or, *see* Golden Fleece
Toisy, *see* Geoffroy de
Toul, Bishop, *see* Guillaume Fillastre
Tournai, Doornik, 106, 120, 199, 230, 235
Tours, Gregory of, *see* Gregory
Treves, 21 f., 63, 235
Troyes, 16 ; Treaty of, 9, 113

Ulrich von Lichtenstein, 93
Utrecht, 87, 182 ; Bishop of, *see* David

Vacquembach, *see* Peter of Hagenbach
Valenciennes, 18, 30, 106, 178
Valentine, Visconti, wife of Duke Louis d'Orléans, 45, 47, 49, 111
Varagine, Voragine (Varazzo), Jacobus de, 218
Varennes, Jean de, 102
Vasco Fernandez, Count of Lucena, 86, 173
Vasco Mada de Villalobus, 86
Vaud, Pays de, Waadt, 190
Verdun, Bishop, *see* Guillaume, Fillastre
Villon, François, 117 f., 171, 234, 241 ; mother, 219
Vliet, van, 226
Vrelant, Willem, 168
Vyt, Josse, Jodocus, Lord of Pamele, 209, 217 f.

Waleran de Wavrin, 144
Wauquelin, Jean, 64, 136, 138, 171, 180, 236
Wenzel, King, 7

Werve, Claus van, 26, 33, 35, 213
Weyden, Rogier, Rogelet, van der, de la Pasture, 17, 175, 229 ff., 236
Wiclif, John, 181
William III, Duke of Saxony, 83

William VI (IV), of Bavaria, Count of Osberbant, 35, 106, 211
William, Count of Juliers, 187
Windesheim, Windesheimer, 154, 242
Wydeville, John, 133

Ypres, 4, 5, 23, 27, 202, 235

DATE DUE

2/28/75			
APR 12 1975			
GAYLORD			PRINTED IN U.S.A.